The Psychology of Executive Coaching

The Psychology of Executive Coaching

Theory and Application

SECOND EDITION

Bruce Peltier

Routledge
Taylor & Francis Group
New York   London

Routledge
Taylor & Francis Group
270 Madison Avenue
New York, NY 10016

Routledge
Taylor & Francis Group
27 Church Road
Hove, East Sussex BN3 2FA

© 2010 by Taylor and Francis Group, LLC
Routledge is an imprint of Taylor & Francis Group, an Informa business

Printed in the United States of America on acid-free paper
10 9 8 7 6 5 4 3

International Standard Book Number: 978-0-415-99341-8 (Paperback)

Library of Congress Cataloging-in-Publication Data

Peltier, Bruce.
    The psychology of executive coaching : theory and application / Bruce Peltier. -- 2nd ed.
        p. cm.
    Includes index.
    ISBN 978-0-415-99341-8 (pbk. : alk. paper)
    1. Executive coaching. I. Title.

BF637.C6P37 2009
658.4'07124--dc22   2009009266

Visit the Taylor & Francis Web site at
http://www.taylorandfrancis.com

and the Routledge Web site at
http://www.routledgementalhealth.com

To the son who didn't cry.
1924–2006

Show up, or choose to be present.
Pay attention to what has heart and meaning.
Tell the truth.
Be open to outcome, not attached to results.

THE FOUR-FOLD WAY: WALKING THE PATHS OF THE WARRIOR,
HEALER AND VISIONARY
ANGELES ARRIEN (HARPERCOLLINS, 1993)

Contents

Preface

The main purpose of this book is to translate psychological theory for executive coaches. Its goal is to make the principles, research, and wisdom of psychology accessible to the practice of executive coaching. This theoretical information can and should form the basis for effective coaching in the organizational consulting environment.

Much has happened in the United States since the publication of the first edition of this book in 2001. The most significant events of the period—the attacks of 9/11, the invasion and occupation of Iraq, the flooding of New Orleans, the near collapse of the financial credit system, and the election of a new American president—highlight the importance of leadership, integrity, and competence. Executive coaching during this period has grown and become mainstream in many business sectors worldwide. Coach-training organizations have also grown and thrived across the globe. It looks like coaching is here to stay.

Executive coaching has become a popular way for companies to assist and develop talent, and there is a growing body of literature on how to do this kind of work. Most coaching books do not effectively establish a direct relationship between psychological concepts and coaching practice. Many are written in the popular style of business self-help books, and they occasionally exhort more than they enlighten. This book begins with psychological theory and is written to provide a conceptual foundation for the organizational coach. It is not a handbook or how-to-coach book.

The author is a counseling psychologist with 30 years of clinical and organizational experience, as well as an MBA and entrepreneurial, small business experience gained over a 20-year period.

There is a primary and a secondary target reader for this book. It is first written for psychotherapists, including psychologists, psychiatrists, master's-level psychotherapists, marriage and family therapists, and social workers who would like to expand their practice into the corporate, nonprofit, or small-business environment. Opportunity clearly exists in the business world, and psychology has plenty to offer. But psychological concepts and methods must be translated for the corporate world first before it is applied in that setting. The business point of view and its vocabulary must also be accommodated if psychologically trained coaches are to be successful.

The second audience includes businesspeople, managers, leaders, and human resources directors who want to improve their coaching skills with enhanced knowledge of psychology. Coaching is an important part of their present jobs, and they may lack an adequate understanding of the psychological bases for effective coaching. Some organizations now view coaching as a mainstream, in-house management skill. This book takes essential lessons from psychology and makes them available to the management coach. These ideas and principles, when properly applied, can help grow a promising employee, develop a young leader, remediate one who has run into difficulties or limitations, head off derailment, and perhaps enhance the entire organizational environment.

The book is organized in the following way. Good coaching usually begins with an assessment, and Chapter 1 describes the application of principles and methods of psychological testing. Chapter 2 reviews the developmental psychology literature as it applies to adults. Chapters 3 through 8 each describe an important psychotherapy theory or theoretical viewpoint, beginning with a brief history and a description of its essential components. Examples are provided to demonstrate how each model can be optimally applied to executive coaching. Strengths and weaknesses are discussed in terms of the theory's applicability to the business world. Chapter 9 reviews the important research done by social psychologists since World War II, emphasizing the power of the social context on human behavior. Chapter 10 defines hypnotic communication in a way that makes it powerfully useful to coaches. Chapter 11 describes the now-popular research on emotional intelligence, sorting out the most useful aspects from the hype. Chapter 12 summarizes lessons from athletic coaching books, as there is much to be gleaned from this intriguing body of literature, a source widely read by business executives. Chapter 13, on the coaching of women in business, points out that in the still-male world of corporate life, there is a need to understand gender politics and differential gender communication patterns, values, and tendencies. Chapter 14 has been added to this edition describing the psychopathology likely to be encountered by business coaches. Coaches are well advised to study this chapter and handle such unfortunate situations with care. Chapter 15, another new chapter, reviews the popular and scientific literature on leadership and leader development. Chapter 16 describes the important but poorly understood differences between managing and leading. Chapter 17 translates well-established ethics codes and ethical principles from psychotherapy into the executive coaching setting, where formal ethics codes are now evolving. The final chapter describes how to make the transition from therapist to coach, and it provides essential business information for psychotherapists unfamiliar with the business culture and point of view. Most chapters end with a list of summary points for readers in a hurry to translate their skills and get going. Extensive references and additional recommended readings are listed at the end of each chapter for the reader who wishes to study in greater depth.

If you are a psychotherapist with established counseling skills, you may want to skip selected parts of the text and go directly to your areas of relative weakness. These might include theories you learned years ago but have forgotten. Many of the chapters will provide a useful *brush-up*. You will certainly want to study the chapters that focus on the business world and how it works, as well as the chapter on leadership.

If you are a manager or executive, you should focus on the psychotherapy theory chapters to gain essential background on their development, evolution, and core ideas. You may even want to seek additional training or find a mentor from the psychotherapy field.

These are exciting times in psychotherapy and in executive coaching, and there is an increased openness in organizations to the value of psychological interventions. Each of these two worlds has much to offer the other. This book strives to help you make the most of the available opportunities and to make a positive impact on workers and on the organizational culture as well.

Acknowledgments

Again, there are many people to thank.

First, to Tracey, Drew, and Carly for their support and flexibility and love. What a great family. It's been a terrific ride over the past 20 years. I hope you guys read this book from time to time and get something of value from it. You have all contributed: Tracey with your work challenges, examples, successes, and special point of view (and kindness and support); Drew with your love for Dostoevsky and willingness to do whatever is necessary; and Carly with your extended essay and insights into gender, and uncanny ability to challenge the ideas I thought I had settled long ago.

Thanks to Cindy Lyon for crucial support, and to many other wonderful colleagues at the Arthur A. Dugoni, University of the Pacific School of Dentistry. What a great place to work. One more big thank you to Art Dugoni—lifelong student of leadership—for all of his mentoring and positive reinforcement. A shout-out to Carp for his friendship and intuitive appreciation of the absurd. Special thanks to Seberiana Hernandez for all she did to help, which was a lot.

Thanks to Terry Patterson, Faith Otis, and other colleagues at the University of San Francisco. Much of what I have learned about psychology came from teaching there.

Students deserve serious appreciation, as they have challenged me to refine and clarify my thinking so that it is more or less comprehensible.

Thanks also to Caroline Horner and Mike van Oudtshoorn of i-Coach Academy for their support and collaboration. They provided an opportunity for me to travel to London and South Africa to continue to work on the ideas in the book, encouraging me to produce a second edition.

Much appreciation goes to Dana Bliss for opening the door, nurturing the project, nudging and indulging me, and providing just the right editorial touch and positive support.

Special thanks to the Bomber for consistently being in my corner.

John Vriend, the writer, died since publication of the first edition, but his big paw prints are all over this one as well. He wrote that "It goes," and it went.

Author and Contributor

Bruce Peltier, Ph.D., is Professor of Psychology and Ethics at the Arthur A. Dugoni School of Dentistry, University of the Pacific. He is a licensed psychologist and an executive coach in San Francisco, California. He is a 1970 graduate of West Point. His MEd and PhD are from Wayne State University, and his MBA is from the Eberhardt School at the University of the Pacific. His postdoctoral internship was completed at the University of Southern California, and he served for 2 years as a research assistant at the Center for Educational Research at Stanford University. Dr. Peltier has served as President of the San Francisco Academy of Hypnosis and has taught psychotherapy classes at the University of San Francisco for the past 25 years.

The author can be contacted at: b.peltier@sbcglobal.net or bpeltier@pacific.edu. His Web site can be found at: http://brucepeltier.com/.

Alan Hedman is a management consultant and psychotherapist in Corrales, New Mexico. His undergraduate degree is from Pacific Lutheran University, where he was inducted into the University's Athletic Hall of Fame. He served as the Associate Director of the Health and Counseling Service at the University of Southern California for 5 years. For the past 25 years, he has been an executive coach and organizational consultant, primarily to nonprofit organizations.

His Web site can be found at: www.dralanhedman.com.

Introduction

Take a course in psychology, rather than technology.

—Tom Peters (Weinstein, 1999, p. J2)

Coaching activities, training, and literature have flourished since publication of the first edition of this book, and it appears that executive coaching is here to stay. There are now many books in print that describe coaching and how to do it. There has been an explosion of coach-training programs as well as organizations willing to coach people in a wide variety of areas including business coaching, life coaching, and health coaching. Coaching psychology seems to have emerged as a legitimate new subspecialty of psychology in Great Britain and Australia. There is now a substantial body of literature on executive coaching in academia (Kampa-Kokesch & Anderson, 2001) and *The Executive Coaching Handbook* (Executive Coaching Forum, 2008) lists 55 journals that publish research articles on executive coaching worldwide. Nonetheless, it is still difficult to sort things out. What is real? What is bogus? What is coaching and what is psychotherapy? Where does psychology fit into coaching practice? Who should coach? And how?

This book is for two audiences. It is written primarily for psychologists, counselors, social workers, and other trained psychotherapists who seek to apply their clinical experience to the corporate workplace. The second reader is the executive coach or management coach who would like more background on the psychological theory underlying the practices of executive coaching. A 2004 survey (Grant & Zackon, 2004) of International Coach Federation members ($n = 2,500$ with 67% American respondents) revealed that only 5% of coaches came into the field from psychology and only 19% had training and background in mental health fields (psychology, social work, or counseling). The other coaches came from a variety of fields—predominantly management consulting, and applied executive or management experience. Similar results were reported in a recent Harvard survey of 140 experienced coaches (Coutu & Kauffman, 2009). That survey revealed that more than 75% of coaches have assisted clients with "personal issues." The interested reader is directed to this important study of coaches for more comprehensive information about the current state of coaching practice in industry.

The goal of this book is to translate psychological theory into practical executive coaching skills.

Two Forms of Coaching

This book limits its focus to the application of coaching and psychological theory to organizational settings in general and more specifically to the coaching of executives. Coaching has become a popular, mainstream way to improve executives and organizations. Although little has been written on the subject, two basic forms of coaching have evolved. *Executive coaching* provides one-on-one services to top-level leaders in an organization on the principle that positive changes can be leveraged to filter down and enhance the entire organization. The alternative view is that a toxic executive can pollute an organization and cause widespread damage. There is evidence that the primary reason coaches are used has shifted in the past decade. Previously, coaches were hired to "fix toxic behavior at the top" (Coutu & Kauffman, 2009, p. 27), whereas the current trend is to use coaches to develop high-potential performers. One thought leader made this recent observation:

> As coaching has become more common, any stigma attached to receiving it at the individual level has disappeared. Now, it is often considered a badge of honor. (Charan, 2009, p. 93)

In the present economy, many are promoted into leadership positions based on previous diligence and technical excellence. They never intended to have a leadership position and did not prepare for it, but they could not resist the money and prestige that came with a promotion. Others simply had a great idea and boundless creative energy, so they started a company. Now they have to figure out how to lead. At the same time, companies are well aware of the importance and cost-effectiveness of retaining their best people, even when it means spending money to develop them in a down cycle.

A second approach, called *management coaching*, views coaching as a set of day-to-day skills exercised by managers at all levels of the organization. Some even view coaching as a primary way for managers to conduct their work. It replaces standard ways to manage people. Managers coach rather than control. In this view, workers are all seen as team members and assets to be continuously developed for promotion. This version makes coaching an integral part of succession planning, for employees must be proactively coached to move up into more demanding positions as the organization and its human capital evolves.

Although this book accommodates both views of coaching, and the principles and techniques can be used throughout the organization, the primary focus is on coaching the executive. Basic psychological theories are described, reviewed, and focused specifically on coaching the corporate or organizational executive.

Much executive coaching is presently atheoretical when viewed from the point of view of mainstream psychology. This book is for those who desire a framework for what they do. The Center for Creative Leadership in

Greensboro, North Carolina, recently published an annotated bibliography of executive coaching (Douglas & Morley, 2000, p. 39). It defines the executive coach as "a consultant who uses a wide variety of behavioral techniques and methods." This text describes many of the available methods for coaching along with their theoretical background. Readers of this book are likely to also be interested in a new coaching book that parallels the one you are currently reading. *Handbook of Coaching Psychology* (Palmer & Whybrow, 2008) is focused on coaching and psychology in wider settings (rather than just business and executive coaching) and is written from a British perspective. That text also has chapters on the application of psychotherapy theory and it includes several approaches not covered in this book. Coaching is quite popular in Britain, Ireland, Spain, and other European countries, as well as in Australia and New Zealand.

Psychologists and other mental health counselors are facing significant changes in work patterns, and many psychotherapists are seeking alternative ways to apply their hard-earned skills. Much of the change is driven by the powerful influence of managed care health plans, which have driven downward payment for and access to psychotherapy. Some of the change reflects current social and cultural values, which deemphasize personal therapy and perhaps introspection as well. Biological psychiatry has demonstrated an increased power with new medications, and managed care organizations are quite happy to take advantage of the associated cost savings. The "talking cure" has lost its place in mainstream American culture. It is too slow, too personal, provides no guarantees, and lacks the punch and focus demanded by those in the fast lane.

What Business Do Therapists Have in Executive Coaching?

Why should psychotherapists consider coaching? Is it within their training and scope of practice? Is it appropriate? Who should consider the practice of coaching? Is it for everyone? The business strategy literature is helpful in addressing these questions. Two strategy questions are especially useful.

Strategy Question 1: What Business Are You In?

What business are you in? is a question that strategists insist must be answered with care because it aligns all future efforts of an organization. The answer can open doors or it can close them.

> You can miss the strength of competitors by looking only at their end products, in the same way that you miss the strength of a tree if you look only at its leaves. (Prahalad & Hamel, 1990, p. 82)

By way of example, if a railroad views its business as running trains, it runs into severe constraints as airlines grow and penetrate new locations, driving down the time and cost of transporting goods and people. A railroad may benefit by thinking of itself as being in the business of transportation. This lesson is not lost on tobacco companies. They cannot continue to view their business as the making and selling of cigarettes, as recent events have made cigarettes difficult to sell in the United States. They are tobacco companies, always looking for ways to market and sell tobacco. This view has helped them develop new tobacco-delivery methods that include convenient little pouches that can be slipped between the cheek and gums. Such a shift in viewpoint opens doors and potential new markets and services. A business is best viewed as a "customer-satisfying endeavor" rather than a specific product or service (Kerin & Peterson, 1998). Products and services are transient. They must change as customers and environments change. If you are a psychotherapist, you probably define yourself on the basis of this single thing that you do: psychotherapy. That begs the second strategy question.

Strategy Question 2: What Are Your Core Competencies?

No company can do everything, and it is unwise to stretch oneself too thin. Railroads do not own or fly airplanes, and they do not employ pilots. They are in a poor position to compete directly with airlines, if they interpret that to mean buying and flying planes. A core competency is that set of skills that you know best, and it represents your collective learning. When companies are clear about their core competencies, they can function in a variety of lucrative markets, as long as their products and services derive closely from those competencies. Companies sometimes get into trouble when they wander too far from their core competencies, and there is risk in diversification. But few businesses can survive without occasionally reinventing themselves or refreshing their products or services, as the market is dynamic and competitors are always lurking.

The reader may want to read Prahalad and Hamel's 1990 essay in the *Harvard Business Review* titled "The Core Competence of the Corporation." In it they list three defining attributes:

1. A core competence provides potential access to a wide variety of markets.
2. A core competence should make a significant contribution to customers.
3. A core competence should be difficult for competitors to imitate.

The Core Competencies of Psychotherapists

Core competencies are the wellspring of new business development.

—**C. K. Prahalad and Gary Hamel (1990, p. 91)**

Although the definition of core competence varies somewhat between psychologists, marriage and family therapists, social workers, and psychiatrists, it varies more between individuals in those fields. Someone who identifies as a psychotherapist is likely to view her basic competencies more narrowly than, say, a psychologist, who may engage in a wide variety of assessment and consultative activities.

Nonetheless, here is a definition of the business of the psychotherapist that opens the door to executive coaching:

> *The psychotherapist uses psychological methods to facilitate the growth and development of individuals in intrapersonal and interpersonal functioning, as well as the remediation of problems in those areas.*

Core competencies may include one-on-one interpersonal interaction and problem solving, cultivation and use of empathy, development of insight, behavior analysis, cognitive restructuring, hypnosis, or psychological assessment.

You may not agree with the aforementioned definition, and you may choose to tweak it to suit you, but you need a clear idea of your core competencies along with a definition of your business in order to focus your transition from therapy to coaching. You may even decide, as a result of this values-clarifying exercise, that executive coaching is not for you.

There is dispute in the coaching literature about the relevance and importance of formal psychological training and experience. Those who come into coaching without formal psychological training sometimes question the need, validity, and utility of such training. The 2009 Harvard study of coaching (Kauffman & Coutu, 2009) revealed that only 13% thought that psychological training was essential and nearly half thought it did not matter at all. Although it seems likely that some coaches who lack a background in psychology are able to provide excellent coaching, it seems certain that training in psychology is useful if not essential. Coaches in the Harvard study noted that although they were almost never (3% of the time) hired to help an executive with a personal issue, they actually addressed a personal issue in coaching 76% of the time.

> Over the past 15 years, it has become more and more popular to hire coaches for promising executives. Although some of these coaches hail from the world of psychology, a greater share are former athletes, lawyers, business academics, and consultants. No doubt these people help executives improve their performance in many areas. But I want to tell a different story. I believe that in an alarming number of situations, executive coaches who lack rigorous psychological training do more harm than good. (Berglas, 2002, p. 86)

The Potential

Executive and management coaching are ideal ways to bring the positive potential of psychology into the workplace. Psychologists have always recognized that the workplace has a powerful influence on a person's mental health, and efforts to make the work environment more humane can have a healthy impact on large numbers of people, as well as on the bottom line. There is a large and growing interest in coaching (on the part of psychotherapists and others), as evidenced by many numerous recent publications. A search of Amazon.com reveals no fewer than 20 books with the term *executive coaching* in the title. In addition, there are many other books on coaching psychology and leadership coaching. It is no wonder that providers of psychological counseling, accustomed to focusing their skills on individuals in private sessions, now look to corporations and small businesses for a new market.

Coaching seems popular in the mainstream business press as well. A 2000 study of media perceptions in 72 articles revealed that "favorable views of executive coaching far exceed unfavorable views" (Garman, Whiston, & Zlatoper, 2000, p. 201).

Many of the experienced executive coaches surveyed in the Harvard study were optimistic about the future of coaching (Coutu & Kauffman, 2009, p. 24):

> [There is] a huge need among executives to build leadership skills, most specifically to manage people—a level of emotional maturity and introspective capacity that very few senior executives have.

> [There is] a growing recognition that most executive development is achieved through customized individualized ways [rather than through] programmatic efforts.

> Executives can lead very lonely lives. Coaches allow for conversations they cannot have with superiors, peers, employees, or family.

> Coaching is a safe place to have difficult conversations.

> I expect the profession to grow and for credentialing to become more rigorous over time.

> I believe [coaching] is on the rise: More and more executives and teams are facing issues too complex to deal with on their own without outside perspective.

Counseling and clinical psychologists, as well as marriage and family therapists, social workers, and even psychiatrists, possess powerful interpersonal change skills. This book puts old wine into new bottles, so that more can appreciate the vintage. It is written to help psychotherapists adapt their valuable skills to the corporate culture and to provide theoretical and practical tools for coaches who lack formal psychological training.

Coaching: What Is It?

For all of the work that has been done to illuminate the subject of coaching in the past 15 or 20 years, what actually happens in coaching engagements remains quite mysterious.

—Richard R. Kilburg (2004, p. 203)

It is no accident that management consultants often start by declaring what coaching is not. "Coaching is specifically not therapy," they typically state. Although some business practitioners include "counseling" in the repertoire of skills used by managers on a day-to-day basis, counseling is reserved for troubled employees with "psychological problems." Counseling is personal and it is aimed at personal problems. Coaching carries a much more positive implication in the corporate world. High-performance athletes are coached; sick, weak, neurotic, or crazy people get therapy. Such thinking goes like this: "Anyone with a lick of sense seeks coaching, but competent people don't need therapy. They can handle things on their own." Competent people, however, want coaching. High performers seek it out. Tiger Woods apparently works with his swing coach regularly, even after a stellar performance. Elite tennis professionals have personal coaches, and TV cameras spotlight those coaches during important matches.

Carol Macmillan (1999) performed an extensive literature review as part of her dissertation on role definitions of management consultants. She concluded (p. 75):

> As more mental health clinicians move into organizational consulting positions, it becomes more important to establish what the role of the organizational consultant is, particularly when the consultant is trained and experienced in clinical work. The consulting literature in general is poorly defined, poorly documented, and poorly integrated, particularly as it relates to clinical theories, which may be relevant and useful for consulting work.

Despite the unsavory implications of psychotherapy in the corporate culture, there is no denying that the literature of psychotherapy is important and highly relevant to executive coaching. The baby can't be thrown out with the bath water. Here is an example of the relevance of psychological theory in executive coaching:

> Within this systems orientation, we draw from the frameworks of humanistic, existential, behavioral, and psychodynamic psychology and choose our techniques eclectically to fit the client, the situation, and the need.

This quote is from the article "Coaching at the Top," by Kiel, Rimmer, Williams, and Doyle (1996, p. 68) of KRW International, a firm that specializes in the coaching of CEOs at Fortune 500 companies.

Lester Tobias (1990, p. 1) made the following observation in his book *Psychological Consulting to Management*:

> Consulting psychology, management psychology, or corporate psychology, as it is variously called, is the application of the principles of psychology to help people in organizations become more effective.

The Center for Creative Leadership (Douglas & Morley, 2000, p. 40) provides the following descriptions of coaching:

> Reduced to its essence, executive coaching is the process of equipping people with the tools, knowledge, and opportunities they need to develop themselves and become more effective (Peterson, 1996). Executive coaching involves the teaching of skills in the context of a personal relationship with the learner, and providing feedback on the executive's interpersonal relations and skills (Sperry, 1993). An ongoing series of activities tailored to the individual's current issues or relevant problem is designed by the coach to assist the executive in maintaining a consistent, confident focus as he or she tunes strengths and manages short-comings (Tobias, 1996).

Anyone interested in a serious exploration of executive coaching, its nature, and future directions is urged to read The Executive Coaching Forum's *Handbook* (2008). The definition of executive coaching found there is:

> Executive coaching is an experiential and individualized leader development process that builds a leader's capability to achieve short- and long-term organizational goals. It is conducted through one-on-one and/or group interactions, driven by data from multiple perspectives, and based on mutual trust and respect. The organization, an executive, and the executive coach work in partnership to achieve maximum impact. (p. 19)

In a 1998 essay in *The Family Therapy Networker*, W. T. Anderson of the Meridian International Institute highlighted the interaction between psychological thinking and theory and executive coaching (p. 36):

> Although management thinkers are notoriously eclectic in their plundering of intellectual resources … there's really no way the modern discipline of management would have evolved as it has without theories and practices borrowed from psychology.

Coaching Defined

Executive coaching, as described in this book, is defined in the following way:

Psychological skills and methods are employed in a one-on-one relationship to help someone become a more effective manager or leader. These skills are typically applied to specific present-moment work-related issues (rather than general personal problems or psychopathology) in a way that enables this client to incorporate them into his or her permanent management or leadership repertoire.

Examples of skills derived from psychotherapy literature include active listening and empathy, self-awareness, process observation, giving and getting feedback, assertive communication, conflict resolution, cognitive restructuring and learned optimism, effective use of reinforcement, hypnotic language, functional analysis, stimulus control, social learning, resistance management, detriangulation, reframing, motivational interviewing based upon stages of change, and even paradoxical directives. These skills and others are described in the chapters that follow, with examples to demonstrate their application to the workplace. Other essential skills that can be coached include more basic elements of leadership and management such as delegation, public speaking, presentation of self, time management, strategic planning, goal setting, writing skills, phone skills, strategic planning, sales skills, use of information technology, and project management. Consulting that focuses directly on a business's content skills or technical skills is not included in the scope of this book, nor is it seen as a typical coaching focus, although there is a significant and growing demand for coaches who can provide specific business or project-related expertise as well. Examples include dentistry, law, sales, and technology industries.

The skills that psychotherapists possess are of enormous potential to business executives and corporate leaders. They ought not go to waste. That said, therapists cannot hope to succeed in this arena without serious exposure to key business concepts and culture.

The most important workplace skill was, is, and always will be the ability to get along with people. If you don't have that skill, any success you will have will only be temporary. (Murphy, 2000)

Coaching Executives

Things change at the top. As a manager or executive rises in a hierarchical organization, information does not flow the way it previously did, and some executives complain that it is tough to get a straight answer any more. This results in troublesome blind spots for leaders. Research on 1,214 managers and executives by Sala, documents one important component of this problem:

> The results of this study demonstrate that higher level employees are more likely than lower level employees to have an inflated view of their emotional intelligence competencies and less congruence with the perceptions of others who work with them often and know them well. This information is valuable because ... previous research has firmly established that high-performing managers tend to have more accurate self-perceptions. (2003, p. 225)

Organizations are often willing to spend time and money on the ongoing development of top executives. They assume that such a commitment will, down the line, pay compounded dividends. The organization will perform more effectively, profits will increase, and life will be more comfortable for everyone in the organization. The company's reputation will be enhanced, and key people will be retained. Intervention is especially important when a top executive has a blind spot or some poor quality or tendency that drives others up the wall. Organizations suffer when exceptional technical workers, who do not have leadership skills, are promoted into leadership positions. It is common for companies to promote people who have an excellent technical record into leadership positions on the assumption that they will be able to learn how to lead on the job. This is a ridiculous notion. Some of these newly minted "leaders" do not even possess much interest in leadership, but they take the "promotion" because it is a step up and it means that they will be paid more money. Some young executives actually find interpersonal interaction to be distressing. Many are not even aware that a distinctive set of essential leadership skills exists! At the same time, leadership theorists and experts do not even agree on a basic definition of their core concept. They do agree that no adequate or commonly accepted definition of leadership exists. It is unreasonable to expect those promoted into leader positions to be able to quickly and smoothly make the transition without help. It must also be noted that excellent leadership is rare and difficult to do.

Organizations are often willing to give coaching a try at top levels because it is at top levels that important strategic and operational decisions are made. One or two critical strategic decisions can literally make or break a company. Good strategic thinking is also rare and difficult. Sometimes the decision-making process is risky and lonely, and an executive can often use a trusted adviser—someone who is not inside the organization. This is where therapeutic methods, translated to fit the corporate culture, can be enormously valuable. There is real potential for the win–win result. Therapists get to use existing skills to coach and make a good living, and executives benefit from a source not previously available in the corporate setting.

Where Coaching Can Help

There are at least four general situations that call for executive or management coaching. Coaching works best when it is seen as a *benefit* for high achievers, key people, and those with great potential. When it is seen only as remedial, executives are likely to run from it, and a coach then becomes the "angel of death"—the last step before you are shown the door. No one in an organization wants to be stigmatized or marked for elimination, so they avoid coaching or resist. If coaching is going to work it must be framed as a benefit—an *opportunity* for the most promising or valuable executives and managers.

Here are four general ways that executive coaches can help:

1. *When big things in the organization change*—Coaching is extremely useful when an organization realizes that it must change. This decision might be an adaptation to evolution in the market environment or it could be a decision to respond to a perceived opportunity. Such changes usually require new executive approaches, and a coach can help leaders adapt. Coaching is of special importance during mergers and acquisitions. Organizational sea change can become a disaster without outside help.

2. *Skill development for individual transitions*—Coaches can help high performers acquire the necessary new skills as they move to positions of greater authority and responsibility. When someone is rewarded for technical excellence and given a promotion into a leadership position, he or she typically needs to learn new leadership skills. This person may even need to learn a whole series of new and sophisticated social skills (e.g., delegating, public speaking, or entertaining clients or board members at dinner). This is likely to require a solid assessment or self-evaluation. A coach can facilitate and accelerate this process. The essential leadership skills do not come naturally and must not be taken for granted. They must be identified, evaluated, taught, and discussed.

3. *Specific skill development*—Sometimes an executive realizes that he or she has never learned one specific critical skill, such as how to work with an advisory board or board of directors. A coach can be extremely cost effective in such a case, especially if the coach has expertise in that specific area. Sometimes executives realize that they lack one important leadership or social skill, such as speaking in front of large audiences or working a cocktail party. Sometimes they must improve the way they present themselves in public settings. Others must learn the difficult skill of delegating. Many lack the difficult knack of strategic planning, a crucial leadership function for all organizations.

Frequently, executives have been able to hide a shortcoming for years, but are now faced with awareness of the limitation. The time has come to deal with that shortcoming and fix it. Sometimes they are only dimly aware that they have a skill deficit, but know that something is getting in the way. Sometimes others have to inform them of deficits or specific weaknesses.

4. *Resolving specific problems*—Frequently, a powerful and successful person possesses one or two sets of dysfunctional behavior that cause repetitive difficulties. He or she may have an annoying or abrasive habit or a gap in self-esteem or self-confidence that didn't show before. Perhaps the increased responsibility is a heavy burden, and the person lacks stress-management skills, resulting in negative work interactions or missed deadlines. Perhaps the person finds it difficult to trust. In this situation, the coach is called on for specific remedial help. When done well, this kind of help can save a career and a lot of corporate expense. It can also eliminate considerable human friction and misery.

The Harvard survey (Coutu & Kauffman, 2009, pp. 6–7) found that coaches had been engaged for the following purposes at least once in their careers: helped develop a high-potential manager or facilitate a transition to leadership (about 95% of coaches); acted as a sounding board (94%); enhanced interactions of a team (91%); addressed derailing behavior (87%); addressed personal issues or issues in the client's nonwork life (76%); and assisted in outplacement (41%).

The survey revealed that coaches were most frequently engaged in the following ways:

1. Develop capabilities of high-potential managers or facilitate an upward transition (48% of coaches reported frequently doing this)
2. Act as a sounding board on organizational or strategic matters (26%)
3. Address derailing behavior (12%)
4. Enhance the interactions of a team (11%)

Steps in the Process

Effective coaching involves a four-step process.

Step 1: Get Things Started

Either the company must find a coach or a coach must find the company. Regardless of how this happens, the coach must, in some way, sell the service. This means that he or she must call attention to a deficit, make a case for skill enhancement, or offer a solution to a problem. Coaches have to be able to define their work in terms of outcomes and solutions. What will be better as a result of coaching? How will we know, and what difference will it make? Ground rules and parameters such as confidentiality, reporting relationships between coach and sponsor, and dimensions of the project (targeted people, time, and money) must be established. A contract must be negotiated and signed. The Harvard survey reported that 90% of experienced executive coaches establish an up-front agreement about the proposed time frame for the engagement before they began the work (Coutu & Kauffman, 2009, p. 11). Much of this is discussed in detail in Chapter 17 "Ethics in Coaching" and Chapter 18 "Making the Transition."

Step 2: Gather Information and Make a Plan

Step 2 typically includes an assessment of the executive to be coached—the client. The assessment process is described in Chapter 1. Supervisors, colleagues, direct-reports, and customers are often called upon to provide input to the coaching process. Extensive data are carefully fed back to the client. A clear plan is developed, and the plan includes measurable outcomes. This plan is locked in and written down. The coach and client agree on the focus and what will change.

Step 3: Implement

The coach has an extended period (typically 3 months to 2 years) to produce tangible results. This process includes regular contact between the executive and the coach (e.g., in person, through e-mail, and over the telephone). The focus of meetings may be to solve problems, to develop new skills, or to work on objectives described in the plan for change. Good coaching often includes shadowing, where the coach goes to the executive's workplace and observes the person in action.

Step 4: Lock in the Changes; Arrange for Ongoing, Continuous Improvement and Support

Improvements that do not last are of little value. Without effective arrangements for permanent long-term change, coaching will take its place on bookshelves full of other trendy, passing management fads. Activities of value to organizations are those that have a lasting influence, long after the consultant has left. Steps must be taken to cement short-term gains.

The Harvard study of coaching behavior reported that coaching engagements typically last from 2 to 18 months (Coutu & Kauffman, 2009, p. 10). Forty-five percent of engagements lasted between 7 and 12 months. Only 4% continued for more than 2 years.

Outcome evaluation is sorely lacking in executive coaching. Most coaches are not documenting their work. According to the Harvard survey, "Fewer than one-fourth of the respondents said they provide any kind of quantitative data on business outcomes of the coaching" (Peterson, 2009). Coaches must learn how to do this and establish systems for ongoing assessment of client performance and their own coaching work.

Coaching as a Mainstream Leadership Skill

Coaching can have an egalitarian influence on organizations. When its premise is that each employee is valued, time and money are justified, as they will benefit the entire organization in the end. When people are viewed as assets worthy of development, coaches can be employed to stimulate growth in areas of organizational importance or weakness. Such areas might include regular, on-the-job coaching in the following:

- Interpersonal communication
    Listening skills
    Assertiveness skills
    Ways to read other people
    Effective use of language
    Giving positive and negative feedback
- Delegation skills
- Team-building skills
- Diversity in the workplace
- Running an effective meeting
- Writing skills for business and management
- Planning skills
- Decision making
- Project management
- Conflict management
- Cultural competence
- Organizational culture
- Dealing with difficult or problem employees or colleagues

Referring Pathology Appropriately

Executive coaches can certainly identify and occasionally remediate personality pathologies but the corporate coach typically refers such cases to professionals and psychotherapists outside of the organization. There are good reasons, discussed later, to keep the activities of coaching and therapy separate. Coaches must possess skills that allow them to make such referrals in an effective way. In his summary of the Harvard survey of executive coaches, Anthony Grant (2009, p. 32) came to the following conclusion:

> Given that some executives will have mental health problems, firms should require that coaches have some training in mental health issues— for example, an understanding of when to refer clients to professional therapists for help.

Coaches need to be able to recognize common psychopathologies, use appropriate referral techniques, and possess some familiarity with local referral sources. The Harvard survey reported that (Kauffman & Coutu, 2009, p. 14)

> coaching is unsuccessful when executives have severe behavioral problems, when they are unwilling to look inward, or when they have fundamentally different values from those in the organization. The behavioral challenges coaches cited as resistant to coaching include narcissism, deep resentment, a sense of resignation, and very serious self-esteem issues. ... Executives who are chronic blamers, are attached to the victim mentality, or have an ironclad belief system often do not respond well to coaching.

Common psychopathologies found in the organizational workplace are described in more detail in Chapter 14 of this book.

Do Not Throw Out the Therapy Baby with the Bathwater: Coaching and Psychotherapy

Some business consultants and executive coaches go out of their way to distance themselves from the symbols and language of psychotherapy. This is easy to understand, as therapy brings with it all kinds of baggage in the form of negative images and implications in the corporate world. If you need a psychotherapist, according to this way of thinking, you are sick or crazy or weak; strong people can solve their own problems, and effective executives do not have those kinds of problems, anyway. "We hire stars, not mental cases," some might say. But to run from the therapy model, to abandon it completely, would be a serious mistake. The core ideas from accepted therapy theories have significant value for executive or management coaches. The trick is to apply these methods effectively in an arena where they are not always welcomed, understood, or appreciated.

Numerous unfortunate impressions of therapy linger in the management world, and many still attach a stigma to therapy. Therapy is seen as appropriate for Woody Allen types who would rather sit around and whine than go out and make things happen. This is hardly an attractive image for the corporate executive charged with the task of moving "market mountains." Therapy is viewed as slow, expensive, tedious, often ineffective, or only appropriate for people with "real" problems. It can drag on for years, with no attempt at evaluation or accountability. Therapists are sometimes seen as complex, wimpy, gloomy types who do not live in the real world—they will not give you a straight answer, they have never really accomplished anything significant in the real world, and they are probably a little goofy themselves. Business executives sometimes believe that in therapy you just talk a lot about your feelings and complain. You go over and over things. Many businesspeople have no real experience with psychotherapy, and some are uncomfortable with the idea that they might have to confront themselves, their feelings, and their behavior. Others dread the negative feedback they might get from a coach or from coworkers. At the same time, introspection is not always valued in the pragmatic business world where many focus on day-to-day survival, usually achieved through direct, immediate action.

If executive coaches allow themselves and their work to be defined this negative way, they are dead before they get through the door.

Differentiating Coaching from Therapy

A coach must be able to provide a good working definition of coaching and articulate the difference between coaching and psychotherapy. Table I.1 summarizes the major differences, and the distinctions can be challenging. On the other hand, this all could turn out to be a case of a distinction without a difference in actual practice.

As can be seen in Table I.1, coaching is typically action oriented, data driven, present-moment focused, and designed for a high-functioning client. Confidentiality is complex and much less secure than it is in therapy. Even the definition of the concept of "client" is complicated, as the sponsoring organization (that pays the bill) has a stake in the outcome. Doesn't that make them a client? Boundaries are much less rigid, as the work usually takes place outside of the coach's office, and it often includes social events, large business meetings, and company outings.

Certainly there are aspects of therapy that are inappropriate and counterproductive when dragged into the corporate environment. If a therapist attempts to provide coaching without significant knowledge of the business world or the corporate environment, including its vocabulary, its motivations, its assumptions, and its bottom-line orientation, he or she is destined to fail. A psychotherapist who has spent all of his or her time in the therapy world, isolated from the corporate environment, is likely to face significant difficulties in coaching. If you have spent your entire professional life at universities, in counseling centers or clinics, in a private therapy office, and at professional meetings with psychologist colleagues, you are going to have to make a significant transition.

Values As a starting point, mental health professionals must often overcome their own serious value biases about the business world. Psychologists sometimes do not respect a bottom-line profit orientation. Money is a primary method for evaluation in the business culture, and many therapists do not think in those terms. Some are actually uncomfortable with this orientation. Psychotherapists must be able to talk directly about money.

Competition Business executives compete and expect others to compete with them, moment-to-moment, day-to-day, all the time. Their position is

Table I.1 Differentiating Coaching from Therapy

Therapy	Coaching
Focus on the past	Present and future focus
Passive orientation (listening), reflective	Action orientation
No presumption about client mental health	No psychopathology assumed to be present
Data from client	Data is information from key others, as well as from the client
Pathology or remediation orientation	Growth or skill development orientation
Therapist competency in mental health	Coach competency in facilitation and business
Personality orientation (examining and altering personality characteristics)	Performance focus (enhancing performance)
Problem is intrapsychic (found in the person)	Problem is found in person–environment mix
Information not shared with others	Information sometimes fed back to key members of organization (with great care)
Client is clearly the person you work with	Definition of *client* unclear (may be the organization that is paying coach's fees)
Client (person) must feel enriched	Organization must feel enhanced by the coaching
Confidentiality is clear, nearly absolute, legal	Confidentiality is complex, less absolute
50-minute sessions typical	Meetings of variable length
Work in therapist's office	Meet in executive's workplace or a neutral site
Rigid boundaries	Flexible boundaries, including social settings
Work through (resolve) personality issues	Work around personality issues
Client chooses therapist	Organization often chooses coach
Client pays therapist (sometimes through health care plan)	Sponsoring organization typically pays coach

See also Sperry's chart in *Corporate Therapy and Consulting* (1996, p. 184); Bachkirova's similar chart in *Handbook of Coaching Psychology* (2008, p. 357); and another similar chart in Coutu and Kauffman (2009, p. 22).

rarely secure, as others are trying to best them or replace them. Companies cannot stand still. They are expected to grow and improve and make more money every year. Competition is a way of life; it is accepted and expected—even welcomed by effective executives. Counselors are not used to this focus as they tend to think cooperatively. It is easy to underestimate the depth and significance of this difference.

Appearance Corporate executives are used to dressing for success, on the assumption that the way you look carries real weight. If you appear successful and powerful, they believe that others will give you respect and you will be taken seriously. They know that appearances send powerful messages. Mental health workers often ignore this part of life, dressing for comfort on the assumption that appearance is superficial and insignificant.

Pace Things move fast in the corporate world, and decisions must be made now, without enough information. Therapists are trained to reflect, to work through, and to give things time to settle out.

Venue Therapists nearly always conduct their work in their own offices. Clients come to them. It is very different in the coaching arena, where coaches often meet with clients in the client's work setting. Sometimes the work is done off-site at meetings or retreats. Sometimes a coach actually sits in on client business meetings. A coach may even travel with a coaching client. The Harvard survey also reported that 20% of executive coaches use the telephone for coaching interactions (Coutu & Kauffman, 2009, p. 11).

What Therapists Can Offer the Business World

In spite of these significant differences, psychotherapy has much to offer the corporate world. Here are some of the most important general things that therapists can bring to business:

1. *Insight*—At its best, therapy produces hard-earned wisdom about how life really works. The executive who knows how to study the undertow of psychological currents and patterns in a work environment has a significant advantage. This includes insight into self and insight into the dynamics and motivations of others. An executive who cannot read and understand other people does not stand much of a chance in the long run. One who is ignorant of self is at a real disadvantage. Some people develop these skills on their own; others must work at them in a structured way with help. It is difficult to learn these things alone or in isolation. Everyone can use another set of eyes and ears, and another point of view. It also helps an executive to have someone to talk to about what is really true. Much corporate and organizational conversation is stilted by a need to shade things one way or another. Most people manage conversations with a boss carefully. Such interactions are rarely authentic in any deep way. It is extremely valuable to have someone to talk to in an honest way about reality.

2. *Adult Development*—Each of us goes through a series of expectable changes in life. To behave like a 30-year-old when you are 50 is to ask for trouble. It just does not work, and an understanding of development

brings an important expertise to the mix. Developmental changes and urges are important motivators, and they must be considered when making significant corporate decisions. Executives must continuously develop along several dimensions. Many exceptional young executives are promoted ahead of their contemporaries, only to find themselves in a new cultural milieu with new rules and priorities. Their previous scorn for conformity or self-promotion or social schmoozing puts them at odds with their new colleagues. Such leaders may need help to move through this developmental phase within their career. Adult development is described in detail in Chapter 2, a new chapter in this edition.

3. *Modeling Effective Listening Skills*—Most psychotherapists are far better listeners than most business executives. Therapists have taken courses in graduate school on how to listen effectively. Many have read research on listening and how it functions, and most have experienced internships or traineeships where they received feedback on their listening skills. At the very least, ex-counselors can serve as a useful model of these skills for executive clients. Simple listening techniques such as restatement, paraphrasing, reflection of feelings, summarizing, and physical listening are new to executives and highly valued, once they are experienced and understood.

4. *Resistance*—People do not change when they say they will. People do not grow when they decide they need to. Therapists are used to resistance, and they come to expect it. It does not throw them; they do not find it discouraging or annoying. It simply comes with the territory. It is actually useful in some theoretical ways.

5. *Cooperation*—The therapist–coach is not competitive in any way with the executive client. When the executive succeeds, the coach succeeds. Therapists bring this rather unique slant to the business world, and it is rare and valuable in that context. Sometimes executives compete compulsively, when they would be better off to cooperate from time to time. There is evidence that cooperative models of leadership are advantageous with modern workers in the present economy.

6. *Psychopathology*—Coaches with mental health training and background experiences have the advantage of knowledge about common psychopathologies and how to detect them. Although this is certainly not the most common activity of an executive coach, it comes in handy from time to time, especially with leaders or followers who have personalities that are destructive. A chapter describing psychopathology and how to spot it has been added to this edition (see Chapter 14).

Table I.2 Positive and Negative Themes from Psychotherapy Related to Coaching

Positive Themes (Useful in Coaching)	Negative Themes (Leave These Behind)
Insight	Passive approach
Awareness as a goal	Data from client only
Self-examination	Slow movement
Intrapersonal understanding	Focus on feelings or intrapersonal
Talking about things is superior to:	information
• not talking about them	Meeting only in office (of clinician) at a
• ignoring them	regular time, for a standard period of
• pretending things are OK	time (50 minutes)
• hoping things will get better	Reliance on the coach
Rapport building/special relationship	
Feedback from impartial party	
Confidentiality	

7. *Interpersonal Aspects of Leadership*—The most important components of leadership are interpersonal. Psychologically oriented coaches bring important techniques and unique experiences to the table in this area. Chapter 15 examines leadership theory in detail.

Other, more specific themes must be considered in the coaching–therapy mix. Table I.2 summarizes some important themes to keep in mind.

Positive and Negative Themes from Therapy (What to Keep and What to Throw Out)

As shown in Table I.2, there are aspects of psychotherapy that must be left behind if the coach is to be perceived as useful and relevant in the corporate world. This is most often true at the beginning of a coaching relationship. Once trust and effectiveness have been demonstrated, a coach can be less wary about being confused with a psychotherapist, although this issue never completely goes away.

The Overall Purpose of This Book

Simply stated, the goal of this book is to help the reader synthesize the best lessons from psychological theory in a way that they can be quickly understood and effectively applied to executive and management coaching. There are two target audiences: the psychotherapist who wants to enter the world of executive coaching and organizational consultants seeking to enhance their understanding of the psychological components of coaching. Most chapters begin with a history of the theory and its basic concepts, followed by examples of the way that the theory can be applied to coaching in the workplace. Strengths and weaknesses of theories are discussed, along with situations that are well suited or poorly suited for each approach. Four new chapters have been added to the second edition. One describes the kinds of psychopathology that might be encountered by a coach in an organization (Chapter 14). Another summarizes relevant contributions from developmental psychology (Chapter 2). Emotional intelligence is introduced and evaluated in Chapter 11. Leadership theory is described in Chapter 15. There is a rewritten chapter specifically aimed at coaching female executives, and it explores the unique problems that women face when they enter the corporate arena and move from survival to thriving in the executive suite (Chapter 13). Chapter 16 describes the important differences between workers, managers, and leaders. Another summarizes the lessons an executive coach can learn from successful athletic coaches (Chapter 12). A final chapter provides tips for the psychotherapist who is just getting started in the coaching world (Chapter 18). References and recommended readings follow each chapter.

References

Anderson, W. T. (1998, January/February). New kid in the boardroom. *The Family Therapy Networker,* 35–40.

Bachkirova, T. (2008). Role of coaching psychology in defining boundaries between counseling and coaching. In S. Palmer & A. Whybrow (Eds.), *Handbook of coaching psychology* (pp. 351–366). London: Routledge.

Berglas, S. (2002, June). The very real dangers of executive coaching. *Harvard Business Review, 80*(6), 86–92.

Charan, R. (2009, January). The coaching industry: A work in progress. *Harvard Business Review, 87*(1), 93.

Coutu, D., & Kauffman, C. (2009, January). What can coaches do for you? *Harvard Business Review, 87*(1), 91–97.

Douglas, C., & Morley, W. (2000). *Executive coaching: An annotated bibliography.* Greensboro, NC: Center for Creative Leadership.

Executive Coaching Forum. (2008). *The executive coaching handbook.* Available at: www.executivecoachingforum.com

Garman, A. N., Whiston, D. L., & Zlatoper, K. W. (2000). Media perceptions of executive coaching and the formal preparation of coaches. *Consulting Psychology Journal: Practice and Research, 52*(3), 201–205.

Grant, A. M. (2009, January). Coach or couch? *Harvard Business Review, 87*(1), 97.

Grant, A. M., & Zackon, R. (2004). Executive, workplace and life coaching: Findings from a large-scale survey of International Coach Federation members. *International Journal of Evidence Based Coaching and Mentoring, 2*(2), 1–15.

Kampa-Kokesch, S., & Anderson, M. Z. (2001). Executive coaching: A comprehensive review of the literature. *Consulting Psychology Journal: Practice and Research, 53*(4), 205–228.

Kerin, R., & Peterson, R. (1998). *Strategic marketing problems: Cases and comments.* Upper Saddle River, NJ: Prentice Hall.

Kiel, F., Rimmer, E., Williams, K., & Doyle, M. (1996). Coaching at the top. *Coaching Psychology Journal: Practice and Research, 48*(2), 67–77.

Kilburg, R. R. (2004). Trudging toward Dodoville: Conceptual approaches and case studies in executive coaching. *Consulting Psychology Journal: Practice and Research, 56*(4), 203–213.

Macmillan, C. (1999). *The role of the organizational consultant: A model for clinicians.* Unpublished doctoral dissertation, Massachusetts School of Professional Psychology, Boston.

Murphy, D. (2000, June 25). On the fringe: Survival lessons. *San Francisco Sunday Examiner and Chronicle,* pp. J1–2.

Palmer, S., & Whybrow, A. (Eds.). (2008). *Handbook of coaching psychology.* London: Routledge.

Peterson, D. (1996). Executive coaching at work: The art of one-on-one change. *Consulting Psychology Journal: Practice and Research, 48*(2), 78–86.

Peterson, D. (2009, January). Does your coach give you value for your money? *Harvard Business Review, 87*(1), 94.

Prahalad, C. K., & Hamel, G. (1990, May–June). The core competence of the corporation. *Harvard Business Review, 68*(3), 79–91.

Sala, F. (2003). Executive blind spots; Discrepancies between self- and other-ratings. *Consulting Psychology Journal: Practice and Research, 55*(4), 222–229.

Sperry, L. (1993, June). Working with executives: Consulting, counseling and coaching. *Individual Psychology, 49*(2), 257–266.

Sperry, L. (1996). *Corporate therapy and consulting.* New York: Brunner/Mazel.

Tobias, L. (1990). *Psychological consulting to management: A clinician's perspective.* New York: Brunner/Mazel.

Tobias, L. (1996). Coaching executives. *Consulting Psychology Journal: Practice and Research, 48*(2), 87–95.

Weinstein, B. (1999, November 21). Career search: Peters sees black hole for white collars. *San Francisco Sunday Examiner and Chronicle,* p. J2.

Recommended Readings

Benton, D. (1999). *Secrets of a CEO coach.* New York: McGraw-Hill.

Block, P. (2000). *Flawless consulting: A guide to getting your expertise used* (2nd ed.). San Francisco: Jossey-Bass (Pfeiffer).

Doyle, J. (1999). *The business coach: A game plan for the new work environment.* New York: Wiley.

Hall, D., Otazo, K., & Hollenbeck, G. (1999). Behind closed doors: What really happens in executive coaching. *Organizational Dynamics,* 39–52.

Hargrove, R. (1995). *Masterful coaching.* San Francisco: Jossey-Bass (Pfeiffer).

Kauffman, C., & Coutu, D. (2009). *HBR research report: The realities of executive coaching.* Available at: coachingreport.hbr.org

Kilburg, R. (2000). *Executive coaching: Developing managerial wisdom in a world of chaos.* Washington, DC: American Psychological Association.

Kilburg, R. (Ed.). (1996, Spring). Executive coaching [Special issue]. *Consulting Psychology Journal: Practice and Research, 48*(2).

Martin, I. (1996). *From couch to corporation: Becoming a successful corporate therapist.* New York: Wiley.

Miller, J., & Brown, P. (1993). *The corporate coach.* New York: St. Martin's Press.

Richard, J. (1999). Multimodal therapy: A useful model for the executive coach. *Consulting Psychology Journal: Practice and Research, 51*(1), 24–30.

Segal, M. (1997). *Points of influence: A guide to using personality theory at work.* San Francisco: Jossey-Bass.

Spector, E., & Toder, F. (2000, March). Coaching 101: A primer for psychologists. *The California Psychologist, 33*(3), 18.

Stern, L. R. (2004). Executive coaching: A working definition. *Consulting Psychology Journal: Practice and Research, 56*(3), 154–162.

Stevens, J. H. (2005). Executive coaching from the executive's perspective. *Consulting Psychology Journal: Practice and Research, 57*(4), 274–285.

Thach, L., & Heinselman, T. (1999, March). Executive coaching defined. *Training & Development,* 35–39.

Vriend, J. (1985). *Counseling powers and passions.* Alexandria, VA: American Association for Counseling and Development.

Wallace, W., & Hall, D. (1996). *Psychological consultation: Perspectives and applications.* Pacific Grove, CA: Brooks/Cole.

Witherspoon, R., & White, R. (1997). *Four ways that coaching can help executives.* Greensboro, NC: Center for Creative Leadership.

1
Assessment

Whatever exists at all, exists in some amount and can be measured.

—Edward L. Thorndike (1918, p. 16)

There is one essential area where psychologists have a clear edge over all other kinds of consultants: psychological testing and assessment.

Testing is central to the professional identity of psychologists, and to some extent it represents psychology's historic core competency. Psychologists in the 1950s and 1960s often defined themselves as psychometricians, and psychological testing was their single important professional activity. Among mental health providers, only psychologists are formally trained to conduct and interpret psychological testing and assessments. Psychologists study testing in school, receive supervision in residencies, and are licensed to conduct formal evaluations and submit them as evidence in court. Psychologists are often identified with psychological testing in the eyes of the consuming public. Most psychologists possess a basic understanding of the important elements of assessment, including knowledge of the important tests and how to choose them, the clinical interview, concepts of validity and reliability, and how to inform people about the results of testing in ethically effective ways. Other psychotherapists (psychiatrists, family therapists) are familiar with assessment methods, and all assess their clients in some (less formal) fashion as a regular component of individual treatment.

The Role of Assessment in Coaching

Assessment is an essential element of executive coaching. It is important because people in the workplace tend to avoid frankness when they deal with one another, especially when they interact with people to whom they report— bosses and those who formally evaluate and pay them. The higher leaders get in an organization, the less frank feedback they receive. Leaders at the top of organizations rarely get any negative feedback at all, and sometimes—because of flattery or fear—they have a distorted sense of their strengths, weaknesses, and abilities. Structured assessment is important because people are generally not accurate self-reporters, in spite of how certain they may be about themselves (Erdberg, 2000). We cannot rely on what people tell us about their own qualities and behaviors.

Dissemination of assessment information must be negotiated and clarified at the beginning of the coaching relationship. Anticipate that clients might be wary about revealing information when they do not know exactly where that information will go. Therefore, it is essential to have a clear discussion about confidentiality and the kinds of reports that coaches will make. Clients are to be the first and most thoroughly briefed, but there are typically two other interested parties, the senior manager of the client, and perhaps the human resources (HR) department if that unit plays a role in coaching in the organization (such as coach selection and evaluation). A recent international survey of 140 experienced executive coaches conducted at Harvard University revealed that 68% of coaches kept their client's manager apprised of progress and 56% briefed HR personnel. Twenty-seven percent provided information to others such as the chief learning officer or the person responsible for leadership development in the company (Kauffman & Coutu, 2009, pp. 12–13). These other parties typically have an interest in information that might help them understand and improve organizational operations and culture. Coaches and clients should design a formal plan for dissemination of assessment data and findings, and it should include regular meetings to evaluate progress. Goals are tracked at these meetings and renegotiated as appropriate. Clients must be apprised of any discussion between their coach and others. They should be included in feedback discussions whenever possible.

Stages of Change

Prochaska and DiClemente's extensive research in addiction (Prochaska, 1979; Prochaska & DiClemente, 1983; Prochaska, DiClemente, & Norcross, 1992; Prochaska & Velicer, 1997) led them to the development of an important stage theory of change, commonly called stages of change or the transtheoretical model. They studied hundreds of people struggling with addictive behavior and were seeking "common principles that can reveal the structure of change," especially intentional change, in human behavior (Prochaska et al., 1992, p. 1102). While observing the ways in which people tend to change, they developed a normative model with five or six progressive stages, and this model provides an important vehicle for executive assessment. These stages of change are:

1. *Precontemplation*—People at this stage have no intention of changing. They may not even perceive that there is a problem. Although others may think that something is wrong or needs attention, the subject does not.

2. *Contemplation*—At this stage subjects are aware that a problem exists. They are thinking seriously about making a change, but have made no commitment and have taken no action. People can remain in this stage for years. They are not quite ready yet. They may be weighing pros and cons and may be ambivalent.

3. *Preparation*—At this stage there is a commitment to change and plans are made to accomplish it. Goals are set.

4. *Action*—The plan is put into effect and change is made. Clients behave differently than they have in the past. This stage, like several others, can be uncomfortable. Goals are assessed.

5. *Maintenance*—Changes are consolidated and reinforced. Relapses are corrected.

6. *Termination*—Changes become normal and are seen as a natural part of one's identity. It feels as if it has always been this way, and the old behavior holds no interest.

It is easy to grasp the importance of Prochaska's work for coaches. One of Thorndike's three learning principles (1932) was the law of readiness, which helps explain the importance of Prochaska's stages of change. Thorndike asserted that (Lindsay, 2000, p. 237):

1. When someone is ready to act, doing so will be experienced as satisfying.
2. When someone is ready to act, not doing so will be experienced as annoying.
3. When someone is not ready to act, but is forced to do so, this will be experienced as annoying.

The Harvard survey of coaches inquired about client "coachability" and found that out of 10 factors cited, the most important one was *change readiness* (Kauffman & Coutu, 2009, p. 18).

This means that timing is everything. Coaches must time their interventions correctly or risk annoying their clients. Careful assessment allows a coach to determine the stage of readiness of the client and respond appropriately. The question of who initiated the coaching process is often instructive. Did the client request help or was the client pressed into coaching by the sponsoring organization? Does the client perceive the situation in the same way that his or her boss perceives it? What is at stake; what happens if coaching does not take place or is unsuccessful?

When clients are in a precomtemplative stage, clients are unlikely to be interested in getting help and may, in fact, be defensive or offended, as others have probably already tried to point out their shortcomings. They may employ some of the psychological defenses described in Chapter 3, such as denial, projection, intellectualization, or reaction formation. They may prefer that other people change. This is a difficult stage for coaches, as they are under pressure to get results but are faced with a client who is uninterested in participating. Honest, authentic, Rogerian interaction (described in Chapter 5) along with potentially powerful results from a 360-degree assessment (described later under the heading "Assessment Methods for Coaches") may open a door, especially if accompanied by an employer mandate for change. Consciousness-raising and values clarification are appropriate at this stage. Clients in this stage can become the best and most highly motivated clients once they trust that a coach is truly interested in the client's point of view and does not intend to push an unwanted agenda from the outside.

Clients in the contemplative stage are typically easier to work with, as thoughts about change are already in motion. They may, however, be ambivalent, perfectionistic, or procrastinators. People can get stuck in this phase for years. Values clarification exercises or discussions may be useful, and the data from 360-degree evaluations is still likely to be productive. It is a good idea to "normalize" ambivalence at this stage, meaning that a coach can call a client's attention to the fact that ambivalence is common and expectable. Coaches may employ Lewin's force-field analysis (described in Chapter 9) or a functional analysis (found in Chapter 4) to examine the pros and cons of change. Self-efficacy, the extent to which a person feels that he or she can actually accomplish something once they start, should be examined and enhanced when possible (also described in Chapter 4). Sometimes clients do not have much confidence in their ability to make a change, so they avoid it and put it off and make excuses. Having a coach at this stage can really make a difference, especially if people feel that they have someone who will stick by them if things get tough. Change nearly always entails risk, and it is good to have someone with you to share some of that risk. Persuasive methods are tempting at this stage and coaches must carefully assess the appropriateness of efforts to urge the client to change, as these can be counterproductive or productive, depending upon the circumstances. Coaching judgment is key at this stage.

Things begin to happen in the preparation stage, where good intentions are converted into a plan for action. Obstacles are identified, timelines are established, and activities are designed and prioritized. Goal setting is now called for.

Then comes the action. In this phase, plans are activated and real change begins, optimally in small, achievable steps. The best plans consist of small, feasible activities that are acceptable to the client and the organization. This can be a time of great discomfort, and coaches can help to provide important support. It is also helpful if important others can recognize and support early improvements. Coaches can hold clients' feet to the fire and cheerlead at the same time.

The maintenance stage consolidates gains in ways that avoid relapse or backsliding. Coaches continue to provide appropriate positive reinforcement and recognition. If relapse occurs, coaches help clients get back on track using the relapse as a useful guide to improving the plan. Coaches, when appropriate, can help arrange positive organizational responses to the changes made by their client.

If all goes well, clients eventually make it to the termination stage where the new behavior is more or less completely integrated into daily life. The changes are comfortable and there are no urges or inclination to go backward or revert to old ways. New behaviors are integrated into the client's identity and are seen as "normal."

Miller and Rollnick (2002) have integrated the stages of change into a formal treatment method and called it *motivational interviewing*. The method is summarized for coaches in Palmer and Whybrow's *Handbook of Coaching Psychology* (2008, pp. 160–173).

Most executive coaches fly by the seat of their pants when it comes to assessment, and many use an informal 360-degree process. This chapter outlines the important components of an effective executive assessment process along with ways to incorporate them in coaching.

A Brief History of Psychological Assessment and Psychometric Instruments

Attempts at objective assessment have been around for centuries, and there is evidence that formal mental testing has roots in the 16th century, if not earlier (Drummond, 2000). Psychologists have always used the clinical interview to assess patients and clients, but modern clinical practice has moved toward structured interviews, which have the potential to be more reliable and more consistently comprehensive than unstructured ones. Objective psychometric instruments were first conceived out of the need to standardize the way that psychologists collect and interpret client information, particularly during wars and times of rapid educational or economic expansion in the United States. It was thought that standardized instruments would yield better results than interviewer preferences and prejudices.

Alfred Binet was studying the relationship between palmistry, phrenology, and intelligence when the Ministry of Public Education in Paris commissioned him to develop procedures to distinguish between students who could be educated and those who could not (Drummond, 2000). This work led to the development of the first standardized IQ tests. Testing was originally conceived as an objective and fair way to allocate precious educational resources (even though it has not generally accomplished that purpose. If anything, widespread standardized testing in education seems to have served to maintain the status quo and distract from learning).

World Wars I and II led to accelerated activity in test development, as the American military establishment sought to quickly and efficiently screen out "dull" young men using the Army Alpha test. They added the Army Beta when it became clear that many immigrant recruits could not be accurately tested using a format written in English. Standardized testing seemed successful, and the Army eventually moved toward personality testing to screen out recruits with character problems.

Hathaway and McKinley (1943) pioneered the Minnesota Multiphasic Personality Inventory (MMPI) at the University of Minnesota as a way to differentiate between normal, neurotic, and psychotic people. They combined questions from the best existing personality inventories and developed comprehensive norms that became widely accepted in the psychological community as the gold standard for personality testing. The test was taken over by a commercial testing corporation who partnered with the University of Minnesota in the 1980s to revise and restandardize the test (update norm groups). Another recent revision has produced a restructured form that allows users (psychologists) to administer a shorter test on a laptop, making the MMPI a potentially useful tool for coaching. Pearson Assessments offers narrative scoring versions that could be valuable to executive coaches interested in assessing the personality of their client.

In 1921, Hermann Rorschach developed a projective method to assess personality using inkblots. Several scoring systems evolved and devolved until John Exner consolidated the best features of those systems and subjected them to rigorous systematic, data-based evaluation in the 1970s. His system can be used to enter data into a computer that produces information on an extremely wide range of cognitive-behavioral factors. Exner moved the inkblot test dramatically forward in terms of validity and reliability, although skeptics remain. The Rorschach is an excellent, comprehensive instrument that produces a large amount of important personality information, but it is difficult and time consuming to use, and it lacks a certain face validity in the corporate world (it seems odd to the test taker).

Just after World War II, Raymond Cattell used the *lexical hypothesis* to develop an important personality test called the 16PF. The lexical hypothesis asserts that any important human quality will eventually be coded into language or made into a word (or words) so that we can speak to one another about it. If that is so, he reasoned, then analysis of available words can lead us to understand personality. Cattell employed factor analysis, a computer method used to reduce a large number of variables to the smallest possible number of variables that are discrete and cannot be reduced any further. He eventually claimed that the thousands of words describing various qualities of human behavior could be reduced to 16 pairs of words whose definitions were distinct from one another. Using these factors Cattell developed a test to map personality in 1949. Other scientists claim to have subsequently reduced these factors down to five. These are now called the *Big Five* personality factors, and they are described in Chapter 15 in a discussion of leadership. The 16PF now offers scales and narratives on personality, vocational factors, and leadership qualities and its proprietary owner (IPAT) offers a "Leadership Coaching Report" and a "Management Potential Report."

In the early 1950s, Harrison Gough designed a major psychological inventory, the California Psychological Inventory or CPI, using many of the questions from the MMPI. His instrument was different from the MMPI in that it was written to assess for normal personality factors. (The MMPI is a test for psychopathology.) CPP (formerly Consulting Psychologists Press) publishes the CPI and it gets generally positive reviews from psychometricians. It is well suited for executive and leadership coaching, and there are now shorter versions available along with a "Coaching Report for Leaders."

No report on psychological assessment in business coaching and development would be complete without mention of the MBTI, the Myers-Briggs Type Indicator, as it is so popular and well accepted in management consulting circles. Most coaching clients have heard of this test and have probably taken it at one time or another in their career (one Internet site estimates that 2 million people take this test each year). The test was based upon Carl Jung's ideas about personality types. Two women with no professional training in psychometrics— Isabel Myers and her mother, Katharine Cook Briggs—developed the test in reaction to events related to World War II. Briggs noticed that many people, women in particular, had taken jobs based upon a patriotic impulse only to find that they hated their work. She sought a way to efficiently match people to jobs based upon their personalities. Myers and Briggs built their instrument by investigating perception, judgment, and attitude and eventually settled on four dimensions: Extraversion–Introversion (E–I), Sensing–Intuition (S–N), Thinking–Feeling (T–F), and Judgment–Perception (J–P). The combinations of these dimensions led them to 16 types of personalities based upon the ways that a person prefers to focus attention (EI), acquire information (SN), make decisions (TF), and orient oneself toward the outer world (JP). Many consultants love this test, but psychometricians possess deep skepticism, particularly about its validity and reliability (Healy, 1989; Pittenger, 2005). Clients may inquire about the test and coaches should be able to articulate an educated point of view about the MBTI when asked. The inventory is now owned and sold by CPP.

Recently, the convergence of extensive historical norms developed over the past century using the data reduction power of the personal computer has produced some extraordinarily convenient and useful tools. Testing via the Internet appears to have great potential value to psychologists and executive coaches. Data can be entered on an office computer, uploaded to a testing service, and the results can be downloaded back to the end user within moments. Numerous testing companies are standing by to sell you their assessment products, and Table 1.1 lists the major companies. Coaches have an obligation to examine and evaluate any test they choose, especially if results are used to make important decisions. There are many attractive but dubious tests available for purchase.

Assessment Methods for Coaches

Assessment is one of the early steps in any successful coaching effort. There are at least five ways to get the assessment information needed for good coaching. An optimal evaluation of your client would include all four, although all four are not always feasible. Effective assessment generally implies that coaches are able to conduct productive one-on-one interviews with clients and key others.

Method 1: Multipoint, Multirater, or 360-Degree Feedback

This is an area of accepted organizational development practice that is different from the normal practice of psychotherapy, and is likely to seem strange and even a little uncomfortable to a coach first trained in psychotherapy. It is not new, as it apparently has roots in assessment centers developed by the German military in World War II (Fleenor & Prince, 1997). The method solicits feedback from people all around your client. Since there is some controversy over whether the term *360-degree* is proprietary, many use the terms *multipoint* or *multirater feedback* or *full-circle evaluation*, or even *multisource assessment*. This method represents a diminished approach to confidentiality and an expanded view of client data collection, in that significant others are brought into the mix right at the beginning of the coaching process. Most business organizations are familiar with the 360-degree process, as it has become widely used (and misused) in the past decade. The Harvard survey of executive coaches reported that 77% of experienced coaches thought that 360-degree feedback was of very high value in their work (Kauffman & Coutu, 2009, pp. 16–17). Some businesses use this process routinely in organizational development and personnel evaluation, and they use it as an organizational change method. Everyone in the organization contributes feedback to everyone else, and the information is passed along to organizational consultants and members. A comprehensive description as well as research evidence for the efficacy of the 360-degree process can be found in Morgeson, Mumford, and Campion (2005).

Dangers, Caveats, and Solutions in Multirater Feedback

More often than not, it exacerbates bureaucracy, heightens political tensions, and consumes enormous numbers of hours.

Maury A. Peiperl (2001, p. 3)

Although 360 degrees of feedback are extremely useful in coaching, there are some important caveats that coaches must consider. Coaches from the world of psychology may not be aware of the negative feelings associated with recent misuse of multipoint feedback systems. These evaluation methods have become popular and widespread, and there are many consulting firms and proprietary systems available to help administer them. Problems arise, however, when multirater evaluations are used for compensation and promotion purposes rather than for development. There is a good case to be made for avoiding the use of multipoint feedback for selection and promotion purposes, as you cannot count on its validity (a concept discussed later in this chapter). Halo effects cause other important problems. When your client is an upbeat and kind person, these global positive attributes spill over and influence other unrelated bits of feedback. If your client is somewhat grumpy or tense or moody, these qualities affect ratings in unrelated areas. There is simply no way to know exactly how valid 360-degree ratings are, and it can be extremely unfair (and perhaps illegal) to use the information for personnel decisions. Most 360-degree evaluations are not validated against specific job content. It is the job of the coach to filter the inherent bias and help clients make accurate sense out of the data, so that they can apply it to the process of self-improvement.

Many people cringe when the idea of a 360-degree evaluation is suggested, and one can encounter fierce resistance, some direct and some covert. This is an especially difficult problem when clients feel a powerful anxiety about evaluation but do not express it. 360-degree evaluation is an extremely useful tool, but it has to be introduced and used carefully. Coaches are in a perfect position to do just that, as they can manage the process, exploiting its advantages and buffering clients from typical mishaps. The main mishaps include choosing the wrong raters, overloading a few supervisors with a demand for continuous input to the process, and providing feedback in a way that reveals its source (who wrote it or said it). Sometimes raters use the feedback as an opportunity to retaliate or extract revenge for a previously perceived slight. Sometimes clients behave in ways that will ingratiate themselves with colleagues or direct-reports rather than offer a difficult or unpopular rating.

Coaches can avoid most or all of these problems by observing the following guidelines:

- Use 360-degree feedback for development and not for appraisal, hiring, promotion, or salary consideration.

- Let your client have a say in who will serve as raters. There are many good reasons to do this, not the least of which is that corrective feedback is powerful when it comes from someone you chose.

- Let your client have input to the questions and topics for feedback and collaborate on the design of the process.

- Give feedback to clients in gentle, positive, supportive ways. Be clear and direct with accurate feedback, but present it in small doses when necessary and in actionable terms. Frame feedback in ways that set the stage for constructive action. Coaches may choose to buffer any harsh criticism received. Feedback must be given in person—or if that is not possible, verbally over the telephone or on a video hookup. Do not simply send a report to your client or another person. If there is a report, send it after you have reviewed the results in person. Be open to client input to any written reports.

- Be scrupulous about confidentiality. Be clear with your client about the extent and limits of confidentiality and stick to your agreements. Missteps in this area are deadly.

Although organizations sometimes use a large 360-degree system for overall evaluation, coaches tend to use multirater feedback to get information for their single client, one client at a time. In this method, all the important people in a client's world are solicited for input. This includes people your client reports to, people who report to your client, and peers. It should also include internal customers (people within the organization to whom your client provides a service) and, when feasible, outside customers. It may also include family members, if there is a chance that they can provide useful information, and it should include self-assessment input from your client. The receptionist and the custodial staff can be included if their point of view has a chance to be useful.

Figure 1.1, the Johari window, created by Joseph Luft and Harry Ingham (Hanson, 1973; Luft, 1970), is a helpful model. It is also called a "disclosure-feedback model of awareness." It can be used to orient the executive and coach, and it can be used to organize and understand 360-degree information. In coaching, the general goal is to move knowledge from cells II, III, and IV toward cell I and to make cell I larger. The Johari model teaches us the following (Luft, 1970):

- A change in one quadrant causes a change in other quadrants.
- It takes psychic energy to keep information in quadrants II, III, and IV.
- Threat tends to decrease awareness, whereas mutual trust tends to increase movement to quadrant I.
- Forced awareness (exposure) is usually counterproductive.
- The unknown, hidden, and blind quadrants are maintained by social training, custom, and fear.

Assessment requires coaching clients to agree to receive feedback that may be uncomfortable and negative. Do not underestimate how difficult and threatening this can be. It is easy for a coach to become inured to the painfulness of unflattering feedback that clients may get from colleagues. Remember: When they first hear it, it can break their heart.

Create a set of questions that will be posed to all participants in the 360-degree evaluation. You can get these questions from various sources, including your client, and you can suggest several of your own. First, check the coaching goals and see which questions naturally derive from them. Then ask supervisors, bosses, or mentors what the best questions would be. Then ask your clients what they think they would like to learn. Good

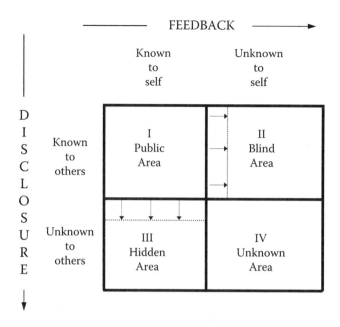

Figure 1.1 The Johari window.

questions are not difficult to create, especially if you intend to ask them in person or over the phone. Most multipoint evaluations include questions like the following:

1. What are this person's strengths? What does he or she do well?
2. What are this person's weaknesses or skill deficits?
3. What is it like to work with this person? Do you enjoy it or look forward to it?
4. What would you like this person to know about how to best work with you?
5. Give an example that would be instructive to the client (about coaching and the client's development).
6. What does this person need to learn to be successful at the next level?

Method 2: Homemade Instruments

Although there are many commercially available instruments, you can certainly develop your own. For example, you can create Likert-type scales based on interviews with your client and important others using the format in Figure 1.2.

There are numerous electronic ways to collect information about a client. Although personal interviews or phone interviews are probably the best method, they are time consuming. Personal contact offers several clear

Example Question 1:

How much does Joe Executive allow you to operate autonomously?

0	1	2	3	4	5
None	Some	Moderate Amounts		Quite a Bit	Lots

Example Question 2: *How well does Joe delegate?*

0	1	2	3	4	5
Poorly	Needs to Improve		Adequately Moderate	Quite Well	Wonderfully

Figure 1.2 Likert-type scale.

advantages in that they allow a coach to be thorough and to offer tailored follow-up questions and get a feel for the impressions that a subject offers in addition to data. Personal contact typically results in better information, and it certainly seems more confidential than purely electronic methods. E-mail questionnaires are likely to be perceived as more convenient and colleagues can complete them from home or a hotel room if they wish. However, they create obvious potential problems with confidentiality. No one ever knows for sure where e-mails end up.

Coaches might consider creating an online survey using a service such as Survey Monkey (www.surveymonkey.com). These surveys are inexpensive and relatively easy to build. If kept short, they are convenient for respondents, and they often result in high return rates relative to other survey methods. The survey company claims that data are secure, but it is the coach's responsibility to ensure that this is true in each case. Wariness is warranted.

The question of confidentiality must also be addressed with those who provide the feedback data to coaches. They have a stake in it. Although it is usually possible to tabulate and synthesize the information into a "group" consensus so that your client cannot tell who said what about whom, this is sometimes tricky. A coach cannot assume that people will not be able to correctly connect comments to specific people—or worse, to erroneously do so. People who report to your client, whose job may depend upon the goodwill of your client, may understandably be nervous or reticent about providing precise negative information, even though that information might be extremely useful to the coach and the executive. It is wise to have a conversation about this with each person who provides information. Warn them that even though you intend to completely disguise what they say, there is a possibility that you might not be able to guarantee it. Ask them for direct, useful input, but recommend that they take care of their own position and comfort level. Certain parties will not be able to provide information in a disguised or confidential way when there is only one person with certain information. For example, if a supervisor tells the coach that a client does not meet deadlines, that client will know exactly where that piece of feedback came from. It is the coach's job to effectively combine and synthesize the information so that a few important points are made without indicting those who contributed. When this is not feasible, it may be possible to simply warn the rater and get his or her permission to pass feedback along to your client anyway.

Method 3: The Interview

Psychotherapists have a special skill and advantage in this area, as they have relied on assessment interviews throughout their career. They know how to create rapport quickly in a one-on-one interaction, they know how to ask difficult personal questions, they are used to carrying a checklist in their head, they know how to focus a rambling person in a brief period of time, and they know how to bring out a shy client.

The one-on-one interview is a powerful and important coaching skill, because it sets the scene for most of the coaching that will follow. Harvard executive coach survey respondents rated the interview as their most important tool, with 86% reporting that it is highly valuable (Kauffman & Coutu, 2009, pp. 16–17). Rapport must be established, goals must be set, guidelines laid down, and, while all of this is happening, coaches can assess their client. Check out the client's interpersonal skills such as the ability to listen, ability to speak clearly and concisely, ability to focus, their openness and defensiveness, sense of humor, and the general interpersonal impression that they make, along with the reactions they invoke (in you) in the interview.

The First Meeting The first interview in coaching is different from a counselor's intake interview. Many psychotherapists focus much of their attention on history and intrapersonal development. This is unnecessary and probably counterproductive in coaching. Certainly, the coach is interested in how a client developed, especially as it pertains to the matters at hand. "I am interested in how you came to be this way" is a fair statement that most clients will welcome. But an extended interest in psychosocial history is liable to detract from the action focus that executive coaching requires.

There are essential aspects of the first interview with a coaching client, and clients are assessing coaches during that meeting, as well. This interview can last anywhere from 45 minutes to several hours, depending on the circumstances, and it might actually take place over the telephone. Often, executive clients want to move quickly, so a longer first meeting can be a good way to cover a lot of ground at the outset.

Here are some important components of the first coach–client contact.

1. Get off on the right foot. Present yourself confidently and calmly. Assure yourself that you can make an important contribution, because you can. Think carefully about how to dress for the situation. Some companies are formal; some are casual. Some expect consultants to dress the same way that they do; others expect a more professional, dressed-up look. Feel free to ask about how people dress at the company if you do not know. Determine the meaning of coaching to your client, especially whether he or she considers it to be a growth opportunity for those on the fast track, a remediation effort, or a way for the company to shed executives who are not working out. Make sure that you reach an understanding about reasonable expectations. Deliver a clear working definition of what you have to offer. It is imperative that you get clear about this definition and rehearse it ahead of time, if necessary, for if you cannot do this, you are in trouble. Your client probably has some ideas about who you are and what you intend to do, but these notions may not be accurate. One coaching expert puts it this way: "If a coach can't tell you what methodology he uses—what he does and what outcomes you can expect—show him the door" (Scoular, 2009, p. 31).

2. You may have to *sell* the assessment to your client. Executives are sometimes skeptical of consultants, as most have had poor or mediocre experiences with them in the past. This is especially important when coaching has been suggested or mandated by the boss. Find out what your client thinks of coaching before you start. Check out his or her previous experiences with consultants, and see if mistakes were made that could now be avoided. Find out if your client is interested in the coaching process. There is extensive evidence that client motivation is one of the most important variables determinative of coaching success (Peterson, 2009; Scoular, 2009). Find out if he or she trusts, values, or believes in the information you could provide through an assessment. See if the client welcomes feedback and coaching.

3. Discuss and agree upon the level of confidentiality that is optimal and possible. Do not promise more than you can deliver in this area. Consider making an expressed, written agreement about how information will be shared, how much, with whom, and when. Stick to this agreement, even if it becomes difficult to do. You will gain respect in the organization if you can do this.

4. Set reasonable, important, achievable goals, and agree to help your client meet them. Conceptualize these goals in a way that can be measured, so that you both will know, points in the future, whether

they have been met. This may require creativity. Although everything can be measured, the metrics of coaching are not always obvious. For example, if you are working with someone's feelings of inadequacy, your client can count the number of times that he or she thinks a specific thought or feels a specific feeling. If you are working with listening skills, you can evaluate his or her empathy behavior using a Likert-type scale (for example, from "none" to "perfectly empathic"). You can count almost anything. You can express most questions using a *scale-from-1-to-10* format. For example, "On a scale of 1 to 10, how nervous do you feel about speaking in front of the directors next week?"

5. Establish ground rules and a structure for the coaching. This includes scheduling, cancellation policies, and the amount of face-to-face time you will spend together to accomplish goals, along with the efforts expected of both of you outside of your meetings together. This requires that you describe a clear and useful definition of coaching to your client. Discuss your views of what coaching is and is not, what it can and cannot accomplish, as well as a preview of its methods, as you see them.

6. Continuously assess your clients. How do they treat you? Rate their interaction skills, listening skills, and speaking skills. Do they interrupt? Do they talk on and on long after their point should have been made? Do they have annoying behaviors? Do they ask questions about you (can they get outside of self)? Are they able to focus in a calm manner, or are they jumpy and all over the place? Do they think positively or negatively? Is their thinking expansive or constricted? Check out their vocabulary. Is it appropriate? Do you like being with them and look forward to meetings, or do you feel uncomfortable or dread them? These observations will be useful later. Make notes and remember them.

7. Prepare a written memo to yourself or letter to the client after the first meeting. Doing so documents agreements and goals and provides a starting point for later benchmarking.

Method 4: Direct Behavioral Observation

Most psychotherapists will find this area new. Executive coaches get important information about their clients by observing them directly and in context. This happens in several settings, including the one-on-one contact that coaches have with them. Begin your evaluation from the very first contact you have, including the voice-mail message that initiated your relationship. Notice your reaction to this person's message, as it is likely to be instructive.

Write it down so that you can compare it to your impressions later in the relationship.

Seek opportunities to observe your clients as they work. Listen to them on the phone, read their e-mail messages if you can (with their permission, of course. You may even need to get permission from the larger organization to do this as well). The best way to get a comprehensive and accurate sense of your clients is to shadow them. Accompany them at work, sit in meetings with them, watch them as they interact with people in the hallways, and sit in as they give instructions to people who report to them. This is an aspect of coaching that is very different from psychotherapy, and it offers a tremendous advantage. Forty-six percent of executive coaches in the Harvard study (Kauffman & Coutu, 2009, p. 16) reported that shadowing was a highly valuable tool and 20% rated it a perfect 10 on a 1 to 10 scale of usefulness. The information that counselors get from their therapy patients is useful but flawed, in that it is nearly all self-reported. It is filtered through the needs, defenses, and biases of that person. Direct observation is so important and powerful that coaches must forcefully advocate for its use. This usually means that they must push through their own natural inclination to be shy about shadowing. It is a powerful assessment technique, and clients accommodate to it more readily than most coaches expect, especially when having a coach is seen as a benefit for high-potential executives rather than as a remediation. It makes sense to paint the coach as a status symbol for those with a bright future rather than as the "angel of death." You and your client can decide how you should be introduced to others in the workplace. For example, "This is my coach. She will be joining us this morning to observe how I operate at team meetings. We're working on ways to make these meetings more effective." You will be surprised at how quickly a coach can fade into the background.

It is important to create key questions for shadowing. Some examples are:

- How do others behave around this client? How do they react?
- Do you see deficits or signs of target behaviors for coaching (those to be changed)?
- Does your client's behavior match his or her self-perception?
- Does your client do what the client says he or she is doing?
- How does this person reinforce others, consciously and unconsciously?
- What unintended messages does your executive send to others?
- Is this someone you would want to be around? Why or why not?

Create your own questions based upon the circumstances and goals.

Method 5: Formal Objective Assessment Instruments

A wide variety of standardized, prepackaged instruments are available to the coach, some of which were described earlier in this chapter. They can be of extraordinary value, but they can also be a significant waste of time and energy. In fact, they can serve to *turn off* a client and damage rapport. Before purchasing and using instruments off the shelf, evaluate them carefully.

Testing Tools: The Basics   There are two important ways that formal instruments can add value to the coaching process:

1. *Accuracy*—Interpersonal interviews and even behavioral observations are subject to several sources of distortion, including bias and missed data. Formal, structured instruments can minimize these problems. A structured instrument can ensure that all bases are covered.

2. *Efficiency*—Large amounts of information can be quickly obtained and tabulated. Data can be digitally *crunched* in a way that is virtually impossible to accomplish otherwise. Clients can be compared to extensive norms that answer the question "Compared to what?"

For testing to make a legitimate contribution to the coaching process, the following components must be in place. If you are going to use a standardized or commercially produced instrument, you need to address the following issues.

Selection   The coach must be familiar with the available tools and instruments and must be able to match them with their client and with the task at hand. This is not easy to do, as there are thousands of tests and inventories out there. Coaches have to experiment with tests to determine which instruments are legitimate and which are optimal for their purpose. New instruments appear on the Internet and in the literature on a regular basis, some of which are excellent and many which are weak. Most are expensive, at least at start-up. They become relatively inexpensive once initial costs (for booklets, manuals, licensing, and software) have been met.

Evaluation of the Instrument   Most testing tools are proprietary, and the seller of the instrument cannot be counted on as a valid source of information. Testing companies hype their products. There are hundreds of inventories that are, at best, a worthless and whimsical distraction, and at worst, a source of distorted information accompanied by the patina of technical or scientific truth. Coaches, at the very least, should try the instrument out on themselves before using it with clients.

The Construct   The first, and perhaps most important, task is to decipher the basic concept that the instrument supposedly tests. (Personality is an example of a construct. Leadership is another.) Clients rely on coaches to do a good job with this. They count on us. They naively assume that we have done this adequately, yet it is a daunting task. Tests do not always test what they sound like they are testing, so you have to do a little checking to get a good feel for what the results really mean. For example, there are several available scales and measures of depression, but they do not all test the same thing. Each test starts with a different conception or definition of depression (the construct). You have to understand the test maker's definition of depression to be able to understand the results. This is true about tests of leadership. You have to know how the test makers defined leadership when they designed their test. Similarly, if you plan to use an instrument that assesses emotional intelligence (EI), you must find out how the makers of that test define EI. Clients do not know this, and they are liable to swallow results without scrutiny. It is easy to confuse matters when you get test results that do not make sense. This can happen when a test is not measuring what it purports to measure. Test developers use a particular theory or viewpoint from which to develop their instrument, and it is important to explore the conceptual underpinnings. For example, many consultants use the MBTI without a clear understanding or explanation of the theoretical basis for the instrument, or even a clear sense of what the essential concepts (e.g., sensing or perceiving) mean. This leads to confusion and misinformation, especially when the test is a relatively simple one.

Validity   Aside from the question of construct validity, there are a couple of other questions that must be answered before an instrument is used. Validity asks the questions: Is this test measuring what it says it measures? Is it accurate? Do the questions address content that is relevant to the results that the test produces? Is there evidence that the results tend to accurately predict things in the future in real life? Will the results work in the specific environment at hand? Do the results work better than a cheaper or easier method of getting the same information? Was this instrument developed for people similar to your client? Does the test appear (to your client) to be asking important and relevant questions, or do the questions seem mysterious or incomprehensible (face validity)?

Reliability   Another set of evaluative questions has to do with the stability of the instrument: Can *you* use it and get the same results that the designers get? Can you use it in your coaching setting and get accurate results, or is it only useful in specific, narrow settings and circumstances? Do you get consistent results when you use the instrument with different kinds of clients? (Was it designed for nurses, for example?) Is it a *sturdy* instrument; can your client take the test at home or on an airplane, or in a hotel room? Can your client take the test again a year from now and get relevant and valid results for comparison purposes? Can you ask a member of your staff to administer the test (rather than you) and expect valid results?

Acceptable levels of validity and reliability depend upon the situation, and they are reported on a scale from 0 to 1, where 0 means no correlation or relationship and a correlation coefficient of 1.0 (or –1.0) is "perfect." Correlation coefficients in the range of 0.4 to 0.5 are considered moderate in strength, whereas scores of 0.6 or 0.7 are typically thought to be high.

Standardization   Standardization is the norms question. To whom or to what is your client compared? Every judgment in life is a function of "compared to what?" You are smart when compared to some people, but not so smart when compared to others. How does the test determine and present results to the consumer? As an example, it typically makes little sense to use an MMPI for business coaching, because the purpose of the test is to assess psychopathology, and because norms were developed in clinical and hospital settings. The best tests for coaching employ business and executive norms, meaning that your client's responses are compared to similar people in the same kind of circumstances. If you get a result that puts your client at the 95th percentile, you must be able to answer the question: the 95th percentile of what or whom? Were all members of the norm group from the Midwest? Were they about the same age as your client, the same gender, and (the most vexing problem) similar in race, culture, and ethnicity? If the answer to these questions is yes, then your results will be more accurate, more relevant, and more cogent. A second concern, in addition to the similarity question (Is the client similar to the norm group?) is norm-group size. How many people were used to establish the test's norms? Is the size adequate? Larger is generally better, to a point.

Practical Issues   Is the test written in a way that sounds smart and competent? Many are not, and they sound silly or trivial or strange (for example, "I have black and tarry stools" or "I like to play drop-the-handkerchief"). This can be a turnoff to a client. Are the questions clear and coherent? Are the questions written in a way that is difficult for your client to understand? Is the inventory too long to hold your client's attention, or so long that your client will not make time to get it done? If you are going to ask an executive to spend a couple of hours filling out questionnaires, the results had better be worth it. Most formal instruments can now be taken online or on a laptop computer. The most practical systems allow the end user (your client) to log in with a password and take the test at their own desk or home. It is wise for coaches to take these tests themselves prior to inflicting them on clients. Once you have taken the test, evaluate the quality and form of the feedback for its usefulness and coherence. Think about this from your client's point of view.

Also, determine whether or not the administrator of the inventory will need to be trained, especially if the task of administration or scoring will be delegated to a member of your staff or your client's team.

It is a bad sign when the information you need to evaluate an instrument is not readily available or if the testing vendor is unwilling to help. It is also problematic when the available information about a test is incoherent or written in a technical style that is difficult to decipher. Think about rejecting this test and seeking other instruments. There are alternatives for every inventory or test that is currently available. Testing companies should be able to provide you with a sample packet so that you can adequately evaluate their instrument. Care is necessary because many vendors are not always eager for you to know about these essential qualities of their tests. Sometimes they just want you to buy them. There are resources available for use in evaluating existing psychometric instruments. One highly regarded resource is the Buros Center for Testing, which has regularly published the *Mental Measurements Yearbook* and *Tests in Print* since 1938. These evaluations are now available at a small cost online at: www.unl.edu/buros. The reader can find validity and reliability data for nearly every test in print, along with one or two reviews written by unbiased experts. A coach unfamiliar with psychological testing is advised to consult with an experienced psychologist prior to the use of such instruments.

Specific Instruments   There is a wide range of prefabricated, proprietary, self-report instruments available. Most suffer from the problems associated with self-report data, although some incorporate a mechanism for input from those who work with your client. Also, it is important to seek tests that provide results in the form of relative strengths and weaknesses rather than psychopathology or only weaknesses.

There are a few well-known and well-respected companies that have produced and sold instruments for years. Listed in Table 1.1 are the names and contact information for five of the oldest and most widely used companies. Each of these companies has created products that can be extremely useful in assessing executives and managers. You can generally rely on their instruments to be adequately valid and reliable.

Each of the companies listed in Table 1.1 produce a wide range of instruments designed to assess the "normal" population. Results are presented in several formats that can be used to help executive clients understand their personality strengths and weaknesses relative to their current job or career aspirations. Formal instruments that test for emotional intelligence are described in Table 11.1 in Chapter 11. Although executives typically find lengthy questionnaires to be annoying, they are often persuaded by data. The combination of standardized test data, input from 360-degree evaluations, and their coach's professional opinion can be particularly persuasive. Coaches should triangulate data whenever possible, meaning that any finding that is consistent across all sources (360-evaluation data, formal inventory, coach's observation) is likely to be valid and important.

Administration   Remember that assessment, especially by a psychologist, can be threatening. Most people have unrealistic views of what psychologists can *tell* about them, and they may be wary that a coach may pathologize or

Table 1.1 Key Sources for Assessment Instruments and Products

Company	Products	Internet Address	Telephone
Pearson Assessments and PsycCorp	Various personality inventories (MMPI)	www.pearsonassessments .com	(800) 627-7271
Institute for Personality and Ability Testing (IPAT)	Various personality inventories (16PF)	www.ipat.com	(800) 225-IPAT
Consulting Psychologists Press (CPP)	Personnel inventories (MBTI, CPI, Strong, FIRO-B)	www.cpp.com	(800) 624-1765
Center for Creative Leadership (CCL)	360-degree instruments and assessment tools	www.ccl.org	(336) 545-2810

diagnose. Take care not to oversell formal testing if you decide to use it. Clients sometimes think that tests have powers that they really do not have. There is no magic in a psychological test. Results must be tempered by the judgment of the coach and client. In the end, it is the coach's judgment, not the test scores, that matters.

Presentation of assessment results is critical. Engineering and business management vocabulary is optimal when discussing the evaluation process. For example, the term *instrument* is likely to fare better than *psychological test*. Corporations are used to thinking in terms of *metrics* (data from the measurement of outcomes), and *benchmarks* (goals considered to be excellent and achievable). The term *data* is preferable to *information*. This is not true across the board or for every client, so consider the circumstances and mirror the organization's vocabulary. Popular local vocabulary evolves in any culture, and business and organizational cultures are no exception. Track the language that is used and mirror it appropriately. Avoid clinical vocabulary unless you can think of a good reason to use it.

Make sure that the purpose of assessment is clear to all parties, and that there is agreement about what will happen to the data. If the information is to be used for "developmental" purposes (to develop the executive-client), make certain that this agreement is clear and honored. Your client must know that data will not be used for selection, promotion, or retention purposes (assuming that this is, in fact, the case). Such a use of data is certainly not part of a coaching process.

Set the scene for realistic, truthful data collection that is aimed at discerning goals that you and your client can use. Emphasize strengths and weaknesses (or areas for future growth or development). Find one or two things to work on, rather than a whole bunch at once, even if your client seems to be interested in changing many things. Prioritize, if necessary; one thing at a time. Create goals that are simple and easy to remember. Early successes tend to energize the process.

Confidentiality in Assessment

The issue of confidentiality must be dealt with early on, and some executives might not seem concerned about this at first. (Executives in other countries often tend to be more cautious or private about personal information than clients in the United States.) Clients may even understate their real concern about confidentiality when they first speak to a coach, as they strive to seem confident and willing, rather than insecure. A clear understanding of what is at stake is essential, along with an agreement about where the information goes or does not go. Coaching is different from therapy in that it often has more than one purpose, and the organization that is paying for the coaching has a legitimate stake in the outcome. This implies that the organization, in the form of a boss or supervisor or human relations professional, has some claim on the information that would otherwise be confidential if the client were seeking private counseling (and paying for it). This does not mean that some level of discretion is not possible or important. It is possible, and many coaching clients are actually quite interested in how and where information will be shared. Some coaches insist on a confidential relationship with their clients, whereas others do not offer such an arrangement, as it is not always feasible or realistic to do so. One of the experienced coaches reported the following in the Harvard survey (Kauffman & Coutu, 2009, p. 12):

> I maintain strict confidentiality regarding the content of coaching. Reporting to human resources is a given in terms of general themes of organizational value. Any reporting concerning progress to HR is with the coachee present and led by the coachee.

A discussion about confidentiality must take place at the beginning of the relationship, and the coach must not overestimate the ability to manage information flow. If a coach is uncomfortable with the situation, he or she should reconsider the appropriateness of the assignment and perhaps decline to proceed.

There are several important steps to managing confidentiality. Check out your client's assumptions. Temper their expectations at the onset, and perhaps assert that a coaching client cannot count on absolute confidentiality as would a psychotherapy client. The coach can follow that statement with a commitment to *discretion*, making it clear that the coach has the client's best interests in mind. The question of whose interests prevail (the organization's or the person's) must still be discussed and determined honestly and openly. It will often be possible to provide great discretion to the individual client, but in some cases very little. The key is to figure this out at the onset, reach a clear understanding, and stick with it. Do not promise something that cannot be delivered, and do not reveal anything unnecessarily. If your client wishes assessment information to go forward to support his or her career, think carefully about the request. If it will change the balance of feedback and make accurate or hard-hitting information impossible to get in the future, rule it out. But if you and your client decide to forward some of the information to others, consider a written agreement specifying the details.

The level of feasible confidentiality will vary from organization to organization, but all managers (of the clients being coached) will expect some information about the progress of the coaching. Are goals being met? Is the coaching productive? What can the boss do to help? What can the organization learn about itself from this client's assessment? Take care to provide appropriate ongoing information to those who pay the bills. If you go too long without contact with your sponsoring organization, you risk losing that client. They need some evidence or assurance that their money is being well-spent.

What to Evaluate

Circumstances, clients, and goals determine the variables of interest. There is an extremely wide range of dimensions along which a client can be studied, and it is smart to give these some thought before you begin. Targets are determined by the circumstances that led to the coaching. If coaching is necessitated by a client's deficit, the evaluation must begin by focusing on what is lacking, what is "wrong." When coaching is offered as a developmental benefit to an executive with great potential, choice of evaluation variables is open for discussion and careful selection. It might start with a discussion of the particular strengths and assets that have served that executive well thus far. It might also begin with an evaluation of the attributes required for someone to be successful at the target level (the level or position your client is aiming for in the organization).

The following section describes examples of variables typically assessed by coaches and executive clients. Many of these skills or qualities are essential to high performance in business.

Interpersonal Skills

Interpersonal skills might be the area in which the coach possesses the most valuable expertise. It is common in business for a valuable executive to lack certain areas of interpersonal development. Most of us have interpersonal blind spots and relative weaknesses. A person who feels that he or she could not use input or improvement in some area of interpersonal interaction is a fool. Many successful executives have been promoted because of their drive, their content skills, or their technical track record. Some never intended to be managers or leaders, but they have taken a promotion into such a position because of the money attached. They now need additional skills to continue to succeed. The skills they developed in technical excellence are inadequate for a manager. The skills required to propel a person to middle management or to a vice president position are different from the skills needed to lead a company. Some of the important interpersonal skills required of effective executives are shown in Table 1.2.

Table 1.2 Assessment Variables

Skill	What to Look For—Sample Components
Listening	Does client value listening? (Or is it lip service?)
	Amount of listening
	Active or passive listener?
	Does client participate, ask questions, rephrase?
	Physical listening/attending skills? (Client appears to be listening.)
Speaking	In front of large audiences?
	In small groups or meetings?
	One-on-one?
	On the telephone?
Empathy	Notices other people?
	Grasps the concept?
	Cares about others and their point of view?
	Is capable of putting self in others' shoes?
Management/self-management	Is well organized?
	Can control things?
	Delegates appropriately?
	Has clear communications?
	Is loyal?
Leadership	Is passionate about the work and organization?
	Presents a confident image?
	Has a positive attitude, point of view?
	Knows how to motivate others; is persuasive?
	Understand leadership role?
	Has strategic vision?
	(See Chapter 15)

(Continued)

Table 1.2 (Continued)

Skill	What to Look For—Sample Components
Self-awareness	Has an accurate sense of self?
	Values self-understanding?
	Is open to input from others? (see Chapter 11)
Self-presentation	Overall appearance is appropriate for the situation?
	General impression they give?
	Optimistic?
	Energetic?
Sense of humor	Is this person too serious?
	Appropriate sense of humor?
	Can the person make light of himself or herself?
	Can they see the funny side of things?
	Is their humor out of control or over the top?
	Sarcastic?
	Do they tell racial or sexual jokes?

Intrapersonal and Self-Management Skills

Intrapersonal and self-management skills are another area of core coaching competency. *Intrapersonal* refers to events that happen within a person; in this case, emotions, urges, feelings, energy levels, conflicting or competing thoughts, communication with self, and levels of stress or relaxation. Coaches offer uniquely valuable help to executives in this area. Effectiveness in a career involves self-understanding and self-management. One must be aware of one's own emotional reactions and energy and tendencies. These reactions must be managed so that they represent an overall asset rather than a liability.

Psychological-mindedness is perhaps the most important overarching quality of interest to the coach when first sizing up a client. Psychological-mindedness is an informal term from psychoanalytic lore. It has not attracted a significant line of formal research, even though most would consider it important, if not essential. It refers to an interest in self-exploration and a capacity for self-observation and self-awareness. Psychologically minded people find emotions important and intriguing. They wonder about what others are thinking and feeling. When trying to understand what is going on around them they consider psychological factors, can spot and label them, and can use insight to make sense of things. They tend to have good social skills. Some executives lack this psychological-mindedness or disparage it, and this is a problem, as they are unlikely to be interested in coaching or in self-exploration in any serious way. When a coach notices a deficit in psychological-mindedness, this challenge must be addressed early. The problem might be insurmountable, but it cannot be ignored. Although a psychometric instrument (Shill & Lumley, 2002) exists to measure it along with the psychological-mindedness (Py) scale on the CPI, personal observations of the coach combined with data from a 360-degree assessment should suffice.

Daniel Goleman's view of emotional intelligence (EQ or EI) (1995, 1998) can be helpful, and executives can be assessed along his five categories (self-awareness, self-regulation, motivation, empathy, and social skill). There are numerous Web sites that provide tools and ideas about how to use EQ for executive coaching, many of which are cited in Chapter 11 along with information about formal assessment instruments for emotional intelligence.

Content Skills

A successful executive who can contribute to organizational effectiveness possesses a high degree of *content skill;* he or she understands the core competency of the organization in a deep way and knows how to enhance it. It is helpful if key executives understand the history of both the organization and the product. For example, if you are an executive in the coal industry, do you understand and appreciate the history of coal and mining operations in this country and around the world? Do you know about the history of union activity in coal mining? Can you clearly articulate the difference between so-called *clean coal* and other types of coal? Does the topic excite you? Do you understand how historical factors influence the present culture and environment? Do you look forward to technical discussions with colleagues or subordinates?

Leadership Skills

Much has been written about specific qualities and behaviors that are associated with good leadership. Much of this is described in Chapter 15 where the reader will find checklists for use with their clients. That said, it must be emphasized that there is no such thing as a universal set of leader traits or skills that will be optimal in all organizations and situations. The leader-context fit or match is key.

Political Skills

Success requires the ability to understand the organizational culture and a willingness to honor related overt and covert rules. There are *political* dynamics that are common to most organizations and there are dynamics that are unique to each. An effective executive is adept at both kinds. This requires an attitude of acceptance of a modicum of political game playing (with integrity). Some executives never accept the necessity to play the requisite organizational games, and skillful executive coaching can be extremely useful in helping clients reexamine and decide how to reframe such a posture. Technical workers who possess contempt for organizational politics have little chance for success as managers or leaders. They may be able to thrive for a while in some organizations as a *rebel*, but their demise is pretty much inevitable, especially if they are promoted.

Personal and Industry Vision

It is useful to have a view of where one is going, what is possible, and how to get there. For some, this comes naturally. Others need coaching. Vision becomes incrementally more important the higher one goes in an organization. At the top, it is essential.

Discussing the Results

When it comes time to provide feedback to a client, think carefully about how to do it. Clients and circumstances vary, and some would be well-served to get information in a direct and hard-hitting way. Others need it to be softened, and the feedback must be framed in gentle, positive terms, so that it can be heard. Take care to avoid overwhelming your client with too much negative information. Titrate it if necessary. Mix positives in with the negatives. Like a good piano teacher, do not overload your client with too much information at one sitting. It may be best to choose one important piece of feedback and focus on it alone, rather than passing along everything that you learned. There is no rule mandating that you transmit every bit of data. Sandwich negative comments between two positive ones. Watch for signs of feedback fatigue. Often, executives will not show their feelings of hurt or disappointment, because they have learned to hide those feelings at work. You must be aware of the impact that negative feedback can have. If you give negative feedback, assume that it hurt more than it appears. Assume also that even though you presented many examples of positive qualities, clients often remember only the single negative comment that you made. They focus on that comment and grind on it, feeling worse the longer they grind.

The 360-degree evaluation can be repeated at set intervals or at the beginning or ending of coaching phases. For example, you can set goals to be accomplished in 3 months, and then conduct a mini-360-degree evaluation to check progress. You can even begin each coaching meeting with a review of the most important or relevant 360-degree finding.

Feedback and Goal Setting

When you have tabulated all of the assessment information (from initial interviews, from the 360-degree evaluation, from written instruments, and from your own reactions and observations) sit down with your client and go over it all at length. Focus on a discrete number of factors rather than every single data point. Compare your client's own perceptions with the information you got from other sources. Does your client accurately understand his or her strengths and weaknesses? (Remember to emphasize strengths!) How accurate is your client's self-perception? Is any of the assessment information surprising to you or to your client? Use this information to help your client set a small number of achievable and measurable goals, and to evaluate progress along those goals on a regular basis.

Coaches must remember that business clients tend to have a great deal of faith in formal psychometric instruments and may uncritically accept whatever a coach tells them. Bourne (2008, p. 393) reminds us to honor the P. T. Barnum effect ("There's a sucker born every minute") and Stagner's (1958) research indicating that most people—and personnel managers in particular—are astonishingly gullible when it comes to acceptance of vaguely worded feedback from psychological testing. Analyze results carefully and package them in a way that accurately energizes your particular client.

Overarching Assessment Questions

The Harvard survey (Kauffman & Coutu, 2009, p. 23) asked experienced executive coaches about factors that determined success in coaching. They reported three such key factors, and each must be assessed throughout the coaching process, especially at the onset.

1. *The executive's motivation and commitment to change*—Successful clients were described as possessing a "fierce willingness" to learn and evolve even if it required personal and professional vulnerability. When clients are ambivalent or resistant, coaches must bring motivational stage–appropriate methods to the task. Match your approach to the client's readiness.

2. *Support of the sponsoring organization*—Senior management must buy in to the coaching initiative. Without senior support, all kinds of unfortunate things can happen. Coaches must assess the level and quality of support at the beginning of the initiative and react with honesty and clarity. It may be best to decline a coaching job from time to time, depending on organizational interest and motivation.

3. *Clarity of goals*—Coaching has a much higher likelihood of success when goals are clear, achievable, measurable, and agreed upon by all parties. It is helpful to write these goals and revisit them often, adjusting and renegotiating when appropriate.

Summary

An accurate assessment is essential for good coaching. You have to learn much about a client and the sponsoring organization in order to provide excellent help. Interview checklists, behavioral observation (including shadowing at the work site), a 360-degree evaluation, and prefabricated pencil-and-paper instruments can all ensure that assessment meets three important criteria: accuracy, efficiency, and comprehensiveness. Psychologists are in an excellent position with their training, background, and point of view to provide such an assessment, but they have to work with a diminished level of client confidentiality when third parties are involved in data collection and when the organization has a share in the outcome. Social workers and other psychotherapists may need to enhance their formal assessment skills as they learn executive coaching, and assessment must be adapted to the organizational culture. Coaches lacking psychometric training are advised to consult with a psychologist for help in this area.

References

Bourne, A. (2008). Using psychometrics in coaching. In S. Palmer & A. Whybrow (Eds.), *Handbook of coaching psychology* (pp. 385–403). London: Routledge.

Drummond, R. J. (2000). *Appraisal procedures for counselors and helping professionals.* Upper Saddle River, NJ: Prentice Hall.

Erdberg, P. (2000, March). Assessing personality: Psychology's unique contribution. *The California Psychologist, 26.*

Fleenor, J., & Prince, J. (1997). *Using 360-degree feedback in organizations: An annotated bibliography.* Greensboro, NC: Center for Creative Leadership.

Goleman, D. (1995). *Emotional intelligence.* New York: Bantam.

Goleman, D. (1998). *Working with emotional intelligence.* New York: Bantam.

Hanson, P. (1973). The Johari window: A model for soliciting and giving feedback. In J. Jones & J. W. Pfeiffer (Eds.), *The 1973 annual handbook for facilitators* (pp. 115–119). San Diego: Pfeiffer & Company.

Hathaway, S. R., & McKinley, J. C. (1943). *The Minnesota Multiphasic Personality Schedule.* Minneapolis, MN: University of Minnesota Press.

Healy, C. C. (1989). Negative: The MBTI: Not ready for routine use in counseling. *Journal of Counseling and Development, 67,* 487–488.

Kauffman, C., & Coutu, D. (2009). *HBR research report: The realities of executive coaching.* Available at: coachingreport.hbr.org

Lindsay, S. R. (2000). *Handbook of applied dog behavior and training: Principles of behavior adaptation and learning.* Ames, IA: Blackwell.

Luft, J. (1970). *Group processes: An introduction to group dynamics* (2nd ed.). Palo Alto, CA: National Press Books.

Miller, W. R., & Rollnick, S. (2002). *Motivational interviewing: Preparing people to change.* New York: Guilford Press.

Morgeson, F. P., Mumford, T. V., & Campion, M. A. (2005). Coming full circle: Using research and practice to address 27 questions about 360-degree feedback programs. *Consulting Psychology Journal: Practice and Research, 57*(3), 196–209.

Palmer, S., & Whybrow, A. (2008). *Handbook of coaching psychology.* London: Routledge.

Peiperl, M. A. (2001, January). Getting 360-degree feedback right. *Harvard Business Review,* Reprint R0101K.

Peterson, D. B. (2009). Does your coach give you value for your money? *Harvard Business Review, 87*(1), 29.

Pittenger, D. J. (2005). Cautionary comments regarding the Myers-Briggs Type Indicator. *Consulting Psychology Journal: Practice and Research, 57*(3), 210–221.

Prochaska, J. O. (1979). *Systems of psychotherapy: A transtheoretical analysis.* Homewood, IL: Dorsey Press.

Prochaska, J. O., & DiClemente, C. C. (1983). Stages and processes of self-change of smoking: Toward an integrative model of change. *Journal of Consulting and Clinical Psychology, 51,* 390–395.

Prochaska, J. O., DiClemente, C. C., & Norcross, J. (1992). In search of how people change. *American Psychologist, 47,* 1102–1114.

Prochaska, J. O., & Velicer, W. F. (1997). The transtheoretical model of health behavior change. *American Journal of Health Promotion, 12,* 38–48.

Scoular, A. (2009). How do you pick a coach? *Harvard Business Review, 87*(1), 31.

Shill, M. A., & Lumley, M. A. (2002, June). The Psychological Mindedness Scale: Factor structure, convergent validity and gender in a non-psychiatric sample. *Psychology and Psychotherapy: Theory, Research and Practice, 75*(2), 131–150.

Stagner, R. (1958). The gullibility of personnel managers. *Personnel Psychology, 11,* 347–352.

Thorndike, E. L. (1918). The nature, purposes, and general methods of measurements of educational products. In G. M. Whipple (Ed.), *National Society for the Study of Educational Products: Seventeenth yearbook* (pp. 16–24). Bloomington, IL: Public School Publishing Co.

Thorndike, E. L. (1932). *The fundamentals of learning.* New York: Teachers College, Columbia University.

Recommended Readings

Atkinson, M. J. (2003). California Psychological Inventory (3rd ed.). In B. S. Plake, J. C. Impara, & R. A. Spies (Eds.), *The 15th mental measurement yearbook* (pp.159–161). Lincoln, NE: Buros Institute of Mental Measurements.

Berens, L. V., Cooper, S. A., Ernst, L. K., Martin, C. R., Myers, S., Nardi, D. et al. (2002). *Quick guide to the 16 personality types in organizations: Understanding personality differences in the workplace.* Huntington Beach, CA: Telos Publications.

Cattell, H. E. P., & Schuerger, J. M. (2003). *Essentials of 16PF assessment.* Hoboken, NJ: John Wiley & Sons.

Craig, R. (1999). *Interpreting personality tests: A clinical manual for the MMPI-2, MCMI-III, CPI-R, and 16PF.* Hoboken, NJ: John Wiley & Sons.

Greene, R. L. (2000). *The MMPI-2: An interpretive manual* (2nd ed.). Needham Heights, MA: Allyn & Bacon.

Groth-Marnat, G. (1997). *Handbook of psychological assessment* (3rd ed.). New York: Wiley.

Kaplan, R., & Palus, C. (1994). *Enhancing 360-degree feedback for senior executives: How to maximize the benefits and minimize the risks.* Greensboro, NC: Center for Creative Leadership.

Lepsinger, R., & Lucia, A. (2009). *The art and science of 360-degree feedback* (2nd ed.). San Francisco: Jossey-Bass.

Lyman, H. B. (1997). *Test scores and what they mean* (6th ed.). Needham Heights, MA: Allyn & Bacon.

McAllister, L. (1988). *A practical guide to CPI interpretation* (2nd ed.). Palo Alto, CA: Consulting Psychologists Press.

Passmore, J. (2008). *Psychometrics in coaching: Using psychological and psychometric tools for development.* London: Kogan Page.

Prochaska, J. O., Norcross, J., & DiClemente, C. (1994). *Changing for good.* New York: William Morrow and Co.

Van Velsor, E., Leslie, L. B., & Fleenor, J. W. (1997). *Choosing 360: A guide to evaluating multi-rater feedback instruments for management development.* Greensboro, NC: Center for Creative Leadership.

2

Developmental Psychology and Adult Development

Theories of normal development provide parameters to help make sense of personal lives, showing what we might generally expect at different stages of life and anticipating potential crises.

—Sonia G. Austrian (2008a, p. 4)

The vast field of developmental psychology has much to offer the executive coach. Developmentalists help us understand what we are doing and why we do it by examining the ways we grew and were forged. Their premise is that we share distinctive and discernable patterns of growth and development, that these patterns shaped us, and that a clearer understanding of the developmental process can be instructive in understanding present behavior. Models of development provide a coach with several practical frameworks for assessment and practice.

Although philosophers have always had an interest in these matters, modern developmental psychology really began about a century ago with Freud's psychosocial stages. Subsequent theorists made major adjustments to Freud's work. Others simply parted ways. Developmental psychology is now a legitimate specialty area within psychology, and there are hundreds of master's- and doctoral-level programs in universities around the world. It is a popular and important field of study.

This chapter reviews several of the most powerful development frameworks and recommends ways for coaches to effectively use these models to understand clients and have a powerful impact. It focuses mostly on adult development, a relatively recent subspecialty area in the field of developmental psychology, because executive coaching is most interested in the development and behavior of adults rather than that of children or adolescents.

There are several different ways that developmental psychologists describe their findings and organize their observations. For example, it is typical (but not universal) for theorists to present their work in a series of progressive stages. This format is called a *stage theory*. People are thought to pass through discrete stages or steps, one after another, to move from childhood to adulthood and then old age. Stage theory has been applied variously to physical growth, identity formation, language development, moral development, intellectual and cognitive development, development of spirituality, and even progression toward acceptance of death.

Sometimes the stages are continuous; in other theories, they are discontinuous, lurching forward suddenly and unexpectedly. In some theories, people pass through the stages smoothly and seamlessly. In others, a crisis must be resolved before moving to the succeeding stage. Some stages require that a "task" be accomplished before one can move along. Typical stage theorists assert that mastery of one stage precedes progression to the next. It is usually possible to get bogged down in one stage or another. Sometimes people get stuck in a stage without awareness. They go on with their life just like everyone else, only to struggle with a certain kind of problem or inadequacy over and over again, somewhat mysteriously. They may have trouble finishing projects that they have begun, they may have trouble sustaining close or intimate relationships, they may feel that nothing matters, or they may possess a vague sense of anxiety when faced with everyday tasks and duties. Some people have trouble with authority, whereas others are uncomfortable with trust. Some seem unnecessarily rigid, whereas others are too safety oriented. All too often there is no rational explanation for their dysfunctional patterns. Developmental psychology has something to offer about each of these mysteries.

Temperament

Prior to a discussion of development influences, it is essential to acknowledge that humans bring "baggage" with them into the world at birth. Any psychologist with children can describe how astonished they were to discover that each of their children seemed different from the day they were born (or earlier). We were taught about nurture in graduate school, but unprepared for the force of nature. Nearly all parents marvel at how different siblings seem from a very early age. These inborn qualities of temperament seem to be innate, and they must be accounted for in personality assessment. References date back to Hippocrates and his four temperaments—(1) choleric, (2) phlegmatic, (3) melancholic, and (4) sanguine (Little, 1996–2007)—and much work has been done to try to accurately assess temperament over the years. The Myers-Briggs Type Indicator is the best known assessment instrument in this area.

The most influential researcher in temperament is probably Harvard psychologist Jerome Kagan who observed two qualities in infants that seemed inborn and relatively immutable. He called the infant types *high reactive* and *low reactive* or *inhibited* and *uninhibited*. Others have referred to them as *fearful* and *fearless*, and they seem somewhat similar to Jung's introverts and extroverts (Alic, 2001). Throughout his lengthy career, Kagan has argued, more or less, that genes play a major role in personality development alongside parental and social influence. He faulted mainstream personality theory and developmental psychology for straying too far from empirical data. Others have taken an even stronger view for inborn temperament over parental influence (Harris, 2009; Rowe, 1994).

Temperament must be factored into coaching, as most clients will possess qualities and personality characteristics that are fundamental and essentially immutable. There is no sense in criticizing these qualities or attempting to change them. They must be accepted and perhaps embraced. In fact, an accepting point of view toward "negative" parts of one's personality may turn out to be the most powerful perspective that a coach can offer. It can be liberating to embrace difficult aspects of one's own personality, and such acceptance can occasionally (and paradoxically) enable change. At the very least, such personality characteristics must be acknowledged and discussed. There is little worse than pretending that something obvious is not actually happening—or that it is happening but is not discussable. Acceptance of the notion that we are all born with enduring or unshakable "positive" and "negative" qualities can be quite helpful. Once this happens, a person makes workable accommodations. Coaches can help clients decide to put themselves in positions that might take advantage of positive personality characteristics and minimize or sidestep other personal qualities. It is always better to have a job that fits. In fact, the leadership literature described in Chapter 15 emphatically emphasizes leader–task fit.

Freud's Psychosexual Stages

Developmental psychology in the West begins with the work of Sigmund Freud. His psychodynamic view of psychotherapy is described in Chapter 3, and his stages of childhood development are described next. The description is brief and offered mostly as historical backdrop. Much of Freud's work on psychosocial stages has been discarded by modern psychology, and most of it focused on childhood and adolescence (rather than adult development). Nonetheless, it is uncommon to go through a week in the workplace without hearing the term *anal* used to describe a compulsive or obsessively organized colleague or *oral* to describe someone who smokes or drinks too much. Others are described as having a *big ego*, a term that originated with Freud's work.

Freud's psychosexual stages are really stages of personality development and his overall theory focused on infantile sexual urges that are aggressive, unacceptable, and repressed. He organized stages around the erogenous zone he thought was primary at that stage of personality organization. What follows is a simplified description of the stages and their characteristics. One can get stuck at any of these stages, and such a "fixation" is problematic thereafter. Remember that these views are no longer widely held in psychology.

Oral (birth to 18 months or so)—Gratification in this stage derives from the mouth. A child's earliest experiences with feeding are central to development. If feeding and oral gratification do not go well, a child becomes orally fixated, resulting in neediness, dependence, helplessness, or problems in overt oral behaviors such as overeating, smoking, or drinking.

Anal (age 1 to about age 3)—In this stage, gratification and pleasure involve the anus and elimination. Toilet training is the organizing task to be mastered. If it is not mastered, problems such as anal retentiveness, stinginess, stubbornness, difficulty expressing feelings, or lack of control persist.

Phallic (age 3 to about age 6)—Focus shifts to the genitals at this stage, and successful resolution of Oedipal and Electra challenges result in satisfactory sex-role adaptation and identification. Successful development of the superego then leads to adequate moral judgment and behavior.

Latency (age 5 to about age 12)—This is a quiet period where sexual forces are supposedly dormant. Young adults shift their focus from parents to peers, and they incorporate community values and standards along with an ability to manage urges.

Genital (age 12 and beyond)—Puberty ignites a renewed interest in sexuality. Successful resolution results in mature sexual identity and capacity. The ability to engage in satisfying relationships is associated with this stage.

Jung's Contributions

The Swiss psychoanalyst Carl Jung was on track to be Freud's intellectual successor until he disagreed with core Freudian concepts, particularly the sexual underpinnings of personality development. Jung's thinking took off in several different directions, and although his work is intriguing and popular with some, it can be difficult to comprehend and to research. He is thought to be the father of *adult* developmental psychology because he was the first to assert that significant growth and change take place after adolescence.

Jung felt that humans are faced with a series of opposite forces that must be reconciled. We have a *persona* that expresses the public self, an image we would like the world to perceive, and this image is at odds with the shadow, our darker side. We are driven by masculine forces (anima) and feminine forces (animus) as well, and these must be reconciled and managed. We all have introverted and extraverted inclinations that compete, and we also possess a personal, individual unconscious that conflicts with the collective, group unconscious. To Jung, management of these normal conflicts, reconciling opposites, and individuating had to be done to live a unique life and avoid the trap of ambivalence. He believed that this could only happen after the age of 40, the age he called the "noon of life" (Austrian, 2008c). Prior to that age, younger people are busy differentiating from parents and figuring out how to fulfill mundane responsibilities. During the second half of life, one has the time, internal capacity, and relaxed ability to sift through things and develop a personalized sense of self in the world.

Piaget's Stages of Cognitive Development

In the 1920s, the Swiss psychologist Jean Piaget famously described four sequential stages of intellectual development, and his work provided a foundation for much subsequent theorizing about human development. Cognitive development, in his view, referred to the ways that human thinking, reasoning, problem solving, and conceptualizing evolve, starting in infancy. Early in his career he worked with Alfred Binet on the development of the first IQ tests, but he became interested in the patterns of thinking responsible for consistently wrong answers, which led him to study cognitive development in children. He observed thousands of children, including his own. Piaget theorized that humans create *schemas* (mental constructs, frameworks, structures, or models) to order and understand things. When confronted with a new thing or experience, humans seek to fit it into an existing schema. If it fits, it is *assimilated*. If it cannot fit, the new thing is rejected or *accommodated* by adjustment or expansion of our schema so that it can fit. As our schemas continue to accommodate, we continue to develop. This process is extremely active in children, and it continues at a less frequent pace throughout one's life.

Here is a very simple description of Piaget's stages:

Sensorimotor (birth to about 2 years of age)—In this stage toddlers learn about the world through direct physical experience. They touch, feel, see, smell, taste, and mouth things. They use their bodies and reflexes to figure things out. Piaget thought that children in this stage make no distinction between self and the world outside of self. Life is all one global mass of experiences. They do not understand cause-and-effect relationships.

Preoperational (age 2 to about 7)—At this age children learn to use symbols (words and numbers) to think and to make sense of the world. Although still egocentric, they observe and imitate adults to figure out how to get what they want. They begin to discern predictable patterns in life and develop complex mental representations of the patterns.

Concrete operational (age 7 to about 11)—At this point they begin to use *operations*, methods that yield consistent results when applied repeatedly. Children begin to actively categorize things. Egocentrism fades as children recognize the importance of others in the world, and they begin to be able to take the perspective of the other. Thinking is still quite concrete.

Formal operational (age 11 onward)—This stage brings abstract thought. One can imagine solutions that cannot be seen. Complex, logical reasoning methods such as induction, deduction, implication, comparison, and hypotheticals become possible.

Each stage involves a characteristic challenge related to egocentrism, meaning that children have to distinguish inside things from outside things to advance their understanding of the world. Piaget conducted hundreds of experiments and wrote 60 books to describe his findings. Examples of Piagetian characteristics that might be of interest to a coach include egocentrism, abstract reasoning capacity, language development, moral reasoning, cognitive flexibility and concreteness, centrism (the tendency to see only one aspect of a situation), and the capacity to take a broad, inclusive view. Even one's relationship to humor is related to Piaget's developmental models.

Erikson's Psychosocial Stages

Erik Erikson was the first modern figure to focus on the psychological development of adults. His thinking clearly derives from the work of Freud. In fact, he had been a student of Freud's daughter, Anna, and gone through an analysis with her (Watson, 2002). He built his developmental framework on a rather different premise than Freud and took a different point of view in the end. Whereas Freud focused on basic biological, psychological, and even sexual forces that were internal, Erickson turned his attention to social and relationship forces that were external. He described human development along eight stages, the first five using Freud's work and the last three focused on the development of adults.

Erikson's early personal history probably had a direct influence on the content of his theories. Erikson had Danish parents, but was born in Germany. His mother never married his father, and Erikson never knew him. Subsequent to Erikson's birth, his mother married a German pediatrician named Theodor Homburger, and Erikson took Homburger's family name. Erikson was a tall, blond, Danish Jew in pre-World War II Germany, and apparently found it difficult to be accepted by Jewish and non-Jewish friends alike. "At temple school, the kids teased him for being Nordic; at grammar school, they teased him for being Jewish" (Boeree, 2006). Erikson was not told about the identity of his biological father until he was in high school, and he seems to have struggled quite a bit with his own identity development, at least as a young man. He wandered for a while and never entered university. He even referred to himself as a wanderer and a Bohemian as a young man (Erikson, 1975). In 1933, he left Nazi Germany and immigrated permanently to the United

States where he became the first child psychoanalyst in Boston. He eventually taught at Harvard, Yale, and the University of California, Berkeley, even though his own formal education had ended at about the 12th grade (Watson, 2002). After establishing citizenship in the United States, he changed his name from Erik Homberger to Erik Erikson, a name thought to symbolize ultimate self-definition: Erik, son of Erik (Boeree, 2006).

His most important work is found in his second book, *Childhood and Society*, which was published in 1963. In that book he describes eight hierarchical stages of human development, each based upon the resolution of a crisis between two extremes. External social or environmental events often trigger the crises, and such events could include changing schools, leaving home, getting married, changing jobs, or retiring from work. His theoretical ideas focus on themes of personal independence and on connectedness to others. Each stage requires the achievement of some kind of mastery that enhances the establishment of personal identity. In fact, the common term *identity crisis* stems directly from Erikson's work. Unsuccessful achievement of mastery results in less adequate personal identity and future problems. The process is cumulative, and successful mastery at each stage depends, in part, on mastery at previous stages. In contrast to Freud, Erikson's model allows one to continue to improve on all stages of development throughout the lifespan.

What follows is a brief description of the stages that are shown in Table 2.1. The title of each stage is a contrast between the goal of the stage and the result of a bad outcome (that is, good outcome vs. bad outcome or successful vs. unsuccessful resolution of the stage). The overarching theme of the stages describes an evolution from a sense of *trust* and *connectivity* (to other people) to a *capacity for healthy independence* to *productivity* and, eventually, to *giving back* (Watson, 2002). Note that different authors and sources give slightly different titles to the stages.

Stage 1: Basic Trust vs. Mistrust

Baby humans are the most helpless of the animal kingdom, and they rely completely on adults to survive. If caretakers do their job properly—if they consistently provide food, shelter, warmth, and human contact—this first stage will be negotiated successfully. When that happens, a child establishes a deep belief that the world will consistently and reliably provide what he or she needs. The infant learns he can trust the world. It is a safe place, and one can count on responses from the outside world to be orderly and adequate. When parenting is capricious or inconsistent or lacking in some major way, the infant gets the impression that the world is a dangerous and unreliable place that is essentially uncontrollable. The world they were born into cannot be counted on to provide what is needed. Adults who do not succeed at this developmental stage are likely to focus excessively on control and might experience persistent

Table 2.1 Erikson's Psychosocial Stages

Stage	Optimal Period	Task and Description
Trust vs. Mistrust	Birth to 1 year	Develop belief that the world will consistently deliver what you need. You can count on the world's order and predictability. Security and independence are established.
Autonomy vs. Shame/Doubt	1–3 years	Learn how to do things on your own. If you are criticized for your attempts or if you stumble, you may develop a sense of shame and self-doubt.
Initiative vs. Guilt	3–6 years	Make things happen through relationships. Explore social rules and roles.
Industry vs. Diffusion	6–11 years	Mastery and success in a wide range of skill areas. Rewarded (not criticized) for attempts.
Identity vs. Role Confusion	Adolescence	Resolution of the "identity crisis." Integrate many sources of identity data into a unified sense of self.
Intimacy vs. Isolation	Young adulthood	Strong sense of identity allows one to take a risk to be vulnerable and intimate, to commit to others.
Generativity vs. Stagnation	Middle adulthood	Focus on giving back to others or producing something to leave behind. Teaching, parenting, community service.
Ego Integrity vs. Despair	Old age	Reconciliation of all of the plusses and minuses of one's life into an overall positive view of self and life. Comfortable with prospect of death.

unfocused anxiety. They may have trouble taking risks and making big decisions. They may not take enough appropriate action on their own behalf. They may cling to others or tend toward dependency in relationships. They are unlikely to feel secure, no matter what happens in the real world.

Stage 2: Autonomy vs. Shame and Doubt

At some point in the second year of life, children begin to explore the external world on their own. This is why parents childproof the house, covering electric outlets to protect young, probing fingers. This is the stage where children try things out and strive to do things on their own. They attempt to feed themselves, to learn to clothe themselves, and they do not like others to do everything for them. It is important that caregivers support these attempts appropriately and that children are not criticized, laughed at, or humiliated when they fail or fall down. When a child is criticized for an attempt to do something new or to learn a new skill, they suffer feelings of shame or self-doubt.

Stage 3: Initiative vs. Guilt

At this point, children try to learn new ways to manipulate the world through other people and relationships, and failure can be perceived as a moral failure. They try out new roles and learn about gender-appropriate behaviors. They may explore new ways to interact and relate to others, and if criticized may feel a sense of moral guilt for having failed to properly incorporate social standards and skills. The risk they took in being purposeful is blunted, and this produces feelings of guilt. Successful resolution of this stage results in a person who is relatively unafraid to try new ideas, to meet new people, and to establish new relationships. It is also possible that too much unrestrained initiative can produce a person who lacks adequate self-control and is ruthless or uncaring about his or her impact on others. Healthy resolution also produces a person with a sense of purpose.

Stage 4: Industry vs. Inferiority

Stage 4 involves mastery in a vast variety of new skill areas. Young people are invited and expected to learn math skills, sports skills, history facts, and social skills. Accompanying this expectation is the possibility of failure, and if a child fails too much or perceives that they are failing more often and more comprehensively than peers, he or she may end up feeling a sense of inferiority. Children at this age are able to make more accurate self-assessments than previously, and they tend to compare themselves to others to make those determinations. If they do not get good enough grades, if they do not make the team, or if they are not popular they run the risk of feeling inferior. If parents push children too hard to master too much, too soon, there is also a risk of inertia, where children lose interest and lose desire to take the risk to compete and to try. On the other hand, if things go well, if enough mastery is achieved, a lasting sense of competence results.

Stage 5: Ego Identity vs. Role Confusion

Stage 5 takes place in adolescence and requires resolution of the first big "identity crisis." One's body and brain are changing, and hormones are pumping.

Prior to this stage, children did not have to decide the large question of "Who am I?" They were busy with other essential tasks, most involving exploration and mastery of new skills. Now with most of those skills more or less in place, the challenge is to figure out which of the old childhood ways to leave behind and which to embrace forever. There are many aspects of life that have to be integrated into some sort of central identity. There are skills to put in place, values to ponder, friends to consider, personality qualities to evaluate, political views to question, gender characteristics to sort out, and strengths and weaknesses to manage. There is also the huge factor of the opinion of others, always powerful in the life of the adolescent. How does one integrate all of these factors (and more) into a sense of a single person? Should commitments be made and, if so, in which direction and to whom? What educational or career path should be taken? Should I conform? To what and to whom? Should I rebel and let the world know that I am in control, that I have autonomy?

If this stage does not go well, a person is left with identity confusion. There are two common ways that this can happen (Watson, 2002). The first is called *role diffusion*, resulting in a vague, lifelong lack of focus and a sense that nothing matters and that the person does not really count. No commitments are made and one's life simply drifts. The second way is called *role foreclosure*. This happens when some other person or other force or institution makes the identity decision for the adolescent. Family tradition (all the men in the family were firefighters) or a forceful parent sometimes makes this happen, and it can result in a person who is *half in* and *half out* of his or her own life, never having actually decided (personally) to be who they became. Those who solve the identity crisis are later able to make commitments and stick to them, investing fully in one's own life and career. Their values and goals are aligned and embraced. They have a solid sense of self; there is a there there.

Stage 6: Intimacy vs. Isolation

If a solid sense of self-identity has been established, it is possible to go on and take the risk involved in making a commitment to others or to another. Real intimacy requires openness; openness puts one in position to be vulnerable. A person with whom we have shared intimate secrets or personal details is now in a position to potentially hurt us. This is a risk that can only be taken by someone with self-confidence, with a solid sense of identity. Commitment is seen as essential if one is to avoid lifelong self-absorption, loneliness, and isolation. Those unable to resolve this crisis are thought to become habitually competitive rather than cooperative, not so accepting of others, and threatened by gestures of closeness. They may behave in very social ways, but they do not commit to substantial relationships. Indeed, they never really figure out how to do this.

Stage 7: Generativity vs. Self-Absorption and Stagnation

Stage 7 is the first of Erikson's two stages of adult development, and they represent truly groundbreaking thought in the field of developmental psychology, as previous theoreticians simply did not address development after adolescence.

To Erikson, generativity meant giving something back to future generations. In this stage, one builds on the solid relationships that have already been established and contributes to others outside of self and intimate relationships. One takes responsibility for the development of children or students. One creates art or useful products or institutions or structures or schools or buildings or literature. One can mentor others. The questions in this stage are: Who do you take care of? Who do you teach? What do you leave behind? How do you contribute to others? The contribution need not be earthshaking, but it must involve sharing what you have learned or accumulated with others who can benefit now or after you are gone.

If this stage does not take place or does not go well, one lives only for self, stuck in selfishness. He or she continues to focus on what they can get rather than what they can give. They then stagnate and fail to develop any further.

Research indicates that generativity is associated with a wide range of benefits including low levels of anxiety and depression, high levels of self-acceptance and life satisfaction, capacity for leadership, and involvement in civic and community activities along with a sense of belonging and fulfillment (Berk, 2004, p. 513).

Stage 8: Integrity vs. Despair

The big task in this final stage is acceptance. The question is: How did you do? How do you like what you did with your life? Did you do a pretty good job with what you had to work with or did you make a mess of it? Did you leave some tasks unfinished? Did you go in the wrong direction? More important though, can you accept both the positive and negative aspects of what you see when you look back?

There are inevitable losses at this stage, including the loss of power in the world of work and relationships, the loss of financial growth, and the loss of energy. These losses must be integrated into one's identity if this stage is to be negotiated. There's something sad about an older person unwilling or unable to accept what has happened, when it is too late for a "do over." Death is around the corner and that must be faced as well. If one has established a sense of trust in the life process, it is probably easier to trust death, as well.

This stage requires an honest assessment and an overall acceptance. All of the complicated aspects and components of one's life must be integrated into some sort of whole. When this process goes well, the older person lives more or less cheerfully, accepting fate and sharing accumulated wisdom. When it goes poorly, the result is a bitter older person who is full of contempt for self and for others, an outcome Erikson calls *despair*.

Summary

Erik Erikson was the first developmental psychologist to make a serious study of adult development. All of his stages are relevant to coaching because, unlike Freud's earlier model, the issues are never totally resolved or out of play. One can always go back and continue to work on the issues in any of the stages. In Erikson's model, development is never finished. You have many chances to improve on what you have got, and developmental crises or challenges provide an opportunity to do just that. Coaches can discuss client development in terms of these stages when appropriate, and it is relatively easy to spot areas of importance to coaches and clients in the Eriksonian stages of development. Just look for issues of trust, control, cooperation and competition, commitment to projects or to people, ability to receive feedback and take criticism, relationships, and mentoring. When clients have difficulties in these areas, it can be extremely helpful to pull out a chart of Erikson's stages and use it to start a discussion. There is always work to be done, and identifying stage issues can be a good beginning. It is typical for humans to unconsciously act out stage conflicts, and a discussion of those conflicts can be extremely helpful if done discretely, gently, and in a positive frame.

Attachment Theory

There are several other theories of development that derive, more or less, from Freud's psychoanalytic work. These theories come from modern branches called ego psychology or self-psychology or object relations theory. They all place importance on very early relationships between infants and the caregivers charged with nurturing these infants.

Historically, psychoanalysis legitimized the use of focused attention on parenting and early childhood experiences. It viewed these early social experiences as causative and contributory to adult development as well as to difficulties, but it focused almost exclusively on traumatic events or fantasized trauma or even instinctual drives, to the exclusion of most other environmental influences. Psychoanalysts studied feeding, toilet training, sexual trauma, and internal conflicts. Freud himself eventually focused on Oedipal arrangements and conflicts, especially unconscious and fantasy components, rather than real-life aspects of the familial relationship environment. Early psychoanalysts were almost exclusively interested in the internal world of the child, not the real world. "They were not interested in making a serious science of the way that parents treated a child or of the quality of relationships in the family" (Karen, 1994, p. 35).

This left a big gap. Other theorists asserted that in addition to a need for food and sex, humans had a primary need for meaningful connectedness to other people. They moved their interest away from psychosocial conflict toward the ways that early nurturing interaction influenced later character development.

It is often difficult to discern the usefulness of such theories for business coaches, and one source even asserts that "attachment theory has little to tell us about work relationships" (West & Sheldon-Keller, 1994). But attachment theory is important to coaching because it has been subjected to serious empirical research and it directly addresses adult development and several components of successful work life. As a result, it has been widely embraced by psychotherapists, and coaches ought to be familiar with it. Attachment theory focuses on the quality of the first essential relationship that humans have with a caregiver. Coaches are likely to find it useful to know what attachment theory has to say about understanding and interacting with clients. It is of special importance when coaches are faced with clients who have trouble with trust, relationship management, self-confidence, or introspection.

History and Development

Attachment theory began with the British physician-psychoanalyst John Bowlby. In the 1950s he departed from Freud's thinking and used emerging ideas of ethology to try to understand human attachment to caregivers. Ethology is the study of instinctive, adaptive evolutionary animal behaviors. Darwin is the grandfather of that field, and the subsequent work of Konrad Lorenz influenced Bowlby. Lorenz studied imprinting in ducks, and was able to show that ducks will attach to the first suitable living entity during the critical period for attachment (roughly the first 36 hours of duck life). He was able to get ducklings to attach to him, and photos of Lorenz and his ducks are memorable. Subsequently, several aviators have been able to hatch migratory birds under the wings of a hang glider and get them to "attach" to the aircraft for flights together over long distances later in life. This work can be seen in several amazing documentary films (*Le Peuple Migrateur, Winged Migration,* and *Fly Away Home*).

Bowlby asserted that human attachment to a primary caregiver was a biological imperative and that the quality of that attachment forged important aspects of one's personality. Austrian (2008b, p. 365) put it this way:

> Children are born with a predisposition to become attached to their caregivers, and early disturbances in primary attachment relationships can lead to lifelong feelings of insecurity and to a distorted capacity to develop and sustain meaningful relationships.

Bowlby established several essential points. First, he noted that human infants are more helpless than those of any other species. Human babies rely on caregivers for much longer periods than other animals. Humans must attach, one way or another, for better or for worse. It is an extremely rare person who forms no attachments at all. Second, attachment results in what Bowlby called a relatively stable internal *working model* of relationships. This working model is an internal representation of the way that interaction with the caregiver (and by extension, with others) works. It is a system of expectations, beliefs, memories, experiences, rewards, and punishments derived from early attachments to caregivers. It represents a model of the rules, the benefits, the dangers, and the probable outcomes to be found in subsequent relationships. It is constantly under revision, and it provides a framework for all important future relationships (Watson, 2002).

In about 1950 Bowlby began a lifelong collaboration with Mary Salter Ainsworth, a Canadian–American psychologist who made significant contributions to attachment theory, many of which derived from her research technique called the "Strange Situation." In this innovative and controversial method, she observed infants and mothers as she put them through a series of physical exchanges in a laboratory. She placed the parent and child in a room and brought a stranger into the room. She then had the parent leave the room and had the parent return, all the while observing the behavior of parent and child in various coming, going, and reunion situations. After considerable experimentation, she concluded that a satisfactory attachment with a primary caregiver provided a *secure base* for an infant, a potentially important concept for coaches. Here's what Bowlby (1988, p. 62) wrote about the secure base: "All of us, from the cradle to the grave, are happiest when life is organized as a series of excursions, long or short, from the secure base provided by our attachment figure(s)."

Caregivers provide a secure base when they give adequate care characterized by sensitive, timely, and consistent responses to an infant's needs. Such caregivers are emotionally available, appropriately responsive, and not overbearing. They are attuned to the needs of their child and able to regulate their own positive and negative emotional reactions (Sable, 2008). A secure base allows a child to become independent, knowing that he or she can return, as needed, to safety. They can come and go, making forays into the world with little worry that their base will not be there. This allows them to reach out into the world and to trust, to have confidence in their actions. As an infant develops into young adulthood, the secure base function shifts from the parental figure to others of importance.

One of Ainsworth's students, Mary Main, later became an important contributor to attachment theory through the use of the Adult Attachment Interview, which she developed and used to help further classify attachment styles.

Attachment Styles

By the late 1990s theorists had settled on a rough typology of four primary attachment styles. These attachment styles describe the ways that we tend to connect and relate to important others in our lives. They characterize how we manage close relationships, trust, and intimacy. Although theorists have given them a wide variety of slightly differing names, they consist of the following categories:

Secure Attachment—People with this level or type of attachment tend to be confident, comfortable with themselves and others, can take risks, and are able to be independent and engage in close relationships. They balance needs for closeness with an ability to be autonomous. They require and make good use of "alone time." They are capable of effective introspection. Those with secure attachment are comfortable with trust; they are able to trust others and are generally trustworthy. They do not worry much about whether others like them or not.

Anxious–Ambivalent–Preoccupied Attachment—This attachment style involves insecurity and feelings of inadequacy. People with this style are uncertain about whether relationships are safe or reliable. They may develop dependent relationships and preoccupation with jealous fears of betrayal or abandonment. They often try to control or smother others, and typically respond to relationship challenges with anger or passivity.

Dismissive–Avoidant–Resistant Attachment—These people tend to value autonomy over closeness. They may be uncomfortable with closeness or intimacy and as a result, keep their relationships superficial. They may not even value close relationships, and they are unlikely to possess the ability to understand their own reactions and emotions. They seem detached or distant and tend not to trust others.

Disorganized–Disoriented Attachment—Main is credited with the addition of this fourth category, which was added 20 years subsequent to the previous three. It includes people whose attachment style is strange, irrational, odd, confused and confusing, contradictory, and difficult to comprehend. People with this attachment style may lapse into dissociative states to cope. They seem peculiar, especially in their interpersonal interactions.

All of these categories evolve over the lifespan, but are thought to be somewhat restrictive once established. An observant coach is likely to be able to recognize observable patterns indicative of their client's working model of relational attachment. The patterns regulate comfort levels and interpersonal closeness, dictating how people manage to keep others close or distant. Trust, intimacy, and control are involved.

Table 2.2 Adult Attachment Model

		Thoughts about Self	
		Positive	Negative
Thoughts about Others	Positive	Secure attachment Higher self-esteem Higher sociability Comfortable with intimacy and autonomy Trusting, accepting	Preoccupied with relationships Anxious attachment Strives for self-acceptance through others' acceptance Lower self-esteem Higher sociability
	Negative	Dismissing of intimacy Counterdependent Higher self-esteem Lower sociability Independent-vulnerable	Fearful attachment Socially avoidant Lower self-esteem Lower sociability Feels unlovable Does not trust others

Source: Table modified from Bartholomew and Horowitz (1991).

Adult Attachment

Psychologists Bartholomew and Horowitz (1991) used circumplex analysis (a statistical method for organizing related data points) of relationship patterns of 77 college students to conclude that an additional attachment category was justified, that of fearful attachment. They began with the observation that Bowlby's original construct of a working model consisted of two essential components: a person's perception of the *quality of the attachment figure* (the other) and the person's *judgment of self.* Their four attachment styles (secure, anxious, dismissive, and fearful) are summarized in Table 2.2.

Attachment and Coaching

There are several ways that coaches can productively use attachment theory to help clients. The need for a secure base and its ongoing utility continues from childhood into adult functioning. Sable (2008) observed that adults often find a secure base *outside* of one's family of origin, and adult attachment behavior is "developmentally more organized, diverse and sophisticated" (p. 22). Adults seek the support of a secure base in times of stress, uncertainty, adversity, and danger. When a mentor or parental type of figure is available, adults seek physical or emotional proximity. At other times, when a real attachment figure (a person) is not available, support can be found simply by thinking about the secure base and allowing internal feelings of protection to provide the needed sense of comfort. Recall the occasions when you felt overwhelmed but were able to soothe yourself by imagining a supportive person who had confidence in you.

Coaches should be aware that they can (and often do) serve as a surrogate secure base, or attachment figure, especially if the coaching work takes place over an extended period of time. As rapport evolves and strengthens, the secure base phenomenon is likely to become more important, and the quality of the coach–client relationship becomes critical. In this way of thinking, coaches must be accessible and reliable, consistent, dependable, and perceived by clients as safe and comforting. Like a good parent they must be emotionally available and appropriately responsive, able to regulate their own positive and negative feelings (Sable, 2008). They should be supportive without being critical or negative, and, most important, it is crucial that coaches be perceived as trustworthy. A secure base eventually leads to client independence and effective risk taking. Clients can study and develop relationship skills from the vantage point of the base. Attachment theory points out that adults typically notice the availability of possible attachment figures, wondering whether this person would respond in a positive way if called upon for support. Many clients will explore their coach for potential attachment. Coaches may want to explore their own capacity and willingness to serve as an attachment figure for clients. This would involve a coach's capacity for intimacy and comfort with the ability to provide a calming influence during periods of stress and adversity, dependability and reliability, along with a willingness to listen without judgment. If we are to believe attachment theory, clients are likely to seek the proximity of "a person regarded as 'stronger and/or wiser'" in times of stress or difficulty (Wallen, 2007, p. 12). The validity of this premise seems obvious.

Coaches can also use attachment theory and its categories to evaluate clients. Suboptimal early attachment is thought to exert influence that continues throughout adulthood, creating client problems with relationships, trust, openness, independence, risk taking, persistence, emotional management, and even self-confidence. Some adults who had a problematic attachment history find it difficult to rely on other people or to confide in them. Your client's personality was profoundly influenced by early attachment (in this theory), and you can use it to make sense out of that client's strengths and weaknesses. These factors are truly important when a client attempts to move into significant positions of leadership, and they can enhance a career or undermine it. Coaches are not therapists, and no one would expect a coach to attempt to resolve these attachment difficulties or cause a change in their client's attachment style. In fact, in some cases, a referral for psychological counseling will be appropriate. But coaches can adjust their interpersonal approach based upon their assessment of a client's capacities in the areas listed (for example, trust, intimacy), so that they respond to clients in ways that are perceived as comfortable. They can also call attention to these difficulties in the interest of finding a good job-personality "fit."

Third, attachment theorists assert that more secure people are better at something called *metacognition*, the ability to think about thinking and to use it to reflect productively on oneself. Wallen describes this as "the capacity to adopt a reflective stance toward experience," and it is a capacity essential to the coaching process. Although this capacity sounds much like psychological-mindedness, Fonagy and Target (1997) call it *mentalization*. It is "the ability to self-reflect, identify internal emotional states, and perceive the impact of one's emotions and behavior on others" (Austrian, 2008b, p. 405). Some people, especially those preoccupied with interpersonal safety, seem to either lack this capacity or have a "defensive inhibition" toward it (Wallen, 2007, p. 2). They are so concerned with what others think that they cannot take time to notice their own thinking. Coaches can observe a client's capacity for effective introspection and may even be able to promote mindfulness. This recommendation implies that coaches value and cultivate their own meta-cognitive capacity.

Stages of Adult Development: Gould and Levinson

Prior to about 1970 there was little formal psychological interest in human development that might take place after adolescence. It has even been reported that the study of adult development was considered a vaguely taboo subject, as it invited frightening and depressing discussions of the aging process (or death) by researchers themselves in middle age (Austrian, 2008c, p. 214). Youth was celebrated; middle-age ignored. That all changed when Roger Gould and Daniel Levinson, without any serious theoretical guidelines, simultaneously took on major investigations of adult development. Gould used data from a sample of White, middle-class men and women at the University of California, Los Angeles (UCLA) to come to the conclusion that adulthood was a time of "active and systematic changes" in a "series of distinct stages" (Walsh, 1983, p. 47). Publication of his research in 1972 opened a floodgate of interest in the topic, and his work was followed by a best-selling popular book *Passages* by Gail Sheehy (1976). Prior to the publication of his own book on adult developmental stages, Gould sued Sheehy for plagiarizing his research and won a significant monetary award ("Passages II," 1978). Gould's work is a mix of the psychoanalytic and the cognitive, emphasizing the impact of childhood experiences along with an interest in assumptions, beliefs, and myths. He described a natural "maturational push" that motivates us to "transform childish dependencies into self-responsibility" (Walsh, 1983). Stages of development contain age-related "illusions of safety" that must be outgrown. He divided adult life into five time periods, each involving a move from a position of dependent security to a position of greater independence and autonomy. We begin life assuming that our parents will protect us. Once we abandon that view, we still assume that the ideas they passed along will serve a protective function. Still later, we realize that parental ways are inadequate and we must develop our own hybrid tools.

At that same time, Daniel Levinson began a study of 40 men between the ages of 35 and 45 at Yale University (he expanded the age cohort later). Using a procedure he called "biographical interviewing," he conducted a series of structured and informal interviews and combined them with formal psychological testing. His subjects were laborers, novelists, business executives, and biology professors, and he conducted interviews with their wives and coworkers as well. In 1978, he published his results in a popular book called *The Seasons of a Man's Life*. Levinson had no preexisting theories to work with, and he did not build his theory on Freudian or Eriksonian principles. Instead, he focused on underlying patterns that constitute a design of a person's life at any one point in time and called these the "individual life structure" (Levinson, 1978). Transitions are defined as the termination of one life structure and the beginning of a new one. He reported that "the life structure evolves through a relatively orderly sequence during the adult years" (Levinson, 1978, p. 49). He focused his research on the time between adolescence and age 65, noting that gerontologists were already actively at work on the years that came later.

His interviews led him to divide this age period into four broad "eras," each lasting about a quarter of a century and each with its own distinctive set of unifying qualities. The eras are:

- Childhood and adolescence (birth to age 22)
- Early adulthood (age 17–45)
- Middle adulthood (age 40–65)
- Late adulthood (age 60+)

In Levinson's view, transitions from one era to the next are "neither simple nor brief," and they require a "basic change in the fabric of one's life" (Levinson, 1978, p. 19). The period of transition involves a boundary zone that is in between and might be lengthy. His model includes a sequence of developmental periods within each era. There are tasks to be accomplished, and these enable one to grow out of one period and into the next. Successful development includes the defining of a personal dream (and subsequent modulation of that dream), the securing of a mentor, development of a career path (and the implications for identity), and establishing intimacy and satisfying friendships. As in Jung's model, there are polarities to be resolved, including differentiation between young and old, destruction and creation, masculine and feminine, and attachment and separation. Successful negotiation of these tasks and challenges are not assured in Levinson's view. He noted that "for large numbers of men, the conditions of work in early adulthood are oppressive, alienating and inimical to development" (Levinson, 1978, p. 338). He also pointed out that most men do not receive effective mentoring if they get any at all, that workplaces tended to be hypermasculine, that the workplace can be downright oppressive, and that there is not much support for human development once a young person leaves the family (or college).

Levinson's work was immediately criticized for its exclusive focus on males. He subsequently conducted companionate research, again using biographical interviewing with a cohort of 45 women, including 15 business executives, 15 academics, and 15 homemakers. His results were published in *The Seasons of a Woman's Life* (1996), which was completed by his wife, Judy, after his death in 1994.

Both of Levinson's books on adult development reflect the zeitgeist and the social and cultural transitions that were taking place in the period between 1960 and 2000 in the United States. As expected, the career trajectories and experiences of women were different from that of men. Levinson wrote that "I was surprised by the extent and power of the differences revealed by this study" (1996, p. 38). Although eras and periods from his research on men could reasonably be applied to the lives and career paths of women, there were significant differences. He used the term *gender splitting* to describe the differences, and he intended a very serious point (p. 38):

> My central concept is gender splitting. This term refers not simply to gender differences but to a splitting asunder—the creation of a rigid division between male and female, masculine and feminine, in human life.

He described the impact of gender splitting in four basic forms:

1. In the domestic and public spheres
2. In traditional marriage as it relates to work roles (domestic or outside of the home)
3. Between "women's work" and "men's work" in society
4. Between feminine and masculine components of the individual psyche

Gender was found to have an important impact on the essential tasks of young adulthood that had been described in *The Seasons of a Man's Life*. Women's experiences were different. In contrast to men, the dreams of women were split and complicated. Only the homemakers had unified dreams—as men tended to have. Women in business or academic careers weighed and incorporated a desire to raise children along with the career demands of their spouse. They found this integration to be difficult. They also found fewer opportunities to be mentored effectively. There were fewer female mentors available, and they found male mentoring relationships to be complicated. Their career trajectory was different, in that their novice period seemed to last longer than that of men. As a result, women viewed their own careers as somewhat less successful and less satisfying than men. All of these observations were made during a period of significant gender upheaval in American society. See Chapter 13 ("Coaching Women") for a more complete discussion of these issues.

Moral Development

Although corrupt and self-centered CEOs dominate the current news cycle, it is most likely the case that a solid career is best built on a foundation of personal integrity. Coworkers and colleagues quickly size up one another to determine trustworthiness, honesty, and integrity in small and large matters. Coaches can evaluate their clients' moral development, and this can provide fertile ground for career enhancement.

Classic philosophers like Confucius, Socrates, and Aristotle provided foundations for moral values, and moral development is addressed in all of the major religious texts. But the 20th century produced important new psychological models to describe how humans develop ethical reasoning skills. This body of work implies that humans go through stages of moral development at the same time that we develop in other important ways. An effective coach can observe the thinking and behavior of their client from a moral point of view to assess levels of moral motivation, reasoning, and skills. Coaching in this area poses significant challenges.

Piaget also applied his stage model of cognitive development to moral development, theorizing that a person's views of right and wrong go through stages in a way similar to cognitive development. He described two broad stages of moral reasoning (Craig & Baucum, 2002) and found that our methods of moral reasoning change dramatically at about the age of 10 (Crain, 1985). The stages are:

Moral Realism—Thinking in this early-to-middle childhood stage is rule bound, and the rules are treated as concrete and absolute. Good behavior is judged by the authority of others and solely by consequences (if you broke a rule, you were bad).

Moral Relativism—Toward the end of middle childhood (after the age of about 10) children begin to notice that there is no absolute right and wrong in real life, and that rules are useful but cannot be relied upon in an absolute way. Behavior is judged by socially agreed upon reciprocal arrangements that require perspective taking. Intentions are factored into moral judgments (What was the actor trying to accomplish? Did they mean to do a bad thing?).

Psychologist Lawrence Kohlberg began with Piaget's basic ideas and built a theory of moral reasoning that extends well beyond the youthful age periods of Piaget's work. Although Kohlberg's methods and conclusions have been challenged, his is the most influential model of moral development in Western thought. His theory was based on research conducted with 72 male children and adolescents using a dilemma faced by a husband named Heinz. Heinz is faced with the problem of whether to steal a drug to save the life of his sick wife. Kohlberg examined the thinking and reasoning found in children's responses to the dilemma and sorted patterns into a hierarchical set of stages. His research revealed two important trends along with his six stages. He witnessed development from a focus on *external forces* (such as laws or authority figures) toward *internalized moral principles* (developed by individuals for their own personal use). At the same time he observed movement from *concrete* reasoning toward the *abstract* (Craig & Baucum, 2002, p. 358).

A summary of Kohlberg's stages is provided in the following outline. Keep in mind that these are stages of *reasoning* and not necessarily *behavior*, although Kohlberg claimed that there is surely a connection between thinking and action.

Level I: Preconventional morality (based on external rewards and punishments)

Stage 1—Obedience and punishment orientation. Behavior is judged by the physical consequences. If rules prohibit a behavior, it is thereby wrong. One obeys rules to avoid punishment. The fact of punishment makes the action wrong or proves that it was wrong.

Stage 2—Instrumental purpose orientation (exchange relativism). Right action flows from pragmatic self-interest. You do what it takes to get what you want or need, and that makes it "right." Other people do the same, and you might make deals with them that are mutually self-satisfying. Punishment is a risk that naturally should be avoided in the process.

Level II: Conventional morality (based on social conformity, loyalty to social structures)

Stage 3—Approval-of-others (good boy/good girl) orientation. Starting in the teen years, this view is that family, schools, and community expectations matter. Good behavior involves trust, concern for the welfare of others, harmony, and social approval. Stealing would bring dishonor upon yourself and your family or school or peer group, therefore, it is wrong. How others would judge you is an essential element in determining morality.

Stage 4—Social order maintenance orientation. Norms, conventions, rules, and laws are obeyed to maintain social order and institutions. What would happen if everyone decided to break a law they personally disagreed with? Members of communities have a duty to conform for the sake of the overall community.

Level III: Postconventional or principled morality (autonomous reasoning)

Stage 5—Social contract orientation. Laws are not necessarily good or fair to all people in all circumstances. They are to be followed for the good of society, but should be open to examination or change when they do not benefit members of the community. According to Kohlberg, "Right action tends to be defined in terms of general individual rights and in terms of standards that have been critically examined and agreed on by the whole society" (1981, p. 18). There are occasions when a human "right" could take precedence over a law, but laws represent a social contract that citizens freely enter into and, as a result, conform to. Ethical behavior is motivated by a concern for the "good society," which evolves from a democratic process.

Stage 6—Universal principle orientation. Rightness is a matter of individual conscience, guided by abstract principles that are self-chosen. The principles are unassailable in the abstract (e.g., justice, in particular) and widely endorsed. The final arbiter of what is right and wrong is oneself, and right action is chosen to avoid self-condemnation. Right action might include civil disobedience of unjust laws or situations.

Kohlberg's view of moral development involved an active process of reflection. Transition from one stage to another does not occur naturally or without serious thought and discussion. One cannot assume that moral reasoning will evolve without active effort and direct discussions about right and wrong. Development is also likely to require perspective taking, as one must imagine what it is like to being in someone else's shoes in order to advance the capacity for moral reasoning. Moral development, in Kohlberg's view, is much more likely to be successful when it takes place in an open and democratic atmosphere (Crain, 1985).

Criticisms

Two powerful criticisms of Kohlberg's work have emerged. The first is that his stages are based upon Western philosophical foundations and may not be applicable or especially useful outside of that cultural perspective.

A second important challenge came from Carol Gilligan, one of Kohlberg's (and Erik Erikson's) protégés. She noted that Kohlberg's stage theory was built on research with young White males exclusively, and found that females tended to be classified lower than men when they were plugged into his stages. She concluded that Kohlberg's premise was limited and biased toward a masculine view, as men tend to view problems through a rule-bound justice perspective. Women, she wrote, tend to focus on relationships and have a caring point of view. Males and females, therefore, use different criteria and come to somewhat different moral conclusions. Boys are trained to be independent, whereas girls are taught to take care of the needs of others. A full description of her ideas can be found in her 1982 book *In a Different Voice*. Nancy Eisenberg subsequently found few differences between adult men and women, arguing that girls typically offer empathic moral judgments, but that boys eventually catch up (Craig & Baucum, 2002).

Implications for Coaching

Although implications of a developmental view may not be obvious to coaches, the stages and concepts in this chapter can be useful. A developmental point of view allows a coach to sidestep judgment and think about how a person's behavior makes sense in a psychological framework, rather than a punitive or pathological way. We are all on a path of personal evolution and growth, and we are all at different points on different scales. It helps just to have some kind of explanatory framework at all, and the stages described earlier may well provide the best explanation for a client's capacities and tendencies. It may also be useful to call a client's attention to one or more of these developmental paths and to see if he or she has an opinion about his or her status along that path. Coaches can remember that development is often instigated by crisis, and that movement from one stage to a more advanced stage is often accompanied by strife. In spite of the discomfort, strife is not always an entirely bad thing, and career crises can result in significant personal growth. This is one more way to turn lemons into lemonade.

A developmental view of client behavior can be helpful in the following specific client areas:

- Capacity for empathy
- Ability to trust others
- Self-concept and self-esteem
- Self-absorption
- Comfort with interpersonal closeness
- Moral judgment, moral behavior, and integrity
- Capacity for introspection
- Difficulty with authority figures
- Capacity for and comfort with independent thought and action

Attachment theory reminds us of the important impact that a trustworthy, emotionally dependable, nonjudgmental person can have during difficult times. Coaches are quite likely to be viewed and experienced as a *secure base* by many executive clients, especially during trying times. Coaches would do well to review the qualities that attachment theory associates with a "good-enough" attachment figure.

No coach is expected to remediate clients with serious developmental deficiencies, but it can help to identify such clients. This may result in a referral to psychotherapy or it may cause a coach to have second thoughts about the possible efficacy of coaching or the wisdom of taking on a particular client. Remember that all humans have temperament, a built-in set of personality characteristics that are more or less impossible to influence or modulate. In those areas, it may be helpful to simply acknowledge problematic characteristics and help clients build a career by taking advantage of strengths and avoiding areas of intractable difficulty. Similar decisions may be appropriate when a developmental stage is fixed and unlikely to change.

References

Alic, M. (2001). Kagin, Jerome. In *Gale encyclopedia of psychology* (2nd ed.). Detroit: Gale Group. Retrieved January 25, 2009, from: http://findarticles.com/p/articles/mi_g2699/is_/ai_2699000518.

Austrian, S. G. (2008a). Introduction. In S. G. Austrian (Ed.), *Developmental theories through the life cycle* (2nd ed., pp. 1–6). New York: Columbia University Press.

Austrian, S. G. (with Mandelbaum, T.). (2008b). Attachment theory. In S. G. Austrian (Ed.), *Developmental theories through the life cycle* (2nd ed., pp. 365–414). New York: Columbia University Press.

Austrian, S. G. (2008c). Adulthood. In S. G. Austrian (Ed.), *Developmental theories through the life cycle* (2nd ed., pp. 201–283). New York: Columbia University Press.

Bartholomew, K., & Horowitz, L. M. (1991). Attachment styles among young adults: A test of a four-category model. *Journal of Personality and Social Psychology, 61*(2), 226–244.

Berk, L. E. (2004). *Development through the life-span* (3rd ed.). Boston: Ally and Bacon.

Boeree, C. G. (2006). *Personality theories: Erik Erikson.* Retrieved January 25, 2009, from: http://webspace.ship.edu/cgboer/erikson.html.

Bowlby, J. (1988). *A secure base.* New York: Basic Books.

Craig, C. J., & Baucum, D. (2002). *Human development* (9th ed.). Upper Saddle River, NJ: Prentice Hall.

Crain, S. C. (1985). *Theories of development.* New York: Prentice Hall.

Erikson, E. H. (1963). *Childhood and society* (2nd ed.). New York: Norton.

Erikson, E. H. (1975). "Identity crisis" in autobiographical perspective. In E. H. Erickson (Ed.), *Life history and the historical moment* (pp. 17–47). New York: Norton.

Fonagy, P., & Target, M. (1997). Attachment and relative function: Their role in self-organization. *Development and Psychopathology, 9,* 679–700.

Gilligan, C. (1982). *In a different voice: Psychological theory and women's development.* Cambridge, MA: Harvard University Press.

Harris, J. R. (2009). *The nurture assumption: Why children turn out the way they do.* New York: Free Press.

Karen, R. (1994). *Becoming attached: First relationships and how they shape our capacity to love.* New York: Oxford University Press.

Kohlberg, L. (1981). *The philosophy of moral development: Moral stages and the idea of justice.* San Francisco: Harper & Row.

Levinson, D. (1978). *The seasons of a man's life*. New York: Ballantine Books.

Levinson, D. (with Levinson, J.). (1996). *The seasons of a woman's life*. New York: Ballantine Books.

Little, D. (1996–2007). *Hahnemann on constitution and temperament*. Retrieved January 25, 2009, from: http://www.simillimum.com/education/little-library/constitution-temperaments-and-miasms/hct/article01.php.

Rowe, D. C. (1994). *The limits of family influence: Genes, experience, and behavior*. New York: Guilford Press.

Sable, P. (2008). What is adult attachment? *Clinical Social Work Journal, 36*, 21–30.

Sheehy, G. (1976). *Passages*. New York: E.P. Dutton.

Passages II. (1978, August 14). *Time*. Retrieved January 25, 2009, from: http://www.time.com/time/magazine/article/0,9171,946984,00.html.

Wallen, D. J. (2007). *Attachment in psychotherapy*. New York: Guilford Press.

Watson, M. (Speaker). (2002). *Theories of human development*. (Audio CD recorded lectures, course # 197). Chantilly, VA: The Teaching Company.

Walsh, P. B. (1983). *Growing through time: An introduction to adult development*. Monterey, CA: Brooks/Cole.

West, M. L., & Sheldon-Keller, A. E. (1994). *Patterns of relating: An adult attachment perspective*. New York: Guilford Press.

Recommended Readings

Axelrod, S. D. (2005). Executive growth along the adult development curve. *Consulting Psychology Journal: Practice and Research, 57*(2), 118–125.

Berger, J. G. (2006). Adult development theory and executive coaching practice. In D. R. Stober & A. M. Grant (Eds.), *Evidence based coaching handbook* (pp. 77–102). Hoboken, NJ: John Wiley & Sons.

Cassidy, J., & Shaver, P. R. (1999). *Handbook of attachment; Theory, research, and clinical implications*. New York: Guilford Press.

Kail, R. V., & Wicks-Nelson, R. (1993). *Developmental psychology* (5th ed.). Englewood Cliffs, NJ: Prentice Hall.

Newman, B. M., & Newman, P. R. (2009). *Development through life: A psychosocial approach* (10th ed.). Belmont, CA: Wadsworth Cengage Learning.

Rholes, W. S., & Simpson, J. A. (2004). *Adult attachment; Theory, research, and clinical applications*. New York: Guilford Press.

3

The Psychodynamic View

Psychoanalytic consulting maintains the position that the presenting problem may at best be a symptom and often is an issue that serves to protect the real problem.

—William M. Czander (1993, p. 183)

No text on the application of psychological theory would be complete without a chapter on psychoanalysis. It is the oldest of the psychotherapies, and there are several modern variations, including object relations theory and self-psychology. Virtually all psychotherapists trained in the 20th century have been exposed to psychodynamic ideas, and for many it was the foundation of their training. This can be an asset and a liability, and this chapter discusses both aspects. Although many variations of Freud's thinking can be extremely useful to the executive coach, the psychoanalytic psychotherapist is the butt of Woody Allen jokes and the source of stereotypes that can seriously damage a coach's attractiveness and credibility. Indeed, some coaches go out of their way to distance themselves from Freud and from psychotherapy, especially when it is stereotyped as endless probing in search of childhood memories. Some psychotherapists actually have more to *unlearn* than to learn when it comes to the application of psychodynamic principles to executive coaching. Prior to about 1990, even clinical training that was not explicitly analytic contained artifacts of psychoanalysis. The 50-minute hour, the transparent therapist, strict adherence to boundaries, and the therapist's inclination to interpret everything are examples of methods likely to be more useful for the couch than the coach. One classic and unexamined example is the assumption that "depth" equals "strength" (Harrison, 1970/1994). Many clinicians operate on the unchallenged assumption that deeper interventions or interpretations are, de facto, better. This assumption can ruin a coaching relationship, where analysis is often less trusted than action. Deep interpretations may actually be too threatening for the coaching relationship.

Many of the essential rules and conventions of psychodynamic therapy are violated in executive coaching. For example:

- Coaching is goal- and action-oriented rather than reflective or introspective. Business executives move at a pace not generally comfortable for psychotherapists.

- Coaching usually takes place on the client's turf, not the therapist's office.
- Time frames are flexible, and the 50-minute hour is irrelevant or counterproductive.
- Client–coach contact includes a mixture of professional and social interactions in various settings.
- Confidentiality is almost assuredly weakened or threatened.
- Coaches are typically active rather than passive in interactions.

There is danger when a coach becomes associated with Freud, because coaching can then be viewed in the organization as corrective action mandated for losers, a remedial effort for damaged executives just before they are moved out. Coaching works best when it is seen as an activity for executives who are looking for an edge, some additional way to push their limits and expand their effectiveness.

The trick is to integrate "analytic" or "dynamic" thinking into coaching without pathologizing the client or relationship. The task is to think analytically and behave proactively. That said, the action-oriented and psychodynamically informed coach can be very effective. Psychodynamic therapists and coaches often understand things in a unique and important way.

Usefulness

Psychodynamic ideas can be extremely useful in coaching. Here are some examples:

1. When an executive wants to develop political or interpersonal skills:
   - To understand the behavior of board members
   - To deal with people above in a hierarchical power structure
   - To sell work
   - To develop effective relationships
   - To lead and manage team members
   - To choose key personnel for important tasks

2. When an executive desires enhanced self-understanding:
   - Of his or her own behavior, especially when it does not make logical sense
   - Of strengths and weaknesses
   - Of future development
   - Of optimal career choices

3. When an executive behaves in ways that are self-defeating:
   - Overcontrolling or underempowering
   - Abrasive
   - Self-centered
   - Disorganized

- Angry or hostile
- Poor listener
- Perfectionistic or rigid
- Authoritarian
- Too timid in certain situations
- Distrustful
- Easily threatened
- Procrastinates

4. When an executive needs to deal with difficult colleagues or employees:
   - Working with talented or key people who are difficult
   - Dealing with people who are self-centered or narcissistic

Theoretical History and Basics

Sigmund Freud was a pioneer—even a revolutionary—in his time and place. He broke ranks with philosophers and physicians in his day by insisting that reason could be used to fearlessly explore deterministic forces motivating human behavior. He believed that behavior could be understood, if only we looked closely and clearly enough. He pinpointed strange and even ugly impulses, and exposed us to the fact that we do not run our lives on a rational basis. We are all irrational, in spite of our rational pretenses. And we are irrational in predictable patterns and configurations. Central to this viewpoint is the idea that we rarely deal directly with external reality. Instead, we interact with the world based on internal representations. We "see the outside world in terms of internal concerns" (Czander, 1993, p. 45).

What follows is a very basic summary of Freudian ideas, simplified and presented based upon their utility in executive coaching. Many of Freud's ideas will be discarded, as they seem more useful to therapists than to coaches. (Mainstream psychotherapists have already rejected some of Freud's ideas as well.) The views of Freud and related theories, such as object relations theory and self-psychology, will be presented here in ways they can be useful to the executive coach.

What Motivates People?

Business thinking is essentially economic; that is, it sees enlightened self-interest as the primary motivational force. We work hard (and smart) because we want to thrive. In this view, when we work hard and smart, we will get what we want. We get houses, cars, and financial security. Others admire us for our success. There is a linear relationship between thoughtful, goal-seeking behavior and success. Psychoanalytic thinking rejects this view (Czander, 1993), replacing it with an irrational set of motives and causes for human behavior.

In the psychodynamic view, behavior is the result of the interplay of conflicting internal forces. The view is *dynamic* in the sense that when two forces come into conflict, a third, and different, force is produced. (Freud was influenced by the dramatic advances that were taking place in the physical sciences of his day, such as thermodynamics and the steam engine.) Human psychic energy is expressed through one of three channels: the id, the ego, and the superego. The *id* is the original way that children control energy, and it is motivated by the desire for pleasure as well as the avoidance of pain. It is primitive, simple, and instinctual, and is called the "Pleasure Principle" (Czander, 1993). The *ego* is reality oriented and pragmatic, and its main job is to control the id and still satisfy needs. The ego is sensible, and it rules with the "Reality Principle." The *superego* is the moral channel, and is often thought of as the seat of the conscience. Its goal is the ideal, rather than the real, and it strives for perfection. It subdues the impulses of the id and attempts to substitute moralistic goals for realistic ones. It rewards a person with feelings of pride. It punishes with feelings of guilt or inferiority (Corey, 1982).

The Role of Fantasy

Fantasy is important to psychodynamic theory. In the workplace context, we strive to gratify fantasies about our career aspirations (Czander, 1993). We have an idealized notion of who and what we are in the world of work (called the *ego ideal*), and often it is pretty fantastic. In most cases, the workplace cannot fully service our fantasies, especially when we work in a hierarchical organization. By definition, only a few make it to the top. Few are able to sustain status as a *rising star*. The rest are disappointed, and they experience psychic conflict and perhaps hostile or aggressive impulses. Such conflict is rarely discussed openly or directly. It manifests itself in frustrated, disguised, and camouflaged forms. Psychodynamic thinking can help sort it all out.

The Unconscious at Work

Freud contributed the idea of the *unconscious* to modern behavioral science, the idea that we do not know much of our own mental activity. Recent research by cognitive scientists has essentially confirmed the existence of unconscious psychological processes, so we now know that the unconscious is real (Cramer, 2000). A central goal of psychoanalysis is to make the unconscious conscious; that is, to become more self-aware, to understand more about how we think, feel, and react. In that way, we can exercise conscious choice and make decisions in line with our espoused values and the interests of the organizations we lead.

Defense Mechanisms

One of the most durable ideas in Freud's legacy proposes that we have many ways to protect our ego or sense of self. We use defense mechanisms to distort or deny reality so that we are not too hurt or too threatened. The id, ego, and superego compete to control available psychic energy, and the urges of the id often feel dangerous. Anxiety is a signal that we are struggling to control these desires. When we cannot rationally control these primitive urges (to attack or to flee), we use defense mechanisms to keep threatening feelings out of consciousness and painful thoughts out of awareness. Defenses protect us from painful emotions or realizations. They are ways to distort reality by behaving irrationally to protect one's ego ideal or sense of self. These are typically useful in the short-run and self-defeating in the end. We use defense mechanisms like we use aspirin: to temporarily blunt pain until we get a better handle on things. Defenses smooth out the emotional bumps in the road and are useful unless they become extreme or habitual. Like aspirin, they work well in small amounts, but become toxic if we consume the whole bottle at once or become too reliant on them. When a person clings to defenses, when they are too quick to defend, or when defenses interfere with accurate perceptions of reality, they become troublesome. There are many such mechanisms in the psychodynamic literature, and a knowledge of them can be extremely useful in an organizational setting. People are not usually aware when they are using them, but the alert coach or executive can spot the use of defense mechanisms in the business setting. Some defenses are healthier than others. Clients and others tend to regress to more immature or primitive defenses when stressful situations threaten them. Detailed descriptions of all the defenses can be found in the back of the *Diagnostic and Statistical Manual of Mental Disorders* (4th ed., text rev.; American Psychiatric Association, 2000, pp. 811–813). What follows is a description of defenses most likely to be employed by healthy executives in the workplace. Coaches must be able to spot them and incorporate them into their understanding of clients.

Adaptive Defense Mechanisms

Altruism   Rather than experience feelings that are threatening, you dedicate yourself to actions that benefit others. You use this difficult psychic energy to help. This allows you to avoid your own uncomfortable feelings. Instead of taking care of the business that is right in front of you (because you are intimidated by it or because you are scared that you do not know quite how to do it) you spend time mentoring a younger executive or you help someone with a project of his own. No one could criticize you for this, including yourself. But the primary motivation is to avoid something that must be faced.

Sublimation   In this case, you channel uncomfortable emotional energy into something socially acceptable. Rather than feeling hurt or angry, you "get busy." You redirect energy toward a positive goal. When you are anxious or upset, you focus on a big project that needs to be done and seem to have boundless energy for it, even though the true source of energy is avoidance. Channeling aggressive impulses into athletics is a common example. Sometimes executives inexplicably head for the golf course or the gym when the pressure gets extreme. This mechanism is less of a problem when you are taking on a challenge that is worth doing, even if it means that you are not facing a different primary task.

Humor   When faced with painful or threatening feelings, you emphasize the funny aspects of the situation. This defense works quite well unless it gets out of control and becomes an irritant to others. It can also be a problem when humor is sarcastic, hostile, or, alternatively, too self-deprecating. We laugh and joke about things rather than face them. Gallows humor is an example; the person who makes jokes in the emergency room is another. It is occasionally misunderstood to mean that a person is not taking a difficult problem seriously or that he or she does not care about it. Constant or inappropriate humor is a tipoff: maybe this person is actually anxious about something she does not care to face. Consider that possibility. The overall level of humor in an important meeting can indicate that a problem is overwhelming. Some organizational cultures allow for more humor than others. If a client's main defense is humor, but he finds himself in an uptight organization, he will certainly be uncomfortable, and perhaps misunderstood. Laughter when someone else is panicking is rarely appreciated.

Substitution   We substitute one (comfortable) behavior for a threatening one. This happens when, instead of sitting down and writing a difficult memo, we clean our desk, refile things, or make telephone calls. In this way, we can tell ourselves that we are accomplishing something with our time. Such behavior can be productive, but it can also mean that we are winning a small battle while losing the war. It can be very helpful for a coach to find a way to point this out to a client who is stalled or inadequately productive.

Compensation   We overstrive in certain areas as a way to handle a perceived weakness. For example, when a business client is weak in the accounting area, he overcompensates by spending excessive time on the shop floor, where he is comfortable. Sometimes people with extraordinary skills in one narrow area have done this. As executives move up in a hierarchical organization, they need to expand their repertoire or change the few things that they are very good at. For example, the transition to partner often requires a person to learn how to find new clients and to sell work. If psychic compensation throws energy in those directions, all the better, but this defense usually invests effort in the same old direction, causing a person to get better and better at something he or she is already good at.

Rituals   Although rituals can sometimes be negative, the repetition of behaviors can effectively cover or manage anxiety (for example, bouncing the ball three times before you shoot a free throw; using a preshot routine in golf; always sitting in the same seat in important meetings; parking in the same spot each day; taking the same route to work; using a certain pen to sign documents or write important notes). Many companies could not survive without their organizational rituals. A coach must quickly learn the rituals and decide how to accommodate to them. They are an integral part of any organizational culture, they do not always make rational sense, and executives are often quite reactive to the rituals of the CEO. Occasionally, a leader's rituals are damaging to others, and it may be a coach's job to find a way to point this out.

Identification   One way to avoid feelings of inferiority is to take on the identity of the organization or the leader. We become company men and we give up our own values or independent judgment. In this way, we do not have to face negative things that we think about ourselves. People take on aspects of important cultural or sports figures, allowing them to feel good without actually accomplishing much. Rooting for a sports team—fan behavior—is a form of projective identification. This can be good or bad, depending on how one identifies. Sometimes a coach can actively help a client consciously choose good models.

Affiliation   Rather than suffer threatening or negative feelings, you turn to others for support and comfort and you share your perceptions. You do not expect them to solve your problems, you just hope they will be a comforting ear. Organizations need people who will serve as such an ear, and coaches can provide some of this service. Clients will expect much more than just listening and affiliation from their coaches, however.

Defense Mechanisms That Deny

Denial   Denial is a simple defense, and it amounts to an unconscious ignoring of the facts. Things happen and we simply pretend they are not there. They can be obvious to everyone else, but we still exclude harsh truth from our reality. We behave as if something does not exist, even though it is directly in front of us. Entire organizations can indulge in group denial, especially if things are going poorly or if there is a huge looming crisis and no one has an answer. Coaches can often spot the denial before others in the organization, and sometimes they are in a good position to point it out. Sometimes, however, a coach would be a fool to "make the unconscious conscious" even when the temptation is great. Here is an example of how one coach handles psychoanalytic insights in executive coaching (Macmillan, 1999, p. 142):

> So I feel that I have a sophisticated understanding of analytic thinking and I know that I bring it into the world of work. But it is never directly spoken about. ... I see a lot of connections to what goes on in corporate consulting ... as long as it stays in the mind of the consultant.

Repression   Repression is an extreme version of denial, in that we banish a particular thought or line of thinking from our reality. This can happen at an organizational level, when certain topics are known to be off limits for discussion. Once again, it may well be the coach's job to point out areas of organizational or personal distortion. Such a mandate requires exceptional interpersonal tact and courage, and when things go well, a coach can make an extraordinary contribution in this way.

Isolation   Isolation can be helpful or harmful, but it is an essential one when we have to perform a distasteful task, such as firing someone we care for. We simply detach the feelings from a behavior. A good surgeon probably uses this defense extensively. Isolated leaders are usually not healthy, however, and it is rare that someone inside of the organization can effectively intervene. Coaches sometimes can.

Defense Mechanisms That Twist Reality

Rationalization   Rationalization may be the most common of all the defenses. We simply change the explanation to make it more acceptable, make excuses, or explain things away. We come up with excellent reasons for the things already done. "I really didn't want that promotion anyway. I would have had to move to Los Angeles, and my family would have hated that." "It's just as well," we say. "We didn't need that account, anyway. It would have been an enormous headache."

Intellectualization   We use intellectualization when we ignore feelings and are able to discuss pressing matters only as intellectual arguments. Even the most obvious emotional or difficult aspects of a situation are swept under the rug of complex, logical arguments. A coach is likely to be called upon when a bright executive is promoted to a position requiring excellent communication. It is then that the coach must discern whether complex jargon is defensive or is just a matter of a learned communication habit. Style can be attacked directly, whereas defenses must be explored and understood if they are to be acknowledged at all.

Projection   When we experience a desire that is unacceptable, we sometimes put it out of mind by attributing it to others. It is present but in someone else. Instead of saying "I hate him" we say "He hates me" (Hall, 1954). There is ample room for projection in the daily life of an organization. The trick is to understand the difference between projection and reality. This is no mean feat.

Defense Mechanisms That Cause People to Behave Strangely

Reaction Formation   To tolerate a threatening impulse, we express its opposite. That way we do not have to notice it, and we have terrific deniability.

We express great affection for someone we actually despise. Conversely, when we have a crush on someone at work, we behave inexplicably rudely toward them. (This mystifies people and hurts their feelings.)

Help-Rejecting Complaining   People use this defense when they complain or make repetitious requests for help that are not sincere. No actual help could suffice, and offers are rejected without consideration. These behaviors actually cover feelings of hostility that cannot be expressed directly. This defense is very common, and it drives others crazy. Some people seem to always complain. It is not so much that they object to things, but that they are covering up their own unacceptable feelings of inadequacy or even rage.

Displacement   We express hostile urges toward safer targets. Instead of yelling at a boss, we yell at our kids. Hardly anyone takes on the CEO. We snap at one another, or worse, at the administrative assistants or the consultants.

Regression   When anxiety becomes unmanageable, we revert back to earlier, less mature behavior. For example, an executive stops delegating under pressure and regresses to a time when she took care of all the details herself. One's worst developmental habits sometimes return under pressure (Kernberg, 1979).

Conversion   Instead of dealing with anxiety through appropriate action, we express it through a physical response. Examples include coughing uncontrollably when you have to speak at a meeting, getting a rash, getting the flu, or even cold sores. Some people yawn when they are nervous. Many people become sick when difficult or threatening tasks loom. Remember: This is an unconscious mechanism; they are not simply weaseling out or malingering.

Passive Aggression   When we feel hostility, anger, or other negative emotions toward someone dangerous, or when it would be difficult or inappropriate to express those feelings directly (as it usually is in business), we behave in passive ways that have the effect of being aggressive or negative. We can then remain blameless, because we did not actually do anything aggressive. An example: You are upset at your boss. Rather than saying something, you forget to set up a hotel room for her when she is on the road. She gets stuck with the problem and you can simply say "I'm sorry." You did not actually do anything aggressive, you just forgot. And she had to scramble around for a hotel room in Cleveland in the winter at midnight. The *silent treatment* is the ultimate common example of passive aggressive behavior. You just do not speak to someone. If they ask about it, you just deny your feelings and act like everything is fine. You did not do anything obviously hostile or wrong. In fact, you did not do anything at all.

Provocative Behavior   Provocative behavior is associated with adolescents, but sometimes seen in grown-ups as well. It is a way to express hostility without feeling guilty about it. You simply behave in a way that provokes the other person to behave poorly so that you can (justifiably) retaliate. Coaches may encounter clients who have inexplicably goofed up, blown an assignment, or created a rift in the team or department.

Usefulness

There are two ways that an understanding of defense mechanisms can be useful in coaching. First, a coach must be able to recognize defenses in his or her executive client. The coach must then decide whether to call attention to those defenses or to simply integrate them into an overall understanding of the client. Some executives may resent the mention of defenses. The tricky part of this process is that it can raise defenses itself. People use defenses precisely because they feel threatened, so sophisticated communications skills are essential here. Coaches can add important value by making executives aware of their characteristic defenses. Normalize these mechanisms. *Everyone* uses them from time to time. Give examples of how you, the coach, have used a defense recently and how things worked out (positively or negatively). Make it easy to discuss defenses by normalizing such a discussion. Use humor, where appropriate. Many of our standard defenses seem pretty silly when we isolate and discuss them, even though they serve important functions.

Nonetheless, some coaching assignments preclude the overt discussion of defenses. A clearly understood set of coaching goals can determine how defenses are handled or discussed. Some goals might preclude analysis of defenses, as might some client personalities. If a client is averse to introspection, discussion of defenses might even be counterproductive.

The second important use of defense mechanisms in coaching is to teach clients how to observe them in other people. That way, your client does not need to react stupidly; that is, to go for the bait. When an employee complains and complains, even after the executive makes serious efforts to solve the problem, it is useful to consider *help-rejecting complaining* as a cause. Maybe they really feel hostile or afraid, but cannot express the feeling. It often helps to simply label someone else's defenses in your own head to avoid taking things personally. An understanding of the use of defenses can help in a greater understanding of organizational politics, and it can prevent you from "spinning" or acting foolishly. This process might also result in development of specific strategies for specific workplace defenses.

It is important to note that in Freud's model, one cannot simply look in the mirror to discover these things. A second, impartial party is required, and that is where the coach comes in. A coach has a special mirror for the executive, and the clinically trained coach is armed with theoretical assets not generally available to clients. A coach also has a vested interest in the development of the executive and is willing to inform him or her about these tricky psychological games.

Social Defenses

Defense mechanisms are not exclusively intrapersonal. Organizations use them as well, and they use them to the same ends: to manage threat and anxiety. They employ them to reduce uncertainty and to handle uncomfortable feelings of inadequacy, intimacy, and dependency. Sometimes a corporate culture is organized to protect against the uncomfortable feelings its members resist. Bureaucratic structures are used to stabilize the difficult inner world of leaders and managers. Rules for interaction serve to buffer people from one another. The physical layout of offices even reflects these defensive rules. In many organizations, top leaders have their own floor.

Older organizational cultures are more able to "get away" with such social defenses, and modern companies are less likely to offer the safety of a rigid bureaucracy. The postmodern company has a flat (rather than hierarchical) structure, and technical workers can (and do) readily interact with chief executives. The days are mostly gone when a boss could hide behind closed mahogany doors or extensive layers of memoranda. Roles are less rigid now, and they do not protect people from contact with one another. Modern companies are discarding the old routines. Communication rituals (which are used to protect and stabilize our inner world) are changing, and the absence of social defenses makes interpersonal skills more important. Companies depend on the sophisticated interpersonal ability of its leaders and managers, and it is unreasonable to expect most members of modern organizations to possess them. Coaches are of great importance in the modern, fast-moving organization, because they can help people develop adaptive social skills.

Core and Related Concepts

Object Relations Theory

The object relations theory point of view emphasizes the ways that people use one another to stabilize their own inner world. In this theory, humans develop internal representations of people and of things with which they can *connect*. These internal, symbolic connections help us to manage our inner lives and are called *objects*. Humans are seen as *object seeking*, and these objects are both real and fantasized. The object can be a person or an organization or even an idea that we hold dear. For example, many people use football teams for this purpose. When their favorite team does well, they identify with the team's success and feel competent and comfortable, even though they might otherwise feel inadequate or insecure. We use these objects to feel safe and to manage fear and internal conflicts that derive from the complexities of real life. One common, less optimal way to do this is to *split* objects into good or bad. This is something of an infantile tactic that allows us to manage threatening or complex feelings. It is difficult to think of a person as having a combination of good qualities and bad qualities at the same time, and the ambivalence can be intolerable. So we idealize them or we disparage them, depending upon whether they conform to our wishful expectations or meet our own internal needs. We also do this to ourselves, in the way that we represent ourselves internally. It is difficult to think of oneself as an integration of good aspects and bad aspects all at once, so we tend to move back and forth between them in absolute ways, depending upon how things are going (and according to deeply entrenched cognitive habit patterns). When something negative happens at work, we are threatened with the possibility of a *narcissistic injury*, an injury to our sense of self or our self-esteem. We then have to figure out how to integrate this information into our perception of self. If we are "good," how could this new (negative) information be true? There are many ways to respond, some healthy and some unhealthy. One common way is to project the negativity to the outside, onto someone else. Another is to take it in and collapse, on the presumption that we are now totally bad. It is just easier and simpler (and more childlike) to do this all-or-nothing thinking.

It is important for a coach to observe the way that clients handle negative events as well as the ways that they idealize themselves and others. Sometimes coaches are called in to help with negative psychological or interpersonal situations. Observe how key players respond to negativity, loss, and disappointment and look for this splitting.

A Developmental Point of View

Psychodynamic thinking is developmental, and it can help set goals for growth. This means that we all go through rather predictable stages of development, both personally and in our career, and these stages were described in Chapter 2. In the developmental view, there are several qualities associated with healthy development. They provide us with a psychodynamic framework for sizing up executives.

Trust The healthy person is able to trust others, the world, and himself. Every executive must be evaluated along this dimension, as a deficit in this area manifests itself in ways that handcuff a leader. The ability to trust is a relatively rare quality, and it implies solid self-esteem. It is virtually impossible to succeed without enormous trust in others, in the market, and in one's own abilities to get things done. At the same time, effective executives must identify those who cannot be trusted, and there are plenty of them around in typical business environments. Most clinicians-turned-coaches are able to evaluate the level of trust their client feels for them and then to extrapolate that trust level to others in the corporate arena. In other words, coaches must evaluate their client's characteristic ways of trusting (or not trusting) based upon how he or she treats and reacts to the coach.

Accurate Perceptions   The fully functioning person is able to accurately assess surroundings, including threats, opportunities, and the strengths and weaknesses of others as well as their motivations. Effective people do not distort things much. They are clear-eyed observers. They do not exaggerate the faults of people they do not like; they do not idealize those in the inner circle. An accurate perception of others implies accurate empathy, beginning with a natural interest in others, followed by the ability to correctly guess what others might be thinking and feeling.

Psychodynamic theory points out that humans perceive the world, particularly other people in the world, based upon their own internal needs, wishes, fantasies, and personal development. This inevitably produces a distorted view of things. It is the wise executive who can cut through his or her own internal filters to understand things in a relatively objective way. This is a valuable skill, and coaches can help clients develop it, for they come to the organization as an outsider, and they are not constrained by the normal pressures of the organizational culture. Most coaching will not overtly include a detailed examination of the development of distortions, but it may be useful to point out distinctive patterns to clients, normalizing them along the way.

Independence and Autonomy   Executives and leaders must be able to operate independently. This important dimension must be evaluated and strengthened. The independence–isolation balance has to be just right. It is important to be able to *team up* and function cooperatively, but at the same time it is essential to be able to think for oneself. This balance is difficult for most people. Our temperament typically dictates that we lean one way or the other.

Some jobs or tasks require more autonomy than others, and a good match between personality and position makes a big difference. Sometimes coaches are called in to help an executive who is not comfortable with the level of autonomy required by her position. The CEO's position can be very lonely. Some jobs require interdependence and great cooperation. Still others demand that many are kept *in the loop*, and a lone wolf will not fare well in such a job. The management literature is increasingly turning away from models that stress an isolated, hierarchical leader-at-the-top organization. Some industries seem to require an *interdependent* style of leadership at the top (and throughout the organization).

Self-Awareness and Self-Management   An effective executive cannot function without self-awareness and self-management, and they are often hard earned.

As Clint Eastwood (playing Dirty Harry) observed, "A man's got to know his limitations." An executive has also got to know his or her strengths and inclinations as well. Executives must be able to discover their own areas for growth. They must be willing and able to take advantage of strengths. And they must be able to find ways to minimize the impact of personal weaknesses. A coach can really help when executives are not realistically aware of their own strengths or weaknesses. Coaches can provide a venue and vehicle for safe introspection. Any leader with a future must be capable of some measure of psychological-mindedness, and coaches can help with this important area of development.

Comfort with Power and Authority   Many people never reconcile power and authority. They chafe when others have authority over them, or are unwilling to exercise appropriate power when it is called for. Ambivalence about power and authority can render an otherwise capable executive impotent. Willingness to accede to a boss's decisions, even when you think that he or she is dead wrong, is an essential (if infrequent) element of a successful career. At some point in each career, the ability to assert power, even when others disagree, is an absolute necessity. Graceful management of these two important scenarios can make or break an executive. To do so requires other qualities found in the healthy person: accurate empathy, a solid sense of self-confidence, and a clear perception of reality.

Energy and Focus   A person's internal forces must be aligned for him to accomplish his goals. When they are not, a coach can use psychodynamic principles to figure out what's getting in the way and how to get them back into balance. Sometimes, when an executive cannot get going, there is an intrapsychic reason. This is important when an executive seems inexplicably stuck, or when she is spinning her wheels or is frustrated with a lack of success. This becomes especially important when an executive provokes negative or hostile feelings in others. More often than not, this is a good time to consider a referral to therapy for such an executive. A clinically trained coach can be of great help in the referral decision.

Reiteration of Family Dynamics   Sometimes an executive behaves in ways that are easier to understand when family background is known, and often a person can adjust her behavior once she considers the influence that family has had on present behavior. This important aspect of coaching does not give the coach a free pass to spend lots of time digging away at the roots of a client's family tree, as one might do in therapy. The exploration must be focused, limited, and goal directed. Connections must be made quickly between the past and the present situation, so that coaching does not get lost in a therapeutic conundrum.

Resistance Freud observed that humans do not exactly leap at the opportunity to acknowledge and change their behavior. Mostly we resist change, because we are doing the best we think we can, and because change is threatening, and because change means that we have to acknowledge that what we have been doing and what we are doing now is "wrong." Most people would rather feel *right* than be effective. So, clients will resist change, resist advice, and will take good advice and drop it into the dumpster as soon as they walk out the door, in spite of the fact that they are paying serious money for that advice. Many hard-charging executives and most males resent help and advice in all of its forms, including coaching. Psychodynamic theory would say that many people feel ambivalent or even resentful about using a coach, no matter how enthusiastically they behave on the surface. A coach should expect such resistance. Executives can be excruciatingly difficult to schedule, partly because they are very busy and partly because coaching does not always seem to be of immediate importance (as is an essential customer or impatient board member). Sometimes executives cancel coaching meetings with annoying regularity. There is no need to take this personally or to blame the executive when it happens. It is normal and expected, and sometimes it is an unconscious expression of a natural resistance to change. Change can be threatening. Coaches need to work with resistance and build rapport, so that defenses are lowered, trust is established, and the executive gets himself into a posture that allows the acceptance of help. Occasionally a coach must confront client resistance or ambivalence. This implies that coaches must be trustworthy, both with information and with the important feelings that arise. Sometimes canceled meetings mean that the coach does not have an effective working contract with the executive client. It can also mean that there are conflicts between the coach and the executive that are unspoken, or that the client is uncomfortable in some way but has never mentioned the discomfort. It can also mean that the coach and client are getting too close to a sensitive and important issue. Even so, inexperienced coaches tend to get more client cancellations than experienced ones, just as inexperienced clinicians do. This can be remedied with a clear discussion about time and the importance of coaching, along with the simple confidence that comes with experience. Nonetheless, a reasonable cancellation policy, clearly articulated at the onset, is prudent. Then when cancellations occur, there is a context for meaningful discussion, when appropriate.

Transference and Countertransferance

No discussion of Freud would be complete without mention of transference:

> As important as it is, the concept remains little understood outside clinical psychoanalysis. This is unfortunate, because transference is not just the missing link in theories of leadership—it also explains a lot about the everyday behavior of organizations. (Maccoby, 2004, p. 78)

People bring their psyche and personal history to every relationship. Therefore, executives will behave toward coaches in the same ways that they behave toward other significant people, especially their parents. They may have reactions to their coach that are best understood as reactions to authority figures or maternal figures in general. *Transference* is a term that describes a reaction one has to a real-life person with feelings associated with someone important from the past. When you have feelings of resentment for a boss who is actually quite nice, those feelings may be left over from your relationship with a parent. Some people have difficulty with all authority figures as a reaction to the parenting they received years ago. In therapy, the clinician exploits this phenomenon. It is noted and analyzed. Transference is important in understanding all of a client's reactions to others, including reactions to bosses, direct-reports, colleagues, and the coach. Coaches do not use transference in the same way as therapists, but they still must be aware of the ways that clients behave toward them, for this behavior provides important clues about the way they behave in important work relationships. Transference can be a good or bad thing, depending upon how it plays out, but it is usually confusing, as feelings do not directly or accurately relate to the present situation. Transference reactions are often more obvious (if not more clear) in times of stress and distress (Maccoby, 2004). Psychodynamically oriented thinkers argue that many, if not most, of our important decisions are powerfully influenced by transference. When people make a personnel decision using intuition, they are probably expressing some measure of transference without awareness.

Countertransference—correspondingly irrational coach reactions to clients—is also of interest to coaches, who must manage new countertransference reactions and still learn from them. In that regard, it may be novel and challenging for some coaches to find that, instead of treating patients who are in pain or who are ineffectual, they are suddenly faced with executives who are successful, self-assured, powerful, and wealthy. Some coaches may even experience an envy of high-flying executives who earn much more than the coach could ever command. Some coaches might even feel intimidated by the trappings of power, after having left a small clinician's office for a meeting in a CEO's top-floor suite (overlooking Central Park or the Golden Gate Bridge).

On the other hand, it is still true that a clinician's reactions can be instructive, not just to the clinician, but to the executive as well. The trick is to figure out how to translate a countertransference hunch into a useful coaching intervention.

Narcissism

Psychoanalysts have contributed a great deal to the understanding of a vexing and complex mix of difficult behaviors called narcissism, a topic described at length in Chapter 14 (concerning psychopathology) and in the leadership chapter (Chapter 15). Named after the tortured young man who wasted away with love for his own reflection, the narcissist thrives on the attention and admiration of others. At its extreme, it is a personality disorder, but narcissistic forces have driven many effective, powerful, and charismatic leaders. Most of us have some narcissism in our personality. Absent narcissism, we would be drab, meek, and subject to the whims of others to the extreme. Excessively narcissistic executives must manage surging feelings of self-importance, a sense of entitlement (this can be especially dangerous), a fragile ego, and wariness about being exposed. They can be envious. Narcissists often lack empathy and seem only superficially interested in others, usually to the selfish extent that the other can help them. They can be interpersonally exploitive, Machiavellian, and they tend to be "high-maintenance" bosses. They require admiration and attention, and they can come across as arrogant and grandiose (American Psychiatric Association, 2000, pp. 714–717). Narcissists frustrate and annoy others, and if people do not have to put up with them, they won't.

Great leaders probably need some of the qualities of a narcissist because of the enormous self-confidence (and perhaps audacity) needed to move mountains and take great risk (Maccoby, 2000). They need charisma, and they need vast amounts of energy, some available for vision and some for self-promotion. The coach is invaluable to such a person, but narcissists tend to distrust and devalue mentors, so it is likely to take considerable time and effort for a coach to become a trusted guide for the narcissist. Even then, a relationship with a narcissist is challenging and confusing. Consistent empathy over extended periods of time seems to be the key. The coach must typically endure an extended series of tests before he or she will be trusted. Narcissists are likely to be exquisitely sensitive to betrayal or misunderstanding throughout the coaching relationship.

The coach's task with narcissism is twofold. First, assess your clients. Decide whether their level of narcissism is appropriate to their career path. (Carefully consider an open discussion.) Second, help them manage narcissistic behavior so that it whisks them along without dragging them down or damaging other people along the way.

Coaches must also keep an eye on the thoughts and feelings they have for executive clients. Always mull over the question: Do those feelings derive strictly from the relationship at hand, or have I (as coach) brought some baggage along? It is the coach's duty to attend to this matter and to keep the present relationship as clear as possible.

Containment

Psychoanalysts pay great attention to the quality and conditions of the therapeutic relationship. One function of this relationship is to provide a safe "container" for placement and storage of a client's upsetting and unfinished emotional reactions. This requires that the therapist establish and maintain a safe and consistent way for this to happen. Boundaries (and confidentiality) must be negotiated, established, and maintained so that clients know that there is a place where they can safely dump (and discuss) their most challenging feelings. This is one way to manage threatening feelings and to eventually understand and integrate them. Coaching, no doubt, can serve such a helpful function. Clients are likely to test the quality of the containment by offering an example of a dangerous or otherwise negative feeling or story to see how the coach will receive it. If that test goes well, the door will be opened to more challenging and important issues and feelings.

Parallel Process

Psychodynamic thinking adds yet one more important idea to the coaching mix, and it comes from the world of psychotherapy supervision. This is the notion that dynamics that occur in coaching mirror the dynamics that the executive-client experiences in the regular world of work. In other words, what you experience with your client is likely to be the same thing that others experience when they interact with that same client on a daily basis. Therefore, the coach's reactions to this executive are liable to be important and valid clues about this person's work behavior. If you, as a coach, feel intimidated or annoyed or bored with your client, it is possible that many others do as well. Pay attention to reactions like these. They can inform you about necessary adjustments to the coach–client relationship and they can represent the best, most powerful data you will get.

On Theory and Application

> *Psychoanalysis was probably the most interesting thing that I've ever done.*
> *I learned an enormous amount about myself. Only problem is, I was more*
> *depressed when I finished than when I started.*
>
> **—Anonymous patient**

Psychoanalysis and psychodynamic approaches to therapy have traditionally been long on inquiry and short on implementation. The central assumption—that insight leads to change—is no less true in executive coaching. But the coach has a greater obligation to facilitate action and observable change than does the psychoanalyst, and few business organizations are likely to hire and retain a coach who simply enlightens. Corporations expect to see clear and effective changes in their executives when they spend money on coaching, so the task of the psychodynamically trained consultant is to translate observations into *deliverables*. It is unlikely that psychoanalytic principles alone could possibly be adequate to that challenge.

Summary

1. Remember that executive coaching must be results oriented and positive in tone. Long efforts at introspection are liable to be unattractive in the workplace, as will coaching that is seen as exclusively remedial.

2. Much of what people do and feel is not rational or conscious. Learn how to study people from a psychodynamic perspective, even if you do not often mention your observations or hypotheses. Psychodynamic thinking is most useful when things do not add up in a logical way. When your client behaves in ways that do not make sense, or when he or she has inexplicable reactions, or when others react to him or her in consistently unexpected ways, consider the psychodynamics.

3. Anticipate resistance. Expect that clients will have ambivalent feelings about being coached, even if they express great enthusiasm. Do not become disappointed or angry when they behave in ways that seem resistant. It is perfectly normal and predictable.

4. Assess the quality and nature of the interpersonal interaction between coach and client. Determine whether it is frank, open, and reasonably honest. Check for distorted interaction such as idealization (i.e., your client treats you as if you were a king or queen or genius, which you are not). This can be a sign of resistance. It can be a way that clients keep you at arm's length from the matters that need to be addressed. It can be a distraction. The reactions you have to your client are also important clues about how this client affects others.

5. Check to see how capable your clients are at "getting outside of self." Do they only talk about themselves? Are they only interested in themselves or their own concerns? Are they curious about you at all? Do they wonder what others are thinking or feeling (for reasons other than self-protection or self-promotion)? Are they capable of empathy? Are they able to stop talking and really listen? Look for a healthy balance. When that balance is absent, figure out why. Consider confronting your client about it.

6. Evaluate your clients' ability to accept negative feedback. Are they balanced in their response? Thoughtful? Do they seek it? Or do they reject it and punish the messenger? Conversely, do they wallow in it, as if they thrive on it while it crushes them? Monitor this capacity and help your clients seek and use feedback in a balanced, productive way.

7. Assess the defenses used by your clients. Are they healthy and appropriate or destructive and rigid? Are your clients aware of them? Teach your clients to observe defenses in key others.

8. Remember that most clinical training in counseling and psychotherapy (especially prior to 1990) contained theoretical and stylistic artifacts of psychoanalysis or psychodynamic psychotherapy (for example, hour-long meetings in the clinician's office, or the stubborn unwillingness of a clinician to answer a direct question with a direct answer). Reliance on this ingrained style can be detrimental to effective executive coaching.

References

American Psychiatric Association. (2000). *Diagnostic and statistical manual of mental disorders* (4th ed., text rev.). Washington, DC: Author.

Corey, G. (1982). *Theory and practice of counseling and psychotherapy* (2nd ed.). Monterey, CA: Brooks/Cole.

Cramer, P. (2000). Defense mechanisms in psychology today. *American Psychologist, 55*(6), 637–646.

Czander, W. (1993). *The psychodynamics of work and organizations.* New York: Guilford.

Hall, C. (1954). *A primer of Freudian psychology.* New York: New American Library.

Harrison, R. (1994). Choosing the depth of organizational intervention. In W. French, C. Bell, & R. Zawacki (Eds.), *Organization development and transformation* (4th ed., pp. 413–424). Boston: Irwin/McGraw-Hill. (Original work published 1970.)

Kernberg, O. (1979, February). Regression in organizational leadership. *Psychiatry, 42*(1), 24–39.

Maccoby, M. (2000, January–February). Narcissistic leaders: The incredible pros, the inevitable cons. *Harvard Business Review.*

Maccoby, M. (2004, September). The power of transference. *Harvard Business Review, 82*(9), 77–85.

Macmillan, C. (1999). *The role of the organizational consultant: A model for clinicians.* Unpublished doctoral dissertation, Massachusetts School of Professional Psychology, Boston.

Recommended Readings

Allcorn, S. (2006). Psychoanalytically informed executive coaching. In D. R. Stober & A. M. Grant (Eds.), *Evidence based coaching handbook* (pp. 129–149). Hoboken, NJ: John Wiley & Sons.

Diamond, M. (1993). *The unconscious life of organizations.* Westport, CT: Quorum.

Freud, S. (1916). *The complete introductory lectures on psychoanalysis.* London: George Allen & Unwin Ltd.

Freud, S. (1951). *Psychopathology of everyday life.* New York: The New American Library.

Goldman, G., & Milman, D. (1978). *Psychoanalytic psychotherapy.* Reading, MA: Addison-Wesley.

Hirschhorn, L. (1997). *The workplace within: Psychodynamics of organizational life.* Cambridge, MA: MIT Press.

Kernberg, O. (1978, January). Leadership and organizational functioning: Organizational regression. *International Journal of Group Psychotherapy, 28*(1), 3–25.

Kets de Vries, M. (Ed.). (1991). *Organizations on the couch: Clinical perspectives on organizational behavior and change.* San Francisco: Jossey-Bass.

Kets de Vries, M. (1995). *Life and death in the executive fast lane: Essays on irrational organizations and their leaders.* San Francisco: Jossey-Bass.

Kilburg, R. R. (2004). When shadows fall: Using psychodynamic approaches in executive coaching. *Consulting Psychology Journal: Practice and Research, 56*(4), 246–268.

Kline, P. (1972). *Fact and fantasy in Freudian theory*. London: Methuen.

Levinson, H. (1972). *Organizational diagnosis*. Cambridge, MA: Harvard University Press.

Levinson, H. (1996). Executive coaching. *Consulting Psychology Journal: Practice and Research, 48*(2), 115–123.

Roberts, V. Z. & Brunning, H. (2008). Psychodynamic and systems-psychodynamic coaching. In S. Palmer & A. Whybrow (Eds.), *Handbook of coaching psychology* (pp. 253–277). London: Routledge,.

Shapiro, D. (1972). *Neurotic styles*. New York: Basic Books.

Tobias, L. (1990). *Psychological consulting to management: A clinician's perspective*. New York: Brunner/Mazel.

4
Behavioral Concepts

People have used rewards both knowingly and unknowingly, since the beginning of recorded history.

—Gary Martin and Joseph Pear (1978, p. 34)

Behaviorism has a long and honored place in the history of psychology and psychotherapy. It is a powerful way to understand human behavior, yet it is widely misunderstood and routinely misrepresented. Behavioral psychology offers powerful tools to the executive coach. This chapter reviews the basics, clears up myths and misrepresentations, and outlines ways that methods of behavior therapy can be effectively used in executive coaching.

The forces studied and described by Pavlov, Watson, and Skinner influence us all the time whether we acknowledge them or not. In fact, if something happens to you repeatedly, with regularity (even though you say that you do not like it or understand it), it is almost certainly being reinforced in some way. It makes sense, then, to explore and understand the cues and contingencies that serve to maintain our behavior, as well as the behavior of those with whom we work. The central theme of this point of view is that *behavior is a function of its consequences.* This chapter focuses on the environment that stimulates one reaction over another and the consequences that maintain or promote behavior. A careful study of those specific forces can help a coach and client take charge and make change. Often, attention to a few simple principles, at little or no cost, can turn things around. Alternatively, it is possible to make things progressively worse through well-intentioned efforts that misuse or fail to incorporate the principles described in this chapter. Ignore behavioral principles at risk of great peril.

History: From Rat Mazes to Cubicles

Ivan Pavlov

Ivan Pavlov, the Russian physiologist, explored the reflexive reactions experienced when a physician taps us below the kneecap or when we flinch because someone puts a finger near our eye or when we hear a loud noise. He called these automatic responses *respondent*. He showed that we can pair a previously neutral stimulus with a loud noise and eventually elicit the respondent reaction without the original noise itself. The automatic response he used in his experiments was drooling, as he was studying gastric responses in dogs at the time. He paired the drooling with various sounds and was able to cause his dogs to drool when he rang a bell. This is called *classical conditioning*. The ability of living things to develop such associations is adaptive; that is, it helps us survive. We do not have to eat bad food after one bad experience. We can simply smell it and feel repulsed. The things that we pair with reflexive responses, however, are not always good for us. Sometimes they get in our way. For example, consider the person who has a humiliating experience the first time she speaks in public. It is common for people to have a debilitating reaction whenever a public speaking situation arises; in fact, many people feel dizzy at the *thought* of speaking in public. Their heart races, their breathing changes, and their sweat glands start pumping. This reaction can be understood as classical conditioning. The fear is paired with the idea of speaking in public and certainly with the appearance of a podium and a crowd. Naturally, they then avoid such situations, the reactions become more powerful, and they never learn to speak in public. Respondent conditioning is not something to be trifled with.

John Watson

The father of modern behaviorism was John Watson, who insisted that human behavior be studied and measured objectively and scientifically. He translated Pavlov's ideas for practical human use and insisted that we attend to *observable matters* rather than the internal psychological states and abstractions (such as egos or anxieties) that had occupied Freud's attention. If it could not be counted or measured, it did not matter to Watson. He was specifically interested in how to use behavioral principles in child rearing and in industry, and asserted that if given complete control over the environment, he could turn any child into any kind of person he desired. He eventually left Johns Hopkins University and academia (apparently as a result of an affair with his graduate assistant) to pursue a career in advertising. Modern business practitioners share his interest in measurability.

B. F. Skinner

The best-known and most controversial modern behaviorist was B. F. Skinner (1948, 1971, 1976), who was as much a philosopher as he was a psychologist. He took Pavlov's and Watson's ideas, and refined and expanded them to come up with something he called *operant conditioning*. He observed that most of human behavior could not be explained as reflexive reaction, and he focused on the contingencies of behavior. Things that happen after we do something have an impact on whether we do it again. Or, as the early behaviorists explained it, behavior followed by something perceived as pleasant is more likely to recur; behavior followed by something unpleasant or uncomfortable is less likely to recur. This concept is known as *reinforcement,* and it forms the basis for modern behavioral techniques. Skinner was able to teach pigeons to do amazing things using well-shaped reinforcements, and he advocated careful use of behavioral principles to make society better. His central idea was this: "If you want people to be productive and active in various ways, the important thing is to analyze the contingencies of reinforcement" (Evans, 1968, p. 10). He experimented with and refined most of the basic ideas described in this chapter.

Albert Bandura

Stanford psychologist Albert Bandura (1969, 1977) added observational or *social learning* to the mix in the 1960s. Watson's and Skinner's views were too mechanical and narrow for Bandura, who observed that people do not always need to experience reinforcement contingencies themselves in order to learn. You can watch your big sister touch the stovetop and learn not to do it yourself, without having to personally get burned. You learn the contingencies through social observation. Bandura added rehearsal and modeling to the behavioral repertoire, both of which were internal or cognitive processes associated with learning. He also added the obvious but complicating observation that reinforcement goes both ways. We reinforce one another in a process he called reciprocal influence. When you yell at your kids, they stop jumping on the furniture. This rewards your yelling behavior, so you tend to yell again in the future. Your kids have reinforced you while you were reinforcing them.

O. B. Mod

Most of behavioral psychology was housed in the academic departments of psychology until Fred Luthans (1998; Luthans & Kreitner, 1973, 1984, 1985) began to apply it to organizations and management practices in the 1980s. He termed his early ideas *organizational behavior modification* or *O. B. Mod* for short. Luthans translated the work of behaviorists into management models and language, and his books are listed in the References section of this chapter.

Usefulness in Coaching

There are two general ways that a coach can use behavioral principles. First, a coach can use the laws and methods of behavior therapy to help clients understand themselves and to change (as people and leaders). Second, a coach can teach clients how to use behavioral methods to manage and improve their own organization. Thoughtful application of behavioral principles ought to form the foundation for any healthy and productive organization. Both of these applications will be discussed in this chapter.

Behavior therapists honor Occam's Razor, the principle of parsimony, and this is a good thing for corporate coaches. It says that "one should never employ a more complex explanation when a less complex one will do" (Craighead, Kazdin, & Mahoney, 1976, p. 13). When something as simple as reinforcement explains someone's behavior, there is no sense embarking on a complex intrapsychic wild-goose chase.

Another element of behavioral thinking is important for executive coaches: Behavior therapy is experimental. "Research is treatment and treatment is research" (Thoresen & Coates, 1978, p. 5). This means that each effort to work with a coaching client is viewed as an experiment. Interventions are used with clear goals in mind. Progress toward the goals is checked, and the experiment is adjusted, based on the measured progress. This method fits well into modern organizations interested in continuous quality improvement.

Basic Principles

Principles from the world of behavior therapy must be considered. They explain much of what happens to us from moment to moment, yet most people do not think about them on a regular basis. Many managers misuse these principles, and they work to the disadvantage of those who are ignorant of them. What follows is a review of the basic forces and relationships that behavior therapy makes available to the coach.

Reinforcement

Reinforcement is a powerful influence, whether you notice it or believe in it or not. Many people feel as if they are swimming upstream, against the flow all the time, and it is because they are doing what Steven Kerr (1975) has called "the folly of rewarding A, while hoping for B."

A functional definition of *reinforcement* is *anything that influences the likelihood or strength of a response or tends to produce repetition of the response.* In plain English this means that a reinforcement is anything that, when it follows a behavior, tends to strengthen (or weaken) that behavior. Reinforcements are only known through systematic observation. You can guess at what they are, but you will be wrong some of the time, because a reinforcement is not always what people assume it is. Some things that people think might be a reinforcer turn out to be merely *rewards*, which are different. Rewards are *desired* by the person who is behaving. The person likes the rewards, but he or she does not reliably produce repeat behavior. Reinforcers by definition produce more behavior, whether they are liked or not. If you want A, you must reinforce A with something that has demonstrable power to produce more of A. It is crucial that patterns of reinforcement not be random. Random reinforcement patterns wreak (mystifying) havoc in an organization. Contingent reinforcement gets the results we desire, as long as we align our desires with the reinforcements or the reinforcements with our desires.

Reinforcements are all around us, readily available and powerful, and people rarely get tired of them. There are a variety of reinforcements, and distinctions must be made between them so that you can get the results you really want.

Intrinsic and Extrinsic Reinforcement

The first set of distinctions is between intrinsic reinforcers and extrinsic reinforcers. Although the behavioral literature is not completely clear about this distinction, the best way to think about them is as follows: *Extrinsic* reinforcement comes from outside of us and is a little artificial. Money is a classic extrinsic reinforcer. It does not mean anything by itself, but people quickly learn to work hard to get it. Bonus miles, given by the airlines, are another example of extrinsic reinforcers. The airlines are trying to get people to repeat the choice of their company. The miles do not mean anything themselves, but people quickly learn to associate them with something good.

Intrinsic reinforcement comes from within. It takes place inside of the person, in his or her mind or value system or feelings. Intrinsic reinforcements are unique to each of us. An example of an intrinsic reinforcer is the good feeling you get when you accomplish a difficult task or when you have solved a problem that others cannot seem to solve. Even without verbal praise, the internal feelings are reinforcing, as they are liable (for most people) to cause you to do more of this kind of problem solving in the future. The act of learning a new skill can be intrinsically reinforcing. Some reinforcers can be both intrinsic and extrinsic. A certain look on someone's face can act as an extrinsic or intrinsic reinforcer, depending on what it means to the person who reacts to it.

Research is equivocal about the power and implications of these two types of reinforcers. Many think that intrinsic rewards are superior, because the person experiencing the reinforcement is more likely to take credit for the behavior, whereas people reinforced extrinsically might just attribute the behavior or learning to the external reward system (e.g., "I did it for the money"). Some also say that extrinsic rewards can wear out, whereas intrinsic ones never do. One never tires of doing something that is deeply satisfying.

Primary and Secondary Reinforcement

Another distinction has to do with whether the association between the behavior and the reinforcer is natural or learned. A *primary* reinforcer is innately reinforcing, whereas a *secondary* reinforcer must be "figured out." The connection between the behavior and the reinforcement must be repeated until they are associated or *learned*. The thrill of a kiss is primary; the absence of a kiss (as negative reinforcement) is secondary, as it must be learned. Cash bonuses in the workplace are secondary; the smile of a boss is primary.

It is not always essential to create a new, extrinsic, or secondary reward structure in an organization or coaching situation. There are many "natural" primary reinforcers in the work environment, most of which are available for thoughtful use. Most cost nothing to apply. Some examples are (Luthans & Kreitner, 1985):

- Simple greetings ("Good morning!" and "How are you?")
- Simple attention (Listening to someone is generally reinforcing. It may also be specifically reinforcing of the speaking behavior itself.)
- Informal recognition of an employee

- Recognition of an employee at a meeting
- Compliments ("That report you gave today was excellent.")
- Praise ("That was a terrific meeting you ran.")
- A visit to someone's office to say hello or to get information you could have gotten over the telephone
- Asking for advice from someone you want to reinforce
- A smile in the hallway
- A friendly and encouraging telephone greeting ("I'm glad you called.")
- Taking someone out for coffee or lunch

Positive and Negative Reinforcement

The difference between positive and negative reinforcement is widely misunderstood. Negative reinforcement is often confused with punishment (a verbal or physical spanking, for example).

Positive reinforcement takes place when something satisfying follows a desired (or *target*) behavior. You do something I favor, so I tell you that I am impressed. Negative reinforcement happens when I withdraw something aversive when you perform the target behavior. If I stop giving you the silent treatment when you clean up your office, I am using negative reinforcement. The classic laboratory example is that of animals in a cage with an electrified floor, an uncomfortable environment. When they push on the correct lever, the electricity stops, along with the discomfort. This is called negative reinforcement. You make the bad thing stop by performing the correct, desired behavior. You get relief.

Punishment

Punishment is different from negative reinforcement and is just what it sounds like. When you do something undesirable, you receive a punishment, something that is aversive to you. When you say something indiscrete at a staff meeting, your boss gives you a dirty look. This is punishment. It is also called punishment when you stop applying a pleasurable reinforcer when someone does something you do not want repeated. Taking away privileges in response to poor performance is an example of this type of punishment. Punishment tends to get immediate results, but it has serious undesirable side effects. Research indicates that when punishment is used as the primary vehicle for learning, two things happen. First, learners are more likely to attribute the learning to the teacher (or setting) rather than to himself or herself. Second, learners are less likely to enjoy the learning process and might even develop resentments related to the teacher. They may then avoid the teacher and the learning environment. Also, punishment often creates an uncomfortable atmosphere, where people are tense or anxious as they struggle to perform. This clearly creates an undesirable outcome in the workplace. People do not generally perform well when they are anxious.

Punishment can become confusing and difficult to control, and the attention one gets when being yelled at can (paradoxically) turn out to be a positive reinforcement to them, which then serves to strengthen the undesired behavior. Sometimes negative attention is better than no attention at all. The way to decide whether this is happening is by looking at the results. Is punishment working? Is behavior changing in a desired direction? Sometimes people yell and cajole, only to complain that behavior never changes. That only means that the contingencies are incorrectly arranged or applied or understood.

The other intriguing problem with punishment, as mentioned earlier, is that it can be rewarding (and reinforcing) to the punisher. The person administering the punishment can feel rewarded, either by the feeling of power that accompanies yelling or punishing, or by the fact that the objectionable behavior ceases immediately (but only temporarily).

Reinforcement Schedules or Patterns

Table 4.1 (a table that can be found in various forms and text such as Luthans & Kreitner, 1985) shows the relationship between applying and withdrawing something pleasurable or undesirable.

Timing is crucial in the application of reinforcement, and poorly timed rewards or punishments can inadvertently strengthen unwanted behavior patterns. For example, imagine that you have asked an employee to clean up his desk. He does so, and then proceeds to surf the Net. You walk by and tell him "Great job!" It is quite possible that, instead of strengthening the target behavior (desk clearing), you reinforce Web surfing. Reinforcement must be immediate and clearly understood by the receiver to be reinforcing of the desired behavior. *Clear* and *immediate* are the keys.

Behavioral researchers have worked hard to explore the timing of reinforcement, and they have established a literature on reinforcement schedules or patterns. The use of one pattern or another affects the speed and power of reinforcement and learning. Here are some examples of the available patterns of reinforcement and their characteristics.

Fixed Ratio In a *fixed ratio schedule*, positive reinforcement is applied on every nth iteration of the desired behavior. The ratio could be 1:1 (reinforcement is given each time the desired behavior occurs) or 1:n (where reinforcement is applied every nth time the desired behavior is seen). It is not necessarily

Table 4.1 Types of Reinforcement

	Something Nice	Something Noxious	Nothing (No Response)
Apply It	Positive Reinforcement	Punishment	Ignoring or Extinction
Withdraw It	Punishment	Negative Reinforcement	

true that a 1-to-1 ratio is the most powerful. A fixed ratio is a steady and predictable pattern. It tends to be powerful, and it is generally comfortable for the person being reinforced. Piece-rate incentives are an example of this when the worker figures out that there will be no more reinforcement schedule. But when the reward goes away, the behavior stops pretty quickly.

Variable Ratio In a *variable ratio schedule*, positive reinforcement can be applied in an unpredictable ratio, given an average *n*. So, if the set reinforcement rate is 1 to 10 (reward is given, on average, every 10 times the person produces the target behavior), the reward might come after the second response, then after the twelfth response, then after the seventh. Rewards are irregular but consistent in amount over time (on average, every tenth time). The classic example of this schedule is the slot machine. People will sit in front of those "one-armed bandits" and pull the lever all night long, while the house knows exactly how much it will pay out over an extended period of time. Variable ratio reinforcement produces a powerfully learned response and great persistence, but tends to be less comfortable for the worker. They do not know when they will be reinforced again. (Perhaps the cheap drinks in Las Vegas are designed to take the edge off the experience at the same time that they lower inhibition.)

Fixed Interval Rewards are time-based in a *fixed interval schedule*. A reward is given after a consistently set period that the person worked or produced the target behavior. Hourly pay, a salary, and a monthly paycheck are examples of a fixed interval schedule. This schedule is comfortable for the worker, but tends to produce clock-watching behavior. It is not known for producing high volumes of work. A monthly check is hardly immediate enough to influence day-to-day effort. It does, however, create an organization where everyone tends to show up on time and hang around. It can also produce uneven effort, perhaps stimulating better work just before the time for annual evaluations or accreditation.

Variable Interval A *variable interval schedule* occurs when you provide reinforcement at irregular periods, and the person has no idea about the schedule. The worker has no clear idea when the next reinforcement might come. This produces powerful and resilient behavior, but tends to be uncomfortable for the person being reinforced. Most of life's natural and social reinforcers operate on this schedule. For example, we know that there will be another earthquake in California; we just do not know when it will come. So, we retrofit buildings and feel vaguely uncomfortable while we wonder about the next one.

Individual Differences

It is also important to understand the perceived reinforcement structure of those you want to influence. A reward to one person is aversive to another. A trip to the big league ball game might seem like a great reward to a father, but to a young child it can mean a long car ride, a boring walk through the parking lot, exposure to loud crowds, hot sun, and a situation that is impossible to understand (the rules of the game and what is going on). As mentioned before, verbal criticism can be perceived positively (as attention) by some people starved for attention or by those whose parents only interacted with them when they criticized them.

The Premack Principle

David Premack's (1962) principle says that you can use a high-probability or frequently occurring behavior to reinforce a lower-probability behavior. For example, if you know that you are going to run the disk defragmenter on your computer at some point in each day, you can make a rule that you will not run it until you get at least one project done first. This is especially useful if you prefer one of your routine tasks to the others. You simply use the more attractive task as a reinforcement for accomplishment of the other tasks. If you enjoy checking your e-mail, you can make that contingent upon completion of some of the more difficult or less attractive tasks that you face. You can use the e-mail as a "reward" for accomplishing the other tasks. This is the opposite of what most people ordinarily do when they prefer one task over the other, as they usually start with the task that they like the best (and the less attractive task may never get done).

Leaders can use the Premack principle organizationally. For example, you can reward high performance with promotion to a job with more responsibility (a more difficult job). You can reward positive behavior with the opportunity to work on pet projects. The possibilities are right there in the workplace. Remember individual perception, of course. The person being promoted must view the new job as attractive if it is to serve as a reinforcement.

Successive Approximations and Shaping

When the target behavior is so difficult or so different that it seems out of reach, gradual small steps can be devised and rewarded to build up to the desired response. For example, when teaching a child to ride a bicycle, it does not make sense to wait to reward the child until she rides the two-wheeler successfully the first time. So, we take the child through smaller, successive approximations of the end behavior, rewarding her for small successes along the way. Start by rewarding the child when she simply asks about the bicycle. Then offer praise for getting on the bike, then for rolling along while we hold on and guide her, then for small periods when we let go. Then start the child off and let her ride to another adult. Gradually the child's behavior is "shaped" by rewarding successes closer and closer to the desired end result.

Successive approximation is useful, for example, when a coaching client needs to learn how to make an important speech in front of a large number of people. The task is broken into many small parts. Each part is rehearsed and learned and rewarded. Eventually, the parts are integrated into the entire speech and it is finally presented in front of the actual audience. This event is (hopefully) immediately followed by applause.

Stimulus Control

Reinforcement is something that is applied *after* the behavior occurs. There is another way to control behavior, and it occurs prior to the behavior itself. It is important to attend to those things that *precede* behavior and have a probabilistic controlling effect. Factors in the environment that make it more or less likely that a target behavior will happen are called *stimuli,* and skillful arrangement of them is called *stimulus control* or *stimulus management* (arrangement of reinforcement is called *consequence management*). We examine the environment and arrange the cues so that the behavior we desire is more likely to occur. A simple example: If you want to lose weight, surround yourself with exercise equipment, not bowls of candy. And change your route so that you do not walk by the doughnut shop on your way to work.

Effective stimulus management involves analysis of the environment and an examination of how things increase or decrease the likelihood that we will behave in the way that we wish. We remove those things that are likely to retard progress and replace them with stimuli that are likely to help us. We limit our exposure to those that we cannot remove. All parties must be involved in stimulus management. Those who work in an environment must have input to the way that the environment is arranged.

Table 4.2 shows the relationship between stimulus control and reinforcement in the management of behavior. When we take a combined look at the things that happen before a target behavior and the things that happen after it, we call this process *functional analysis.*

Table 4.2 The A–B–Cs of Behavior Management (Functional Analysis)

Antecedent	Behavior	Consequent
Thing that precede the behavior of interest. They increase (or decrease) the likelihood of the behavior in the near future.	The behavior we are interested in changing or eliminating or increasing.	Things that happen right after the behavior that tend to increase (or decrease) its chance of happening again.
	Example	
Provide "hot" leads for salespeople, along with encouragement.	Sales calls are made; sales happen.	Commissions are paid. Salespeople are praised privately and publicity.

Social Learning

Albert Bandura's social learning theory adds much to the behavioral mix by including social and mental events in the process. He pointed out that covert events, things that cannot be seen with the eye, serve as cognitive mediating processes in learning and motivation. Humans can learn through vicarious reinforcement, and they do not have to experience the reinforcement personally. Observational learning is usually more efficient (and less painful) than the process of direct trial-and-error experience. He also advocated self-control, the application of behavior modification procedures to self, and the use of covert processes. Here are some of the methods he introduced to the behavioral literature.

Modeling   Modeling is sometimes called *imitative learning*. Humans can learn by observing what happens when someone else learns. It may even be true that imitation is built into our genetic fabric. We imitate without even realizing it. Think about how fashion trends grow in organizations. Powerful people are emulated, and when the boss wears a certain kind of clothing, others follow suit. We observe the contingencies, see how the reinforcements work, learn about the model's emotional responses, and figure out the rules without having to experience any of the pain or discomfort. Research indicates that it is important to choose the right model; that is, someone who is similar to us but is better than we are at the task in question. Coaches and executives benefit by choosing a good model and using him or her as a way to learn a new skill or combination of skills.

There are three basic modeling processes that can help the coach and the manager (Luthans & Kreitner, 1985). They are:

1. *Learning from imitation* (you watch and then do the same thing that was successful for someone else). This happens when you carefully observe someone who is expert at something you want to learn. You can improve your tennis stroke by watching professional matches. When new salespeople follow a great salesperson around before they take on their own accounts, this kind of modeling is at work.

2. *Learning from the consequences of others* (you discern contingencies). When you notice how a coworker is punished (or does not get a promotion or good assignments) and you can see how the punishment relates to his or her behavior, you are the beneficiary of this type of learning.

3. *Using the behavior of others as a cue for your own behavior* (the behavior of others tells you when to initiate behaviors you have already learned). For example, when experienced coworkers start to come in to work on the weekend, this may be a cue for you to do the same.

It is also important for the leader and manager to understand that all members of the organization are watching to learn about how contingencies operate in the environment. When one employee is reprimanded, everyone else learns about the contingencies of punishment in the organization. Leaders must remember this when they decide to reward or punish managers or employees. It has an instructive impact on the rest of the organization.

Rehearsal and Covert Rehearsal   Once a strategy has been chosen, it is often useful to rehearse and practice new behaviors or parts of new behaviors. When learning how to speak to someone in a new way, executives can benefit by practicing this behavior with the coach first. Coaches can then provide feedback, and the practice can continue in a nonthreatening situation. Once the skill is well learned in this setting, the executive is in a better position to take it out into the real world. An even better approach to using rehearsal of new skills is with audio- or videotaping. Clients can practice phone or interpersonal messages digitally first, then review them with a coach. Executives can also leave practice messages on voicemail for a coach's review and feedback. Video is a powerful way to get feedback about how one looks, speaks, and behaves. Every executive coach should be prepared to use video feedback as an assessment and rehearsal tool. It is essential to coaching.

Covert rehearsal, which is covered in Chapter 6 ("Cognitive Psychology and Cognitive Therapy") and Chapter 12 ("Lessons from Athletic Coaches") of this book, is also a useful skill that coaches can teach to executives. There is ample evidence that a mental rehearsal before a performance can provide much of the benefit of a "real" rehearsal. You simply run a mental movie of yourself performing (better and better, step by step) the behavior in question. This is useful in preparing for sales calls, important meetings or transactions, or for confronting someone about a difficult matter at work. The more vivid and detailed the "movie" the better. Remember that some people seem to lack the capacity to make mental images, but they can still find a way to rehearse in their mind. Work with them to figure out a process that they can use.

The Token Economy   Sometimes the best way to manage an organizational situation is to set up an artificial reinforcement system and use tokens instead of actual extrinsic rewards. In this system, explicit goals are established and agreed upon. A point system is used, and values are set for specific behaviors to be encouraged. Tokens (or points) are awarded when small goals are met. These tokens or points can then be "cashed in" for real rewards, such as money or trips or public recognition (for example, the sales person of the month), or a great parking spot.

Care must be taken to establish clear rules that all participants understand and to which they can agree. The goals must be achievable to all, and tokens have to be awarded fairly and evenly according to the rules. It helps when the system is public and fair to participants.

The Organization as a Conditioning Agent In a way, the organization itself acts like a token economy, reinforcing behavior in powerful patterns. The patterns can be intentional (at best) and random or at odds with the espoused goals (the worst). They can even be inhumane (the absolute worst). A behaviorally conscious coach can help clients analyze actual reinforcement patterns that exist in the organizational environment and advocate for deliberate management of them. It makes no sense to ask for behavior A but reward behavior B, which is often the case (Kerr, 1975). It is confusing and demoralizing as well. It has a degrading impact on the organizational culture.

Sometimes the organization just does not provide enough reinforcement for the things that it strives to promote. Sometimes high-performing executives, managers, and employees yearn for simple acknowledgment from the organization, but just do not get it, and it takes the wind right out of their sails.

> Praising and giving direction to employees can't be left to the goodness of managers' hearts. And it can't be a sometimes thing, saved for the annual performance review. It has to be made part of the corporate culture. (Hymowitz, 1999, p. CL 31)

Using a Behavioral Approach to Coaching

A five-step process can serve as a basic map for behavior change. Discuss the steps with your client ahead of time and develop an overall plan that includes goals, smaller objectives, and benchmarks that tell you whether you are on track. Set modest goals, and remember that if the desired changes were easy, they would have been made long ago. It is likely that existing patterns of cues and reinforcements serve to maintain the present behavior.

We will use the case of B. F. Token as an example. Token was recently promoted to the position of manager of corporate engineering at an aircraft company. He has worked hard and effectively over the years as an engineer, and he is not entirely comfortable with his new leadership responsibilities. His vice president complains that he does not seem passionate or confident, and that he does not have a strong presence at division meetings. The vice president has no problems with Token's technical expertise, but is worried about his leadership potential in the company. He wonders if coaching can help Token.

Step 1: Choose Your Focus

Identify the critical variables or factors. Start large and move toward smaller, contributing factors. For example, you can start with the task of enhancing the overall efficiency of a coaching client. Then identify specific factors that make up the concept of *efficiency*, such as time usage, task prioritization, assertiveness with others (e.g., saying "no" when appropriate), management of mental attention, and specific skills required to get specific tasks accomplished. Then break each of those factors into even smaller parts such as the amount of time spent sitting at a computer versus time spent in meetings. Then pick a small number of the smaller factors as a starting point.

In the example of an ineffective sales force, the sales manager must begin by identifying the factors that control sales. This might include the number of times a salesperson calls a new prospect, the number of miles a person drives each day, the number of hot leads each one is given, or the number of meetings each salesperson has with a potential customer each week. It might include salespeople's scores on a test that measures how well they know their products or how well they know their customers' businesses. Decide whether to focus on one market or another. Be as specific as possible and choose measurable factors. Get the sales force involved in this discussion.

In the example of the impassive new manager, B. F. Token, the coach helps him decide on specific factors that contribute to his boss's perception that Token is ineffectual. The coach conducts a 360-degree evaluation. The results point to several important contributing factors, including the way that Token dresses, the seats he chooses at meetings, the way he sits, the tone of voice that he uses, the negative tack of his comments, his lack of eye contact, and the perception that he never disagrees with the vice president or offers an alternative view.

Step 2: Conduct a Behavior Audit

Systematically measure and collect data on the factors you have targeted. There is a way, if you think about it, to measure almost anything, including thoughts, daydreams, feelings, time spent checking e-mail, number of e-mails answered in an afternoon or week, number of phone calls answered or returned, number of interruptions in a given day, amount of time spent walking the hallways, number of requests a person turns down in a week, or level of discomfort (highs, lows, averages) at meetings with direct-reports. You can assign a 1-to-10 scale to nearly anything in life. Collect data first, and do not attempt to fix things yet. The key questions are: how much, how many, and when (not why). Use tally sheets, charts, wrist counters, hand-held gadgets, even pagers (to catch the client at various times of the day and remind her to self-assess), along with confederates to help collect the data. Go with sales people as they do their work. Observe them in the field. Observe Token as he takes on this project, and be ready to provide feedback on a regular basis. Be creative. Make it interesting and amusing. Insist that Token help with the design of the learning project.

In the Token example, the coach accomplishes this in two ways. First, he shadows Token at various work activities, including important division meetings and meetings with the vice president. Second, he videotapes Token when they get together. They decide to focus on eye contact, tone and volume of Token's voice, seating at meetings, and the offering of alternative viewpoints by Token (including disagreements with the vice president).

Table 4.3 Functional Analysis of Token's Baseline Behavior

Antecedent	Behavior	Consequent
Sits in the back of the meeting room.	Says nothing at the meeting.	Feels safe, relieved that he did not have to embarrass himself.
Feels not respected.	Says nothing at meeting.	Maintains consistent self-perception.

Step 3: Do a Functional Analysis

Use an A–B–C (antecedent–behavior–consequent) chart to discern how it all works. Remember to include stimulus control, the factors that precede the target behavior. Without spending energy on the question of why things happen, map out the contingencies. What happens under what circumstances, and what appears to reinforce it all? As an illustration, Table 4.3 is the chart that Token and his coach prepared to help them understand the operational contingencies in his situation. The first chart contains "baseline" information on preliminary behavior.

As can be seen, antecedents increase the likelihood of the behavior in the middle box, while consequents increase the likelihood that the unwanted behavior will happen again next time. This chart helps Token and his coach learn how the behavior is persistently maintained. It also directs them in their change efforts. They must focus on changing the antecedents and consequents if they want the behavior to change.

Step 4: Develop a Change Strategy or an Action Plan

Begin with a contingency contract, a formal agreement for the change process. This specifies, in detail, the changes sought and the arrangement of reinforcements, rewards, or contingencies. Start small. Go for modest changes at first and get some successes under your belt. This enhances confidence and provides energy for the difficult changes and the long haul. Reinforce, support, and encourage the desired changes (as well as the effort itself). Build on the smaller changes. Once smaller changes are in place, leverage them to make the larger ones. Token and the coach practice and rehearse new meeting behavior using successive approximations. They rehearse scripts for the big meetings, including examples of bright, important contributions that only Token could make (due to his specific area of expertise). Then they sit in the actual meeting room, around the large and imposing table, and video record Token saying things. They start with a video of him purposely saying something silly or stupid. Then they watch it and laugh. They rehearse as he practices saying something simple, direct, and meaningful. They video him as he does the same thing. Then they watch and critique the video. Token watches the tape several times to become familiar with the scene. He goes through a mental version of the tape at home, while relaxing in the backyard.

Table 4.4 Functional Analysis of Behavior Change

Antecedent	Behavior	Consequent
Sits in the middle of the meeting room.	Says two things at the meeting.	Feels safe, relieved that he did not continue dangerous pattern, that he is making important changes.
Feels respected.	Says more at next meeting.	Maintains new self-perception.

In Token's case, he and his coach decide that they will experiment with different seating at important meetings. Seats at the rear are off limits to Token from now on. He decides to check with several key players at these meetings, to let them in on his efforts and to make sure that it is OK for him to take "their seats." They encourage him to do so, and this makes him feel safe about this experiment. He also decides that his previous feelings of safety after meetings (in which he had not spoken up) were, in fact, not safe. He reframed the situation so that he could only feel "safe" if he had spoken at least two times in each meeting. So, the A–B–C chart now looks like Table 4.4.

Step 5: Collect More Data

When you do not see the desired result, measure some more of the important variables. Support positive results and problem solve. When change is not happening, inadvertent reinforcement of old or undesired behavior may be the culprit. Recycle through Steps 1 through 4. Remember that this is an iterative process. One cycle through the steps is usually not enough, and the evaluation step is used to shift the focus after an initial run-through. Perhaps the goals need to be rethought. Remember: If the desired changes were easy, the client would have accomplished them by himself or herself long ago. The fact that behavior change is difficult is the reason a coach was hired in the first place. If behavior change was easy, coaches would not be unnecessary. Change requires tenacity, and it is the coach's job to support (and normalize) tenacious effort. The coach can also sit in on some of the meetings to check progress.

Myths and Misconceptions

Ethical concerns have historically been raised in objection to behaviorism, and those concerns are typically related to the problem of manipulation or control. Most people resent the idea that others could control them, and they view behavior modification as an inhumane control mechanism. The main misunderstandings about behaviorism have to do with its perceived power. Behaviorism frightened people when Skinner popularized it, because it was seen as potentially manipulative. It did not help that he rather publicly put his infant daughter into a "Skinner Box" for a while ("A Skinnerian Innovation,"

1971). People were afraid that behavioral technology could be used to control people without their consent. Behavioral approaches have also been criticized because of their disinterest in motives or internal explanations that people offer about their behavior. It somehow seems inhumane.

Both of these problems are eliminated when clients are involved in the development of the change process. Behavioral self-control is a better way to think of behaviorism in the coaching setting. Internal events, such as thoughts and feelings, are integrated as antecedents and reinforcers. Encourage all members of the organization to be involved in a behavioral audit of the environment. As a group, check the contingencies and reinforcements. Advocate nonrandom reinforcement structures and align rewards with self-selected goals.

The larger argument for behavioral thinking has to do with its inevitability. Behavioral contingencies are operating powerfully everywhere, whether you choose to take a head-in-the-sand view or not. The power of reinforcement and its importance in the workplace cannot be ignored.

> Informed that Margaret Fuller, after much thought, had decided "to accept the Universe," Thomas Carlyle exclaimed, "By gad, she'd better!"
>
> (Allen, 1978)

Strengths and Weaknesses of the Behavioral Approach

Strengths

Behavioral approaches offer several advantages to the coach. First, they encourage measurement and metrics, something that many modern organizations trust and value. With behavioral methods, you can offer a manager a plan for change that includes quantified goals and measurable outcomes. Companies are much more likely to spend money when they can be assured of observable positive outcomes.

Second, behavioral approaches are powerful when small changes are important to highly functioning people. Healthy, active, motivated people tend to make good use of behavioral methods.

Third, when you treat each client situation as an experiment, you have a greater chance of eventual success. When your early efforts do not succeed, frame them as part of the process that leads to new information about how the problem "works." Then adjust your plan and move forward in a different way.

Weaknesses

The greatest difficulty associated with behavioral approaches has to do with the problem of identifying and quantifying specific target and approach behaviors. Sometimes it is hard to isolate the specific reinforcers or the important subparts of a large behavior in question. When someone is having trouble because he or she does not seem enthusiastic or does not possess the social skills required of a leader at the next level, it can be difficult, at first, to break the larger behavior down into small measurable behaviors. But it can always be done. It just requires a bit of serious, creative thinking and a coach with some behavioral experience.

Summary

1. Contingencies of reinforcement are the key to understanding how behavior "works." Examine the environment to see what behavior it encourages and discourages. Pay attention to the patterns of reinforcement, the naturally existing ones, and those you have established. Remember that you can tell when something is a reinforcement by how it works, not by what people say about it or what you might think should be reinforcing (or even by what has been reinforcing in the past, or with other people). Do not hope for A while reinforcing for B. And do not blame things on individual qualities such as "willpower" or "character." (For more on the power of the situation, see Chapter 9, "Social Psychology and Coaching.")

2. Set measurable, achievable goals. Start small and build. Measure everything. Make the measurement process creative and find new and interesting ways to assess matters on a regular basis. Make sure that the measurement process is supportive rather than punitive, and create a measurement system that is simple enough and easy enough to be sustained over time. Conduct each coaching assignment as a small experiment and make adjustments when you get data.

3. Involve people other than your client in the change process. Discuss the reinforcement contingencies with them and get their cooperation. Sometimes the most important factor in a change process is the inadvertent reinforcement of a boss. This process is up to the client, but a coach can strongly influence the process, and it helps to act as if involvement of the boss, spouse, coworkers, and others is a completely normal way to conduct effective coaching.

4. Use audio- and video recording liberally. These are powerful feedback technologies that can be used to enhance successive approximation to difficult learning tasks.

5. Teach all coaching clients about reinforcement so that they can use it to enhance their team and organization. There are inexpensive ways to powerfully enhance any organization through thoughtful application of reinforcement principles. There are many effective natural reinforcements available (in addition to financial rewards for good performance). Use them with clients and teach your executives to use

them as well. All organizations can use a periodic reexamination of the overt and covert operational reinforcements that exist.

6. Help your client recruit and observe useful models. Find ways for them to increase exposure to successful exemplars.

References

Allen, T. (1978). On the reinvention of the wheel, the franchising of science, and other pastimes. *The Counseling Psychologist, 7*(3), 37–43.

Bandura, A. (1969). *Principles of behavior modification.* New York: Holt, Rinehart & Winston.

Bandura, A. (1977). *Social learning theory.* Englewood Cliffs, NJ: Prentice Hall.

Craighead, W., Kazdin, A., & Mahoney, M. (1976). *Behavior modification: Principles, issues, and applications.* Boston: Houghton Mifflin.

Evans, R. L. (1968). *B. F. Skinner: The man and his ideas.* New York: E.P. Dutton.

Hymowitz, C. (1999, September 19). Hard workers often can feel starved for recognition. *San Francisco Examiner and Chronicle*, p. CL 31. (Excerpted from the *Wall Street Journal.*)

Kerr, S. (1975). On the folly of rewarding A, while hoping for B. *Academy of Management Journal, 18*(4), 769–782.

Luthans, F. (1998). *Organizational behavior* (8th ed.). New York: McGraw-Hill.

Luthans, F., & Kreitner, R. (1973, May/June). The role of punishment in organizational behavior modification. *Public Personnel Management, 2*(3), 156–161.

Luthans, F., & Kreitner, R. (1984, Autumn). A social learning approach to behavioral management: Radical behaviorists "mellowing out." *Organizational Dynamics, 13*(2), 47–65.

Luthans, F., & Kreitner, R. (1985). *Organizational behavior modification and beyond: An operant and social learning approach.* Glenview, IL: Scott, Foresman.

Martin, G., & Pear, J. (1978). *Behavior modification: What it is and how to do it.* Englewood Cliffs, NJ: Prentice Hall.

Premack, D. (1962). Reversibility of the reinforcement relation. *Science, 136,* 255–257.

Skinner, B. F. (1948) *Walden two.* London: Macmillan Press.

Skinner, B. F. (1971). *Beyond freedom and dignity.* New York: Alfred Knopf.

Skinner, B. F. (1976). *About behaviorism.* New York: Random House.

Thoresen, C., & Coates, T. (1978). What does it mean to be a behavior therapist? *The Counseling Psychologist, 7*(3), 3–21.

A Skinnerian innovation: Baby in a box. (1971, September 20). *Time.* Retrieved January 3, 2009, from: http://www.time.com/time/magazine/article/0,9171,909996,00.html.

Recommended Readings

Baldwin, J. D., & Baldwin, J. I. (1981). *Behavior principles in everyday life.* Englewood Cliffs, NJ: Prentice Hall.

Bellack, A. S., & Hersen, M. (1985). *Dictionary of behavior therapy techniques.* Elmsford, NY: Pergamon Press.

Hersen, M., & Barlow, D. (1976). *Strategies for studying behavior change.* New York: Pergamon.

Krumboltz, J., & Thoresen, C. (Eds.). (1969). *Behavioral counseling: Cases and techniques.* New York: Holt, Rinehart & Winston.

Thoresen, C., & Mahoney, M. (1974). *Behavioral self-control.* New York: Holt-Rinehart.

Whaley, D., & Malott, R. (1971). *Elementary principles of behavior.* Englewood Cliffs, NJ: Prentice Hall.

Whitely, J. (Ed.). (1971). The behavior therapies—circa 1978 [Special issue]. *The Counseling Psychologist, 7*(3).

5

The Person-Centered Approach

ALAN HEDMAN

The therapeutic relationship, then, is the critical variable, not what the therapist says or does.

—Gerald Corey (1982, p. 90)

Carl Rogers, the originator of the person-centered approach, was a defining spokesperson for humanistic psychology for nearly 50 years. His ideas provided a dominant methodology in counselor education and have widely influenced both individual and group counseling during the last half of the 20th century. Although it is not widely known, a main feature of his therapy has been the empirical testing of the core conditions associated with personal change in high-functioning individuals. This would seem to make the Rogerian approach an obvious choice for executive coaches, but for some reason it has not gotten much attention. In the world of executive coaching literature Doctor Rogers receives about the same level of respect as Mister Rogers!

Len Sperry (1996), for example, has written extensively about translating and extending clinical expertise to the dynamics of organizational settings. Although he describes the psychodynamic, cognitive, behavioral, and family systems literature, he makes no reference to the extensive contributions of Rogers. The *Consulting Psychology Journal* (Kilburg, 1996a) dedicated an entire issue to executive coaching, describing coaching in the foreword title as an "Emerging Competency in the Practice of Consultation." A distinguished group of authors in the coaching field reviewed the literature and attributed exactly one reference to Rogers.

There are a number of reasons for this consistent slight. Many professionals see Rogers in the way that they see Mister Rogers: kind and well meaning, but simplistic and clearly out of touch with the hard realities of the business world. If they gave a thought at all to his theoretical contributions, they would likely dismiss them as being too obvious or irrelevant to the work of executive coaches. This lack of attention and respect does a profound disservice not only to Rogers, but also to the executive coach who is looking to improve his or her core competencies. Research by Daniel Goleman (1995, 1998; and described in Chapter 11) and others on the application of emotional intelligence in the workplace has helped to restore some luster to the person-centered approach, as does the work of Stephen Covey (1989). His "Habit 5" addresses this matter directly and in-depth ("Seek First to Understand, Then to Be Understood; Principles of Empathetic Communication").

Robert Cooper (1997) has worked extensively with business leaders and organizations, and he suggests that trust is one of the driving forces for competitive advantage. He quotes a former leader of the Ford executive team, who says, "Emotional intelligence is the hidden advantage (in business relationships). If you take care of the soft stuff, the hard stuff takes care of itself" (p. 31).

This so-called *soft stuff* (empathy, trust, listening, and communication skills) has consistently been shown to produce gains, innovations, and accomplishments by individuals, teams, and organizations. Its absence is frequently the cause of organizational mediocrity and even disintegration. If you think about it, most of the embarrassing gaffes described in *Dilbert* cartoons are directly related to problems of empathy, trust, authenticity, genuineness, and communication.

In his book *If Aristotle Ran G.M.: The New Soul of Business*, Tom Morris (1998) writes that "relationships rule the world." His working principle is: "People first; projects second. If you have good relationships with people, the projects will come." He suggests that the most important factor in business leadership is *relationship*. "What used to be called the 'soft issue' of business will increasingly be the differentiator of sustainable excellence of every industry in the world" (p. 199).

Rogers was a champion of the soft-stuff in counseling. Healthy application of soft skills has consistently been shown to be a critical factor in success or failure of executive coaching. Modern-day gurus of organizational psychology seldom give direct credit to these concepts presented by Rogers. But the centrality of these soft skills as Rogers presented them remains very much alive and well today.

The importance of soft skills often comes repackaged in another form. For example, the concept of emotional intelligence, made popular by Goleman and others, includes a recapitulation of many Rogerian concepts. And the title of Covey's new traveling road show for leaders is "Leading at the SPEED of Trust." That sounds very Rogerian, although Rogers may have been curious to see how his principles can be honored speedily.

In 2006 Daniel Pink published an influential book titled *A Whole New Mind: Why Right-Brainers Will Rule the Future*. He asserts that there are six essential aptitudes that will determine professional success and personal satisfaction in the future. One of the six? *Empathy*. He writes that the ability to empathize with others and to understand the subtleties of human interaction are part of the right-brain qualities that will increasingly determine who flourishes and who flounders.

Look, for example, at how empathy is helping to reshape medicine. Since the discovery of sulfa drugs and antibiotics the medical field has followed a detached scientific model, with little or no emphasis on empathy. Recently, however, some medical and dental schools are now teaching courses like "The Craft of Empathy." Empathy is not taught simply for political correctness. Research using the Jefferson Scale of Physical Empathy (Hojat et al., 2002) indicates that high scores on the empathy test are correlated with high marks in clinical care. Lucian Leape's shocking 1994 essay on error in medicine pointed out that the high rates of death resulting from hospital error in the United States is directly related to interpersonal interactions: "The reasons are to be found in the culture of medical practice" (p. 1851).

Continuing research on the right-brain functioning will have a powerful effect on the way that empathy is viewed in organizations. No longer will empathy be seen as merely nice (but benign). It will be seen as a powerful force in the delivery of all human services.

Graham Jones (2008) in "Coaching Real Leaders," notes that "real leaders," those willing to step up to the plate and stop playing it safe, need authentic coaches who are empathetic and trustworthy. It is only when a caring relationship is established that executives will be willing to go beyond their comfort zone.

The well-known dental practice consultant L. D. Pankey advised his clients to "never treat a stranger," meaning that doctors should get to know their patients before they put an instrument in their mouths (Wright, 1997, p. 13). Other giants of organizational consulting, including Tom Peters (Peters & Waterman, 1982) and W. Edwards Deming (1986), have repeatedly stated that although technique and technology are important, *trust* is the key issue when working with an organization. The words of these modern-day gurus of organizational consulting sound surprisingly similar to the mostly forgotten or abandoned concepts of Rogers. Beginner coaches as well as seasoned professionals will certainly find the work of Rogers important.

The following questions are key to this approach and are examined in this chapter:

- What core competencies are required for successful executive coaches?
- What are the necessary ingredients for a successful executive coaching program?
- What factors contribute to negative coaching outcomes?
- How can the principles and concepts of the Rogerian, person-centered approach assist the executive coach?

Historical Background

Carl Rogers received his PhD in clinical psychology from Columbia University in 1931. By the 1940s, Rogers had grown increasingly frustrated with the behaviorist and psychoanalytic approaches that were dominant at the time, and he was especially bothered by the accepted role of the therapist as the directive expert. He began writing and developing what was then known as nondirective counseling or client-centered therapy. Rogers created a furor by challenging the basic assumption that "the therapist knows best," as well as the validity of commonly accepted therapeutic procedures such as advice, suggestion, persuasion, teaching, and even diagnosis and psychosocial interpretation.

The person-centered approach is both relationship-oriented and experiential, growing out of the existential tradition in philosophy. Its underlying humanistic vision can be captured metaphorically by considering how an acorn, if provided with the appropriate nurturing conditions, will automatically grow in positive ways, as its potential pushes toward actualization (in this case, as a very large tree).

Rogers's basic assumptions about people and the therapeutic process are distinctly American: pragmatic, optimistic, and believing in unlimited potential. People are essentially trustworthy; they have vast potential for understanding themselves and resolving their own problems without direct interventions by the therapist. Individual autonomy is deeply respected. Humans are capable of increasing growth toward self-direction if they are involved in a healthy therapeutic relationship. In his writings from the 1940s until the 1980s, Rogers consistently emphasized that the attitudes of the therapist as well as the quality of the client–therapist relationship are the prime determinants of the outcome of therapy. At its core, Rogerian theory requires that the therapist listen with acceptance and without judgment, if clients are to change (Heppner, Rogers, & Lee, 1984). The therapist's knowledge of theory and techniques were relegated to a secondary position in the Rogerian approach, behind nonjudgmental acceptance of the client.

View of Human Nature

A consistent theme underlies most of Rogers's writing: deep faith in the tendency of people to develop in a positive and constructive manner if a climate of respect and trust is established. He had little use for any system based on assumptions that people could not be trusted or must be directed, motivated, instructed, punished, rewarded, controlled, and managed by others who are in a superior or "expert" position.

He maintained there are three therapist characteristics for a growth-promoting climate in which people can realize their inherent potential:

1. Congruence or genuineness
2. Unconditional positive regard and acceptance
3. Accurate empathic understanding

Congruence or Genuineness

Of the three characteristics, congruence is the most important. Congruence means that thought, feeling, and behavior (action) are all aligned. The therapist must be real, genuine, integrated, and authentic. Rogers distrusted any therapeutic facade. He believed that through authenticity the therapist serves as a model of a human being struggling toward greater "realness." Therapists must be themselves during the time that they are counseling. They must put aside all facades and roles during the counseling process and must be "fully present" for the interaction. This naturally may require the counselor to engage in self-disclosure from time to time.

Unconditional Positive Regard and Acceptance

Therapists need to communicate a deep and genuine caring toward their clients. This caring is unconditional in that it is not evaluative or judgmental of the client's thoughts, feelings, and behaviors. It is an attitude of "I'll accept you as you are" rather than "I'll accept you when …" It was Rogers's observation that a parental view that children will be acceptable when they "behave" is underneath the split between a person's sense of their real self and their ideal self. The result is a vague and chronic feeling of inadequacy. Unconditional positive regard is a tool used to help merge the real and the ideal, so that one's sense of their real self is then accepted and even embraced. This then loosens one's tight clutch on identity and the corresponding self-defeating behavior and allows honest self-examination. Giving up the need to defend one's identity can result in real change. Unconditional positive regard means that clients are accepted as they currently are, right now. Under this condition there is no need for defensiveness, and openness is possible. According to Rogers (1977), research indicates that the greater the degree of caring, accepting, and valuing, the greater the chance that therapy will be successful.

Accurate Empathic Understanding

A main task of the therapist is to demonstrate understanding of the client's experience and feelings as revealed in the therapeutic interaction. The therapist strives to understand the client's subjective reality—trying to walk in his shoes by reflecting, with sensitivity and accuracy, a therapeutic understanding of what was said as well as the meaning and feelings underlying the words. Accurate empathy goes beyond the recognition of obvious feelings to those less obvious feelings, the ones that are only partially recognized by the client. This deeper subjective understanding of the client can only come with patience and careful, caring listening.

If these three therapist attitudes (congruence/genuineness, unconditional positive regard, and accurate empathy) are communicated to the client, Rogers postulates that the client will become less defensive and more open to necessary therapeutic changes. The success or usefulness of the counseling process depends upon these qualities. For a more complete description of these core qualities, see Cormier and Cormier (1985).

Basic Characteristics and the Core Premise

Rogers did not present the person-centered theory as a fixed or complete approach to therapy. Rogers and Wood (1974) describe the characteristics that distinguish the person-centered approach from other models. Two of these distinctions are: First, the person-centered approach focuses on client responsibility and the capacity to discover ways to encounter reality more fully. This approach emphasizes the phenomenal world of the client. *The primary intent is for the helper to comprehend the client's internal frame of reference and focus on the client's perception of self and the world.* Second, the person-centered approach is not rooted in a set of techniques or dogma. Rather, it is best seen as an attitude and belief system demonstrated by the therapist. It is both a way of being and a shared journey in which therapist and client reveal their humanness and participate in a growth experience.

The Process: Therapeutic Goals

The underlying aim of therapy is to provide a climate conducive to helping the individual become a healthy and fully functioning person. The person-centered approach places the primary responsibility for the direction of therapy on the client. The general goals of therapy are as follows:

1. Openness to experience (less defensive, more aware of reality)
2. Achieving self-trust
3. Internal source of evaluation (looking to oneself for the answers)
4. Willingness to continue growing

As can be seen, specific goals are not imposed on clients; rather, they choose their own values and goals.

The Therapist's Function and Role

The role of the person-centered therapist is grounded in a way of being, in an attitude, not in theory, knowledge, or techniques designed to get the client to do something or to change. Basically, the therapist creates a climate that allows the client to grow. First and foremost, the therapist must be willing to be real in the relationship with the client. The therapist does not diagnose or label; nor does the therapist give advice.

Rogers's view (1967) of the therapist's job is "to give a client or person my full, caring attention without judging or evaluating them."

Rogerian counseling places demands on the counselor, and a coach should pay heed to these requirements. A person-centered approach requires a counselor who is able to be "present" in the counseling relationship. The counselor must be able to fully engage with the client, undistracted by personal agendas or roles, so that he or she can accurately experience that client. He or she cannot, therefore, be an agent of the company, attempting to mold their client according to company needs or the dictates of a boss. The counselor must also be able to demonstrate *unconditional positive regard* for the client, establishing no conditions for acceptance. The counselor must take a nonjudgmental attitude and communicate this attitude to the client. He or she must be able to achieve *accurate empathy*, to sense the client's private world as if it were his or her own. These are simple but uncommon qualities, and because they are not easy for most people to learn, many psychotherapists have spent years or even a lifetime practicing and honing them.

The Relationship between Therapist and Client

The person-centered approach emphasizes the personal relationship between client and therapist. Therapy is an active partnership. Rogers (1961) summarized this basic hypothesis in the following way:

> If I can provide a certain type of relationship, the other person will discover within himself the capacity to use that relationship for growth and change, and personal development will occur. (p. 33)

In later writings, Rogers (1967, p. 63) hypothesized in a fairly radical observation that "significant positive personality change does not occur except in a relationship."

The contributions of the person-centered approach, however basic and self-evident they may appear, have had a profound effect on the helping professions. Its core skills (active listening, respecting clients, and adopting their internal frame of reference) are great fundamental tools for the effective executive coach. This will become clearer with a closer look at the basic ingredients for a successful executive coaching program.

Basic Ingredients of Executive Coaching

It is curious to look at the current literature on executive coaching and see the striking similarity to many of the ideas and concepts of Rogers. Although Sperry (1996) never makes direct reference, he surely sounds Rogerian when he discusses executive coaching and consultation. The consultant's role is one of listener, confidant, and personal adviser. Essentially, the consultant serves as a sounding board and as an objective and trustworthy source of feedback. Such consultation sessions consist of directed discussions initiated by the executive-client who sets the agenda.

David Peterson (1996), in discussing the art of one-on-one change in executive coaching, has clearly been influenced by Rogers. He describes the first phase as "forging the partnership." Coaches must build trust and understanding so that people will want to work with them. A partnership requires that coaches earn the trust of people they coach, so they can provide the right amounts of challenge and support throughout the process. If a coach fails here, in Peterson's view people will discount the coach's perspective and will resist opening up, taking risks, or experimenting with new behaviors. To build trust, coaches must learn how people view the world and what they care about. Peterson even quotes Rogers on this last point: "The best vantage point for understanding behavior is from the internal frame of reference of the individual" (Rogers, 1961, quoted in Peterson, 1996, p. 79). This strategy requires effective listening skills, patience, and an understanding of the dynamics of human behavior.

Richard Diedrich (1996, p. 62) from The Hay Group also sounds very Rogerian when he discusses feedback in the coaching process. To be effective, feedback "needs to be two-way, engaging, responsive, and directed toward a desired outcome." One of the most important elements in this process is empathy, which builds trust when expressed through listening and the active sharing of perspectives.

Peggy Hutcheson (1996) proposes tips for coaches that will help them move along the continuum from wanting to control the results to wanting to empower others by helping them take responsibility for change. That sounds like something directly from the Rogerian handbook for executive coaches. Her specific tips include:

1. Accept that the coach is not in control
2. Listen
3. Pay attention to what is not being said as well as to what you hear
4. Coach, do not judge
5. Guide the other person to his or her own solutions
6. Suspend your expertise

When Kilburg (1996b) discusses negative coaching outcomes, as in "insufficient empathy for the client" (the coach did not truly care about the client's well-being or future), his debt to Rogers is obvious. When Witherspoon and White (1996) discuss four distinctly different executive coaching roles—coaching for skills, coaching for performance, coaching for development, and coaching for the executive's agenda—each is premised on the Rogerian concept of establishing a working partnership between equals.

Rogerian Applications to Coaching

Rogers's ideas have always been thought to be ideal for high-functioning, mentally healthy people. From this brief review of current literature, it should be obvious that Rogerian principles are well suited for any successful executive coaching program.

Rogerian coaches have two challenging tasks: to *be* Rogerian (to do the recommended things and to model genuineness, unconditional positive regard, and congruence) and to *teach* these things to clients so that they can become Rogerian in their work settings and lives.

The first task is the general application of the Rogerian principles: (1) create a genuine, authentic, one-on-one relationship with the client; (2) achieve accurate empathy through unconditional positive regard and acceptance; (3) really hear the client and fully accept him or her as he or she currently is; and (4) reflect what you hear back to the client so that he or she can fully appreciate their situation as it is.

The second Rogerian task is useful with most coaching clients, but not all (those rare clients who are excellent listeners are the exception). Teach clients how to listen. Listening is a prerequisite for any worthwhile relationship, and while most people think that they are good listeners, most people are not. Humans will allow themselves to be influenced *after* they decide that they have been heard and understood. Remember the old quote attributed to Teddy Roosevelt, "Nobody cares how much you know, until they know how much you care." Plus, people who do not listen are just not interesting. They do not seem smart and are not taken seriously. Even so, in these fast-paced times, many executives lack solid listening skills, and an effective 360-degree evaluation often points this out. The Center for Creative Leadership (Hoppe, 2006) reports that "assessments of thousands of leaders in CCL's database indicate that many leaders have development needs that directly relate to their listening skills" (p. 8).

Apply active listening with clients and show them how to do it. Active listening includes the following skills and behaviors:

- *Stop and pay attention*—Although this step may seem obvious, it is shocking to observe how often it fails to happen. A good listener takes care to establish a comfortable, nonthreatening atmosphere for interaction, using physical listening, facial expressions, and tone of voice.

- *Use physical listening*—Help clients with their posture and physical mannerisms so that they give the clear impression that they are paying attention. Give them feedback about their eye contact, and the way that they appear when they are listening. Congruence requires that physical messages be aligned and consistent with the verbal ones. When the way you look and what you say are in conflict, your messages become confusing. The listener wonders: *Which message should I believe? He says he is serious, but he does not really look serious or seem to be serious.*

- *Ask appropriate questions*—Take time to ask good questions, questions that indicate that you are following the topic and find it interesting in some way. Use questions to clarify the concerns of the speaker. Take care not to "shotgun" questions or interrogate the speaker with a series of yes or no questions. Use open-ended questions that allow the speakers to express what they have on their mind. Follow up with clarifying questions that seek to sort things out and make them clearer. Consider an occasional probing question that moves the discussion into challenging areas.

- *Restate*—Teach clients how to repeat or summarize what someone says before responding with new information.

  Let me make sure that I've got this right. You think that finance is not allocating enough resources to your project. Is that what you mean?

  This serves to clarify things and demonstrates that the listener is interested and accurately grasps what the other person has said. This implies respect for the speaker, and it becomes even more important as business speeds up.

- *Paraphrase*—Teach clients how to summarize what another person has said, so that an important aspect of the message can be emphasized and explored.

  It sounds like you are having second thoughts about the Acme project.

- *Reflect*—Clients can learn to reflect back feeling states to speakers. Coaches can model this and then teach it. It can be very effective on occasion.

  You don't sound very confident about the timeline. In fact, you seem a little worried about whether we can meet it.

- *Summarize*—Teach clients how to take several statements from a speaker, tie them together into a theme, and check them out with the speaker to see if the meaning is accurate.

  All right. So, on the one hand, you think there is a clear opportunity here, but on the other hand, you are worried about whether we can convince the board to fund the project fully enough to make it work. Am I understanding you correctly?

- *Listen for feelings*—Even when your client does not actually mention an emotion such as fear, hurt, anger, or embarrassment, it is important to *notice* what people seem to be feeling as they speak. You can never rely on what you imagine they might be feeling, but it is, nonetheless, important to wonder and to be interested in emotions, as they tend to drive the encounter. Sometimes the emotional basis for a statement is obvious, once you look for it, and then it reveals something important that you may not have previously considered. Sometimes, if you are paying attention you can spot a tiny flash of emotion. Interest in emotions has an added benefit: It makes conversations more interesting. However, overt talk about emotions is not always appropriate in the business setting, so discretion and judgment are important.

- *Share*—Reveal important reactions appropriately. Use discretion here and share what you think and feel in a way that supports the speaker and moves the conversation forward in a productive direction.

- *Withhold judgment while listening*—Allow the speaker to make their point, and listen with an open mind. Make necessary judgments later, after you have had time to think. A judgmental stance tends to foster unnecessary competition in conversation. This limits what can be accomplished.

- *Acknowledge difference*—In any serious discussion there are likely to be areas of disagreement. It can be useful to politely acknowledge these differences in a matter-of-fact way.

  As you know, we probably differ on this, but my opinion is that such-and-such is true.

Give feedback on specific listening skills as you coach. When your client interrupts, call his or her attention to it. When clients change the subject without attending to what the previous speaker has said, mention this. When they go on and on without noticing the impact on the listener, tell them. Catch them when they argue unnecessarily or when they judge too quickly or when they seem disinterested. Better yet, *show them* on a video made while they were listening or speaking. Feedback about the ways that clients behave around others may be the single most important and valuable service that a coach can provide. Most of us have some blind spots. Remember: Other people are not willing or able to provide such feedback to your client. You may be the only one who can.

Give clients feedback on the impression they make on you. Notice your own feelings as a coach and as a person. Think carefully about this, and when it is appropriate, share your reactions with them (when it will contribute to your clients' development, is not a manipulation, and it does not meet some need of your own). The principle is this: If you have a certain strong reaction to them, it is likely that others have a similar reaction (although this is not always so).

Coach clients on authenticity. Assess their level of genuineness, including how authentically they engage listeners. Discuss this with them and work on achieving just the right amount of personal engagement in each interaction. Some clients may be too personal, revealing too much about themselves, whereas others reveal nothing. Some people grew up in cultures where it is considered impolite to ask personal questions or reveal personal matters, especially in a business situation. To others, however, this can seem stiff and disinterested.

Strengths of the Approach

The person-centered approach provides profound insight into how an executive coach should be with a client. Active listening, respecting the client, and adopting the client's internal frame of reference can provide clients with the opportunity (so rare in the business world) to be really listened to and accurately heard. The power of these so-called soft attributes should never be underestimated as they help build trust, commitment, and loyalty to the executive coaching process. Many business leaders simply lack empathy and listening skills, and the coaching process can provide a living model for empathic listening when done from a person-centered view. This can provide a huge advantage for a leader, especially given that effective leadership typically involves social influence.

Although these Rogerian attitudes are important throughout the entire coaching process, their greatest strength lies in the beginning stages related to "forging the partnership." Unless trust is established and attitudes of respect, care, and acceptance are communicated, most executive coaching interventions will fail.

The Rogerian approach is useful in executive coaching because pathology is rarely the issue at hand. Executive-clients are typically high-functioning, mentally healthy people who need to explore their current working situation and make adjustments or learn new skills. The person-centered way allows for relatively quick rapport and accurate assessment of the coaching situation.

Occasionally, clients are referred for coaching (by a boss or by the organization), but they are not *on board* with the coaching process and do not welcome or trust it. They may superficially cooperate, even though they feel resentful or disdainful. A fast-moving plan for change can be disastrous in such a case, as the executive-client is not likely to put much sincere effort into the process. At worst, a client sabotages the process, and everybody loses. A Rogerian approach, from the beginning, has the best chance for success, for accurate empathy will require the coach to figure this out, without judgment, defensiveness, or blaming. The coach and client can start with the "truth" (that the client resents the coaching or is afraid of it) and go from there to the possibility that coaching can become a positive experience.

Limitations

The Rogerian approach is not a good "stand-alone" theory. This approach is an excellent place to begin a coach–client relationship, but may not be a good place to remain as the coaching process develops. Content knowledge, assessment skills, and motivational techniques all have an important role in executive coaching. The insights from other theoretical perspectives, particularly cognitive-behavioral, family systems, and psychoanalytic theories, are necessary to compliment the core conditions described by Rogers.

Coaching Examples

Two very different examples will help exemplify how best to apply the person-centered approach in executive coaching.

The Case of Bill

Bill is a 40-year-old vice president for human resource management in a midsized, nonprofit organization. He has been required to attend coaching sessions by the new chief executive officer (CEO) who finds Bill to be good on "rules and regulations" but lacking in people skills, namely, an ability to show warmth and understanding. Bill was esteemed by the former CEO, who appreciated his in-depth knowledge of complex administrative procedures. In a sense, Bill is an example of the "what got you here won't get you there" problem described by Marshall Goldsmith (Goldsmith & Reiter, 2007).

Bill represents a typical senior executive, as described by the KRW International Group (Kiel, Rimmer, Williams, & Doyle, 1996), that is, someone who scores 1 or 2 standard deviations above the mean on measures of dominance and need for control. He is not "psychologically minded," and may hold distrust or disdain for the "soft" side of leadership. Therefore, planning for resistance is extremely important with this type of client. We can assume that the coaching process will be "bumpy."

It became clear that Bill was highly resistant to coaching. He did not think the present CEO really understood him and was dubious that anything helpful might emerge from the coaching process. The Rogerian perspective was extremely useful in helping the coach forge a partnership with Bill. Rather than immediately proposing a game plan or rushing to develop a training technique, the coach spent the majority of the first few sessions listening intently to see the issues from Bill's point of view. Generally speaking, working for understanding is more productive than direct confrontation with resistant clients. As a result of his coach's genuineness and accurate empathy, Bill began to see the coach as an "honest broker" and an ally who could actually help him. After establishing trust, the coach developed an anger management and communication skills program, and Bill was able to work diligently with him on developing these skills. The process of empathy caused Bill's resistance to melt. There was then little to resist, and the hard-charging young executive could get to work on the problems at hand. Rogerian coaching also served as a model for enhancement of Bill's interaction skills in the workplace. He improved his interactions by leading in some of the ways he was coached.

The Case of Betty

Betty, age 35, was considered a budding superstar for a large recreational management corporation. She was being groomed to assume more managerial responsibilities, but was encountering difficulty. Her boss noticed that she was very uncomfortable with conflict and often avoided such situations. Betty had many years of successful independent job experience, but limited experience in managing other people. She was also a perfectionist who had great difficulty dealing with perceived failure.

Betty had initially reported being both "excited and scared" about the possibility of a coaching program. A previous (directive) counseling experience made her wary of another similar venture, as she felt that her previous counselor did not understand or appreciate her. Knowing that she was primarily in charge of the direction of the current coaching program, she participated, but without much enthusiasm. Here again, the Rogerian approach helped Betty get past her wariness and hesitation. The coach's willingness to listen, his attitude of caring and respect, and his willingness to let Betty "drive the train" helped establish the trust necessary to begin work on her difficulty with conflict and perfectionism. The coaching began by communicating accurate empathy. This empathy led to an understanding of the way that Betty felt. A coaching program was developed, along with an action plan after Betty decided that she was really being heard and understood. Once her initial resistance diminished, she was able to engage in coaching on her own behalf. She figured out what needed improvement and development, and she got going. Her coach encouraged honest and direct communication during the coaching process and used it as a bridge to foster more direct communication in the workplace. The coach encouraged Betty to confront difficult situations in a direct manner, and they rehearsed the interactions together using video feedback. They worked on establishing and valuing authentic communication. Betty learned some of the Rogerian listening skills and practiced them, so that they would be in place for difficult moments of conflict in the workplace.

Her coach also listened carefully to Betty's concerns about perfection, reflecting back and paraphrasing, so that Betty could hear and think about what it all meant. Gradually, Betty began to accept herself in greater proportions, giving up the need to feel perfect in order to engage projects and people. Betty's real self and ideal self began to merge.

The Future of Genuineness, Acceptance, and Empathy

The future of the principles proposed by Rogers is very bright indeed. But it will come without Rogers attached. Writings on the theory and application of psychology for executive coaching will continue to emphasize the importance of genuineness, unconditional positive regard, and empathy in the coach–client relationship. But you will be unlikely to find any reference to Rogers's groundbreaking person-centered approach. Freud and Jung are still very much alive in the minds of those who write about psychotherapy. But Rogers is lost, no doubt due to a lack of "sex appeal." His ideas are common, sensible, and simplistic, seemingly unworthy of high intellectual regard. His approach, nonetheless, will continue to grow in importance for the executive coach–client relationship.

That said, it must be noted that we have officially entered the world of the sound bite. Executive coaches are increasingly coached to focus on rapid results, so that executives feel that time spent on coaching is justified (Jones,

2008). Rogers's methods do not emphasize speed. As a matter of fact, they may run exactly 180 degrees against a hasty approach to deep human understanding and change.

There is likely to be a continual battle between empathy and quickness. Coaches will be taught the importance of creating genuine empathy in the coaching relationship, with the following caveat: Do it fast enough so as not to lose the interest of the high-energy, fast-moving, short-attention-span executive they are coaching. And remember John Wooden's advice: "Be quick, but don't hurry" (Hill & Wooden, 2001).

Summary

1. The person-centered approach can be viewed as the sine qua non (or ultimate prerequisite) for the successful executive coach. It is a set of threshold skills. These skills and conditions must be in place before other interventions are attempted. Without them, other coaching interventions are unlikely to make a difference. The core skills described by this approach are demanding, but they constitute a core competency for coaches. This approach is essential for the development of a working relationship with clients. The ultimate power of the person-centered approach is realized when it is used in eclectic combinations with other powerful theoretical interventions.

2. Refresh your knowledge of Rogerian skills, if necessary. Review basic listening techniques and actively work on your own interaction skills as a coach. Get feedback from another coach or counselor about your listening skills and interaction style. We all have blind spots.

3. Teach listening skills to your clients. With their permission, give them extensive feedback on the way that they listen and the impact that they have on you and on others.

4. Relentlessly strive to understand things from the point of view of your client.

5. Work on authenticity for the rest of your days.

References

Cooper, R. (1997, December). Applying emotional intelligence in the workplace. *Training & Development, 51*(12), 31–38.

Corey, G. (1982). *Theory and practice of counseling and psychotherapy* (2nd ed.). Monterey, CA: Brooks/Cole.

Cormier, W., & Cormier, L. (1985). *Interviewing strategies for helpers: Fundamental skill and cognitive behavioral interventions.* Monterey, CA: Brooks/Cole.

Covey, S. (1989). *The seven habits of highly effective people.* New York: Simon & Schuster.

Deming, W. (1986). *Out of crisis.* Cambridge, MA: NIT Center for Advanced Engineering Study.

Diedrich, R. (1996, Spring). An iterative approach to executive coaching. *Consulting Psychology Journal: Practice and Research, 48*(2), 61–66.

Goldsmith, M., & Reiter, M. (2007). *What got you here won't get you there.* New York: Hyperion.

Goleman, D. (1995). *Emotional intelligence.* New York: Bantam.

Goleman, D. (1998). *Working with emotional intelligence.* New York: Bantam.

Heppner, P., Rogers, M., & Lee, L. (1984). Carl Rogers: Reflections on his life. *Journal of Counseling & Development, 63*, 14–20.

Hill, A., & Wooden, J. (2001). *Be quick but don't hurry.* New York: Simon & Schuster.

Hojat, M., Gonnella, J. S., Mangione, S., Nasca, T. J., Veloski, J. J., Erdmann, J. B., et al. (2002). Empathy in medical students as related to academic performance, clinical competence and gender. *Medical Education, 36*(6), 522–527.

Hoppe, M. H. (2006). *Active listening: Improving your ability to listen and lead.* Greensboro, NC: Center for Creative Leadership.

Hutcheson, P. (1996, March). Ten tips for coaches. *Training & Development, 50*(3), 15–16.

Jones, G. (2008, August). Coaching real leaders. *Training & Development, 62*(8), 34–37.

Kiel, F., Rimmer, E., Williams, K., & Doyle, M. (1996, Spring). Coaching at the top. *Consulting Psychology Journal: Practice and Research, 48*(2), 67–77.

Kilburg, R. (Ed). (1996a, Spring). Executive coaching [Special issue]. *Consulting Psychology Journal: Practice and Research, 48*(2).

Kilburg, R. (1996b, Spring). Toward a conceptual understanding and definition of executive coaching. *Consulting Psychology Journal: Practice and Research, 48*(2), 134–144.

Leape, L. (1994, December 21). Error in medicine. *Journal of the American Medical Association, 272*(23), 1851–1857.

Morris, T. (1998). *If Aristotle ran G.M.: The new soul of business.* New York: Henry Holt.

Peters, T., & Waterman, R. (1982). *In search of excellence: Lessons from America's best-run companies.* New York: Harper & Row.

Peterson, D. (1996). Executive coaching at work: The art of one-on-one change. *Consulting Psychology Journal: Practice and Research, 48*(2), 78–86.

Pink, D. (2006). *A whole new mind: Why right-brainers will rule the future.* New York: Riverhead Books.

Rogers, C. (1961). *On becoming a person.* Boston: Houghton Mifflin.

Rogers, C. (1967). The conditions of change from a client-centered viewpoint. In B. Berenson & R. Carkhuff (Eds.), *Sources of gain in counseling and psychotherapy* (pp. 71-85). New York: Holt, Rinehart & Winston.

Rogers, C. (1977). *Carl Rogers on personal power: Inner strength and its revolutionary impact.* New York: Delacorte.

Rogers, C., & Wood, J. (1974). Client-centered theory: Carl Rogers. In A. Burton (Ed.), *Operational theories of personality* (pp. 211–258). New York: Brunner/Mazel.

Sperry, L. (1996). *Corporate therapy & consulting.* New York: Brunner/Mazel.

Witherspoon, R., & White, R. (1996). Executive coaching: A continuum of roles. *Consulting Psychology Journal: Practice and Research, 48*(2), 124–133.

Wright, R. (1997). *Tough questions, great answers. Responding to patient concerns about today's dentistry.* Carol Stream, IL: Quintessence Books.

Recommended Readings

Joseph, S., & Bryant-Jeffries, R. (2008). Person-centred coaching psychology. In S. Palmer & A. Whybrow (Eds.), *Handbook of coaching psychology* (pp. 211–228). London: Routledge.

Meier, S. T., & Davis, S. R. (2007). *The elements of counseling.* Florence, KY: Cenage-Brooks/Cole.

Rock, D. (2006). *Quiet leadership.* New York: HarperCollins.

Rogers, C. (1951). *Client-centered therapy.* Cambridge, MA: Houghton Mifflin.

Stober, D. R. (2006). Coaching from the humanistic perspective. In D. R. Stober & A. M. Grant (Eds.), *Evidence based coaching* (pp. 17–50). Hoboken, NJ: John Wiley & Sons.

6
Cognitive Psychology and Cognitive Therapy

Men are not moved by things, but by the views they take of them.

—**Epictetus**

Sometimes executives can benefit by changing the way they think, especially when their thinking limits their success. Coaches armed with cognitive methods can be of great help when this happens. This is true because of the special role that coaches play. A coach can (and should) tell clients that they are thinking incorrectly or poorly, because few others are in a position to do this. One's spouse cannot, their colleagues cannot, and their boss cannot either. A coach can teach a client how to improve the quality of their thinking and, as a result, improve the way they feel and behave. Cognitive therapy focuses on the ways that bad thinking creates negative emotions.

Case Example

Barney Smith, a bright, ambitious operations manager, has gradually made his way up the corporate ladder through hard work, energy, and effort. He is likable, has good intentions, and he knows operations inside and out. But he seems to have hit a ceiling, and this perplexes him, because he is willing to do whatever it takes to continue to succeed. He just cannot seem to figure out what is wrong. He puts in more hours than anyone else and usually takes work home with him as well. There always seems to be too much on his plate, and he feels like he is doing the work of three people. His most recent evaluation sticks in his mind, when he was told that he needs to delegate more. He does not feel comfortable delegating, he has never done much of it, and has chosen to do almost everything for himself, except for the clerical tasks done by his secretary. In short, he is a prolific individual contributor masquerading as a leader. Aware that delegation is likely to become increasingly important as he moves to positions of greater responsibility, he decides that he must learn how to delegate. He takes a seminar and reads some self-help management books, but things do not change. He still cannot seem to delegate effectively, and he is not sure why. Barney is committed and sincere, working as hard as he possibly can, putting in long hours and still making sure that everything is done in exactly the right way. He has his hand in virtually everything in his department. He understandably feels frazzled at times, and his employees do not seem as committed as those in other departments.

What do we do about Barney? Can we help him change this pattern of behavior? What is the best way to approach him? What does cognitive psychology have to contribute?

The Theory

Cognitive psychology is the study of the mind, its ways, and patterns. In this model view, the mind consists of the mental products of the physical brain. The study of cognitive psychology is typically a university-based endeavor, and it has been around since about 1955. As one might imagine, it is a complex area of study, having to do with intellectual processes such as memory, perception, language formation, and the roles of various brain functions.

Cognitive *therapy* is younger and simpler. It uses a few of the core concepts of cognitive psychology, and it has very practical potential in the workplace. Its core concept is this: People can learn to notice and change their own specific thoughts resulting in powerful emotional and behavioral benefits. Its central idea breaks with earlier psychotherapy theories in that it focuses on conscious thinking rather than unconscious processes. It is relatively simple to explain and to teach and, with the right people, can make a quick and profound difference in the way that we feel and behave.

History

There are two key figures in the early development of cognitive therapy. Albert Ellis (1973; Ellis & Grieger, 1977; Ellis & Harper, 1961) was a highly energetic and engaging psychologist who broke with Freudian tradition in the 1960s to forge his own psychotherapy based upon the relationship between conscious thought, emotion, behavior, and happiness. He observed that psychoanalysis (which focused on complex unconscious processes) seemed ineffective and found that patients did better when he actively taught them specifically better ways to think. He was an extremely hard worker and prolific teacher and writer who lectured right up until his death in 2007 at the age of 93.

Aaron Beck (1967, 1976) studied profoundly depressed people at the University of Pennsylvania hospital at about that same time. He experimented with structured programs that taught new thinking patterns to people who were hospitalized and felt extremely hopeless about themselves and their lives. He concluded that *automatic thoughts* (repetitive thought patterns that were incorrect in systematic ways) were responsible for depression and anxiety, and he aimed therapy at changing the mental "rule books" of hospital patients.

One of Beck's protégés, David Burns, wrote a pivotal book for the popular market in 1980 called *Feeling Good: The New Mood Therapy*. His book explained cognitive therapy in a way that is very accessible and it contributed to widespread public acceptance of this approach. Burns has continued to produce materials suitable for people who want to learn how to apply cognitive methods to their own psychological development.

In 1965, a cognitive experimenter named Lloyd Homme described something called a *covert operant*, and this turned out to be a key to the application of Ellis's and Beck's experiences. Homme observed that conscious ideas could be treated in the same way as overt behaviors, that is, they could be observed, manipulated, and managed. Jealous thoughts need not be understood as the product of unconscious processes. They could be observed and changed directly through deliberate and diligent effort using behavioral techniques such as reinforcement and shaping. Thoughts could be treated as mental behavior.

Although these ideas were resisted in the clinical psychology arena for many years, the persistence of Ellis, Beck, Burns, and others, as well as the intrinsic practicality of the approach, eventually won their place in the mainstream therapeutic toolbox.

Philosophical Basis

To understand cognitive therapy it is useful to consider the thoughts of two philosophers. The first is the stoic Epictetus: "Man is not disturbed by events, but by *the view he takes of them*."

The second is from the old Kantian koan:

1. I see a tiger.
2. I think I'm in danger.
3. I feel afraid.
4. I run.

The core idea is that Kantian Statement 3 (as well as 4) derives from Statement 2, *not* from Statement 1, as most people assume. The way that you feel does not come from life. It does not derive from your surroundings or from the things that are happening to you or even from your direct perceptions. The situation cannot make you sad or crazy. Those feelings are a function of thinking, and you can exercise choice. What you choose to think determines what you feel and what you do next. If you are thinking poorly, you will feel bad and you will make poor decisions. This is an extraordinarily powerful and useful principle, one that has not gone unnoticed by motivational speakers. Thinking mediates emotion. Specific thoughts create and control feelings. If you think you are in danger, you are likely to feel afraid. If you feel afraid, you are likely to run. But what if the tiger is in a cage? What if you are a tiger tamer, and you have been around tigers all your life? Simply seeing a tiger does not cause fear and running. You have to *think* you are in danger before those other things happen. As in the caged tiger example, our first thought in a challenging situation is often not the optimal thing to think. Luckily, we are not stuck with that first thought or instinct. Thinking is largely under our control. Humans are capable of observing their own thinking and are even capable of changing what they think. Most people make the mistake of assuming that the events of life, the tigers, make us feel bad or good. This is a problem, because we cannot control most of the important things or forces in life. Life is too big and too mysterious, and it tends to do what it wants, independent of what we think we would prefer. The basic premise of the cognitive approach is: *We cannot control life, but we can control how we think about life.* By controlling our thinking we are then able to manage our emotions and behaviors. If you feel bad, it is not because "life" is bad. It is because you are thinking poorly and inaccurately in systematic ways, and these thoughts and patterns dictate your feelings. It is important to note that cognitive therapy does not advocate "positive thinking." It emphasizes correct or accurate or reasonable thinking. Positive thinking is fine, as long as it is reasonably accurate.

Coaching with Cognitive Approaches

There are three areas of interest available to coaches who want to use cognitive methods, and each involves a different aspect of client thinking. They are: (1) general style of thinking, (2) specific thinking patterns, and (3) specific thoughts. These methods, along with the use of imagery, are described next. Cognitive work starts with an assessment of emotions or feelings. Ask your clients to check within themselves to see if they are feeling angry, sad, afraid, or hurt, or if they associate any of these feelings with the problem at hand. When humans experience these emotions, this is a clue that they are thinking irrational thoughts. A premise is that the events of life are, in fact, neutral. Life is neither intrinsically good nor bad. Goodness and badness involve human judgments. Use the feelings to get to the thoughts or thinking patterns that caused them. Thoughts cause feelings. The first step is to identify and label feelings.

General Styles of Thinking

Beck described four problematic patterns that he consistently observed in depressed people. These four patterns need to be examined, challenged, and changed. Beck (1967) called them *depressive distortions*, which are shown in Table 6.1.

Specific Thinking Patterns

San Francisco psychologists McKay, Davis, and Fanning (2007) contributed 15 patterns of thinking that cause problems on a reliable basis. Table 6.2 is a paraphrasing of their list.

Table 6.1 Patterns of Cognitive Error in Depression

1. *Arbitrary Inference*—A conclusion drawn in the absence of sufficient evidence (or of any evidence at all). For example, you conclude that you are worthless because it is raining on the day that you host a picnic.

2. *Selective Abstraction*—A conclusion drawn that is based on *only one of many* elements of a situation. A worker blames herself entirely for the failure of a product to function, even though she is only one of many people who have produced it.

3. *Overgeneralization*—An overall sweeping conclusion made on the basis of a single, perhaps trivial event or bit of evidence. A student regards his poor performance in a single class on one particular day as final proof of his overall worthlessness and general stupidity.

4. *Magnification and Minimization*—Gross errors in performance evaluation. A woman believes that she has completely ruined her car when she sees that there is a slight scratch on the rear fender (magnification). A man still believes himself worthless by underestimating the value of a succession of solid achievements (minimization).

Source: From Davison and Neale (1978, pp. 197–198).

Table 6.2 Styles of Distorted Thinking

1. *Filtering*—You take the negative details and magnify them while filtering out all positive aspects. Sometimes people have a characteristic theme for their filter, such as *danger* (safety), or *loss*, or *injustice*. They view and evaluate everything through that lens.

2. *Polarized Thinking*—Things are black or white, good or bad. You have to be perfect or you're a failure. There is no middle ground. Things are either awful or they are terrific. They are right or wrong. There is no realistic gray area. This is particularly important in how people judge themselves or others.

3. *Overgeneralization*—You come to a general conclusion based on a single incident or piece of evidence. If something bad happens once, you expect it to happen over and over again. If someone lets you down once, you assume that they are incompetent, and that you could never trust them with anything important again.

4. *Mind Reading*—Without their saying so, you know what people are feeling and why they act the way they do. In particular, you are able to divine how people are feeling toward you. You think that your assumptions about what others are thinking are true.

5. *Catastrophizing*—You expect disaster. You notice or hear about a problem and start thinking of "what ifs." What if tragedy strikes? What if it happens to you? You immediately assume the worst possible outcome. This is your style.

6. *Personalization*—You think that everything people do or say is some kind of reaction to you. You compare yourself to others, trying to determine who's smarter or better looking. You tend to relate everything around you to yourself.

(Continued)

Table 6.2 *(Continued)*

7. *Control Fallacy*—If you feel externally controlled, you see yourself as a totally helpless victim of fate. You do not believe that you can effectively influence the important outcomes. These are out of your control. Conversely, you feel excessively responsible. Everything depends on you, and if things do not go well, it is all your fault. The fallacy of control has you responsible for the pain and happiness of everyone around you. This is a sizeable burden.

8. *Fallacy of Fairness*—You feel resentful because you think you know what's fair, but other people will not agree with you. Fairness is a big standard for you. You think everything should be fair, even though there is insufficient evidence to indicate that life is particularly fair and plenty of evidence that it is not. When things go poorly, you respond with, "That's not fair. It's just not fair. It shouldn't be that way."

9. *Emotional Reasoning*—You believe that what you feel must be true … automatically. If you *feel* stupid and boring, then you must *be* stupid and boring. Your feelings are the truth. They define you.

10. *Fallacy of Change*—You expect that other people will change to suit you if you just pressure or cajole them enough. You need to change people because you feel that your hopes for happiness depend entirely on them. Some of your relationships are based on the premise that you can change the other person. You often talk about how others should change. You give them advice about this.

11. *Global Labeling*—You generalize one or two qualities into a negative global judgment. If you have one bad interaction with someone in a department, you tell others that the whole department is "a bunch of jerks."

12. *Blaming*—You hold other people responsible for your pain or take the other tack and blame yourself for every problem or reversal. When something goes wrong, someone is surely to blame.

13. *Shoulds*—You have a list of ironclad rules about how you and other people should act. People who break the rules make you angry and you feel guilty if you violate those rules. Your shoulds are perfectionistic. No one could really meet these standards, but you hold yourself or others to them.

14. *Being Right*—You are continually on trial to prove that your opinions and actions are correct. Being wrong is unthinkable, and you will go to any length to demonstrate your rightness. This makes you defensive, and you have to hang onto your opinions and justify what you have done.

15. *Heaven's Reward Fallacy*—You expect all your sacrifice and self-denial to pay off, as if there were someone keeping score. You feel bitter when the reward does not come. You work extra hard and sacrifice, and do the right thing, expecting to get a lot of credit later. Often, it does not come, and this upsets you.

Source: From McKay, Davis, and Fanning (2007, pp. 46–49), with material added for coaching.

Specific Thoughts

Ellis, on the other hand, developed a list of 10 specific thoughts that must be recognized, evaluated, challenged, and changed (see Table 6.3). He called them *irrational ideas* (Ellis & Harper, 1961). According to this approach, rigid and thoughtless adherence to these specific ideas causes us problems, not life itself. These irrational ideas are explained in detail in Ellis's 1961 book, with a chapter on each of the following irrational thoughts.

Tables 6.1, 6.2, and 6.3 list examples of the styles, patterns, and specific thoughts that cause negative emotions and problem behavior. Many or most of these thoughts are automatic. People are hardly aware of them unless challenged. The task for the coach is to help clients notice these thoughts and patterns and then to substitute effective ones for the negative and irrational ones. More effective thoughts are typically more accurate or realistic thoughts. Clients need help figuring this out, and coaches provide this specific assistance. Improved executive effectiveness is sure to follow, especially when the new pattern is repeated diligently until it replaces old thinking patterns and feels "natural."

Table 6.3 Ellis's Irrational Thoughts

Irrational Idea 1—It is a dire necessity for an adult to be loved or approved of by almost everyone for virtually everything he or she does.

Irrational Idea 2—One should be thoroughly competent, adequate, and achieving in all possible respects.

Irrational Idea 3—Certain people are bad, wicked, or villainous and they should be severely blamed and punished for their sins.

Irrational Idea 4—It is terrible, horrible, and catastrophic when things are not going the way one would like them to go.

Irrational Idea 5—Human happiness is externally caused and people have little or no ability to control their sorrows or rid themselves of their negative feelings.

Irrational Idea 6—If something is or may be dangerous or fearsome, one should be terribly occupied with it and upset about it.

Irrational Idea 7—It is easier to avoid facing many life difficulties and self-responsibilities than to undertake more rewarding forms of self-discipline.

Irrational Idea 8—The past is all-important and because something once strongly affected one's life, it should indefinitely do so.

Irrational Idea 9—People and things should be different from the way that they are, and it is catastrophic if perfect solutions to the grim realities of life are not immediately found.

Irrational Idea 10—Maximum human happiness can be achieved by inertia and inaction or by passively "enjoying oneself."

Imagery

Cognitive therapy also makes use of images. Mental pictures and other forms of imagery can both hurt and help people. Frightening images constrain us; comforting images soothe. Most, but not all people, visualize and are capable of manipulating the images they see. The first step in using imagery is to make an imagery (capacity) assessment. Coaches must check to ensure that their client makes mental pictures and can call up one image or another when asked to do so. If you discover that your client does not easily visualize or is not capable of imagery, this approach should be adapted to fit your client's mental style or even discarded. A small number of people simply do not seem capable of noticing images or pictures in their minds. For them, a foray into this world can be frustrating and demoralizing, unless you are able to help them use a vague "sense of things" (in place of imagery) to accomplish this work. Most people, however, are quite familiar with their own image-generating process, and some are extremely facile. Imagery manipulation can be very useful to such individuals.

Begin by assessing the specific images that come to mind when your client is at work. In Barney Smith's case, for example, as his coach, you could help him figure out what images he associates with delegating. Next, you would ask him to imagine delegating a task to someone specific. Then have him notice which images pop up. If none come to him, ask him to let an image evolve. Instruct him to observe the image in great detail, and then assess the image and its meaning. Finally, encourage him to make changes in the image and help him practice changing the old image to the new one. The task is to learn from these images and shift from dysfunctional images to ones that are more useful.

Rian McMullin's *Handbook of Cognitive Therapy Techniques* (1986, pp. 272–276) lists many such helpful images, and Chapter 10 (hypnotic communication) in this book describes 10 useful imagery techniques.

Application

The best way to make use of cognitive approaches is to start at the bottom of Kant's paradigm and work backward, as shown below in Table 6.4.

Begin by teaching your client the cognitive model, its assumptions, and principles. Determine how easily your client can access feelings and thoughts—or if they can do this at all. Some people find identification of their own feeling states to be difficult to do. Others do not seem to think in

Table 6.4 Kant's Paradigm

4. I run.	(Behavior)
3. I feel afraid.	(Feeling or Emotion)
2. I think I'm in danger.	(Thinking or Cognition)
1. I see a Tiger.	(Perception)

sentences or words or ways that can be clearly described. If your client is able to notice and label these internal events, observe their behavior or emotion and connect those to the precipitating thoughts. Assess whether their behavior is effective, relative to desired goals or objectives. Identify discrete problematic behavior. Size up negative emotions and feelings. When and under what circumstances does the negative emotion occur, and what problems does it cause? Then—and here is the key step in this method—connect the behavior and feeling back to the specific thoughts, patterns, or styles (from the earlier tables) that produced them. In this model, the thoughts *produce* the feelings and the behaviors. Once you have identified the thinking that produces problematic feeling and behavior, the task is to challenge and dispute it. A person's distorted thinking patterns are rarely obvious to himself or herself. Outside help is usually needed in this process, and it is often necessary for the helper to be tenacious. Most people prefer to be "right" rather than effective or happy, and to feel better they must admit that their thinking is incorrect or ineffective or problematic. Feedback of this sort requires some authority or rapport on the part of the therapist or coach, but it is *the* essential step in the change process. This feedback step also requires skill and finesse, for it can easily be perceived as simple criticism or, worse, rejection. No one likes to be told that his or her thinking is wrong.

Once problematic thinking has been identified and challenged, it must be adjusted or replaced. If a simple cognitive adjustment is possible, an easy, elegant intervention can be the result, especially if the interaction can be framed in a positive way. If replacement thinking is necessary, care must be taken to come up with a thought, pattern, or style that is more "true," more realistic, and more effective than the old one (not necessarily a *positive* thought). And the thinker must buy into the new thinking. All of this typically takes several iterations. Do not expect it to "take" instantly.

The last step is evaluation. Success is judged with the same model. If feelings are good, if behavior has changed, then thinking has improved. Effective thinking leads to powerful positive feelings and effective behavior.

Application: Barney Revisited

A coach who uses the lessons of cognitive therapy might work with Barney using the six-step program, outlined in the following, taking into account the keys to success discussed after the program outline.

Step 1: Gather Data

First, we need Barney's cooperation and commitment. We start by exploring the problem to figure out what is happening. We do not necessarily accept Barney's diagnosis or view of the problem. We might use a 360-degree evaluation, a standard procedure in executive coaching (described in Chapter 1). We ask for input from the people to whom Barney reports, the people who report to him, and from his peers. We ask Barney to provide the names of the people for the 360-degree evaluation, and when the feedback comes in, we correlate it into relevant themes. In Barney's case, the assessment information indicates that people above Barney in the organization view him as bright and hard working, but in a little over his head. They wonder how he could ever take on more responsibility, since he seems swamped now. They cannot put their finger on the source of this impression, but it does seem that Barney is not a "big picture" guy, as one vice president reports. Barney's coworkers confirm his busyness and the frazzled demeanor. He seems pulled in many directions, and it appears that it is always tough for him to have everything done on time. He always appears to be struggling, and he does not seem comfortable, happy, or fun to be around. He often seems distracted and vaguely worried. They acknowledge that he is competent, but he comes across like he is struggling, and they cannot say exactly why.

Barney's subordinates are very helpful in diagnosing the problem. Although they like Barney and they even admire him, citing his work ethic and integrity, they are annoyed with his apparent lack of confidence in them and his inclination to micromanage. They report that they have tried to give him feedback about this, although no one has been very direct with it. They cannot understand why he does not see it himself, and they do not want to hurt his feelings or get themselves into any trouble. He just does not seem to trust them to do anything really important, and he tries to do it all himself. Some of his employees would prefer to see themselves as "team members" (a term that Barney often uses) but they feel more like caddies or assistants to him, rather than full players. Some workers are quite annoyed, some really do not care, and some report that they have given up, and have quit taking responsibility for projects. They just wait for detailed instructions from Barney and do what he tells them, step by step. They feel that he does not have much faith in them, so they do not take any initiative. Most report that theirs is not a very exciting or gratifying place to work, yet they really like their boss and think he is a good person.

Step 2: Study the Data and Develop an Understanding of the Problem

In Step 2, we sit down with Barney and go over our information in great detail, remembering to protect the people who gave it to us, while managing Barney's defensiveness or hurt feelings. Few people really like negative feedback, even when they ask for it and know that it will be good for them. Sometimes feedback needs to be dispensed in small, well-framed doses. Raw data need to be processed and translated into usable, acceptable information. The communications skills and accurate empathy of the executive coach are important in this step.

Here is what we would discover about Barney's thinking patterns:

1. He has a deep-seated notion that it is important to work really hard, harder than anyone around him. Barney's sense of personal worth and integrity derives from the amount of sheer effort he applies to

work tasks on a daily basis. To him, more effort means he is a better person. Delegation seems lazy to him, as if he were shirking his real work. When you mull this over with him, he acknowledges that such a fundamental view of work might make it hard to delegate anything important to anyone else.

2. He thinks he is the only one who can do things properly. "If you want it done right, do it yourself," is something he remembers his father telling him. He also figures it takes more time to show others how to do things than it takes to simply do them himself. It seems more efficient, from his present point of view, to just get on a task and get it done properly.

Step 3: Develop a Plan

The plan we develop will be based on Kant's paradigm (I see a tiger; I think I'm in danger; I feel afraid; I run), meaning that we will focus any efforts on Barney's flawed thinking patterns. The eventual goal will be to help Barney think differently about some aspect of his work so that he can change his behavior.

We go over Beck's distorted patterns, Ellis's self-defeating thoughts, and McKay et al.'s problematic thinking styles. Barney acknowledges some attempts he has made to delegate, as well as his perception that the results were not satisfactory. He also acknowledges that he has given up on the process, for the most part. He deeply believes Ellis's thought number 2 (one should be thoroughly competent, adequate, and achieving in all possible respects). This thought causes him problems when it is time to delegate, because he really thinks that good people ought to do things themselves rather than ask someone else to do them. When he asks others to do things that he could do himself, he gets a vague sense that he is shirking, that if he were really strong and adequate he could (and should) do them himself, rather than "push them off" on someone else. He also thinks that he is the only one who can really do things properly, the best way, the way he would like to see them done. He is even concerned about the steps that someone else might take to get to the same end result. He is concerned that they might not do it his way. He is deeply concerned about what he would say if he were to delegate tasks and end up unhappy with the results. What would he say? How could he tell someone that what they have done does not meet his high standards, especially when he could have simply done it himself in the first place? It just seems easier to do it himself, and it would thus be done properly, and he would avoid all this messiness. Then Barney could feel like a hard worker, deserving of his pay and of the respect of others.

Barney's inability to delegate also stems from his tendency to use two of McKay et al.'s (1981) problematic styles of thinking. The first is number 7 on their list: *control fallacy*. Barney has trouble delegating because he would have to give up some control, and this is not consistent with his current cognitive style. He has no experience with letting go of control, he does not trust others enough to let go, and he does not trust others enough to assume they will evaluate him properly (generously) if things do not work out in the best possible way. He is afraid others will blame him if the tasks he delegates do not work out perfectly. It all seems too risky because of his control fallacy style. Also, he uses the thinking style called *heaven's reward fallacy* (number 15). He deeply believes that hard work and effort, even lots of small efforts, will get one into "heaven." (He does not literally believe in "heaven," but does feel a powerful, if vague, sense that it is important to do a lot of good work and that he will eventually reap the rewards.) Therefore, it would be a mistake to "palm off" any work to others. One simply stays longer at the office and does it oneself. Eventually this behavior will be rewarded.

Cognitive therapy insists that these thinking errors must be spotted, labeled, and discussed. A coach would clearly describe the flaws they contain along with the expectable results. We would then solicit examples from Barney's real-life behavior, and discuss them with him in a neutral way, avoiding blame and seeking humor.

Step 4: Actively Dispute Problem Thinking

The next step in this approach involves active and relentless disputation of the problem thinking. We would work with Barney to begin to actively catch each instance when his thinking is hurting his performance. The key to this effort is to work backward through Kant's model. Examples of ineffective behavior led to an exploration of what Barney was feeling at the time, and to what Barney was really *thinking*, which led to the poor decision. We would teach Barney to notice what he is thinking when it comes time to delegate or do things himself. As a part of this process, Barney can set delegation goals for himself, picking appropriate tasks and times and people to whom to delegate. That way he will be able to pick specific situations for self-study. "What was happening when you were supposed to hand off the telecommunications project? Let's go back over it and review what you were thinking and feeling at the time," we might say. This all must be done in a neutral style. Blaming is banished, so that freedom of expression and exploration are maximized. Normalize irrational thinking. Everyone does it.

Here are some examples of how to dispute Barney's problematic thinking. First, Barney needs to be helped to understand that he does not add value to the company (at his level) by taking care of details. He thinks that by taking care of lots of small and difficult tasks, he is doing the right thing. But this is precisely the *wrong thing*, because his time and skills are needed in other areas, specifically in leadership activities such as coordination, motivating others, strategizing, and reinforcing. He adds value by preparing, teaching, and supporting others as they accomplish day-to-day details, and this becomes even more important when factoring in the learning that takes place when the people he manages figure out how to accomplish new tasks. Barney needs to grasp the fact that when he rolls up his own sleeves, he actually *subtracts* value from the company because he is not taking care of leadership tasks and is actually undermining the efforts and morale of those whose job it is to take care of the details. Second, he must come to see that when he takes care of the detail work himself (thinking that he can do it best) he deprives others of the opportunity to learn.

Step 5: Replace Problematic Thinking with New Thinking

In this step Barney and the coach work together to develop new thinking to replace the old. This new thinking must meet several criteria. First, it must be more accurate and true to real life than the old thinking. This is not a Pollyanna approach and it is not "positive thinking." Although positive thinking is usually a good thing, we first want to get as close to accurate thinking as we can. The world is a neutral place, and it does not care about us. We do not try to think things that are not true. When we carefully examine the old, we can usually discern that the old thinking was, in fact, irrational. New replacement thoughts must pass the tests of truthfulness and accuracy. If Barney cannot accept them as true, the system will not work. Why should he take on the task of thinking something that he really does not believe or something that is made up so that he can feel better?

Second, the new thinking must be reasonable and achievable. Grandiose or extremely radical new thinking is not likely to work. People rarely change their thinking in radical ways (outside of cults), and when they do, we must wonder about their sense of self. Radical change probably will not last. Thought changes made in this setting must be relatively small and not significantly incompatible with the rest of Barney's cognitive map. If large-scale changes in belief seem warranted, a longer-term plan must be adopted, and it should include small steps to get there.

Third, the new thinking must be acceptable to Barney. If it violates Barney's core values or religious views, it probably will not last, even if Barney says it will.

Here is an example of replacement thinking. Barney must learn that he can still put in many hours, and he can still work very hard. But, to add value to the company, he must behave like a leader: He must engage in the activities of *leadership,* such as directing and mentoring others (to leverage Barney's skills), coordinating the work of others, teaching others the skills they need to do the job as well as Barney can do it, and motivating. This is how Barney gets into "heaven." This may require that Barney overcome some fear or resistance to the learning of difficult leadership skills as well.

Step 6: Reinforce and Sustain New Thinking

The new ways of thinking must be rewarded and supported in the real world of work behavior. Behavior change is usually uncomfortable at first, and the coach must support changes in thinking and in behavior. It may be useful at this stage to enlist the active involvement of others in the process of supporting and rewarding Barney's new behavior, especially if others are to benefit from it. The old ways of thinking are likely to be resilient and can easily bounce back before new thinking is solidly entrenched. The coach's job at this stage is to cheerlead and to relentlessly point out the benefits of new thinking to Barney.

Keys to Success

Early on, the coach must discover the best way to influence Barney. There are three possibilities. First, Barney might allow the coach into his mental world because the coach is viewed as some sort of authority. Perhaps Barney perceives the coach as smart or in possession of some special expertise. Second, perhaps Barney figures that it is in his own best interest to listen and take the coach seriously. Barney knows that something is wrong and sees the benefit of a new approach. The third avenue is through rapport. The coach uses interpersonal skills to develop a trusting relationship that allows the coach to remark candidly about the effectiveness of Barney's thinking. Resistance is minimal in each of these three circumstances, but it cannot be taken for granted. It is easy for clients to nod their head and act like they are going along with the program while secretly feeling criticized or not understanding the transformational process.

Using a cognitive approach will be most effective if Barney is the kind of person who can notice or hear or see his own thoughts. Not everyone seems capable of this. Some people, no matter how hard they try, cannot seem to discern their own specific thinking. Cognitive methods do not work well with them. Other people have the capacity to listen to their thinking, but are not tuned in. They are not used to this kind of introspection, but can learn how to do so with a little instruction and practice. This is a valuable life skill in any context. The question for them is: "What am I telling myself?" or "What was I thinking when I felt that way or when I said that?"

Likewise, this method is unlikely to work very well with people who cannot discern their own emotional states. Some people simply cannot. Some people do not have much interest in their feelings, as they are threatened by them or simply do not value their emotional life. Others can be taught how to do this, although it may be more appropriate for a therapist to teach this skill than a business coach. But emotions are the doorway into identifying irrational thoughts. Once a client notices a negative emotion, that emotion can be tracked back to a specific causative thought.

Evaluation

This can be conducted in two ways. First, specific, measurable goals can be established at the beginning of the process. These can be examined at several points subsequent to the coaching. Second, another brief 360-degree evaluation can be conducted. Supervisors, direct-reports, and peers can offer feedback regarding specific areas of progress, and this can be done over the telephone or via voicemail. Written, measurable forms of evaluation are crucial at some point as well. The value of coaching must be clear to those paying the bill. Clear results are also important when the time comes to sell more coaching work in the future.

Strengths and Weaknesses of the Approach

At best, this approach can work wonders in a short period of time. Some people can rapidly learn to notice and label their thinking and then change it to great benefit, especially when they are motivated. Most people can learn this technique with relative ease and can implement significant changes that are sustainable when someone, such as a coach, consistently reminds and reinforces these changes over a period of several months. Some people are able to make rapid changes when new ideas are presented in the "cognitive" format by an "expert" (the coach), even though others have presented the same ideas, in different forms, on many previous occasions. A related advantage is that this approach allows the coach to make direct corrective comments without labeling the client "bad" or "crazy." Everybody's thinking needs adjustment from time to time, and the right cognitive adjustment can produce immediate rewards.

This method is readily adaptable to the business and corporate environment. It is direct, straightforward, and results-oriented. It is easy to explain and managers can quickly see the point and the potential benefits.

Even so, humans tend to slip back into old patterns, and it helps to have reinforcement available for extended periods of time. This can include simple reminders like small signs around the office, a note posted on the refrigerator, a regular journal with a commitment to long-term change, or ongoing intermittent phone calls with a coach. It is useful to recruit team members and coworkers to help with the process, if this can be done without embarrassing the client.

Limitations

There are two main weaknesses or cautions associated with the cognitive approach. First, not everyone seems to be able to notice the ways that they think. Their thinking styles, specific thoughts, and distortions are not readily available to them. Some of those clients can *learn* to access their own thinking, but others do not seem able to do this at all. If a coach approaches all managers or clients in the same way, assuming that they can easily observe, reveal, and catalog their thinking, the coach runs the risk of frustrating or even humiliating clients unnecessarily. A good first step is to ascertain the extent to which a client can access various forms of his or her thinking. This is easy to do and can be accomplished by asking simple questions:

- Are you able to notice and tell me about your own thoughts?
- Do you think in words or sentences or language at least some of the time?
- If I ask you to think about what you are going to do tomorrow, what *form* does the thinking take?
- Is it in pictures or words (that you can *see* or hear)?
- Do you just get a *sense* of things, or do you get feelings?
- Can you tell when you feel angry or sad or afraid or hurt or happy?

Many people use pictures for one kind of mental task or activity, words or visualized words for another, and a sense of things for other mental purposes. Some people talk to themselves all day long. Others never do. Start by helping your clients figure out their mental style. Assume no mental way is better than any other. If your client really does not seem able to access any recognizable forms of thinking, use some of the other approaches in this book. Cognitive approaches can lead to a long, frustrating goose chase when attempted by those who are not good candidates.

This approach seems to work best with people who can quickly tell you what they are thinking and feeling from moment to moment. It is not that others cannot learn to identify these internal states and processes, it is just that a referral to a counselor might be the best place for such foundational learning. Conversely, this approach works better when the coach is also a person who is able to notice and manipulate his or her own thinking as well. Some coaches may not find this method to their liking because they, themselves, do not have a mental style that is well suited to noticing their own thinking. This makes it difficult to explain it all to others.

Packaging Cognitive Therapy

A second cautionary note is related to the way that this approach is presented to clients. Many people feel insulted when their thinking is challenged. This is not hard to appreciate. Nobody really enjoys being told that the way they think is wrong. It is important to package cognitive methods in a positive frame, so that they are not interpreted as "You think stupidly. Let me tell you how you should think." Such an approach is bound to be met with resistance. This challenge is no small task, and some form of positive rapport is an essential prerequisite. Rapport can take many forms, but it must be established, quickly or slowly. The danger of rejection of this method, depending on the social dynamics of the situation, is profound. The presentation of this approach must be tailored to the unique personality characteristics of each client in each workplace situation.

At the same time you frame what you do positively, do not conflate cognitive therapy with positive thinking. Most people are vaguely familiar with positive thinking methods from self-help books or programs, and they may have negative associations. The core premise of cognitive methods is that *accurate* thinking produces neutral or positive feelings.

Bear in mind that this is an approach that has been designed to work with individuals, one at a time. There is no reason that it might not work in groups or with work teams, but not much has been written to describe that process. It might involve a coach who teaches cognitive principles to a work group, which then discovers its own problematic and irrational group thinking. The process could be fun and productive, especially if all members buy into the endeavor with minimal defensiveness.

Summary

The cognitive approach can be extremely useful in management and executive coaching. It requires a manager or executive who can notice and describe his or her own thinking relative to a perceived behavioral or workplace problem. The coach spends several hours on a one-on-one basis with the manager so that the method can be taught and learned. The specifics of that manager's cognitive map are carefully discerned, and changes are made in the specific ways that he or she thinks about an important work-related set of problems or skills. Changes are implemented by the client, reinforced by the coach, and supported in the work environment. Coaches who find this method attractive are urged to study the "Recommended Readings" list, and especially McKay, Davis, and Fanning (2007), Burns (1980), and even the book for dummies (Wilson & Branch, 2006) in the "References."

1. Human feelings derive directly from thoughts, not from events in the world. People can exercise choice in their thinking and, by doing so, can change how they feel. At the same time, it is difficult or nearly impossible to directly change one's feelings (without changing underlying thoughts). Everyone thinks irrational thoughts. Bad feelings or emotions (anger, sadness, fear, or hurt) are the direct result of irrational thoughts. That is where those feelings come from in this model.

2. Ineffective behavior patterns can be quickly and reliably enhanced by examining and changing specific irrational (and incorrect) underlying thoughts. These thoughts are reviewed and challenged by the coach and client.

3. Cognitive approaches are not for everyone. If the client or the coach is not able to learn how to notice specific things that she is "telling herself," the process is unlikely to be effective.

4. Coaching is conducted like an experiment. Cognitive data are collected, analyzed, and a change effort is untaken. Information from the evaluation of results is fed back into the process.

5. Cognitive change does not often take place after one iteration of the process. Repetition is usually necessary.

References

Beck, A. (1967). *Depression: Clinical, experimental, and theoretical aspects.* New York: Hoeber Medical Division.

Beck, A. (1976). *Cognitive therapy and the emotional disorders.* New York: International Universities Press.

Burns, D. (1980). *Feeling good: The new mood therapy.* New York: Signet/New American Library.

Davison, G., & Neale, J. (1978). *Abnormal psychology* (2nd ed.). New York: Wiley.

Ellis, A. (1973). *Humanistic psychotherapy.* New York: McGraw-Hill.

Ellis, A., & Grieger. R. (1977). *Handbook of rational-emotive therapy.* New York: Springer.

Ellis, A., & Harper, R. (1961). *A guide to rational living.* New York: Institute for Rational Living.

Homme, L. (1965). Perspectives in psychology XXIV: Control of coverants, the operants of the mind. *Psychological Record, 15,* 501–511.

McKay, M., Davis, M., & Fanning. P. (2007). *Thoughts and feelings: The art of cognitive stress intervention* (3rd ed.). Oakland, CA: New Harbinger.

McMullin, R. (1986). *Handbook of cognitive therapy techniques.* New York: Norton.

Wilson, R. & Branch, R. (2006). *Cognitive behavioural therapy for dummies.* Chichester, UK: John Wiley & Sons.

Recommended Readings

Auerbach, J. (2006). Cognitive coaching. In D. R. Stober & A. M. Grant (Eds.), *Evidence based coaching handbook* (pp. 103–128). Hoboken, NJ: John Wiley & Sons.

Ducharme, M. L. (2004). The cognitive-behavioral approach to executive coaching. *Consulting Psychology Journal: Practice and Research, 56*(4), 214–224.

Goleman, D. (1985). *Vital lies, simple truths.* New York: Simon & Schuster.

Johnson, W. (1946). *People in quandaries: The semantics of personal adjustment.* New York: Harper.

Ornstein, R. (1986). *Multimind.* Boston: Houghton Mifflin.

Palmer, S., & Szymanska, K. (2008). Cognitive behavioural coaching: An integrative approach. In S. Palmer & A. Whybrow (Eds.), *Handbook of coaching psychology* (pp. 86–117). London: Routledge.

Postman, N. (1976). *Crazy talk, stupid talk.* New York: Dell.

Seligman, M. (1991). *Learned optimism.* New York: Alfred Knopf.

Serban, G. (1982). *The tyranny of magical thinking.* New York: E. P. Dutton.

Sherin, J., & Caiger, L. (2004). Rational-emotive behavior therapy: A behavioral change model for executive coaching? *Consulting Psychology Journal: Practice and Research, 56*(4), 225–233.

Wegner, D. (1989). *White bears and other unwanted thoughts.* New York: Viking-Penguin.

Zastrow, C. (1983). *Talk to yourself: Using the power of self-talk.* Englewood Cliffs, NJ: Prentice Hall.

7

Family Therapy and Systems Thinking

In short, knowledge of cause and symptom is not very productive. Rather, knowledge of the system, its parts, their interrelatedness, the communication feedback between the parts, and the system's homeostatic functioning is far more useful to an understanding of the problem and a search for its resolution.

—Joseph H. Brown and Dana N. Christensen (1986, p. 14)

General systems theory, control theory, and the family therapy models that evolved from them have much to offer the executive coach. They provide specific techniques and a powerful, overarching viewpoint that can be extremely useful. Corporate culture continues to attract attention, particularly as companies merge and economies evolve, especially across national boundaries. Organizational culture can best be understood using the tools of systems thinking. Corporate organizations follow the very same general rules that other interactive groups do, and the dynamics of families are usually quite relevant to work groups.

Many of the core components of family therapy are an ideal fit for executive coaching and the business environment. Coaches will find that corporate clients take to these approaches with ease and comfort, and they are likely to grasp their usefulness immediately. Since family therapy's methods approximate those of organizational development, translation of these therapy methods into business coaching is relatively easy. Some of the pioneers of family therapy even thought of themselves as family *coaches* rather than therapists. The language of family therapy must be transposed carefully, as the language of family life (for example, thinking of the chief executive officer [CEO] as a father and the chief operations officer [COO] as a mother, or referring to a client as the family's "favored son") could alienate business clients. The application of family systems interventions can be tricky at times, as the models used in psychotherapy are rather stylized, superficial representations of the engineering models. Nonetheless, they are extremely useful.

There are now many formal models or approaches to the use of family therapy including structural approaches, solution-focused methods, narrative therapy, constructivist approaches, experiential approaches, and intergenerational and collaborative therapies. One such model, strategic therapy, which is based upon complex ideas about communication and influence, will be reviewed in Chapter 10 ("Hypnotic Communication"). In addition to those, each of the traditional therapies has been adapted to family therapy, resulting in behavioral and cognitive-behavioral family therapy, psychodynamic family therapy, and others. This chapter focuses on the systems thinking that is foundational to these therapies in some small or large way. Systems thinking is a significant departure from previous linear conceptualizations of human behavior and human change, and it is important for coaches to understand the core concepts. Several useful concepts that are common to most family therapies are also described in this chapter.

Family Therapy and Business

Contrary to popular belief, family therapy systems is not about families at all, but rather about individual persons.

—Stephen J. Schultz (1984, p. 58)

There are several reasons why family or systems thinking is so relevant to business coaching. First, family therapy is built on a cybernetic view, a view that imposes the concepts of complex mechanical control processes and feedback cycles onto communications theory. This necessarily places the emphasis on context (or system) rather than on the person. It parts ways with older therapy models, which take a linear, direct, cause–effect stance. In a cybernetic view an individual's behavior is understood in the context of organizational dynamics. When a client behaves a certain way, it is understood as a function of the organizational system rather than a manifestation of some individual quality. Behavior is a response to the demands of the system. The way someone behaves may be a maneuver to influence or protect the system or a reaction to organizational stressors. This view avoids blaming the coaching client, and it is not likely that clients will confuse it with traditional psychotherapy. This makes it useful in dealing with teams of executives. For example, when a manager starts too many new projects and finishes too few, the problem is located (in the cybernetic view) in the culture of the organization, not in some personal flaw of the manager. More precisely, it is seen in the interaction between the manager and the system (the organization). This view is consistent with the view of social psychology, in that the context or situation is dominant. Second, family therapy tends to be present-moment oriented, and this is good, because practitioners are unlikely to show much interest in a client's personal psychological history. This view fits well in the corporate world. Immediate change is a reasonable goal, and many businesspeople find this goal attractive when resources are on the line. A business coach who spends much time wondering about the past or seems too interested in a client's developmental history is in danger of being labeled a "shrink." Third, family systems and organizational systems are typically quite similar. Useful interventions derived from family therapy can often be applied to a business organization as well (Darou, 1995).

And fourth, since individual behavior is seen as a function of the dynamics of the organization, the company itself is considered *fair game* for examination and intervention. This point of view opens the door for coaches to have a positive influence on the organization in a more substantial way and to sell more work.

Background and History of the Approach

The family therapy paradigm began to take shape in the late 1940s and early 1950s in the United States (Goldenberg & Goldenberg, 2007). Norbert Weiner (along with several other engineers) developed a modern version of cybernetics, the study of self-regulating systems feedback. Weiner invented the term *cybernetics*, having derived it from the Greek word *kubernetes*, meaning steersman or governor (Weiner, 1950, p. 23). Many of the concepts were left over from the development of guided missiles late in World War II and the ideas of German theoretical cell biologist Ludwig von Bertalanffy. Cybernetic systems use continuously self-regulating feedback mechanisms (or loops) to correct deviation and restore stability. This way of thinking is circular and it represents a paradigm shift from an older and more common view of linear causality. Causation in this view is circular, and systems thinking is distinctly postmodern. The British anthropologist Gregory Bateson (and others) took Weiner's ideas and applied them to human communication and interaction. He focused on the relationship between stability and change, and, gradually the focus shifted from individual to context, from content to process, and from linear causality to circular (or reciprocal) determinism. Think of the concept of a "vicious cycle." Each of us influences the behavior of others, all the time, in a back-and-forth way. Schultz (1984, p. 64) provides an excellent (if sexist) anecdote:

> For example, wife nags, husband drinks, wife nags, husband drinks, wife nags, etc. Watzlawick, et al. (1974) say that husband and wife are likely to punctuate this stream of events in two entirely different ways: (1) Husband says that he drinks because his wife nags; and (2) wife says that she nags because her husband drinks.

The questions of interest shift from *why* to *how* and from *what is wrong with this person* to *how does this person's behavior make sense in relation to its context*. The study of cybernetics led to postmodern, second-order cybernetics that added the observer to the system. In this view, any observer (or coach) cannot remain outside of the system. A coach becomes a member of the system he or she coaches. We are not able to stay outside of the context; we necessarily become a part of it as we participate. This factor can be a great help or can become a significant liability to the coach and client. Coaches are then influenced by the same factors that influence clients. This is helpful when you get a feel for how people really behave and respond, but it is a liability when you become constrained by the same organizational dynamics that influence your client. It also becomes a liability when you lose your neutral or unbiased view. When you consult for an organization for extended periods, it is nearly inevitable for you to become a member of the system or organization. This then means that the rules of the system will change to incorporate you; you are then controlled by those rules. You will behave (in part) in response to the rules of the system you are studying. Family therapy represents a paradigm shift in counseling theory.

A Review of the Basics

Here are seven important overarching concepts in family therapy that can orient a coach's work with an executive client. This is a review of some of the operating principles of systems thinking applied to the task of executive coaching.

> Family systems is a way of thinking, not a garage for repairing families. (Palazzoli, 1979, quoted in Schultz, 1984, p. 55)

Concept 1: Homeostasis (The Premise)

Groups, organizations, and their members strive to maintain homeostasis, to keep things the same. The thermostat is a classic metaphor for system homeostasis. When the temperature in a room drops below a set point, the thermostat sends feedback in the form of an electric signal to the furnace to turn on and produce heat. When the heat in the room reaches the set point, that same thermostat sends another signal for the furnace to turn off. The temperature of the room remains constant within a certain acceptable range of comfort. A second useful metaphor is the mobile, that cute collection of cardboard animals that hangs over a baby's crib. If you pull on one of the animals, all the other animals start to move around, but eventually they all find their way back to the original resting place once the pulling stops. Groups and organizations are the same way. That is why consultants and initiatives so rarely transform things. Even a "poor" homeostasis is generally preferred to frightening, uncomfortable, or disorienting change. Everyone knows a family or work unit where chaos and pathology are the norm. People complain that they are miserable, but in some strange way they are comfortable. This implies that a group will resist or even sabotage changes that an individual member might try to make, even as they praise the change effort. When forces are applied to try to make change, especially from within, the system fluctuates but makes its way back to the way it was before.

This model explains "ineffective" individual behavior as a function of group pressures. Why does a person do self-defeating or suboptimal things?

In systems thinking, they do things in service of the group homeostasis. They do what they do to keep the system the same. This idea explains why personal change can be so difficult. Even positive, well-conceived changes made by a client are likely to be met with resistance, for change is always experienced as a threat to the balance or homeostasis of the system. This quality or tendency maintains stability but inhibits change. Many corporate programs, or "management fads du jour," fail due to the force of organizational homeostasis. In systems thinking, individual behavior is understood in the context of system forces, which maintain homeostasis or sameness.

Concept 2: Change Does Not Require Understanding

This is another way that systems thinking departs radically from most other therapies. It does not focus on or require insight. You do not have to figure out how a problem came about or what it means. You just need to intervene in a way that produces lasting change. This is not to say that change is easy, just that you can skip steps designed to produce understanding. Insight is nice and people yearn for it, but all psychotherapists have experience with people who possessed deep insight but could not change.

The systems-thinking coach will focus on process more than content. The actual content of a message is of less interest than how it is communicated. The details are of less interest and less importance than the *way* that it all happens. Process is about *how* things happen, how things take place, who talks to whom, when, and in what way. Who never speaks directly to whom (as if prohibited)? What happens before and after certain other things in predictable fashion? What things happen and under what circumstances? What happens under stress when deadlines are near? What kind of behavior is normal at some meetings and unacceptable at others? The coach is interested in the interaction norms. When something happens at one level of the organization, what tends to follow at others? We are not all that interested in the question of *why* they seem to happen, as this question requires someone to speculate on motivations they probably do not understand very well. It can be embarrassing when you cannot answer this question, especially when it is about something personal and important. The question "why" may also be perceived as an indication that coaching will be emotionally intrusive. The demand for an answer to the question "why" tends to produce defensiveness and "reasons." Reasons typically do not get us anywhere, as they tend to be abstractions, intervening explanatory variables that we cannot do anything about. Reasons often lead to speculation, blaming and finger pointing, excuse making, and rationalization. Sometimes they distract us from action. Reasons are actually one of the tools that systems use to stay the same. Our concern in a systems model is focused on redundant patterns of interaction and the repeated use of the same flawed pseudosolutions.

Concept 3: Focus on the Present

A systems approach insists that the coach study the present rather than the past, since it is the relationships and dynamics of the present organizational system that control and maintain the behavior of individual members. Do not worry too much about how things got to be the way that they are, and do not go on long, wild-goose chases down the path of "how I got to be this way" or worse "if only I'd have done something differently." The answers are right here, right now, in the present system. They are right in front of you and all around you. Stay in the present moment.

Concept 4: Start Anywhere

A circular view implies that you can start anywhere and reach the same end point. Systems thinkers refer to this quality as *equifinality*. You can initiate action anywhere in a system or organization and come to the same eventual conclusions and understandings. There are many ways to "skin the corporate cat," and since all of the parts of the system serve to maintain the system, you can use multiple paths to get to the same destination. Eventually all the road signs point the same way. Often a coach is permitted limited access to parts of an organization. Start with the part that is available, since it is usually possible to get to where you want to from there.

Because of another key concept called *wholeness*, a change in one part of a system will necessarily cause changes in the other parts. Return to the metaphor of the mobile, the free-balancing little work of art that hangs over a baby's crib. It seeks and finds its own unique balance, and if you pull on any single part, all of the other parts go out of balance. When one person in an organization has trouble, it is a sign that there is something out of balance in the organization or that the organization has found a dysfunctional or undesirable balance point. For example, when one person is stressed beyond the breaking point, it usually means that something else about the system is unhealthy. Operations cannot function without effective finance. Marketing cannot operate without coordinated information technology, which cannot make it without human resources. This applies to the (more important) informal dynamics of the group as well, the unspoken forces that drive organizational culture. Sometimes market forces change, causing the old homeostasis to be outmoded and counterproductive.

Concept 5: Problem Locus

When something is wrong, family therapists examine the system, not the individual. When one person manifests "symptoms" he or she is identified as the *I.P.*, or identified patient, meaning that the family has decided to label that person's behavior (which is a function of system pathology or homeostasis) as causative and problematic. This shifts the blame and has the effect of permitting the organization to stay the same. As long as the family can blame one person, nothing changes in the system. A systems-oriented approach would lead the coach to examine the system when an "identified client" is having individual difficulties. Human behavior can only be properly understood in its social context (the empirical evidence from social psychology to support this statement is described in Chapter 9). An individual only changes when the system changes, and the system only changes when individuals change. They are interrelated, not independent.

Concept 6: Attempted Solutions Can Become Problems

Paul Watzlawick and others (including Jay Haley and Milton Erickson) describe the idea that attempted solutions can become problems in an intriguing body of work about paradox, communication, and game theory (Haley, 1991, 1993; Watzlawick, Weakland, & Fisch, 1974). Their ideas are complex and extremely interesting, but difficult to put into practice sometimes. The central idea is that our scratching causes the itching to get worse; worrying about a problem inhibits our ability to actually take action to solve that problem. For example, telling children to be careful can cause them to become fearful people, and, conversely, holding children too close to protect them can produce a wild or rebellious child who takes too much risk.

Concept 7: Feedback, First-Order Change, and Second-Order Change

Regulation of a self-correcting system is accomplished with *feedback*, which contains information about the relationship between internal events and the external environment of the system. When the temperature of the room drops below a certain set point, information is fed back to the heater switch so that it will turn on and warm the room. There are two kinds of feedback, and systems theory uses terms differently than behavior therapy. In systems thinking, feedback that keeps things the same is called "deviation-reducing" or negative feedback. Feedback that amplifies deviation is called positive feedback. Schultz again provides a useful example (1984, p. 63):

> If I shout at you (action) and you become quiet and give in to [me] or placate me and I then quiet down (less of my original action), deviation-reducing feedback has restored our system to its original tranquil state. … In deviation-amplifying feedback, on the other hand, the reaction to the original action results in more of that original action. For example, if I hit you (action) and you hit me back (reaction) and I hit you again, harder (more action), deviation-amplifying feedback is occurring.

System change occurs in two categories, first and second order. This is an important distinction for the coach and the client, not to be confused with second-order cybernetics, which has to do with the way the coach becomes a part of the system.

First-order change occurs when an individual member of a group makes a change in behavior from inside of the system that does not influence the way that others in the system function. It is often a form of individual compromise within the current rules of a system and the change tends to be impermanent (because of system forces toward reregulation). System protection of current homeostasis tends to force first-order change back to its original state. It is generally assumed that a system cannot change its own rules (from within). The term *rules* here does not mean the formal rules. It refers to the actual de facto or *real* ways that things happen and the underlying premises of the organization, which are often covert. Second-order change typically comes from outside of the system and has a transformative effect on that system. It is change of another order. The rules themselves change or the structure of the system changes. Watzlawick et al. (1974, p. 10) use the example of a nightmare. When you try to solve the problems of a dream while experiencing the dream (from within the dream), you are unlikely to succeed. But when the alarm clock wakes you (second-order change), everything about that particular dream experience changes radically and permanently.

Figure 7.1 is a drawing that illustrates these two types of feedback. It was originally drawn during a Stewart Brand interview of Margaret Mead and Gregory Bateson in 1973.

Second-order change is initiated from outside of the system, and the organization cannot accommodate the feedback, so it must, therefore, make an adjustment in its structure. Outsiders (such as consultants and coaches) can say and do things that insiders cannot. When an outsider provides feedback that has the effect of changing the rules, the organization is transformed. It is possible that the significant change in the behavior of one key inside person can precipitate a second-order change in the organization, but this is unlikely

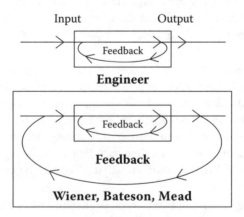

Figure 7.1 Mark Côté. (Redrawn from CoEvolution Quarterly and Cybernetics Society Conference brochure, *CoEvolutionary Quarterly* (Issue no. 10, pp. 32–44, June 1976.)

to happen, and organizational discomfort and resistance usually accompany it, resulting in only temporary or superficial change. Second-order change requires a *paradigm shift* or a change in the basic rules or structure. Think of it this way: If you pull on one of the pieces of a mobile, the pieces all move. Gradually they settle back into their original places. This is an example of first-order change. If you snip off one of the pieces, however, everything changes, and the pieces must find a new way to hang together. This represents a new homeostasis and a second-order change.

Coaches must expect that if clients make a first-order change, that change is likely to be uncomfortable and temporary. Second-order change is the challenge, and coaches can be the alarm clock that alters the dream (or nightmare).

Useful Ideas for Coaching Intervention

Once a coach and client grasp the aforementioned seven concepts, several specific system attributes and ideas can be used to coach effectively.

Systems and Subsystems

Systems consist of subsystems. Families have parental subsystems, sibling subsystems, and male and female subsystems, with boundaries between them. Parents do not drink with or speak about parental sexual matters with their young children. Children do not reveal their sibling's secrets to their parents. Male family members talk about different topics and use a male vocabulary when female members of the family are not around. Every large group (for example, a company or organization) is made up of many smaller groups; each is organized in some way for some purpose, with its own set of rules and norms. The boundaries that exist between subsystems can be rigid, flexible, or permeable. These boundaries dictate when and how members participate and communicate. Subgroups must be acknowledged and boundaries respected. Although all organizations create a formal mechanism for transmission of information, the most important messages often move along informal channels. This is actually true of formal business arrangements as well. In fact, the modern view of marketing as the central hub of a business organization depends upon the effective integration of numerous subsystems (e.g., sales, information technology [IT], customer service, and engineering).

Rules and Norms

Members or participants in each system or subsystem are expected to behave in certain ways. Sometimes it takes an outsider to notice the rules and norms, as they are nearly invisible to insiders. They are crucial, though, and are often considered part of office politics. Some are tantamount to commandments (to be violated at great cost or risk), whereas others can be ignored under certain circumstances or by certain people. Notice which rules are overt and which are unspoken. Who can break which rules? Which norms violate a formal organizational creed? Who sets standards, and why? Organizations are often influenced by powerful personalities who are not formally empowered in the organization. For example, when you look carefully at most organizations, there are a few people who possess much more institutional power than their title would indicate. Everyone seems to understand these people's power and more or less accept it. It is an unwritten rule. Who are these people and what is the source or basis of their power? Coaches must tune into these things.

Myths and Mystification

Companies, like families, collect essential images and stories that serve to define and protect the group during times of stress or uncertainty. These myths are often nearly sacred, and they are rarely challenged, as most members of the group take comfort in them. Many organizations, strong or weak, have stories to tell about their founder or leader. These stories can be very instructive. They can also hold us captive, especially when the realities that created them no longer prevail. The stories of the De Pree family of CEOs at Herman Miller, Inc. (the Zeeland, Michigan, furniture company) provide a great example of the power of myths and stories, and they are detailed in Max De Pree's 1989 book *Leadership Is an Art*. The cult of Jack Welch and developments after he left GE provide another interesting example.

Roles

The systems coach is interested in roles that people take on in organizations. A role is a set of consistent expectations about behavior and reaction. What roles do various people play? What would happen if they stopped playing them? How do these roles serve to keep things the same (the homeostasis function)? After a while, people expect others to continue to behave in the way they always have, and they become uncomfortable when people do not behave consistent with their usual role in the organization. Is it dangerous to behave out of role? A person who holds onto a formal role in the organization can define that role by the way that he or she behaves, but it can be difficult for a new person to take over the same role. For example, tasks are usually not evenly distributed in logical alignment with the company's organizational chart. People have taken on roles over the years that have nothing to do with their position in the formal structure.

Family Roles

It can also be useful to examine the "family" roles that adults seem to take on in the workplace. These familiar roles include: star, blamer, hero, rebel, martyr, scapegoat, distracter, cheerleader, jester, invalid, placater, favored son, mascot, saint, and skeptic (Blevins, 1993). Every family has some, and most people can quickly recall which role or roles they served in their family of origin.

The following are brief descriptions of the roles people take in organizations. Roles are taken on to accomplish something in response to the organizational structure and interpersonal system. Homeostasis applies. When the system changes, people occupying these roles resist the change, unless or until sufficiently powerful forces or second-order changes occur. Their role behavior generally serves to maintain homeostasis, nonetheless.

Star—This person is accorded star status in the organization. He or she is treated as special, and he or she generally performs at a very high level. Inadequacies are minimized and mistakes are ignored. The star's future is assumed to be quite bright. Others may respect or resent this person.

Blamer—This person always seeks to blame someone for everything that goes poorly. When things do not come out the way the organization wants, someone must be to blame. This person reliably points this out.

Hero—This person's job is to "save the day." Whenever the organization is in a tight spot, he or she gets involved and makes things work out. The hero makes the big sale or gets the team through an accreditation or inspection. Others come to rely on them to do so, but they may resent the hero nonetheless.

Rebel—These people do not quite fit in. They are highly autonomous, and they usually do not follow the rules. They dress differently, think differently, and behave differently, and they get away with it, for the most part. Top management finds them annoying, but rebels are often good at what they do or good at one difficult task.

Martyr—This person endures constant suffering on behalf of the organization or its members, typically to get and keep a certain kind of attention.

Scapegoat—This person bears and accepts the blame for the team when things go poorly.

Distracter—This person does things that shift attention away from the team's most challenging or frightening problems. He or she finds other things to which the team should attend.

Cheerleader—This person stays on the sidelines most of the time and encourages others to take action. He or she does not take risks or get directly involved in anything difficult.

Jester—This person creates humor compulsively. Jokes and laughs distract the team from difficulties and problems. This can be delightful and it can be annoying.

Invalid—This person is often sick or damaged or impaired in some way, so that he or she cannot always take on or complete difficult assignments. Additional stress is just too much for the invalid. This behavior would not be tolerated by the organization in others.

Placater—This person can be counted on to appease people when things get difficult. He never confronts things. He always backs down and makes things OK.

Oldest/Favored Son—This person is given special treatment and has extra responsibility. He or she often serves as a trusted go-between for leadership and other layers of an organization. He or she gets subtle benefits and opportunities that others do not get, but is expected to take some responsibility for the behavior of the "younger siblings."

Mascot—This person is kept around for good luck. Mascots are treated as if they were cute and somehow good for the team, but they are not actually expected to contribute much of substance.

Saint or Angel—These people never think, say, or do anything wrong. They are above it all, and they behave virtuously, even when such behavior is not completely appropriate or realistic. They act as if they are better than others. People treat them this way.

Skeptic—This person can be relied upon to cast doubt, especially when optimists or creative people come up with new ideas for the team. The skeptic will throw cold water on new ideas every time. They actively keep the organization from taking risk or making changes.

The coach must remember: The person is not the role. This is true of current formal organizational roles as well as remnant family roles that still hold sway. These roles cause problems because of inflexibility and also because the role-related behavior of one person places extra demands on others. Fixed role expectations, inflexible rules that are not discussible, rigid hierarchies, and well-established coalitions need to be examined and flexed if individual behavior is going to change. Individual behavior is seen as a reaction to these role problems within the organizational system. Table 7.1 is a blank chart for use by coaches and clients to track and figure out which members of the organization fulfill various familial roles.

There is also role strain, role overload, and role conflict with which to contend (Carlson, Sperry, & Lewis, 1997). All three of these problems are prevalent in the corporate world and are likely to become more widespread as corporate work life evolves and speeds up. Workers are increasingly expected to serve in multiple roles in a downsized, superefficient, and nimble organization. Role overload happens when one person is simply assigned too many

Table 7.1 Role Tracking Chart

Role Behavior	Member						
	Jones	Lee	Sanchez	Nguyen	Singh	Shahnaz	Cabanag
Star							
Blamer							
Hero							
Rebel							
Martyr							
Scapegoat							
Distracter							
Cheerleader							
Jester							
Invalid							
Placater							
Favored Son							
Oldest Son							
Mascot							
Saint							
Skeptic							
(Add Your Own)							

different and demanding roles in an organization. Role strain occurs when the expectations of many different roles pull a person in several directions at once, especially when "team play" is expected. This often happens to people who are hard working, reliable, and unwilling to say "no" to new requests. Role conflict occurs when assigned roles are intrinsically incompatible. Appropriate but inexpressible hostility is likely to result, and people behave in all sorts of strange ways under those conditions.

Pseudomutuality

Families often act nice, make nice, and behave politely, even though members are in a state of grave conflict or cannot actually stand one another. Rather than acknowledge conflict, dissatisfaction, or problems, sometimes families (and organizations) present themselves as "perfect" to outsiders. This may be due to a family rule, spoken or unspoken, that members do not air their dirty laundry. An acknowledgment of difference is perceived as a threat to the integrity of the (fragile) system. Many companies are like this. It is considered bad form to say negative things about the organization or culture, especially to outsiders. This pseudopositive pretense allows things to stay the same and members to avoid embarrassment or open conflict. It is another way that the system maintains homeostasis.

Be wary when people only speak in glowing terms about an organization. This is a normal thing to do with outsiders at first, but if the behavior persists and seems odd or artificial or implausible, be wary. A coach is sometimes allowed to say things that could never be spoken by employees or team members. When the coach speaks to them, they can then be heard and acknowledged, and no insider has to take the blame for pointing out that which is obvious but troubling. Be careful, though.

Triangulation

Triangulation occurs when coalitions evolve outside of the formal hierarchy or role structure (Kerr & Bowen, 1988; Segal, 1997). In families, for example, a mother and a son may form an alliance that excludes the husband-father. Information flows (or is kept secret) based upon the coalition. Some people are accustomed to triangulation and can become exceptionally skilled at establishing these unhealthy alliances. They are typically used to manipulate power and information in an unbalanced system, and they can be treacherous. Triangles can be used to exclude someone or gang up on them. Triangles encourage secrets and discourage open communication. They sabotage trust. Sometimes it is the coach's job to tactfully call attention to these triangles and to obvious but unspoken arrangements. That said, coaching, nearly always creates a triangular relationship that must be skillfully managed. Figure 7.2 is the triangle that is formed by the coach, the client, and the sponsoring organization.

Each of the three pairs (coach–client, coach–sponsoring organization, and client–sponsoring organization) can and do form temporary or permanent

Figure 7.2 Natural triangulation in coaching.

coalitions. Information is shared within these coalitions, and the third party is excluded or even talked about. Triangular interactions are normal, but it is easy for them to become toxic and counterproductive. Coaches and clients can agree that the employer is a jerk; coaches and employers can agree that the client is a loser; and clients and employers can bad-mouth the coach. These alignments can undermine the coaching, the client, the coach, and the organization. If there is a "solution" to the problems created by triangulation, it is in clear, up-front contracting about possible future triangulation along with commitments from all three parties to avoid triangulating or to choose a path of openness and integrity. Coaches must be especially watchful and cautious about such situations, and they are often the first to notice and acknowledge them. For an in-depth discussion of this issue with examples from business coaching settings, see Sherman and Freas (2004, pp. 85–88).

Rites and Rituals

There are customary ways that things are done in families and in groups. Some things are always done at certain points in time or in response to other things. These customary ways can ossify and become rituals, unspoken and sacrosanct, to be violated at great risk. They make up a substantial part of the group culture. A simple example is the way that people predictably sit at meetings. In many organizations, people sit in the same seats, meeting after meeting, week after week. No one can say why people sit in the same spots, but it would make everyone uncomfortable if someone sat in the "wrong" seat.

Directives

This is a kind of family therapy intervention. The therapist issues a direct prescription for change and carefully observes the impact. If a client makes the change, all the better. If the client or the system resists, a learning opportunity emerges. This event sheds light on the relationship between the behavior in question and its functional meaning within the system. Ordeals are a subset of directives, and they ask that the client perform something quite difficult as a way to learn about the current problem. The ordeal is usually designed to make the original problem behavior seem small in comparison or to point out that there is little reason to continue the behavior. For example, a coach could ask a client to sit in a different seat at a staff meeting or ask a client to disagree with someone they had never disagreed with before. A fuller explanation along with intriguing examples of directives and ordeals can be found in Jay Haley's book about Milton Erickson titled *Uncommon Therapy* (1993).

Family Life Cycle

Various family systems theoreticians have observed that the structure and behavior of families evolve in developmental cycles, and the management literature includes a similar view of businesses. Behavior that suits a company at one stage can be counterproductive at other stages in the company's life cycle. Employees are expected to behave quite differently when they are at a young, start-up firm than they would behave at an older, well-established, family-owned company or a huge corporation. Clients must occasionally take a hard look at how well they fit the current organizational cycle and then adapt, move, or leave.

Applications

The family therapy model requires us to abandon linear thinking. It is foolish, in this viewpoint, to try to understand the behavior of a person in isolation from the system in which he or she functions. It is counterproductive to attempt to use personal history to understand someone's current behavior. People are best understood in terms of the roles they play in their organization and in the way that things stay the same. The unit of study is the team, the work group, or the entire organization, even though we are obstensibly interested in the behavior of one person. We constantly influence one another, and we are constantly influenced. All of us play roles in the group homeostasis. Although people are often unaware of the role they play, sometimes they are vaguely aware, and occasionally they have a clear understanding of their role and its function. It never hurts to entertain a discussion about roles and the way that these roles function on a team.

This way of viewing things creates limitations as well as opportunities for the executive coach. On the one hand, the entire organization opens up as subject matter. On the other hand, if the coach does not have permission to interact or intervene at a group level, it is possible to feel stuck or helpless within a sick or troubled organization. Interaction with others in the organization runs the risk of violating (or appearing to violate) a client's confidences. Others in the company may wonder about the appropriateness of a coach's interest in a larger group intervention, and they may even feel threatened.

With those caveats in mind, here are seven ways to use family system concepts and thinking in executive coaching. These options must be customized to fit the client organization. More than one option can be used at a time.

Option 1: Teach the Systems Point of View to Your Client

Introduce key concepts as a way to evaluate and understand what is happening. Decide how much of a family vocabulary to use. Some clients will welcome or even introduce the language of families, including terms like parents (dads or moms), kids, older siblings, family arguments, family business, and parental subsystems. Some companies already talk about a "divorce" (divestiture) or about "expecting Dad to solve the problem" (waiting for the CEO to fix everything). Others may find such a vocabulary to be odd. When this happens, simply use a *systems* point of view (homeostasis, cybernetics) that makes little reference to families, per se. You could even change to an engineering vocabulary to explain systems tools if you know that language. Once the systems model is on the table, many options become available.

Option 2: Observe Important Process Variables within Your Client's Organization, or Better Yet, Teach Your Client to Do So

Start with the behavior of team members at meetings. This is the easiest venue for process observation. Table 7.2 is a checklist that can be used to study meeting behavior in an organization. List those present at the meeting across the top of the page and simply tabulate the number of times each person does the things listed in the left-hand column.

Once you or your client have collected these data, analyze them for patterns and meanings. This will not be difficult, as your client will probably have clear ideas about the implications. You can then decide what to do with this new and valuable insight, plus, you have alerted your client to the importance of process variables and how they function (they are often much more powerful than the content or topic of a meeting, and process events and patterns usually go unmentioned). Once clients get into the habit, they can learn to observe process patterns without the help of the chart. The essential idea here is that process explains a lot, often more than what people actually say.

Option 3: If a Client Is Interested and Willing, Explore His or Her Family-of-Origin Experiences

Most of us currently use behavior that was forged in our families; we act out roles, we handle conflict, and we view ourselves in ways that have roots in that era of our development. Most people can derive useful insight from such an examination. The danger in this option is that it may remind a client too much of the worst aspects of psychotherapy, implying that he or she is "damaged" or in need of therapeutic assistance or cannot do anything now about the way that they have been formed in the past. Remember: Insight does not equal change in this model.

Option 4: Help Your Client Examine His or Her Current Organization as If It Were a Family

The family metaphor may help clients understand how their behavior fits in, how they are accepted and treated, and how they can adjust in order to become more effective. In the systems view, your client's behavior makes sense in relation to what it accomplishes or how it reacts to the organizational system. Assess the availability of components of the system, meaning: Figure out how willing others are to participate in the coaching of your client. Is the larger organization willing to participate? Would the organization consider changes if that is what it would take to improve your client's situation? How much can you push these collaborators and how much can you expect from them? Is the rest of the organization off-limits?

Table 7.2 Process Observation Checklist

Behavior to Be Noted	People at the Meeting				
	Jones	Lee	Sanchez	Nguyen	Singh
Silent					
Introduces topics					
Clarifies					
Draws others in (solicits)					
Arrives late					
Interrupts					
Asks questions					
Appears disinterested					
Keeps group on task					
Takes group away from task					
Expresses feelings					
Disagrees					
Leaves the room					
Agrees, supports					
Summarizes					
Suggests					
Proposes options					
Tests for consensus					
Pleads for special interest					
Speaks to one person					
Elephant-in-the-room comment[a]					
Engages in side conversations					

[a] Refers to a remark about something that is glaringly obvious to most members of the group, but is previously unmentioned (because it seems dangerous or embarrassing or too difficult to tackle).

Help your client understand the roles that he or she is expected to assume. Most executives have never undertaken such an inventory. Examine how they feel about the expectations and duties associated with those roles (formal and informal), as well as how they are expected to behave in them. (Are they expected to act like they love the role? Are they expected to behave as if they are burdened, but do it for the good of the group?)

Each family has characteristic communication patterns, and one must understand those patterns to communicate effectively. Interacting against the flow is liable to be met with resistance and confusion. Each work group has its norms, and they must, at the very least, be acknowledged, if not respected. Some families are perfectionistic, some use humor in healthy and unhealthy ways, some have an angry flavor, and family members typically play expected roles. The contributions of some members are more valued than that of others. Some are permitted to speak in certain situations and others are not. Families treat outsiders in characteristic ways, and a coach might expect different treatment by different work groups. Some families wall themselves off from the rest of the world so that they can operate without criticism or resistance, and most families have "unspoken issues" that are essentially off limits for discussion. Success and failure are treated differently in various families, and mistakes are handled quite differently in varying companies and industries. Consider the way that mistakes are treated in the medical community compared to the way they are handled in airlines. In the airline industry, mistakes are routinely examined in the open with the assumption that everyone makes mistakes and the expectation that such an examination will prevent future error. In the hospital culture, error is still denied, hidden, and rarely discussed in the open. Doctors are assumed and expected to be perfect (Leape, 1994) and few are allowed to speak openly, directly, or critically to them. In this way, the system prevents doctors from getting the information they need to head off future mistakes.

Families are usually composed of subgroups, and information is not uniformly shared across these groups. Power or control of various group functions is unevenly assigned to one subgroup or another, and people become uncomfortable when members cross boundaries or step out of roles. Alliances and triangles are formed and maintained between various members for various purposes and at differing times.

Option 5: Give Directives

Ask your client to do something different. If organizations function as systems, any disruption of current patterns of behavior should be instructive. Using the equifinality principle, we should be able to start anywhere in the system to make a change, assuming that the rest of the system will resist the change or change itself to accommodate the new pattern. If your client never attends a particular weekly meeting, for example, instruct him or her to do so. Watch to see if he or she complies or resists or sabotages, and help your client observe the larger system or work group. If your client does not complete the directive, work together to figure out how it happened that the directive was not carried out. What emotions accompanied the situation? What did your client actually do? What images or expectations does your client have about what might happen? What needs to change in order for him or her to complete the directive? If your client carries out the directive, examine the system. Look for system resistance or disapproval and learn from it. New or novel behavior is always instructive in the context of a system.

Option 6: Provide Direct Skills Training

In family therapy, specific communications techniques are often taught to one member or all members of the family. Teach your client specific skills such as active listening, assertion, and public speaking. Video feedback is often a powerful intervention when visual information will help.

Option 7: Explore Solution-Focused Methods

Berg and de Shazer and others have developed a series of simple techniques to help clients learn about the forces that keep them the same (Pichot & Dolan, 2003). They are:

The Miracle Question—Ask your client what would happen if, one night while sleeping, a miracle happened and he or she is now significantly more productive and effective. What changes would that bring? What would it be like? What would it feel like? Who would notice; who would care? How would your client have to behave in the future? What would he or she do? What difference would it make?

Exceptions Question—"Tell me about the times or situations when this current problem does not happen. When is it not a problem? Under what circumstances are you able to function differently?"

The Magic Wand—"If I (the coach) had a magic wand and could change anything about you, what would you like me to change, and why? If I could cast a spell on you or anyone you'd like, what would that spell be?"

Trait Shopping—"Imagine that you find a store that sells personal traits … any trait that can be found. Which one would you want to buy, and why? What would happen after you had this trait?

Option 8: If You Have Permission, Take Action (or Help Your Client to Take Action) on the System Itself

Facilitate second-order change. This is likely to involve discussions with key players in the organizational structure, and requires that they see such discussions as being in the organization's best interest. You or your client can make the following presentation: "We have discovered, as part of the coaching, that our group could benefit from a discussion of how we interact. We would like you to take a look at this with us." Ask others the questions: "What would happen if Joe Client did this or that? What would change? What would you do?" Remember that each group has characteristic ways that it handles "outsiders," and that once you begin to operate within a group you, as coach, lose your outsider status and become a part of the system itself. Remind all parties that change is usually uncomfortable and is predictably met with resistance. Think also about keeping a healthy distance from the system.

Strengths

Family and system approaches are different enough from traditional and stereotyped ways of doing psychotherapy to make them compatible and acceptable to business clients. Most companies are leery about turning a psychotherapist loose in the boardroom. Coaches with a systems point of view behave and think much like a traditional organizational development consultant. They are concerned with the organization—its structure, behavior, effectiveness, and health—particularly as it pertains to the their individual client. Family therapists give directives, and most business clients welcome that from a consultant. Some even figure that if they are getting directives, they are getting their money's worth. Active listening, restatement, and reflection as well as accurate empathy (in spite of their undeniable value) are occasionally viewed with skepticism in the corporate consulting arena.

At the same time, focusing on the organization has the advantage of deflecting blame from the coaching client. As mentioned earlier, coaches must take care to avoid becoming limited to the role of "doctor" who fixes losers or broken employees. When that happens, no one wants to work with you. You become the proverbial *Angel of Death* or last resort before an executive goes out the door. This is why it may be important to avoid becoming the company "shrink."

Occasionally, a systems view can precipitate a shift in the definition of who the client actually is. Instead of an individual client, the organization may choose to view the organization as the "client," causing the coach to shift role and focus. Similarly, one part of the organization could be defined as the client of interest.

A second advantage is that systems approaches can lead to enhanced client understanding of the organizational and political environment, and although this is always a plus, it is of particular value with two types of clients: those who are politically naïve or inept and those who do not value political shrewdness. It is virtually impossible to succeed in a modern organization without attention to the internal political environment.

A third advantage is that a systems approach often opens the door to the rest of the organization, where a coach can make a more significant and lasting difference and, for what it is worth, create more business for himself or herself in the future.

Weaknesses

First, systems approaches can be complex, depending upon which variation you choose. Some of the available interventions are sometimes too complicated to grasp and put into action. It is possible to make a mess if a complex system manipulation goes awry. Some of the family interventions described in textbooks seem to have been invented on the fly and are appropriate only for the old master who invented them. Some systems therapists like to seem mysterious or impenetrable. This presentation may work, but it might also backfire, depending upon the coach's personality and the expectations and egos of clients.

Second, this approach can leave clients in a powerless position if they decide that they are part of a dysfunctional work system that is unlikely to change. This might cause a client to consider leaving the organization (which may or may not be a good idea, both from the point of view of the client and company), or might cause him or her to simply feel bad. Even so, it is always better (for clients as well as coaches) to possess an accurate understanding of the organizational situation and a clear-eyed view of what they are facing.

Third, your client or the organization may not care for the family metaphor. It can be a turnoff in the corporate world, and the way that the model and methods are presented is crucial. If you are going to use this approach, it will be important to find a way to present it so that it will be embraced. A trusted consultant, particularly one who has delivered valued results in the past, can present almost anything and find a responsive audience. A new coach must be somewhat more careful and conventional at first.

Summary

The systems viewpoint is extremely powerful, and the ideas presented in this chapter are likely to be familiar to the organizational consultant. They can be implemented in two ways. First, clients can learn about the family systems model and its key concepts and can apply these to his or her own situation, on the assumption that such an understanding will enable them to make changes in their own approach to things. Second, clients can take these concepts and target second-order change by behaving differently, by overtly requesting system change, or by changing the rules. Discomfort and resistance are to be expected as the organization strives to maintain homeostasis and remain the same. But, like a mobile that becomes weighted differently, a new organizational homeostasis is just around the corner, and the changes are usually worth it.

1. Organizations can usefully be understood from a systems point of view. This means that the principles of family systems therapy can be fruitfully applied to executive coaching. Such principles are likely to be welcomed in most business organizations (depending upon how they are packaged).

2. Individual parts of a system (clients) can only be understood in the context of the organization (the larger system). Behavior is controlled by the system, and behavior changes the system. Circularity replaces

linear thinking in this view. Interventions can focus on the client or on the organization with the same end result.

3. Systems (and organizations) tend toward equilibrium. When pressure is brought on them to change, they respond with feedback mechanisms to put things back into balance. Change is thereby resisted. This is normal.

4. Clients and others often take on roles about which they are only vaguely aware. It is often helpful to discuss and clarify role-related behavior and its meaning and function in the organizational system. Make the covert overt.

5. Coaches, clients, and the sponsoring organization or manager become a communications triangle. This opens the door to tricky interaction possibilities that must be managed carefully.

6. Clients can learn to use process observation and systems principles to understand the organization and to make changes in their behavior to productively influence the larger organizational system.

References

Blevins, W. (1993). *Your family your self.* Oakland, CA: New Harbinger Publications.

Brown, J. H., & Christensen, D. N. (2007). *Family therapy: Theory and practice* (2nd ed.). Monterey, CA: Brooks/Cole.

Carlson, J., Sperry, L., & Lewis, J. (1997). *Family therapy: Ensuring treatment efficacy.* Pacific Grove, CA: Brooks/Cole.

Darou, W. G. (1995). Family systems and organizations. In J. W. Pfeiffer (Ed.), *The 1995 annual: Volume 2, consulting* (pp. 221–234). San Diego: Pfeiffer & Company.

De Pree, M. (1989). *Leadership is an art.* New York: Dell.

De Shazer, S. (1991). *Putting difference to work.* New York: Norton.

Goldenberg, I., & Goldenberg, H. (2007). *Family therapy: An overview* (7th ed.). Monterey, CA: Brooks/Cole.

Haley, J. (1991). *Problem-solving therapy.* San Francisco: Jossey-Bass.

Haley, J. (1993). *Uncommon therapy: The psychiatric techniques of Milton H. Erickson.* New York: Norton & Company.

Kerr, M., & Bowen, M. (1988). *Family evaluation: An approach based on Bowen theory.* New York: Norton.

Leape, L. (1994). Error in medicine. *JAMA, 272*(23), 1851–1857.

Pichot, T. & Dolan, Y. M. (2003). *Solution-focused brief therapy.* Binghamton, NY: Haworth Press.

Schultz, S. J. (1984). *Family systems therapy: An integration.* New York: Jason Aronson.

Segal, M. (1997). *Points of influence: A guide to using personality theory at work.* San Francisco: Jossey-Bass.

Sherman, S., & Freas, A. (2004). The wild west of executive coaching. *Harvard Business Review, 82*(11), 82–90.

Weiner, N. (1950). *The human use of human beings.* New York: Avon Books.

Watzlawick, P., Weakland, J., & Fisch, R. (1974). *Change: Principles of problem formation and problem resolution.* New York: Norton.

Recommended Readings

Bateson, G. (1999). *Steps to an ecology of mind: Collected essays in anthropology, psychiatry, evolution, and epistemology*. Chicago: University of Chicago Press. (Original work published 1972.)

Cavanagh, M. (2006). Coaching from a systemic perspective: A complex adaptive conversation. In D. R. Stober & A. M. Grant (Eds.), *Evidence based coaching handbook* (pp. 313–354). Hoboken, NJ: John Wiley & Sons.

Davis, K. (1996). *Families: A handbook of concepts and techniques for the helping professional*. Pacific Grove, CA: Brooks/Cole.

Gladding, S. T. (2007). *Family therapy: History, theory, and practice* (4th ed.). Upper Saddle River, NJ: Pearson.

Green, J. B. (2003). *Introduction to family theory and therapy*. Belmont, CA: Brooks/Cole.

Hanna, S. M., & Brown, J. H. (2004). *The practice of family therapy* (3rd ed.). Belmont, CA: Brooks/Cole.

Hoffman, L. (1981). *Foundations of family therapy: A conceptual framework for systems change*. New York: Basic Books.

Luft, J. (1970). *Group processes: An introduction to group dynamics*. (2nd ed.). Palo Alto, CA: National Press Books.

Sherman, R., & Fredman, N. (1986). *Handbook of structured techniques in marriage and family therapy*. New York: Brunner/Mazel.

Watzlawick, P. (1988). *Ultra-solutions or how to fail most successfully*. New York: W.W. Norton & Company.

8
The Existential Stance

Existence precedes essence.

—Jean-Paul Sartre (1965, p. 35)

Existential philosophy offers a great deal to the coach who can effectively pick and choose among the many views subsumed under the title of existentialism. This is no easy task, as the existential literature is varied and often complex, meaning different things to different people. The parable of the blind men comes to mind, as they describe an elephant differently based upon whether they felt the trunk or the ear or the tail or the tusk. More often than not, existential ideas are presented in a fictional form, and authors are unwilling to interpret them for readers. Those who subsequently explain their fiction typically do so in language nearly impossible to decipher. Many of the most influential existential thinkers refused to even embrace the label *existential*, as there is very little agreement among them and they tended to be independent in the extreme. Most wrote in revolt or rejection of the ideas of those who preceded them. Whereas classical philosophers advocate reason, existentialists call for passion. One can find numerous books and essays with titles such as "What Is Existentialism?" but one would be hard-pressed to come up with a single tome that adequately captures and digests it all. Existentialism is less an -ism than a way of approaching things, a stance or a "posture." In spite of the fact that existentialism does not lend itself to easy application, existential philosophy has had a powerful impact on psychotherapy theory and practice, and it has enormously useful potential for the executive coach.

The coach's first challenge is to figure out what existentialism is and just what it recommends. This can be a daunting task. The second step is to choose a discrete number of views or principles and decide how to apply them to the workplace. These two tasks are the goals of this chapter. Such an endeavor necessarily requires (useful) oversimplification.

History and Background

It is fair to say that threads of existential thought run from Socrates through the Bible and on into modern culture. The cubicle philosophies of *Dilbert* were surely informed by Franz Kafka, and the motion picture *Groundhog Day* is an illustration of Friedrich Nietzsche's *eternal recurrence*, a test to determine whether any given day is being "lived" properly. (The test: How would you feel if you were to relive this day over and over again?) Prominent existentialists have been a varied lot, and most of them could have been called "characters." Some were Christians, some were atheists, some were Jews, and one or two were Nazis. Most philosophical historians trace the identifiable origins of existentialism to the German philosopher Georg Wilhelm Friedrich Hegel, who lived from 1770 until 1831. Among other things, Hegel wrote about the human spirit and asserted that it is the history of our spirit (as expressed in custom, law, and art) that defines us (Barrett, 1964). Subsequent existential thinkers rebelled against this idea, focusing instead on the view that "existence precedes essence," meaning that each human has no fixed essence, except as it is shown through moment-to-moment behavior, which can always change. Our personality (an example of essence) does not define us; personality is simply a label, and a rather global one at that. Our *choices* define us after we make them, and then we are free to make new ones in the next moment. We choose ourselves. Our essence (or reputation) is defined by our existence (our moment-to-moment choices), not the other way around. Your reputation does not determine your behavior. Your behavior, as manifested by your choices, defines your reputation, and that can change, based upon new choices. Most existentialists steadfastly resist labeling people. Labels are for *things* (like a vase, which has permanent and consistent qualities).

People exist only in the present and can make new choices each day, and people exist in social contexts and roles. A teacher is only a teacher in the presence of students. In a casino, that same person becomes a gambler.

Existentialism raises issues most of us would prefer to ignore. Existentialists tend to be preoccupied with themes of death, anxiety, dread, failure, and the absurd. A brief story (circa 1840) from Søren Kierkegaard (1813–1855) is illustrative. It is about how he became a philosopher while watching his cigar smoke disappear into the air of a Danish café. His friends had all chosen careers and were busy with their work, but he had not.

> It occurred to him then that since everyone was engaged everywhere in making things easy, perhaps someone was needed to make things hard again, and that this too might be a career and a destiny—to go in search of difficulties, like a new Socrates. (Barrett, 1964, p. 21)

Kierkegaard realized that he did not have to look far for these difficulties, as they were right there in front of him in his own life, in his own concrete existence. He was aware of his own pain and choices and anxieties, and to focus on these aspects of his existence would require a rejection of Hegel and spirit. He resolved "to create difficulties everywhere." So, off he went. In the end, he was famous for his epitaph: "That individual" (Kaufmann, 1956).

At about the same time (1844–1849) Fyodor Dostoevsky wrote 10 novels and many short stories before he was thrown into a Russian prison. He wrote of the tragic side of life (a life that he knew all too well), the less attractive qualities of humans (depravity), and the central importance of individual choice and freedom in human existence (Dostoevsky, 1992).

Kierkegaard's work was eventually translated into German, and Karl Theodor Jaspers (1883–1969) and Martin Heidegger (1889–1976) built upon it in the period following World War I. Friedrich Wilhelm Nietzsche was born in Germany in 1844, wrote until the late 1800s, and died in 1900. His work was profoundly influential in his time, is still controversial, and is largely misunderstood. Some of Nietzsche's ideas can be offensive and objectionable. Of importance to this chapter, however, is his emphasis on independent morality, on making the most of who you are, and of excellence over mediocrity. It was his view that humans have a moral obligation to become "excellent" rather than give in to the inclination to inertia and the herd mentality. Nietzsche exhorts us to get up off the couch, get going, and to take life seriously (Solomon, 1995). He tells us to stop preparing for life and start living it, even to live dangerously (Kaufmann, 1956). He also described something he called "the will to power" (Nietzsche, 1968), advocating that each of us do what it takes to have a major say in our own lives, and that we develop, nurture, and use our willpower (King & Citrenbaum, 1993).

German work was translated into French in the 1930s and was met with great enthusiasm by French intellectuals who were turned off by bourgeois culture, and were facing Nazi occupation and another absurd world war. Jean-Paul Sartre (1905–1980) fought against the German army and helped lead French underground resistance during World War II. His essays and fiction put existentialism on the American literary map, and he shocked and confused many readers in the 1950s with themes of authenticity (vs. self-deception), absolute personal responsibility, the inherent conflict in human relationships, and his notion that the existence or nonexistence of God was irrelevant to the human condition.

At about the same time in France, the Algerian author Albert Camus (1913–1960) produced strange fiction about the absurdity and pointlessness of life. He concluded, somewhat paradoxically, that absurdity opens the door to happiness. "One does not discover the absurd without being tempted to write a manual of happiness. ... Happiness and the absurd are two sons of the same earth" (Camus, 1955, p. 122). In an ending too perfect even for fiction, Camus died in an automobile crash at the age of 47. He was not driving the car and had a train ticket and an unpublished manuscript in his pocket.

Key Ideas

This practical summary of essential existential concepts is presented (at great risk of trivializing complex points of view) so that a coach can grasp the basics and choose and use valuable aspects. The interested reader is referred to Olson's *An Introduction to Existentialism* (1962) for a more complete (and still accessible) background and explanation.

Traditional philosophers typically assert that the values of the "ordinary man" (or ordinary person) are bound to frustrate and disappoint. The pursuit of money, physical pleasure, and fame or social approval will not suffice. These values, which most of us seek to some extent in real life, are inadequate on several levels. First, success in attaining these goals is substantially outside of the personal control of most people. The essential determining factors are capricious, beginning with factors having to do with birth and ending with vagaries of luck. Second, even if you do achieve a certain amount of success in finance, physical pleasure, and fame, this can be swept away in an instant, sometimes by factors over which you have no control. Physical satisfaction is guaranteed to dissipate with age. Third, the satisfaction yielded by these values is transient, and they tend to generate a wish for "more." The small number of people who have achieved financial wealth, physical pleasure, and social approval (and are satisfied with these things) might view these observations as "sour grapes," but existential philosophy asserts that this simplistic assessment is unwise.

Philosophers have recommended several ways to emancipate oneself from the pitfalls of traditional values. Stoics and cognitive psychologists advocate that you should "wish for things to be as they are," rather than wishing life to be different (Olson, 1962). We cannot make life deliver what we want, but we can control what we think and desire. Rigorous, self-disciplined thought is key. Enlightenment philosophers advocate the opposite: We should relentlessly strive to change our environment so that we get what we want. A hard look at the world and the history of human happiness quickly negates the likelihood that ordinary people can ever hope that society can be counted on to deliver consistent happiness. For others the secret is in "enlarging our perspective" (Olson, 1962, p. 11) and focusing all of our attention on some object of greater good, such as beauty or nature or love or God. In this way, we are liberated from the problems of unreliable sources of happiness. This was where Hegel entered the picture with his advocacy of the "Absolute Spirit."

Existentialists typically mock and denounce the idea that there is any way for humans to live a completely happy or satisfying life. Life is characterized by frustration, disappointment, and loss. These things are an undeniable and central aspect of everyone's life. They cannot be made to go away, neither by extreme real-world efforts nor by mental denial. They assert that "the only life worth living is one in which this fact is squarely faced" (Olson, 1962, p. 14). To be totally happy is not human. The values and perspectives that derive from this acceptance are the ones worth living for. It is through the acceptance of pain and the ever-present possibility of loss that we become fully alive. We cannot really love without exposing ourselves to the possibility of great loss. Love without such possibility is more like habit or routine. It is a going-through-the-motions way to love. It is likely to be numb. To have a satisfying career is to take risk. Without the risk, work becomes tedium. Existentialism urges us to take the risk (with eyes wide open) and avoid the tedium. Life is to be lived intensely, not tediously.

The values that derive from this point of view include free choice, individual self-assertion, authentic love, and creative endeavor. The practical implications of these and several other existential values will be outlined for the coach in the rest of this chapter.

Six Core Concepts for the Executive Coach

Individuality and Context

Existentialism points out that no one is a fixed person. Things are fixed. A pencil is a pencil in every context, but a person is different in different contexts and different relationships. You think and behave differently when you are with your friends than you do when you are at an important meeting with bosses or potential clients. This is not simple phoniness; it is a function of "background," of role and relationship. Spinelli and Horner (2008) see this notion as a foundational condition of existential life, that of "inter-relation" or "the inter-relatedness of being." Human behavior is best understood in context, and social psychology has highlighted the *fundamental attribution error*, the tendency to overestimate internal (personal) factors and underestimate situational factors. Even though you may have excellent data from a 360-degree evaluation, as well as an earful from key people in the organization, be prepared to encounter your executive clients in a fresh and original way yourself. Clear out your preconceptions before you begin to work with them. Find out what makes them tick and find out what they are like when they are with you. Then compare the "data" you get with those impressions and figure out why they might be different. Understand your clients in the context of their work relationship world.

Choice

To live is to choose, to make endless choices from moment to moment, each and every day. Existential writers call attention to the *anguish of freedom*, freedom made difficult because we have so much choice, with no guarantee that the choices we make will ever work out. Things could turn into disasters, and when we choose one thing, we forgo something else. What if the thing we do not choose would have been much better? This decision-making function of life is central to the existential view of things, and it is the cause of much of the anxiety we all feel. Existence is the process of choosing, and in this view *existence* (the things that we do) precedes *essence* (the "way" we are). We create ourselves by our choices from moment to moment. We are not a certain "way" and must therefore *choose* a certain way. We are free to choose in each present moment, thereby defining our selves. The way we were in the past does not constrain us (except in the form of restrictive thinking), and the future is just in front of us, waiting to be chosen in this way or that.

The ultimate choice is in our choice of meanings. We even choose what things mean. It is human nature to try to figure out what things "mean." In the existential view, meanings are not given or fixed; we *choose* them for ourselves. One must not accept the common explanations. Each of us must figure them out for ourself and assign our own meanings. No one is locked in a previous identity or habit pattern. We are free to learn new ways, to make new kinds of choices. Even when we cannot choose what is happening—or the circumstances—we can still choose how to react and respond to those circumstances. This is a philosophy of independence.

Coaches can observe their clients and notice the ways that they restrict themselves, the ways that they decline to choose, and then encourage clients to notice those things, too. Effective choosing requires constant self-examination, and coaches can teach their executive clients how to do that. As coaches they can serve as a constant reminder for self-awareness and deliberate self-consciousness. Help clients make wise, well-considered choices. Help them notice when they have stopped choosing or when they let others choose for them, or when they move along thoughtlessly from day to day, just to go with the flow.

Intensity

In existential thought, death is the great motivator. Death ends everything, and, since we cannot predict when we will die, it is ever-present in life. Each of us could die today, and some of us will. Death is a possibility at every moment. Therefore, we must make every moment count.

Since death is frightening to most humans, we tend to create ways to avoid thinking about it, to avoid noticing its presence, in spite of the absolute fact that each of us will die. We distract ourselves, make ourselves numb, we become detached. But this does not work. It does not indemnify against death and it makes life less worth living. The existential view is to reject mediocrity and tedium and to become fully engaged in life, as if each day were our last (as it very well might be). This means that we take risks, we get involved, and we become actors rather than spectators. We cannot wait, because we have no assurance that we have much time. We *just do it*, as Nike seems to have noticed.

Death's presence also serves as a values clarifier. If you are aware that your life is time limited, does that influence what you do today? Do you choose A or B? The importance of one thing over another changes when you factor your own death into the picture. You might just make more "authentic" choices, choices that reflect the more "real" values that you possess, the things that you (yourself) really care about. You might make choices based upon the things that are more important to you, instead of the ones that are easier to choose, or the ones that others prefer, or the ones you made yesterday.

As Olson (1962, p. 196) put it, "Death releases human energies only by revealing the insignificance of ordinary pursuits." When we realize that we are going to die, we commit to things, we create things, we connect to people, and we focus. We refuse to fritter time and relationships and consciousness. In this way, death is our ally. It sharpens living. It demands focus.

The Herd Instinct

One of the most misunderstood philosophers of the genre is Nietzsche, and some of what he wrote was clearly objectionable. But one of his key ideas is of great value to the coach. He observed that humans are inclined to be lazy, to be fearful, to seek comfort, and to hide behind habits that keep us safe and the same and distract us from our appointment with death. He also observed that humans in society do not tend to think much for themselves. Instead, they tend to take the mentally easy way and to let others think for them. They accept the prevailing wisdom rather than come up with their own point of view. They take the path of least resistance. He observed that most of us live with a "slave morality." Nietzsche advocated that we instead "live dangerously," that we avoid becoming the "organization man," that we resist being caught up in the corporate shuffle, or in the prevailing attitudes of the times. He would have shouted, "Think for yourself!"

Coaches can take the same point of view, can root out this trend in a client's behavior, and confront clients about the ways they are simply acting out values that are not their own, or taking viewpoints that they have not themselves chosen. Coaches are in a perfect position, as an outsider, to stand outside of the force of the organizational trance state and to help an executive cut through unexamined premises and conclusions. Coaches can be advocates for thoughtfulness and for individual decision making.

Conflict and Confrontation

Sartre's view was that confrontation is the basis for all authentic human relationships. Conflict is not to be avoided—indeed, it is through conflict that we forge real relationships and relationships of trust. He makes this point most dramatically in his play *No Exit*, which takes place in Hell. Three characters are stuck with each other and are constantly in disagreement and disapproval, but, surprisingly, they find that they cannot exist without one another. There is no exit from human conflict and confrontation. The available exits, such as accommodation, denial, placation, and withdrawal, are inauthentic and they result in a numbing tediousness. We need the very people who drive us crazy. Conflict is not only essential to human relationships; it is the very foundation of authentic living. There is no benefit, to the existentialist, in getting along. We must challenge, confront, and be real with others.

Authentic relationships encourage the other person to be free, to make whatever choices they find appealing to become their individual selves. Sidney Jourard observed that "manipulation begets counter-manipulation" (1971, p. 142), and this is wonderful advice for a manager or leader, especially as the American worker continues to evolve toward greater autonomy (in good economic times, at least). Manipulation and control of others simply does not work in the long run, and in the short run, when it does seem to work, it creates unacceptable negative side effects. This makes leadership challenging. Other people are not to be used, and we are not to be used by them. We are not objects or "personnel," none of us.

The Absurd

Several existential writers deal explicitly with the idea that fundamental aspects of life are simply absurd, and there is no escaping this fact, no matter how hard we try, no matter how much we pretend that things make sense. In Kafka's *The Metamorphosis* (1966), the main character is surprised to wake up one morning to discover that he is a cockroach. In *The Trial* (Kafka, 1956), a man is arrested, tried, and convicted without ever finding out what he was accused of. In Camus's *The Myth of Sisyphus* (1955), a man is sentenced to roll a huge rock up a steep hill (eternally), only to have it roll right back down again once it reaches the top. In *The Stranger* (Camus, 1942) a man is convicted of murder, mostly because a jury felt disgusted that he had not properly grieved over his mother's natural death.

Existentialism highlights the utter unpredictability of things (including the fact that we could die at any moment) and celebrates it. The fact that the universe is inexplicable to us—especially when we so desire to make sense of it all—is the ultimate evidence of the absurd (Thody, 1957). We are wired to make meaning, yet we cannot. We wish to understand, but we consistently fail to do so. Life is full of brutal contradictions that we cannot possibly control.

Most of us are tempted to ignore this reality, to deny it, or to pretend it is not true. We create order in things and we insist that our order be honored. But even though it is important to establish order as best we can, it is a mistake to insist that our order prevail. The very nature of life shatters our orderly illusion. The roof can cave in at any moment, and sometimes it does.

This fact is not depressing to the existential thinker, however. In fact, the absurd opens the door to happiness. It is in total acceptance of the uncertainty of life's contradictions that we become free enough to engage ourselves in the regular day-to-day events and pleasures and to really appreciate them. They are our life. They are where we live. Life is crazy, and it is a joy that way. When life turns in a strange direction, we smile. There is a classic anecdote that makes this point:

> You know the story of the crazy man who was fishing in a bathtub. A doctor with ideas as to psychiatric treatments asked him "if they were biting," to which he received the harsh reply: "Of course not, you fool, since this is a bathtub." (Camus, 1955, p. 129)

Ten Existential Guidelines for the Executive Coach

1. *Honor Individuality*—First, approach each new coaching client with a freshness and willingness to see him or her as unique. Reinforce your clients' points of view. Help them figure out what those views are, what they really think and feel, and then support that point of view. Help them learn about themselves and to accept their inconsistencies. Check to see if they value their own personal point of view or, rather, if they diminish its importance relative to the point of view of others in the organization. Strengthen their confidence in their own perceptions and conclusions. Their personal point of view is of intrinsic value, even if they should choose to reexamine and change it as a result of the coaching process. Help them to figure out what is really important to them. Then discern where that fits into their career and their organization's priorities. This process may frighten your clients (or it may not), but it must be done. Help clients avoid a herd mentality and a group morality. Help them choose their own point of view. In the existential perspective, autonomy in self and others is valued and promoted.

   Avoid typing people. Do not put too much stock in what others say about your clients. Experience them freshly for yourself. It is likely that you will have similar impressions and come to similar conclusions, but you must do this for yourself. Look for the truth about your clients inside of yourself.

2. *Encourage Choice*—Remind your clients that they choose their identity each moment of each day. Existence precedes essence. Their reputation need not constrain them. They can remake their "self." They can make new choices and behave or prioritize in new ways, starting now. Once they establish a pattern of different choices and different behaviors, others will eventually begin to look at them differently, and they will establish a new reputation and a new identity, even to themselves. When clients choose not to change circumstances, remind them that they still have the ability to make a more important and powerful choice: that of meaning. They choose what things mean to them, they choose how to react, and they choose how to respond. They even get to choose their attitude.

3. *Get Going*—The time for waiting is over. In Samuel Beckett's 1953 play *Waiting for Godot*, two actors talk for hours about how great it will be when Godot arrives, but he never does. They wait and wait in eager anticipation and shades of intermittent disappointment for naught. Godot finally sends a message that he will surely come tomorrow. The waiters consider suicide (along with the audience, most of whom grew tired of the waiting long before the actors).

Exhort your clients to take risks, to get involved, to act, even to "live dangerously" sometimes. Life is finite, short sometimes, and we do not have any guarantee that we will be alive tomorrow. This means that we must squeeze each day for as much life as possible.

When you enter the world of your clients, look for ways that they have avoided risk or danger, ways that they have made themselves numb, ways that they have withdrawn from the action or narrowed the field. Point these things out to clients and urge them to reconsider. Numb is no way to live, and the existentialist is wary of comfort. We are actors, not spectators in life's adventures.

4. *Anticipate Anxiety and Defensiveness*—Anyone who is a coaching client will feel anxiety. This is expected and "normal." Beware of a client who reports no anxiety, for it means that he or she is not willing on able to notice or discuss feelings or their subjective inner state. It is appropriate for coaching clients to be anxious about coaching or about the situation they face, given that they must change or grow. Change is often frightening, and it adds to the "regular" anxiety associated with a life that is already understood to be out of control, in the existential sense. A coach need not make much of this anticipated anxiety, but can "normalize" or even welcome it.

Resistance and defensiveness can also be anticipated in the coaching process because, as Maslow (1968) pointed out, growth and safety pull in opposite directions, and all humans are drawn to both of those goals. Assume that resistance in clients is always present to some extent and in some form, and do not be disappointed when it erupts. It is an essential part of the change process and coaches must actively contend with it.

5. *Commit to Something*—Existentialism urges us to get involved with the regular activities of everyday life, and to do it with a passion. Do not accept it when your clients hang back. Urge them to get involved with those things that are important to them, even if others do not agree with their priorities. Help them to really dig in to something and to make it important. Such a commitment can lead to excellence and to exceptionality. Mediocrity, especially when it represents a dull, reactive, go-with-the-flow mentality is to be banished. Regular daily activities are understood as a distraction from commitment to something that is really important. Activity and intensity are valued. We only find out what we are made of when we are tested.

6. *Value Responsibility Taking*—Existentialism urges us to take responsibility for the choices we have made. We did it, we chose it, and we now live with the choices and implications. Assess your clients along

this dimension. Ask them what their view is on responsibility, ask others about this in your 360-degree evaluation. Observe them in action. Ask them to describe the last time they publicly took responsibility for something that went wrong in the organization. Help clients take responsibility for the decisions they make and the actions they take. Help them become known as responsibility takers in their organizations. Do not let them duck things. Coworkers and subordinates love people who take active responsibility and scorn those who do not. Certainly the act of data collection—and asking for feedback—along with the changes these might incite, represents an exercise in choice.

7. *Conflict and Confrontation*—In the existential view, interpersonal conflict is unavoidable, yet many people characteristically avoid conflict. This is a mistake, and coaches must assess their clients along this dimension. Ask your clients how they evaluate themselves. Do they enjoy conflict? Do they thrive on it? Does conflict make them feel like they are more fully alive? Or do they hate it? Does conflict scare them?

   Certainly no one would advocate unnecessary conflict, but most people are likely to avoid rather than confront. Existentialism sees conflict as an essential aspect of any authentic relationship, and confrontation is necessary from time to time to keep a relationship "real" and valid. Of course, there are better and worse ways to handle confrontation, and a good coach can help clients learn how to do it. It helps to view conflict and confrontation as a potentially positive aspect of organizational life, rather than merely a symptom of dysfunction. Pseudotranquility and pseudomutuality ought to be of more concern than active confrontation from time to time.

   There is another aspect of the conflict inherent in human relations. Sometimes the very people who drive you crazy are the ones you need the most, so it can be a terrible idea to reject them too readily. There may be important lessons to learn from uncomfortable or annoying others, and as Sartre concluded in *No Exit* (1989), we need each other, even the people we despise.

8. *Create and Sustain Authentic Relationships*—This advice applies to coaches and clients as well. Both will benefit from authenticity in work relationships. Coaches should strive for real relationships with clients, and clients ought to strive for realness in organizational work relationships. An authentic relationship occurs when both parties treat each other as autonomous entities to be respected. The truth is told and neither manipulates for personal benefit. People are not instruments for the accomplishment of some work purpose. They are individuals to be met with respect rather than treated as interchangeable components (personnel) in the labor market (Shinn, 1959). In the existential view, other

people are neither to be manipulated nor obeyed. *Gemeinschaftsgefhül,* or the feeling that we all belong to the community of humans, is the existential view (Jourard & Landsman, 1980).

Authentic behavior with a client means you put into words what you are experiencing with the client as you work. This is the most powerful thing you can do to have the leverage you are looking for and to build client commitment. (Block, 2000, p. 37)

9. *Welcome and Appreciate the Absurd*—Organizations are full of examples of absurdity, and anyone who has ever worked in a large (or small) organization knows how ridiculous things can get. This is simply normal. Assess your clients to see how well they understand this fact and what they do with it. Do they whine or complain when things do not go the way they were supposed to? Do they get angry when their planning goes awry? Help them appreciate how out of control life really is, and help them become more accepting and flexible. Help them find humor in the contradictions. If you can find the absurd to be humorous, you have got it made.

10. *Clients Must Figure Things out Their Own Way*—No one can tell you the answers to the most important questions. You have to figure them out for yourself, in your own way. Coaches have to figure out what this means to them, as well as how to "teach" important things to clients, to help them learn essential lessons or skills. Such teaching is rarely direct, as most humans resist being told what to do. Kierkegaard advocated "indirect communication" and added that truth requires self-discovery. It cannot be handed from one person to another.

Suppose an artist, for example, explains to you that a certain picture is beautiful. You believe him. You go around repeating the conclusion, "That picture is beautiful." But you do not understand what you are saying unless you personally have discovered the beauty. (Shinn, 1959, p. 92)

Strengths and Weaknesses of the Existential Viewpoint in Coaching

The existential way of living and coaching promotes a thoughtful and energetic approach to things. It can be exciting and productive and satisfying. It can promote creativity and action. It can result in relationships that are close, substantial, and enduring. It promotes organizations that are alive and exciting.

There are downsides, however, to the existential stance, and they must be acknowledged. First, the classic existential writers were ineffective at politics and often not so good at social relationships. They have a poor track record, as might be expected, in matters that require finesse, restraint, and compromise, and much of real-life corporate success requires a shrewd political savvy. In fact, it might even be said that the intense, committed person only fits into a small (but important) number of corporate *slots* (chief executive officer [CEO] perhaps being one of them). It is possible, sometimes, for the passionate one to mistake intensity for wisdom. It is true that existentialist writers often seemed to advocate any decision, as long as it was individually and authentically made, without much concern about the wisdom in the decision itself. Decisiveness is sometimes even valued over reason (Shinn, 1959).

The core values of existential thinking are deeply Western, written for the most part by Northern European males. They reflect a belief in individualism and personal autonomy. Taken superficially, an existential view could lead to a kind of individualism that is thoughtless or empty of direction. This kind of individualism for the sake of itself does not work very well in real life or in organizations, and it clashes with core values that have other cultural roots. Some cultures value a more collective view and can find direct interpersonal confrontation to be difficult, counterproductive, and even offensive.

Last, many people have inaccurate negative stereotypes of existential ideas. They associate existentialism with nihilism (a negation of all values or a rejection of law or order) and with godlessness. They also see it as a gloomy point of view, which it most certainly is not. But the ideas of existential writers are complex, and it is easy to see how such misunderstandings arise, and the original writers often did little to clear them up. Nonetheless, it may be simplest and smart to low-key the overt expression of existential ideas and simply bring the best of the existential approach to the coaching process without a label. Coaches might consider the "Recommended Readings" section to decide for themselves what they think.

References

Barrett, W. (1964). *What is existentialism?* New York: Grove Press.

Beckett, S. (1954). *Waiting for Godot: Tragicomedy in two acts.* New York: Grove Press.

Block, P. (2000). *Flawless consulting: A guide to getting your expertise used* (2nd ed.). San Francisco: Jossey-Bass/Pfeiffer.

Camus, A. (1942). *The stranger.* New York: Random House.

Camus, A. (1955). *The myth of Sisyphus and other essays.* New York: Random House.

Dostoevsky, F. (1992). *The best short stories of Dostoevsky.* New York: The Modern Library.

Jourard, S. (1971). *The transparent self.* New York: Van Nostrand Reinhold.

Jourard, S., & Landsman, T. (1980). *Healthy personality* (4th ed.). New York: Macmillan.

Kafka, F. (1956). *The trial.* New York: Vintage.

Kafka, F. (1966). *The metamorphosis.* New York: Norton.

Kaufmann, W. (1956). *Existentialism from Dostoevsky to Sartre.* New York: World.

King, M., & Citrenbaum, C. (1993). *Existential hypnotherapy.* New York: Guilford.

Maslow, A. H. (1968). *Toward a psychology of being*. New York: Van Nostrand Reinhold.

Nietzsche, F. (1968). *The will to power* (W. Kaufmann & J. R. Hollingdale, Trans.). New York: Vintage.

Olson, R. (1962). *An introduction to existentialism*. New York: Dover.

Sartre. J.-P. (1965). *Essays in existentialism*. Secaucus, NJ: The Citadel Press.

Sartre, J.-P. (1989). *No exit and three other plays*. New York: Vintage.

Shinn, R. (1959). *The existentialist posture*. New York: Association Press.

Solomon, R. (1995). *No excuses: Existentialism and the meaning of life, parts I and II* (Audiotaped lectures). Springfield, VA: The Teaching Company.

Spinelli, E., & Horner, C. (2008). Existential approach to coaching psychology. In S. Palmer & A. Whybrow (Eds.), *Handbook of coaching psychology* (pp. 118–132). London: Routledge.

Thody, P. (1957). *Albert Camus: A study of his work*. New York: Grove Press.

Recommended Readings

Cohn, H. W. (1997). *Existential thought and therapeutic practice*. London: Sage.

Spinelli, E. (2005). *The interpreted world* (2nd ed.). London: Sage.

9
Social Psychology and Coaching

How could I have been so stupid ... ?

**—John F. Kennedy (after the Bay of Pigs invasion,
as quoted in O'Brien, 2005, p. 538)**

Social psychology is the study of interpersonal influence—how people influence one another. Although we like to think of ourselves as autonomous and independent, humans do not operate in a social vacuum. The real and imagined thoughts and behavior of people around us have a powerful impact.

The topics of social psychology are directly relevant to executive coaching and the process of influence. This chapter describes how coaches can effectively learn social psychology's lessons and apply them to coaching. Social psychology has contributed much to what we know about leadership, persuasion, conformity, influence, decision making, coercion, and cooperation, and has added concepts like groupthink, field theory, and cognitive dissonance to the management consulting vocabulary.

A Brief History

If I were required to name the one person who has had the greatest impact on the field, it would have to be Adolf Hitler.

—Dorwin Cartwright (1979, p. 84)

Social psychology is a young science, and its origins are in events related to the Second World War. Most of the early studies were motivated by a desire to avoid another fascist catastrophe, and people who escaped the horrors of Nazi Germany conducted many of those studies. The father of social psychology, Kurt Lewin, came to the United States in 1933, the same year that Hitler became chancellor of Germany. Lewin used his research skills to study the consumer behavior of American women to help promote the success of rationing. His mother and most of his relatives perished in a concentration camp. Lewin's protégés studied autocratic and democratic leadership and the authoritarian personality, and they generally came to the happy conclusion that democracy was the most effective way to run an organization. However, Stanley Milgram's (1963) controversial experiments demonstrated that the majority of people would follow simple orders to administer strong electric shocks to others, even when it was clear that their obedience caused serious pain. Solomon Asch (1951) showed that people can usually be convinced to conform to the opinion of others, even when it is clear that the opinion is wrong. Philip Zimbardo and his associates (Haney, Banks, & Zimbardo, 1973) created a fake prison in the basement of the Stanford psychology department and in an experiment that got completely out of control, ended up with prison guards (who had been randomly chosen) behaving quite brutally. Zimbardo himself began to act like a prison warden before calling the experiment off. Social psychologists, like many people in the 1950s, had suspected that there was something faulty about the German character, but they learned from laboratory studies that most of us could fall prey to the worst kinds of human impulses if the conditions were just right (or just wrong). Gordon Allport (1954) and Gunnar Myrdal (1944) undertook a comprehensive description of American racial attitudes and prejudices. Robert Rosenthal and Lenore Jacobson (1968) unearthed the "self-fulfilling prophecy" and showed that teachers can virtually create performance levels in children based upon the teacher's predisposed expectations for those children, even when expectations were randomly assigned. David Rosenhan (1973) took a group of mentally healthy researchers into a mental hospital, got them admitted, and then could not convince authorities that they really were not mental patients. One researcher was stuck there for 7 weeks, because hospital staff interpreted everything he did as confirmation of his mentally ill status.

The Power of the Situation

The main finding that ties together all of these strange and interesting forays into conformity, obedience, and social perception is that *situations* are much more powerful than character, even though we rarely acknowledge that fact. Social psychologists refer to this as the *fundamental attribution error*. Humans tend to overestimate the importance and power of individual personality and underestimate the influence of the social situation. We attribute things to internal forces such as personality or character instead of social forces in our surroundings. But Milgram's subjects could be made to shock others, Asch's subjects could be made to endorse the obviously wrong opinions of others, and Zimbardo's students could be turned into brutal prison guards by the power of the social situation. Social psychology teaches us that we must pay attention to social influences if we are to effectively lead, manage, and change. Coaches must remember the power of the environment, as clients and the bosses of clients are likely to focus too much attention on personality and character. Often the reasons for the success or failure of a client can be found in the way that the culture or situation is structured.

Advertising professionals and organizational consultants use the lessons of social psychology seamlessly and regularly. This chapter applies some of those important lessons to executive coaching.

Field Theory

One of Lewin's many contributions is *field theory*, and it represents a way to help coaching clients cope with the social environment. Instead of focusing on personal qualities or shortcomings, it forces coaches to pay attention to the immediate social surroundings and associated pressures.

Lewin's basic theory was that behavior is a function of the person and the environment, or B = f (P, E) as he coded it. In Lewin's view, action and research were one and the same, and he called his change projects *action research*. Each change project was conducted as a research project. The usual research steps were taken, and this is a great way for coaches to work with executives. The steps are as follows (Krupp et al., 1986):

1. *Identify the Problem*—For coaches, this means identifying one discrete aspect of a client's behavior or skill set to work on. It is best to choose a "problem" that seems especially fixable at first. Start with the low-hanging fruit.

2. *Gather Data and Analyze It*—Feed data back to the client.

3. *Make an Action Plan*—Create a plan that has a high likelihood of success. Get "buy-in" from all parties involved.

4. *Implement Your Plan*—Take action; put the plan into effect.

5. *Collect More Data*—Monitor the situation to evaluate how you are doing.

6. *Problem Redefinition*—Using the data you have collected, make necessary changes in your definition of the problem. Data are used throughout the process to track progress and change or adapt the approach. The question is always: "How are we doing, and how do we need to adjust our focus?" The process is cyclical, and it is important, at the onset, to view the cycling as "normal" and expectable, not as a failure.

Lewin saw things systemically, and believed that in order to change, an existing system must be "unfrozen, moved, and refrozen," and that involves the total picture of influences. Lewin invented the *force-field analysis* (1951), an assessment of all the relevant current social forces. The force-field analysis works like this: Draw a line down the middle of a piece of paper. This line represents the present situation and its balance between the forces of change and the forces that keep things the same. On one side of the line, draw arrows to represent the forces for change (*driving forces*). On the other side of the line draw arrows that represent the forces pushing to keep things from changing (*restraining forces*). This diagram tells you where you need to go to work. The forces for change must be strengthened and the restraining forces must be weakened. Lewin observed that it is often easier to decrease the restraining forces than to strengthen the

Table 9.1 Lewin's Force-Field Analysis: An Example

Forces That Keep Things the Same (Restraining Forces)	Forces for Change (Driving Forces)
Few interpersonal relationships with current partners.	New membership in a country club (could take partners to play golf).
Few previous positions of leadership in the organization.	Enthusiastic supporter of the company.
No current opportunities to sell work for the firm.	Solid performance evaluations throughout career.
No solid mentor or powerful supporter.	Casual relationship with one influential partner (weak, but could be strengthened).
	Serious interest (by the firm) in promotion of qualified women to partner.
	Other female partners doing well.

facilitating forces, and the process of weakening the restraining forces is more likely to reduce tension, whereas a strengthening of enabling forces can increase tension, which makes everything harder (Segal, 1997).

For example, let's say that an executive wants to become a partner in her firm. Table 9.1 illustrates how Lewin's force-field analysis is applied. Once you have completed this analysis it is easier to construct an action plan. Forces for change must be strengthened and forces that tend to maintain the status quo must be weakened or eliminated.

It must be noted that the force-field analysis is not simply a rehashing of the standard problem-solving steps, in that it focuses on the *current* equilibrium situation, and the *present* forces for and against change.

An alternative way (Silberman, 1986) to use force-field analysis is to simply list and address the following:

1. The situation as it is now.
2. The situation as I want it to be.
3. What will keep the situation from changing?
4. What is the most powerful obstacle?
5. Action steps.
6. Resources needed to make the change.

Cognitive Dissonance

A second major social psychology contribution was by Leon Festinger (1957), and it is called *cognitive dissonance theory*. This theory states that humans have a need to feel consistent. We are comfortable when our thoughts, feelings, and behaviors are aligned, and we are uncomfortable when they are in dissonance. Dissonance happens when we think one way but behave in a way that conflicts with our thinking or our values. When uncomfortable, we strive to resolve the inconsistency, either by changing behavior or more typically, changing what we tell ourselves about the situation or the behavior. For example, when you do something that you believe to be wrong, dissonance theory asserts that you must either stop doing it or find a way to explain or rationalize it so that it seems acceptable. A classic example in social psychology research is from a study by Knox and Inkster done in 1968. They found that bettors at a racetrack were more confident in their horse *after* they had placed their bet than before. They had to make their thinking consistent with the action they had already taken.

Thus, you will be in state of dissonance when you snap at an employee if you generally think of yourself as a "nice" person. How could these two apparently conflicting things both be true? The tension created by cognitive dissonance must be resolved in some way, and if the event has already occurred, you cannot go back and erase it, so you tell yourself something that makes it all add up correctly: That employee deserved it. He did something so thoughtless that he required being snapped at. Or you could tell yourself that although you are actually a very nice person, you are under an enormous amount of stress right now and anyone would snap under present conditions. But you must do something to resolve the dissonance between what you think of yourself and your behavior. There are actually many ways to do this. For example, you could discredit a source of conflicting information, you could view problematic information from a different point of view, or you could use selective recall and leave out discordant aspects of the information. But you must do something, and what you do is often irrational or illogical. As Robert Cialdini puts it, "We all fool ourselves from time to time in order to keep our thoughts and beliefs consistent with what we have already done or decided" (1985, p. 53).

Social psychologists also point out that there are two very basic human motives that often invite cognitive dissonance: (1) the need to feel that we have an accurate view of things (the need to be right) and (2) the need to feel good about ourselves. Although these two motives are sometimes naturally or easily satisfied, they often cause conflict. Sometimes, if we view things accurately, we must acknowledge that we have behaved poorly or stupidly or at least, suboptimally.

There are two divergent ways to deal with this problem (Aronson, Wilson, & Akert, 1997). The first is called the *self-esteem approach*. Using this approach, we distort things to feel right and feel good about ourselves. The desire to feel right is a powerful motive for humans. In fact, many people would rather feel right than happy. Depressed people hang onto their irrational thinking even though it causes them to suffer, and they do this to maintain the perception that they are "correct" about life. Sometimes this requires that we justify previous behavior even though, if we thought about it, we would realize how silly the behavior really was. Sometimes it means that we have to go on making the same old poor choices to justify decisions we made before. Sometimes it means that we must sing the praises of something we have suffered for in the past, like a fraternity or sorority that was difficult to break into. For example, companies have been known to continue to use poor software long after it has become clear that the software was no good, simply to justify the decision maker's judgment. If you switch, you must acknowledge that your original decision was wrong, so you trudge along, trying to find something good about the situation and punishing those who criticize it. This is often the reason that people cannot change. If they did, they would be acknowledging that they had been wrong before. We often cling to our views way too long in order to protect our self-esteem and consistent view of ourselves.

This phenomenon causes us to rationalize and justify. Social psychologists have discovered unexpected patterns in this area. For example, they found that if you want someone to like you, it is better to get them to do something for you rather than to do something for them. Ben Franklin actually seems to have stumbled on this "trick" long before social psychology. He referred to it in 18th century writings (Aronson et al., 1997, p. 206). This seems odd at first, but cognitive dissonance provides the explanation. After someone has done something for you, he or she has to be able to explain that behavior. One way to make it all fit is for them to decide that they like you, that you are worth it. Otherwise, why would they have done something for you in the first place?

The second approach is called *social cognition* and it comes from the drive we have toward accurate social perception. Most humans possess the desire to get things right, to figure out what is true. We intuitively understand what is at stake, and we try hard to understand the social world around us. But we theorize imperfectly, and social psychologists have described several classic paths to self-delusion. This becomes a problem when we get stuck on being "right," and being right becomes more important than being effective. Remember: Many people would rather be "right" than happy. To them, at the time, it just seems better.

Groupthink and the Abilene Paradox

Irving Janis was struck by the way that intelligent people made foolish foreign policy decisions at the highest level of American government in the 1960s. His study of four major blunders (Roosevelt's failure to prepare for an attack on Pearl Harbor, Truman's invasion of North Korea, Kennedy's Bay of Pigs invasion, and Lyndon Johnson's escalation of the Vietnam War) led him to the conclusion that rational thinking had been hijacked by the commonly experienced group process dynamics of social psychology. He observed that judgment is impaired in those who become "more concerned with retaining the approval of the fellow members of their work group than with coming up with good solutions to the task at hand." He called this tendency "concurrence-seeking behavior" or *groupthink* (Janis, 1972, p. iii).

Janis (pp. 197–198) concluded that several important symptoms of groupthink could be avoided by thoughtful executives. They are:

- High group cohesiveness and tendency toward agreement and conformity.
- Shared illusion of unanimity.
- Shared illusion of group invulnerability.
- Excessive optimism.
- Insulation of a decision-making group from outside influence or input.
- Persistent attempts by a leader to influence a group's decision.
- Collective efforts to minimize or discount warnings or disconfirming information.
- Pressure against group members who disagree or offer discordant opinions.
- Self-censorship of members who have dissenting ideas.
- Emergence of self-appointed "mind guards" who protect the group from adverse information.

These qualities can cause bad decisions by limiting the information that is considered, limiting the number of alternatives considered, limiting discussion and formal evaluation, biasing available information, and failure to create contingency plans.

Jerry Harvey offered a similar view in his intriguing essay "The Abilene Paradox" (Harvey, 1988). He uses the story of how his family embarked on a long, uncomfortable day trip to Abilene in 104° heat to make his point. No one in the family actually wanted to make the trip, but all agreed because they felt that the others wanted to go. As a group, they did exactly the opposite of what each of the group members wanted to do. Harvey describes the paradox as follows: "Organizations frequently take actions in contradiction to what they really want to do and therefore defeat the very purposes they are trying to achieve." He goes on to point out that "the inability to manage agreement is a major source of organization dysfunction" (p. 18). Harvey asserts that the failure to manage agreement is a more pressing problem than the issue of conflict management in organizations.

Janis and Harvey both offer advice and suggestions about how leaders can avoid or minimize problems related to conformity and excessive agreement. Coaches and consultants would be wise to study this body of work, because of their special outsiders' role. Coaches are in an excellent position to help organizations avoid groupthink if they can avoid becoming too closely identified with insider status. It must be said that those who think they are immune from these dynamics are paradoxically the most vulnerable. We are all vulnerable.

Schemas and the Effects of Expectation

Social psychologists refer to the personal theories that we use to understand everyday events as *schemas*, and these schemas are both useful and treacherous at the same time. They are cognitive simplifications in the form of thought rules. We cannot live without them, but they routinely trick us, and we resist changing these harmful patterns when new information conflicts.

For example, we see things based upon how we expect them to be. If we have an expectation in advance of an event, we perceive it in alignment with the expectation. If you are told that someone or something is positive and special, you are likely to perceive any ambiguities in a positive light. First impressions work this way. Your first impression of someone has a powerful impact on how you evaluate him or her in the future. Reputation works this way. A person's reputation precedes him or her and is a powerful influencer of how that person is perceived in the present moment. Recency also applies. Your most recent interaction with someone is also more powerful than your long-term opinion. The self-fulfilling prophecy is another example of a problematic human tendency. We treat people in line with what we already think of them, and they behave in alignment with expectations. Often those expectations serve as a kind of tunnel vision in that we herald new bits of information that confirm our existing opinion and fail to notice data that would conflict. These judgmental heuristics are useful, as they allow us to avoid having to think through every step of a decision process hundreds of times each day. But they trick us, as well. The following subsections are some examples.

The Availability Heuristic

We use the availability heuristic shortcut when we make a judgment based upon how easily we can bring an example to mind. We tend to think something is truer if we can bring to mind a good, clear picture of it. After seeing photographs you might think that earthquakes are the most dangerous aspect of life in San Francisco even though car wrecks kill far more people there. This is the reason that the drunk (in the joke) looks under the street lamp for his keys, even though he lost them across the street: "The light's better here!" he notes. It follows, then, that if you want to make a good point or you want your view to seem true to others, you would do well to paint a picture, use a metaphor, or connect it to something recent or well known.

The Representative Heuristic

The representative heuristic mental device checks to see if a new piece of information matches information in a category and then assumes that the new information is like all the other cases in the category. For example, you are much more likely to be hired as a CEO if you look and act the way that people think "typical" CEOs do. That is why you sometimes get the advice to "dress like the people who already have the job you want." A recent advertisement by the American Civil Liberties Union makes the disturbing point that Martin Luther King Jr. would have been "75 times more likely to be stopped by the police while driving" than Charles Manson.

Anchoring and Adjustment

Anchoring and adjustment causes us to stick close to the first estimate of a situation. For example, in negotiations, the first offer or bid on the table is a powerful one, because it "anchors" all subsequent perceptions, which must "adjust" from it. If the first offer is in the $500 range, it is very hard to move perceptions into the $5,000 range, even though others may actually be willing to pay $5,000. This phenomenon is also called the *dominance of first impressions*, and it means that executives must get feedback about how they present themselves and pay attention to the first impression that they make. It also means that if you are negotiating a fee it is important to set the starting offer at the optimal level, not too low and not too high.

This heuristic has many other implications. For example, if a real estate agent wants you, a potential powerful buyer, to favor an $800,000 house, she might walk you through a more expensive home first and talk about million dollar homes in the neighborhood.

The Perseverance Effect

Numerous studies have documented the tendency for most of us to think in the same ways, over and over again, even when there is no benefit to the tried-and-true thought patterns. A simple story about this phenomenon, *Who Moved My Cheese?* (Johnson, 1998), sold millions of copies. We think the same things in the same ways as a *style*, not because it is an effective way to process information. We even continue to think in the same way after receiving contradictory feedback. This is an area where a persuasive coach can really earn her fees. If you can bump a client out of an old, worn-out cognitive rut, you will have made a significant contribution, indeed. People can rarely do this for themselves. Change often requires a dramatic event or significant loss.

Lessons in Leadership

Social psychology has been interested in leadership since World War II, particularly in regard to the devastation caused by tyrants and dictators of that era. The first major studies in leadership and group dynamics demonstrated that, when compared to autocratic and laissez faire leadership, democratically led groups were superior. They resulted in higher productivity overall, less in-group conflict, more on-task behavior when the leader was absent, and more creativity (Lewin, Lippitt, & White, 1939). Humans generally do better when they feel that they have a role in the decision making.

Leadership research has often centered on the *great person theory*, which wonders if great leaders possess certain personal qualities that enable them to excel. Not surprisingly, the fundamental attribution error applies here, too, in that no personality or character or intelligence factors have been consistently associated with great leaders. Leaders are only modestly more intelligent than nonleaders, only a little more charismatic, and not consistently more driven toward accumulation of power (Aronson et al., 1997). In a large study of American presidents, one hundred personal factors were matched with historical effectiveness, and only three factors stood out and only one was something that the person had influence over himself (Simonton, 1987, 1992). The factors associated with great leaders were height (tall is better), family-of-origin size (small is better), and number of books published before becoming president. Leadership research is reviewed in more detail in Chapter 15.

Contingency Theory

Of greater importance is the match between the leader and the situation. Some kinds of leaders are ideal for certain times, whereas others are a better fit during other conditions. Some situations call for a certain kind of bold charisma, whereas others require cautious leadership and a focus on the details. Sometimes task-oriented leaders (those who tend to pay the most attention to getting the immediate job done) are best and at other times a relationship-oriented leader is better. Prospective leaders would be well advised to look carefully at situational demands to determine what kind of leadership to apply. Many people are simply not flexible enough to make the changes that a difficult leadership situation requires. A coach might be able to guide a leader through a difficult period or even advise a change of leadership or organizational structure to take advantage of an executive's strengths and weaknesses with regard to the current context.

Emotional Intelligence

Any modern discussion of coaching, leadership, and executive effectiveness must include the work of Daniel Goleman who points out that IQ and the usual technical ingredients are insufficient for lasting success (Goleman, 1998a, p. 93):

> Every businessperson knows a story about a highly intelligent, highly skilled executive who was promoted into a leadership position only to fail at the job. And they also know a story about someone with solid— but not extraordinary—intellectual abilities and technical skills who was promoted into a similar position and then soared.

This body of work is mandatory reading for the executive coach. Goleman asserts that it is *emotional intelligence* (EQ) that makes or breaks leaders, that EQ is the *sine qua non* of leadership, and that it is possible (albeit difficult) to learn the component skills. Goleman defines emotional intelligence as follows (1998b, p. 317): "The capacity for recognizing our own feelings and those of others, for motivating ourselves, and for managing emotions well in ourselves and in our relationships." He claims that his research demonstrates that emotional intelligence is twice as important as IQ or technical skills and most executives are quite bright. Intellectual skills and technical expertise are important, but they are only threshold skills. They get you in the door and onto the playing field. It is EQ that enables you to survive and thrive. The basic components of Goleman's (1995) version of EQ are self-awareness, self-regulation, motivation, empathy, and social skills. These are all natural areas for coaches, and, in fact, Goleman specifically recommends coaching for those who want to enhance their emotional intelligence. Goleman also notes a coming crisis for American corporations and an opportunity for coaches: As IQ continues to rise in children, EQ is on the decline (1998b, p. 11). Coaches are often called on to help executives who have made a name for themselves through years of hard work in front of a computer screen and are now asked to manage or lead people. Goleman provides an *Emotional Competence Framework* for assessment of just such a person (1998a, pp. 26–27). Goleman's claims, the work of other important researchers, and the extensive literature on emotional intelligence are reviewed and evaluated more thoroughly in Chapter 11.

Cooperation and Competition

There is a body of work in social psychology that strives to determine the best ways to enhance cooperation when cooperation is appropriate. Competitive or aggressive reactions are sometimes called for, but more often than not, a potential win–win situation is completely missed because one person behaves competitively when a cooperative response would have been far better. When trust has not been established in human relations, people think in terms of a zero-sum game or condition. They figure that any piece of the pie for others means one less piece for them. This is a condition of scarcity, meaning that there is not enough for everyone. The win–win viewpoint is quite different, and it is predicated on the idea that if we communicate what we desire, there may be a happy fit between what you want and what I want; we might both be able to get much of what we each desire, or we may be able to create more of everything by working together. Such a happy outcome requires honest and open communication, as well as some level of trust. When the chicken arrives, before you start to fight about how much you can actually have, figure out who likes white meat and who likes the dark. Maybe you can actually have it all (all of what *you* want).

Social psychologists have extensively used a game called the Prisoner's Dilemma to test how people cooperate or compete (with competition referred to as *defection* in the literature). In this simulation two people are arrested and held for interrogation. Each is told that if he will testify against his partner, he himself will be set free. A scoring system is set up to highly reward cooperation (i.e., not defecting or ratting on the partner); to reward competition modestly; and to subtract points if one cooperates but one's partner rats on him.

The dilemma is called a *mixed-motive* situation, because participants must decide between total self-interest, trust in others, and benevolent interest in the well-being of others. In this game it is risky (but potentially very rewarding) to look out for someone else. Hundreds of studies indicate that people are inclined to become locked into an escalating series of competitive moves, especially if they feel that their trust has once been violated or that they have been taken advantage of. Trust might be easy to establish, but it is also easy to damage, and it requires ongoing attention. One cannot simply assume that existing trust is stable. It must be monitored and nourished.

It turns out that a strategy called *tit-for-tat* is ideal when tested against all comers in a computerized prisoner's dilemma tournament (Axelrod, 1984). In this strategy, the player begins with a cooperative response and then simply chooses the same option that the other player chose on the previous move. This begins by communicating a willingness to cooperate along with an unwillingness to be taken advantage of. Most people probably respect such a strategy, a cooperative stance by someone who is not willing to be exploited.

In any case, the social environment must be examined along the cooperative–competitive spectrum. Competition is best for some things, but cooperation is essential for others. It is ineffective to compete when cooperation would be better, yet this happens all the time.

Interpersonal Influence

Cialdini (1985) essentially "wrote the book" on influence. He reviewed the available literature on interpersonal influence and conducted participant observation studies in which he and collaborators studied influence in real-life situations. Here is what he learned.

Reasons

First, if you want someone to do something for you, it is best to supply a reason. The reason need not be particularly impressive or compelling. In fact, there is research evidence that the simple inclusion of the word *because* will often do the trick. The nature of the reason does not seem to matter much, but the fact that you gave a reason will greatly increase the odds of compliance. Cialdini points out that children discern the power of the word *because* early on, and they often use it to justify behavior. "Why did you do that?" Answer: "Because!"

Repetition

Second, if you really want to accomplish something, repeat a constant and consistent theme. Say it over and over again in a consistent manner. As long as you do not overdo it, this creates the advantage of making what you are saying familiar, and because of the availability heuristic (we tend to believe that which comes easily to mind), what you are repeating eventually gets attention and credibility. The best way to take advantage of the power of the human urge toward consistency is to combine it with commitment. First, get a commitment to do something, then all subsequent behavior must conform to that commitment. This works for self-change as well. Make yourself state a commitment to something clear and measurable, so that there is no way to weasel out without (you or others) noticing. Then make your behaviors line up with your commitment. This solves the problem of cognitive dissonance.

Owing Favors

Third, the rule of reciprocity calls for us to repay favors. If you do a favor for me, I should try to repay that favor to balance things out. We are *obligated*. It may well be a good idea to keep everyone in your organization in debt to you for something or another. Powerful political figures are well aware of this phenomenon. Cialdini uses the example of the Hare Krishna's gift of a flower in airports in the 1980s. Many people felt woefully indebted, in spite of themselves, after accepting that simple gift. This tactic is used effectively by time-share companies that provide free ski tickets or free stays at a condo as long as you are willing to sit for their sales pitch. People feel indebted. It is important to note that once you have given a gift you must allow the opportunity for the return of the favor. People deeply resent being put into the position of having received a gift that they are unable to repay in some way. (Everybody's doing it.)

Following the Crowd

Another, extraordinarily powerful source of influence is the principle of *social proof*. This principle states that, as social animals, we watch one another to see what the trends are, and then we follow them. We use the mass behavior of others to determine what is true, valuable, and important. It is like the zebras on the Serengeti: When the other zebras run, you'd better run too, just in case, even though you have no idea of why you are running. The human tendency to follow prevailing social trends and patterns is profound, and it explains things like the Jonestown massacre, fashion trends, tattoos, and suicides and homicides subsequent to other suicides and homicides in the news. It also explains why television sitcoms still use laugh tracks, even though everyone says that they hate them. In spite of our expressed dislike for the phony yuks, it works. Crowd behavior is especially important in times of uncertainty and ambiguity, and it is most powerful when the people we observe are similar to us. Keep this in mind next time you find yourself laughing at something that is actually not very funny or clapping for something you do not actually find impressive. Keep this in mind when you are making difficult decisions at work. Guard against mindless conformity and what Cialdini calls *pluralistic ignorance*. Trend following has its value—it tends to keep us safe—but it has many more liabilities, and helps to explain much strange human behavior. Pay attention to the trend, but do not trust it implicitly. Check things out for yourself. On the other hand, when you need to influence someone else, you may want to point out the prevailing trend in the direction of the point of view you advocate.

Similarity and Other "Like" Factors

It is not surprising that we tend to like people and things that are similar to us and familiar. We like people who look and dress like us, and people who are physically attractive have a great edge in life: We tend to believe them and we tend to think all sorts of positive things about them, including the fact that they are "good." This trend is called the *halo effect* in the psychological literature. We also tend to attribute positive qualities to people we like, and people who can make themselves liked in the workplace have a clear and powerful advantage. Although this may seem obvious, this interpersonal liking is often overlooked as a career force. We tend to like people who have a similar background to our own, and it pays to find something in common with someone you are trying to influence.

Choosing Models

The power of similarity is also important in the use of modeling. Modeling is typically found in the repertoire of the behavior therapist or behaviorally oriented consultant (see Chapter 4), but it clearly involves interpersonal influence. When your client wants to change or learn something new, one great way is to find someone who already knows how to do it, to observe that person carefully and to copy them. The best kind of model for your clients is someone similar to them. Similarity makes for a more efficient modeling process. Do not choose someone who seems perfect or who is in total mastery of the sought-after skill. Rather, pick someone who obviously had to work at learning it and is in the process of improving. This tends to make the skill more accessible to the learner and the learner more open to the new skill. Research indicates that it is better to choose a role model from the same gender and ethnic group of the client, and someone at roughly the same prestige level in the organization. It even helps if the model occasionally has to struggle with the learning process, has to work at it, and it is terrific when the model can talk about the process to your client. It is difficult to identify with a flawless model. If you intend to learn golf as a beginner, Tiger Woods may not be the best model for you. It helps if the model has overcome the same obstacles faced by your client and better if they have similar concerns. Multiple exposures to the model and multiple models make for the best learning experience. And remember to encourage the client to adapt the model's approach to his or her style; that is, to do what the model is doing in the client's own way (Cormier & Cormier, 1985, p. 311).

Compliments are powerful. We tend to believe praise when it is lavished on us, even when we should know better, and we tend to like the person who is lavishing it.

The phenomenon called *killing the messenger* has its basis in social psychology, as any television meteorologist can tell you. They often get blamed for the bad weather they announce. One must be careful about taking the role of bad-news messenger, especially if called upon to do this regularly. It can lead to trouble, for you will become associated with the badness of the events communicated. If there are layoffs to be announced, think carefully about who will be the one to break the news.

Social psychologists have even provided data for the *luncheon technique* (Razran, 1938). A series of studies have demonstrated that subjects were more likely to give approval to topics when they were presented along with food. It seems that tax deductions for business lunches actually have a basis in scientific research.

Compliance

Milgram's obedience studies, conducted in the 1960s, placed participants in a situation where they were told to shock other people. The shocks were not real, but participants thought that they were. The subsequent embarrassment and trauma thought to be experienced by those subjects were partly responsible for enhanced protections and increased restrictions on subsequent experimentation using live subjects in psychology. Jerry Burger (2009) recently conducted important partial replications of Milgram's research using added safeguards and limiting the range of subject behavior. His research attempted to determine whether people would still obey at the same rates that Milgram found in the 1960s. Burger included women to see if there would be gender differences. He also studied the effect of several personality variables on obedience. The results of Burger's studies indicated that modern participants were just as likely to obey authority figures—even when it involved hurting other people—as were participants in the 1960s. He also found no significant gender differences, even though he speculated that women might be more concerned about hurting someone else. He reasoned that any such concern was overwhelmed in his study by a lack of assertiveness by women in the face of authority. He found that people who scored higher on empathy scales did express reluctance to continue to shock others, but they did not refuse to continue to obey when told to do so.

Social psychology has carefully studied other ways that people tend to be susceptible to influence. One of the most useful findings comes from a series of studies by Rule, Bisanz, and Kohn, reported in 1985. They created a hierarchy of preferred strategies used to get compliance, and aside from methods that might be called dirty tricks. They found the following:

1. A simple request is the most preferred tactic, for example, "Would you please ..."

2. A reason is compelling, and personal expertise or a role relationship makes a request more powerful. For example, "We've been friends for a long time now ..." or "I really need this because ..."

3. Horse trading is useful. "If you would do this for me, I will be glad to do that for you."

4. Invoking a norm or a moral principle or altruism works. "Everybody else is doing it" or "It's the right thing to do" or "Other people are depending on us ..."

5. A compliment tends to get compliance: "You are so good at this type of thing ..."

6. Negative, deceptive, or threatening approaches are at the bottom of the list, along with the use of force. These should be used only as a last resort, if at all.

The optimal way to ensure compliance with your requests is to allow the targets of your request to save face and to help them feel that they are doing a nice thing of their own volition.

Social psychology has also identified the sources of power that clients possess in the workplace (French & Raven, 1959), and it may be useful for coaches to review these sources outlined in the following with clients. How is the client doing in each of these areas of influence? Does he or she rely on one to the exclusion of others? Are they happy with the compliance they get?

Sources of Compliance Power

1. *Coercion*—Based upon the agent's ability to punish or withhold rewards.

2. *Reward*—Based upon the agent's ability to provide rewards.

3. *Expertness*—Based on the target's perception that the agent has important knowledge or ability.

4. *Legitimacy*—Based on the target's belief that the agent is authorized by a recognized power structure that the target answers to.

5. *Referent Power*—Based on the target's identification with and attraction to or respect for the agent.

Ideally, coercive power is minimized in a modern organization, but clients must be willing to judiciously use that source if necessary. The use of referent and expert influence, however, is likely to create the optimal working environment, along with productivity and creativity.

The Authoritarian Personality

One last social psychology topic deserves mention, even though it is controversial. At the end of World War II Theodor Adorno and several colleagues at University of California, Berkeley (Adorno, Frenkel-Brunswik, Levinson, & Sanford, 1950) approached the problem of Hitler and other demagogues from a slightly different point of view. They described a type of personality that was especially susceptible to authoritarian submission and called it the *authoritarian personality*. Their original ideas derived from psychoanalytic theory, but were grouped with social psychologists who were studying the same problem at the same time. Adorno's team developed a brief questionnaire to use as a screening device—the F scale (F is for fascist)—for people highly susceptible to group influence and excessive conformity to authority. The first question, for example, is "Obedience and respect for authority are the most important virtues that children should learn." Adorno's work was criticized as an attack on conservative thinking. The authoritarian person is portrayed as one who values conformity to prevailing social norms (and is likely to insist that others conform as well); is submissive to authority; intolerant of difference; places a high value on security and stability; and is rigid in his or her views (new or disconfirming information is not welcome). Canadian psychologist Robert Altemeyer (2007) has recently taken an intriguing and more social view of authoritarianism and applied it to current events. The question of interest to coaches seems to be this: Is there a personality type that is authoritarian, and if so, how do coaches recognize and deal with it in the work setting? What if your client seems authoritarian? What if your client has an authoritarian boss? Adorno's and Altemeyer's ideas are engaging and worthy of review.

Summary

1. Treat each "case" and client as an ongoing field study. View coaching as research. Lewin's action research can be described as "research on action with the goal of making that action more effective" (Witherspoon & White, 1997, p. 19). Talk about it that way. Let your clients in on the research, get them involved. Create an optimistic, nonpunitive atmosphere of curiosity. Together, you and your clients commit to study a situation or "problem" so that you can understand it and influence it. Expect that the first interventions will be instructive but will not "solve" the problem. Expect a few iterations of the cycle of assessment, brainstorming, intervention, and evaluation. It's all good.

2. As a coach, remember the power of the situation. Social psychology research makes it quite clear that the *situation* is more influential than personal qualities or individual character. Do not allow your clients to become self-blaming and punitive (but do not let them off the personal "hook" either). It is possible that you could plug almost

anyone into certain situations and he or she will behave in roughly the same way as anyone else would. Examine the social environment as it pertains to the question at hand. Explore the possibility that some aspects of the environment should be adjusted to help clients grow. Teach your clients' organization, if possible, about the organizational climate and culture. Make it open to examination and discussion.

Help your clients examine social situations and how these influence them. Help your clients discern which aspects they are reacting to and why. Explore the ways that your clients are influenced by prevailing social trends and help them think through which trends make sense and which do not. Provide a safe, sane place for your clients to think and talk about these things outside of the social situation that normally influences their behavior.

3. Remember that we all suffer from self-delusion. It is virtually impossible to live in the real and accurate world. It is too much mental work to think through every situation independently from scratch, so we are forced to use mental heuristics to economize and survive. These heuristics are vital and useful, but they often trick us, and cognitive dissonance causes us to make mental adjustments that are inaccurate but comfortable. Help your clients sort through the ways that they are tricking themselves and ways to get back to more accurate thinking. Help clients notice when they are stuck or when they are trapped by their own ideas. An outside view is essential sometimes.

4. Assist your clients with self-presentation. Reinforce the importance of first impressions and physical appearance. Coaches are a crucial source of feedback. *You* can point things out to clients that others cannot (because of prohibitive social mores or role constraints; for example, how do you tell your boss that she has bad breath?). Your role as coach requires that you do just that with your clients. You have a special kind of permission that is extremely valuable. You must skillfully call attention to how your clients present themselves and brainstorm for adjustments. This includes the way they dress, the way they speak (in person and on the telephone), their e-mail messages, the way they stand and sit, the way they make eye contact, the way they listen, and even the amount that they smile. These are all examples of the kinds of self-presentation feedback that coaches are expected to provide to clients. According to social psychology research, it is invaluable.

5. Assess and teach Emotional Intelligence. Goleman's materials are quite useful in selling this concept. Goleman's books, articles from

the *Harvard Business Review*, and cassettes are available to help you and your clients. Technical expertise and intellect are important, but they are threshold skills. They are expected, and they get your clients in the door. Social factors are more important to your clients' long-term success than are the technical factors. These include empathy, self-awareness, self-regulation, and social skills (such as the ability to accurately read the emotions of others). These skills are the bread-and-butter skills of the executive coach, and they are often the reason that coaching is requested in the first place, whether your clients acknowledge this or not. The emotional intelligence format provides a vehicle for the sale of soft skills in the corporate world. EI is described in detail in Chapter 11 ("Emotional Intelligence").

And remember: Do not believe everything that you think.

References

Adorno, T., Frenkel-Brunswik, E., Levinson, D., & Sanford, N. (1950). *The authoritarian personality.* New York: Harper & Brothers.

Allport, G. W. (1954). *The nature of prejudice.* Reading, MA: Addison-Wesley.

Altemeyer, R. (2007). *The authoritarians.* Available from: http://home.cc.umanitoba.ca/~altemey/.

Aronson, E., Wilson. T., & Akert, R. (1997). *Social psychology.* New York: Addison-Wesley.

Asch, S. E. (1951). Effects of group pressure on the modification and distortion of judgments. In H. Guetzkow (Ed.), *Groups, leadership, and men* (pp. 177–190). Pittsburgh, PA: Carnegie.

Axelrod, R. (1984). *The evolution of cooperation.* New York: Basic Books.

Burger, J. (2009, January). Replicating Milgram: Would people still obey today? *American Psychologist, 64*(1), 1–11.

Cartwright, D. (1979). Contemporary social psychology in historical perspective. *Social Psychology Quarterly, 42,* 82–93.

Cialdini, R. (1985). *Influence: Science and practice.* Glenview, IL: Scott, Foresman.

Cormier, W., & Cormier, L. (1985). *Interviewing strategies for helpers.* Monterey, CA: Brooks/Cole.

Festinger, L. (1957). *A theory of cognitive dissonance.* Evanston, IL: Row, Peterson.

French, J. R. P., Jr., & Raven, B. H. (1959). The bases of social power. In D. Cartwright (Ed.), *Studies in social power* (pp. 150–167). Ann Arbor, MI: University of Michigan Press.

Goleman, D. (1995). *Emotional intelligence.* New York: Bantam.

Goleman, D. (1998a, November–December). What makes a leader? *Harvard Business Review,* 93–102.

Goleman, D. (1998b). *Working with emotional intelligence.* New York: Bantam.

Haney, C., Banks, C., & Zimbardo, P. (1973). Interpersonal dynamics in a simulated prison. *International Journal of Criminology and Penology, 1,* 69–97.

Harvey, J. B. (1988, Summer). The Abilene Paradox: The management of agreement. *Organizational Dynamics,* 17–43.

Janis, I. L. (1972). *Victims of groupthink.* Boston: Houghton Mifflin Company.

Johnson, S. (1998). *Who moved my cheese?* New York: Putnam.

Knox, R. E., & Inkster, J. A. (1968). Post decisional dissonance at post time. *Journal of Personality and Social Psychology, 8*, 319–323.

Krupp, S., DeHann, R. F., Ishtai-Zee, S., Bastas, E., Castlebaum, K., & Jackson, E. (1986). Action research as a guiding principle in an educational curriculum: The Lincoln University Master's Program in Human Services. In E. Stivers & S. Wheelan (Eds.), *The Lewin legacy: Field theory in current practice* (pp. 115–121). Berlin: Springer-Verlag.

Lewin, K. (1951). *Field theory in social science.* New York: Harper & Row.

Lewin, K., Lippitt, R., & White, R. K. (1939). Patterns of aggressive behavior in experimentally created social climates. *Journal of Social Psychology, 10*, 271–279.

Milgram, S. (1963). Behavioral study of obedience. *Journal of Abnormal Psychology, 67*, 371–378.

Myrdal, G. (1944). *An American dilemma.* New York: Harper & Row.

O'Brien, M. (2005). *John F. Kennedy: A biography.* New York: Thomas Dunne Books.

Razran, G. H. S. (1938). Conditioned response changes in rating and appraising sociopolitical slogans. *Psychological Bulletin, 37*, 481.

Rosenhan, D. (1973). On being sane in insane places. *Science, 179*, 250–258.

Rosenthal, R., & Jacobson, L. (1968). *Pygmalion in the classroom: Teacher expectation and student intellectual development.* New York: Holt, Rhinehart & Winston.

Rule, B. G., Bisanz, G. L., & Kohn, M. (1985). Anatomy of a persuasion schema: Targets, goals, and strategies. *Journal of Personality and Social Psychology, 48*, 1127–1140.

Segal, M. (1997). *Points of influence.* San Francisco: Jossey-Bass.

Silberman, M. (1986). Teaching force field analysis: A suggested training design. In E. Stivers & S. Wheelan (Eds.), *The Lewin legacy: Field theory in current practice* (pp. 115–121). Berlin: Springer-Verlag.

Simonton, D. K. (1987). *Why presidents succeed: A political psychology of leadership.* New Haven, CT: Yale University Press.

Simonton, D. K. (1992). Presidential greatness and personality: A response to McCann. *Journal of Personality and Social Psychology, 63*, 676–679.

Witherspoon, R., & White, R. (1997). *Four essential ways that coaching can help executives.* Greensboro, NC: Center for Creative Leadership.

Recommended Readings

Benjamin, L. (2009). The power of the situation: The impact of Milgram's obedience studies on personality and social psychology. *American Psychologist, 64*(1), 12–19.

Deaux, K., Dane, F., & Wrightsman, L. (1997). *Social psychology in the '90s* (6th ed). Pacific Grove, CA: Brooks-Cole.

Gilbert, D., Fiske, S., & Lindzey, G. (1998). *The handbook of social psychology* (4th ed.). New York: McGraw-Hill.

Hayes, N. (1993). *Principles of social psychology.* Hove, UK: Erlbaum.

Janis, I. (1986). *Groupthink: Psychological studies of policy decisions and fiascoes* (2nd ed.). New York: Houghton Mifflin.

Stivers, E., & Wheelan, S. (1986). *The Lewin legacy: Field theory in current practice.* Berlin: Springer-Verlag.

Taylor, S., Letita, A., & Sears, D. (2000). *Social psychology* (10th ed.). Upper Saddle River, NJ: Prentice Hall.

10

Hypnotic Communication

You know what charm is: a way of getting the answer yes without having asked any clear question.

—**Albert Camus (*The Fall*, 1957)**

If linear communication and injunctions were effective, there would be little work for executive coaches. When people are *able* to respond to direct suggestions for change or improvement, they do. They take feedback, make an adjustment, improve, and move on. This happy scenario, however, is rare. More often than not, people resist feedback and resent it when they get it. Even when they accept feedback, it is often true that they cannot seem to do anything useful with it. They cannot translate the feedback into effective and lasting action. These sad observations are well known to anyone in the personal change business. Humans have a hard time with change. We say we want to be different, we make New Year's resolutions, we go on diets, and we vow to do better. People know that they would be better off if they maintained a clean desk or if they submitted their expense reports in a timely manner. They know how to exercise, and they know that they should communicate more effectively with their team. But sometimes, they just cannot get themselves to do it.

Influence and Resistance

It is also true that attempts by one human to influence another often create resentment and resistance. "Who does he think he is?" is the unspoken reaction to suggestions to be different. We do not like people who try to change us, and divorce courts are brimming with couples that suffer from the curse of interpersonal influence gone wrong. "If I change, that means he was right, and I am wrong" is another underlying source of difficulty.

Most humans resist injunction ("You do this"). We dislike being told what to do. We resent it, partly because it means that someone else is smarter or better than we are, and partly because it means that we are not presently doing it properly, and partly because it represents a loss of control. We resist out of habit. Once you have done something for a long period of time in the same way, it seems uncomfortable or weird to try to do it a different way, even when you tell yourself that you should change.

This chapter is for those coaching situations when well-conceived change attempts are not working, when clients are stuck and coaches are stalled, and when behavior is refractory to good advice. Such situations are common and frustrating to all involved. They also represent opportunities for the coach to make his or her "mark." One successful intervention in a situation that previously seemed impossible can help establish a reputation that is valuable. Organizations are willing to pay for help that they cannot provide from within. The ability to break a behavioral logjam is the coach's *inimitable competitive advantage*. This is why they will call you back.

Hypnosis and Communication

A universally accepted definition of what constitutes hypnosis is elusive…

Ernest R. Hilgard (1991, p. 86)

At first, the relationship between hypnosis and business communication may seem mysterious, and it requires some explanation. How could trance be used in corporations? The answer is to be found in an understanding of hypnosis; what it is and how it works in its broadest sense.

Hypnosis has a long and storied history and shamans and stage performers have practiced it for centuries. Mysterious figures used trance states to cause witless victims to do strange and embarrassing things. These images have contributed to wide public misunderstanding of hypnosis over the years. The view that most people have of hypnosis probably came from watching a stage show in Las Vegas or at a county fair—or even a cartoon.

There are several ways to define and understand hypnosis, both with and without obvious trance states. Single-factor theories describe hypnosis as a state. One important view is that we are always in and out of trance, or that we are always in one kind of trance state or another, that life consists of a continuous series of overlapping and changing trance states. The late Sidney Jourard captured this view:

> We begin life with the world presenting itself to us as it is. Someone—our parents, teachers, analysts—hypnotize us to "see" the world and construe it in the "right" way. These others label the world, attach names, and give voices to the beings and events in it, so that thereafter, we cannot read the world in any other language or hear it saying other things to us.
>
> The task is to break the hypnotic spell, so that we become undeaf, unblind, and multilingual, thereby letting the world speak to us in new voices and write all its possible meanings in the book of our existence.
>
> Be careful in your choice of hypnotists.

In this view, hypnosis represents the larger trance states that we live in, the ones that define and shape our reality, the fish's water and the bird's air. This view is explored by the constructivists (and cognitive therapists, as well). We live the world of our own personal perceptions and are limited by the boundaries of that perceptual world—boundaries that we have put in place ourselves. Watzlawick, Beavin, and Jackson's 1967 exploration of paradox in patterns of human communication led to several of the interventions described later in this chapter, as well as a basis for some of what cognitive psychotherapists and systems therapists do in their therapy offices. Milton Erickson spent 50 years exploring the ways that hypnosis could be used to communicate, and Jay Haley (1967, 1986) and others (Gordon & Meyers-Anderson, 1981; O'Hanlon, 1987) have documented his complex legacy in detail. There are other theories of hypnosis, referred to as *Socio-Cognitive* (Lynn & Rhue, 1991) that are contextual and social in nature. Coaches are well advised to do their homework in this literature, as hypnosis is difficult to describe (especially in a brief chapter), and the necessary patterns begin to take shape only when one samples several of the available sources over a period of time. The readings are fascinating and well worth reading. Examples are listed at the end of this chapter, and the Zilbergeld, Edelstien, and Araoz (1986) and the Watzlawick, Weakland, and Fisch (1974) texts are special. A more complete definition of the various types of hypnosis, its history, and associated myths can be found in a practical explanation written for the dental literature (Peltier, 2006).

Principles and Attitudes

The hypnosis literature contains a variety of useful viewpoints for coaches. Several come from observations of Milton Erickson (Haley, 1986; O'Hanlon, 1987). Some of these ideas can be found in the book *Change* by Watzlawick et al. (1974). For example:

1. *Human change is nonlinear.* This is a classically postmodern idea. The present does not directly lead to the future, and efforts to direct change in a linear way are doomed to failure. The past did not directly lead to the present situation, and efforts to explore the past (as a vehicle for change) are futile. Paradox is at least as likely to prevail as sensible logic. Study the real patterns (or lack of patterns) if you want to understand how to change.

2. *It is impossible to not communicate.* All behavior, including silence, is communication (Watzlawick et al., 1967). Many ways to communicate do not involve talking or talking about the "problem."

3. *People have (within them) what they need to evolve, to change, and to improve.* It is rarely necessary to actually teach them anything but specific skills. They can figure out the important things for themselves in their own unique way. It is more important to study a person's ways than to try to teach them something. Start from your client's point of view. The way that someone already does things reveals their path

to growth or change. Study, in particular, the ways that people stay the same and keep things the same, even as they declare the need to change. How do they do it? Most limitations are systematically self-imposed and outside of conscious awareness.

4. *It is often easier to influence through implication than injunction.* Injunction here means a directive in the form of "You do this." People listen hard for the implications of things and are curious about them, even when they do not realize they are doing so. They are also more open to implication than injunction. People like to figure out things for themselves and do not like to be told what to do.

5. *More of the same will not produce a new result.* (*Plus ça change, plus c'est la même chose.*) You cannot keep doing the same thing and expect to change. Effective solutions are often "strange" ones. They are also often uncomfortable to initiate. The only solution to difficult problems is often of a second-order nature; that is, the solution violates and changes the rules of the system.

6. *The map is not the territory.* Things are not the way we explain them, nor are they the way that they seem. The explanation is not the reality, and we live in both worlds: the "real" concrete world and the world of our perceptions, attributions, and construal.

7. *The more flexible person gets her way.* It is inflexibility that usually constrains us, not simply a lack of information, or lack of skill, or bad habit. People often continue to do self-defeating things out of a false sense of honor or pride in consistency. All of those deficits can be resolved if we can be flexible and persistent. Encourage and support more choice rather than less. Offer choices even when the choices are somewhat illusory. Most parents understand how to do this with their children: "Would you like to take out the trash first, or would you rather pick up your room?" This is called the *illusion of alternatives.* People respond well to the perception of choice, even if the choices are not so hot. Choice is typically preferable to injunction (for example, "You do this").

Several of these ideas eventually led to what business people have come to refer to as *out-of-the-box thinking.*

Hypnosis without (Obvious) Trance

A view of hypnosis limited to trance is of little use to an executive coach, and much of the work of posttrance thinkers is complex enough to be problematic. But there is a way to define hypnosis that makes it extremely useful to business coaches. Much of what hypnosis offers coaches has this definition in common: *Hypnosis is communication that bypasses critical analytic thought.*

We use hypnotic communication when we influence each other without making a direct request. We bypass resistance. There are many ways to do this, and some people devise ways to influence without realizing it. You may know someone who naively does this—a favorite teacher, an uncle, your mother, or even a local community leader. Somehow these people are influential, and you cannot quite put your finger on why that is so.

Some "Practical Magic"

Here are some techniques that come from the world of nontrance hypnosis. Most of them derive from multiple sources, and when a single source is known, it has been cited. Those sources can be found in the "References" and "Recommended Readings" at the end of the chapter. (Many of these ideas came from a lecture given by Paul Watzlawick at the San Francisco Academy of Hypnosis in 1988.) People who make their living in sales and those who practice neurolinguistic programming (NLP) might find them familiar.

Indirect Suggestion   You can suggest things without directly suggesting them, thereby sidestepping the resistance that accompanies injunction ("You do this"). Indirect suggestions involve a creative process, and there are many ways to do them. The key is to plant an idea or set up a situation that causes someone to do something without being specifically asked or told to do it.

For example, one way to make an indirect suggestion is to "wonder" about something. *Wonder* is a strange and powerful word. It tends to predict the future in a positive way and seems to direct energy and an open mind to the effort. It opens the door to possibilities. "I wonder what would happen if we didn't go to market by the 30th" is entirely different from "You need to get this product to market by the 30th." Other alternative ways to communicate might include "I wonder what it would take to develop a new product to do this," "I wonder how we could get to know someone inside the Acme Company," and "I wonder how you establish contact in a country like Vietnam?" These are not injunctions or even requests, but they plant an idea in a gentle, positive way. To plant an idea is to use indirect suggestion. When executives plant ideas, people who report to them listen and react.

You can make indirect suggestions by *saying things to someone else.* Imagine that you want to suggest to your client that he enhance his appearance in the business setting. Instead of saying it directly to your client ("You dress poorly and should dress differently") and creating resistance or resentment, you could (carefully) say it to someone else while your client is present. "If my client weren't listening, I would tell you that he would be a lot better off if he wore a white shirt to marketing meetings. I think people would take him much more seriously." Although this is certainly a "tricky" way to communicate, when done skillfully it can become a powerful way to say things that could not be spoken directly.

Similarly, you can make your messages more powerful by preempting them; that is, prefacing them with information that makes them paradoxically seem more important. For example, *You know, I'm really not supposed to tell you this, but ...* is a way to make your message very powerful by indirect suggestion. Another way to preempt is to begin your message with "I know that this is going to sound kind of stupid, but ..." Yet another way to say something by not saying it is to start out with "If you tell anyone I said this, I'll deny it, but ..."

You can also create a straw man of the possible resistance by beginning your suggestion with "I don't know, the thing that you want would require an awful lot of work ..." The possibility of extra work is the straw man, easily knocked over by your client who responds, "I don't mind work! I like hard work." You can substitute many other desirables for the word *work* in the equation, such as effort, time, attention, listening skills, or money.

You can use comparisons to your advantage. For example, you can say, "A lot of people don't seem to understand this next part ..." (you've suggested that it is difficult or complex, and further that an average person cannot understand it). This challenges many people to focus their attention and to work hard to get your message. You can also use the indirect effect of comparisons in the following way. Choose a kind of client who is attractive to your current client. Then you can say, "You know, I once worked with a client who was a (insert Rhodes Scholar here), and she picked up on this concept right away. You wouldn't believe how hard she worked at improving." Conversely, you can choose a kind of client who might be unattractive to your client and say, "I once worked with a _____ (prostitute, drug addict, drug dealer, and so forth) when I was working as a psychologist, and he never seemed to be able to get the hang of this." Your present client, not wanting to be grouped with this unattractive kind of person, then works hard to be different. You have set up an indirect suggestion to work hard at something without actually having asked for it.

Specific Language   Certain words have the power of implication built into them and should be used carefully or should be avoided. For example, the word *try* has failure built into it. Failure is implied in the word itself. When you "try" to do something, you are not saying that you will get it done. Rather, you are saying that you will make efforts and attempts that will likely fall short. *Can't* is another such word, as it implies that something is impossible. Often a more accurate word is *won't*. *Won't* carries entirely different connotations, and the connotations are powerful and instructive. *Yet* is a very useful and powerful word, as it can be applied to action that is desired in the future: "You haven't learned how to do this yet" is a way of planting the suggestion that you will learn how to do it in the future. *Right now* is a similar phrase, and it can be used in much the same way: "You aren't putting in the time right now." *As* is another such word, and it implies that you can do something: "Notice how things change as you learn how to listen to your team members." The word *need* is strange and powerful, in that it implies necessity, even when people do not think they are using it that way: "I need more time and resources" implies that you could not exist without them and that it would be disastrous if you did not get them. It is entirely different to say, "If I can get enough time and resources we could finish the project in 90 days. Without them it would take much longer and would result in significant market losses."

The power of these specific words is in their shared implication. They say one thing (in common usage), but they imply something else. Sometimes the implication is clear and shared, and sometimes it is not. But it is always helpful to observe the use of such words, to calibrate one's own usage, and to align one's implications with one's goals. Listen to clients and help them master these kinds of words and use them powerfully yourself. Pay attention to implication.

Specific Nontrance Hypnotic Communications   There are many ways that language can be used hypnotically (outside of explicit trance states). The first principle is to be careful with positive and negative linguistic formulations; that is, use positive words and sentence structures rather than negative ones. For example, think about what happens when you hear the phrase "Don't think of a rooster." You have to do the very thing that you are being asked *not* to do in order to comply. You must think of a rooster to try to accomplish the requested task of not thinking of a rooster. It is automatic and unavoidable. Instead, offer the following: "Think of a big green elephant." When you think of the elephant (which is explicit and interesting enough to capture almost anyone's interest) you have to let go of the rooster image. It gets replaced, using a positive sentence structure. The mind is not able to directly respond to negatives. When you use them you complicate things and make action much more difficult. It is analogous to trying hard to relax.

Storytelling   Effective leaders and persuasive people have always used stories to make their points. This is because we use a different part of the brain to process a story than the part we use when trying to follow linear instructions. Stories are full of indirect suggestion, and the plot of a story is often one great indirect or direct suggestion about how life really works. You can make all kinds of suggestions through a good story. Examples are the same way, as they tell people how things work along with expectations for them. Remember the powerful motivating stories you hear. Write them down and memorize them. If you are a good storyteller, take advantage of this asset. If not, learn how to tell stories. Create opportunities to practice. Make up your own stories, formulated especially for this client or that one. Use previous clients (while maintaining confidentiality) for relevant anecdotes. Integrate one or two important indirect suggestions (along with an appropriate outcome) into each story. Be careful that you do not repeat your stories and never explain them. Let your clients figure out what they mean from their own point of view. In fact, ambiguity is often the most powerful way to react to the indirect suggestions that you plant. Clients often feel compelled to fill in the blanks in the most important ways. Sometimes clients fill in the blanks in wonderful ways that would never occur to you.

Often people can "hear" a message in a story that they cannot hear in any other form. When you tell a story about how someone accomplished something, you can access the principle that goes like this: If it is possible for someone in the world, it is possible for me.

Imagery

If M. Mesmer had no other secret than how to put the imagination into motion effectively, for health purposes, would not that still be a marvelous blessing? If the medicine of imagination is best, should we not practice the medicine of imagination?

—From the original scientific investigation of animal magnetism commissioned by King Louis XVI of France (Franklin et al., 1784)

Be careful how you imagine yourself to be, because you might become that way.

—Sidney Jourard (Jourard & Landsman, 1980)

We process images differently from other kinds of language forms. Images get us. They are powerful and can really move us when well presented. Notice the difference between the *taste of butterscotch* and a recipe. There's no comparison. The sensory experience of taste always wins. Pepper your language and coaching with sharp, compelling images. Exhort your clients to imagine themselves doing something or experiencing something. Help them imagine what it is like to learn something new or to accomplish something difficult or to complete something satisfying. Help them *feel* what it is like to be in that position. Use images and use the word *imagine* regularly.

Find out how your client handles images. Some people have a stilted imaginary life. Help them grow their imagination, and remember, when the imagination and reality come into conflict, the imagination has more power. This is true when people use their imagination to hurt and constrain as well as help themselves. Beware, however, that a small number of people do not seem able to make pictures in their minds. With these clients, help them use images in whatever form is comfortable. Some people can create images without making mental pictures. They somehow use a "sense of things" to accomplish the same tasks that others might do with mental pictures. Begin with an imagery assessment. Discern how clients presently use images and what form the images take.

Here are some specific examples of the ways that imagery can be used. Many come from Rian McMullin's 1986 reference listed at the end of the chapter. These are examples of types of images you can help your client develop as resources for growth and change.

Coping or Mastery Images   Use images that help a person cope with a difficult situation or task. For example, you can help your client create an image of himself or herself successfully asking for a raise or a new assignment. These images can be large, general images or small, detailed ones. The detailed images tend to help when one is learning a new skill or attempting something novel.

Modeling Images   Your client can imagine someone who is already excellent at a desired task or skill. He or she can go through the steps (in his or her imagination) as if he or she were the skilled person. This can serve as a transitional learning experience, making it easier to actually do the new thing when the time comes. "Imagine that you are Andrew Lee asking this client for business. See what it feels like to do that if you were him."

Idealized Future Images   Help your clients imagine how they would like life to be in 5 years. Where do they want to be, how do they want to be, what do they want to be doing, and how do they want to feel? Help them to use their imagination to experience what the future can be like. This can make things more real and can make them more accessible. A variation on this approach is to imagine yourself at the age of 85, looking back on your life. Is there anything to be learned about the current situation?

Leveling Images   Use leveling images when it is difficult for your client to confront or deal with someone else. Public speakers use this technique to successfully get through (or over) their fears. "Imagine your audience in their underwear" is the classic image used for this purpose. "Imagine your boss in his gardening clothes or in his robe, when he has just gotten out of bed." "Imagine your client with you at a baseball game or at a picnic with all of the kids." Then go through the future interaction, and do it successfully. Eventually move to an image that is exactly like the one you have to confront.

Corrective Images   You can use corrective images to undo and redo mistakes that you have made. Go back over the same situation and do it again. This time change something significant and see what difference it makes.

Worst-Case Scenarios   When faced with a difficult or intimidating situation, help your clients develop an image of the absolute worst possible scenario. Help them decide whether they could stand that outcome (they always can, even though it might involve a very undesirable situation). Then back off a couple of notches or levels and determine what the realistic worst case might be. Decide how bad that would be and whether some preparation must be made for it. Then develop a plan for success, knowing that you can handle any conceivable result.

Ultimate Consequences Images   Imagine, in detail, what the outcome might be if you actually do what you are now considering. Imagine what might happen if you take another path. "Imagine what a day or a week would be like if you took that new job with the start-up company." Imagine what might happen if you are able to successfully learn what you are striving to learn. What are the benefits? How will life change? Help your client go through these images in sharp detail.

Cathartic Images   Imagine blowing up at your boss or your team. Just let yourself go in your imagination. See what this is like. Then you will not have to experience it in real life.

Empathy Images   Imagine yourself in the shoes of an important other. Go through a situation in their position and allow yourself to envision what they might be thinking and experience what they might be feeling. This is a great way to learn how to read people better and to become a more cooperative leader or better salesperson. It helps build empathy.

Security Images   Develop and practice images that make your client feel safe. "Imagine that you are in your backyard, at home, on a warm, sunny day." "Imagine yourself in the presence of someone you trust, someone who makes you feel safe." They can then keep those images around for times when things get difficult.

Metaphors   We also process metaphors differently than "regular" day-to-day language. Metaphors help us to understand and to change, and they bypass normal resistance to change. They give us another way to view the same old problems and situations, and they encourage us to engage our intuition. Some of what constitutes great literature is metaphor, as it has no intrinsic meaning or purpose other than to instruct us in larger ways. Metaphors make us think and cause us to notice things that we had never noticed before.

Alice in Wonderland, The Wizard of Oz, Star Wars, Kafka's *The Trial,* and Plato's *Allegory of the Cave* are examples of metaphors. Much biblical material is metaphor. Religious lessons are frequently taught this way. Metaphors are available from Judaism and Christianity, from Asia and India, from science fiction and literature, and even from children's stories. Sheldon Kopp (1971) explored the use of metaphor in his book *Metaphors from a Psychotherapist*

Guru, and defined a metaphor as: "a way of speaking in which one thing is expressed in terms of another, whereby this bringing together throws new light on the character of what is being described" (p. 17).

Kopp also quoted Paracelsus by observing that the guru should not tell "the naked truth. He should use images, allegories, figures, wonderous [sic] speech, or other hidden roundabout ways" (1971, p. 19).

David Gordon, in a metaphor "cookbook," makes the point that "each therapy or system of psychology, then, has as one of its basic constituents a set of metaphors" (1978, p. 8).

Metaphors allow the storyteller to get away with things he or she could never tell us directly. For example, let's say that you are working with someone who dresses inappropriately for the business situation. The way that she presents herself is ineffective, and some relatively simple changes might cause her to be taken more seriously. It might be difficult to give this feedback directly or it might be hard for the client to hear it in a way that motivates or mobilizes change. This is a time to consider a metaphor or anecdote. Create an example of someone who looked or presented herself in a way that did not work. For example, Richard Nixon lost debates and perhaps a presidential election because his makeup and presentation were poorly suited for television cameras. Often the metaphoric message will come across loud and clear and in a way that will not create hurt feelings or resistance. A coach can always use a metaphor or story first, observe its impact, and give direct feedback later, if necessary. But, you usually do not need to explain your metaphors or stories.

Metaphors also encourage risk taking without actually asking for it. Remember how you have felt more daring after having read a good book or watched an athletic event or gone to a movie with an inspiring message.

Humans are always trying to make meaning out of things. With a metaphor, you invite the listener to make sense of what is in it, to pass it through a personal filter and to find the logic and the moral. Great teachers, leaders, coaches, and motivators have always known this, so they build repertoires of metaphors and anecdotes and use them liberally. Moderation is important, and metaphors should be used judiciously, especially by beginners. Too much of a good thing can turn a wise teacher into an annoying irrelevancy. "When I ask you to take an aspirin, please don't take the whole bottle," the old golf teacher Harvey Penick used to say (Penick & Shrake, 1992).

Modeling   As a coach, turn yourself into a model of positive attitude and action. Do this in your own way, with your own style. As a consultant and "expert," others will read you to determine how things are going. If you are confident and at ease with yourself and the process of coaching, problem solving, and growth, clients will read this confidence and feel assured. It is as if you create a small, positive trance state, a set of assumptions about how things are and will be in the future. You do not need to say that you know what you are doing, you do not need to say that things are going to be all right, you simply behave as if that were true. This creates a powerful suggestion. You are then in a position to "predict the future" by stating that goals will most likely be accomplished. You can state them almost casually: "Oh, I imagine you will learn this quite quickly." You assert with calm self-assurance.

This requires excellence on your part. You must do your homework, learn and know your stuff, and make yourself do the right thing. When you lack a certain skill, you must go out and learn it. In this way, you can develop the experience necessary to speak with authority and confidence.

Reframing   Much meaning is derived from context. Standing in your under-wear means nothing if you are home alone. But it has a very different meaning if you are at a corporate cocktail party. Watzlawick et al. (1974) define reframing in a technical way:

> To reframe, then, means to change the conceptual and/or emotional set-ting or viewpoint in relation to which a situation is experienced and to place it in another frame which fits the "facts" of the same concrete situation equally well or even better, and thereby changes its entire meaning. (p. 95)

Coaches can help clients shift contexts to derive new and important meanings. The way we feel is determined by the way that we look at things, how we ascribe meanings, and what we see as the context. It all depends on how we look at it. We can help our clients flex up and change the context. We can offer an alternative context, as no context is ever completely fixed.

There is a great example from the athletic coaching arena, where a coach seems very hard on one specific player. She yells at that player and notes every error, following it with corrective action that sometimes seems punitive. The player finally confronts the coach. "Why do you hate me?" she asks. "I know I'm not a great player, but I work hard, and try to do everything you say."

"I don't hate you," replies the coach. "I yell at you because you have poten-tial. Don't worry when I yell at you. Worry if I stop yelling at you."

Ambiguity   Although you may value clarity and precision in your communi-cations, it is not always the most effective way to coach. Intentional ambiguity has its uses, because humans tend to fill in the gaps. When presented with ambiguous stimuli or confronted with words or situations that have multiple meanings, humans are naturally inclined to complete the picture, to connect the dots, to make sense out of abstractions, and to create personal meaning in unclear situations. Clear and complete communications have their advantages, but ambiguous ones require the listener to work, to sort things out, to think. Sometimes this is exactly what the speaker wants and what the listener needs. Sometimes it is a good idea to let the listener chew on things himself or herself for a while. Often clients will fill the gaps in ways that will surprise. Sometimes clients bring in information that neither the coach nor the client would expect had they approached the problem from a linear point of view. This is not a recommendation to make things intentionally vague, which can be annoying to the learner, but occasional incompleteness and ambiguity can be powerful. You do not always have to fill in all the blanks. Your client is smart, and they have some answers inside. Their answers are usually better than your answers.

The "As-If"   To learn something new or difficult we have to put ourselves in position to do the learning. You cannot learn to ride a bicycle unless you are on the bicycle and moving. You cannot ride a bicycle while it is not in motion. But you cannot sit on it when it is in motion, because that would be riding a bicycle and you don't know how to ride a bicycle. So, how do you make the transition from being a nonrider to being a rider? The key is in the *as-if*. You have to behave as if you already know how to do it in order to learn how to do it. This is true in real (grown-up) life as well. You cannot make a sale as a real estate agent unless you are out there showing homes and writing up offers. You act like a real estate agent before you actually are one. This is how you become one. You cannot become a writer unless you write, and you have to write as if you already know how to write, even though you really do not. You cannot write without starting to write.

The *as-if* is exemplified in the following story told by Paul Watzlawick (1988):

> Three children came to visit their father on his deathbed. Just before he died, he told them that he had divided his estate in the following way:
>
> > Child A gets 1/2 of his worldly goods.
> > Child B gets 1/3 of his worldly goods.
> > Child C gets 1/9 of his worldly goods.
>
> The father then gasps and dies. When the children inventory the father's things, they discover that all that remained from his estate was 17 horses. The horses are worthless as meat, so they couldn't "split" a horse. They began to argue and then to fight, when an old man rode by on his horse. "What's the matter?" he inquired. When the three told him of their plight, he responded, "That's easy to remedy. Here, use my horse." They did, and now having 18 horses, they awarded half to the first child (9), one-third to the second child (6), and one-ninth to the third child (2). That added up to 17 horses, so the old man got back on his horse, which was left over, and rode away.

Final Thoughts

The point is that there are many ways to skin a cat, and that direct, linear presentation of recommendations for change (in the form of injunctions) are not always the most effective or powerful. A good coach must develop a wide repertoire of influencing strategies and must know that just because a client shows up to meet with you, it does not necessarily follow that he or she is ready, willing, and able to change. Most people resist direct injunctions (such as "You should do this; you must be different than you are"). These techniques are called *hypnotic* because they influence in a way that bypasses critical thinking, not because they make use of observable trance states.

Many of the ideas in this chapter are creative and some are manipulative. Most are nonlinear. They do not move in a direct fashion from point A to point B along a straight line. They must be used carefully, with respect for your coaching client. Take care to ensure that no one ends up feeling foolish as a result of your interventions, and make sure that you have your clients' best interests in mind.

These hypnotic approaches require a special rapport, and they help to build rapport as well. Take care of that rapport, as it is the glue that binds your client to you and to the process of growth.

One more thing: Loosen up and have a little fun with your work and your clients. Here's Paul Watzlawick again with the title of his 1983 book: *The Situation Is Hopeless, But Not Serious.*

References

Franklin, B., Majault, M. J., Le Roy, J. B., Sallin, C. L., Bailly, J. S., D'Arcet, J. et al. (1784). *Rapport des commissaires charges par le Roi, de l'examen du magnetisme animal.* (Reprinted in *Skeptic, 4*(3), 66–83, 1996.)

Gordon, D. (1978). *Therapeutic metaphors: Helping others through the looking glass.* Cupertino, CA: META Publications.

Gordon, D., & Meyers-Anderson, M. (1981). *Phoenix: Therapeutic patterns of Milton H. Erickson.* Cupertino, CA: META Publications.

Haley, J. (1967). *Advanced techniques of hypnosis and therapy. Selected papers of Milton H. Erickson, M.D.* New York: Grune & Stratton.

Haley, J. (1986). *Uncommon therapy: The psychiatric techniques of Milton H. Erickson, M.D.* New York: Norton.

Hilgard, E. R. (1991). A neodissociation interpretation of hypnosis. In S. J. Lynn & J. W. Rhue (Eds.), *Theories of hypnosis: Current models and perspective* (pp. 83–104). New York: Guilford.

Jourard, S., & Landsman, T. (1980). *Healthy personality* (4th ed.). New York: Macmillan.

Kopp, S. (1971). *Metaphors from a psychotherapist guru.* Palo Alto, CA: Science & Behavior Books.

Lynn, S. J., & Rhue, J. W. (1991). *Theories of hypnosis: Current models and perspectives.* New York: Guilford.

O'Hanlon, W. H. (1987). *Taproots: Underlying principles of Milton Erickson's therapy and hypnosis.* New York: Norton.

Peltier, B. (2006). Hypnosis in dentistry. In D. Mostofsky (Ed.), *Behavioral dentistry* (pp. 65–76). Ames, IA: Blackwell-Munksgaard.

Penick, H., & Shrake, B. (1992). *Harvey Penick's little red book: Lessons and teachings from a lifetime in golf.* New York: Simon & Schuster.

Watzlawick, P. (1983). *The situation is hopeless, but not serious*. New York: Norton.
Watzlawick, P. (1988, February 25). *Hypnotherapy without trance*. Lecture presented at the Academic Assembly of the San Francisco Academy of Hypnosis.
Watzlawick, P., Beavin, J. H., & Jackson, D. D. (1967). *Pragmatics of human communication*. New York: Norton.
Watzlawick, P., Weakland, J., & Fisch, R. (1974). *Change: Principles of problem formation and problem resolution*. New York: Norton.
Zilbergeld, B., Edelstien, M. G., & Araoz, D. L. (Eds.). (1986). *Hypnosis: Questions and answers*. New York: Norton.

Recommended Readings

Bry, A. (1978). *Visualization: Directing the movies of your mind*. New York: Harper & Rowe.
Camus, A. (1957). *The fall*. New York: Knopf.
Grimley, B. (2008). NLP Coaching. In S. Palmer & A. Whybrow (Eds.), *Handbook of coaching psychology* (pp. 193–210). London: Routledge.
Hoorwitz, A. (1989). *Hypnotic methods in nonhypnotic therapies*. New York: Irvington.
Kroger, W. S., & Fezler, W. D. (1976). *Hypnosis and behavior modification: Imagery conditioning*. Philadelphia: J. B. Lippincott.
Lankton, S. (1980). *Practical magic: A translation of basic neuro-linguistic programming into clinical psychotherapy*. Cupertino, CA: META Publications.
McMullin, R. E. (1986). *Handbook of cognitive therapy techniques*. New York: Norton.
Sheikh, A. A. (1984). *Imagination and healing*. Farmingdale, NY: Baywood.
Watzlawick, P. (Ed.). (1984). *The invented reality*. New York: Norton.
Watzlawick, P. (1988). *Ultrasolutions: How to fail most successfully*. New York: Norton.

11
Emotional Intelligence

The term emotional intelligence *conveys some aspects of present-day zeitgeists; it captures something of the many competing interests or spirits of our age. In some contexts, it refers to an integration in the war between emotion and rationality throughout human history.*

—John D. Mayer, Peter Salovey, and David R. Caruso (2000, p. 97)

Currently, EI mostly serves a cheerleading function, helping to whip up support for potentially useful (though seldom substantiated) interventions focused on a heterogeneous collection of emotional, cognitive, and behavioral skills.

—Gerald Mathews, Richard D. Roberts, and Moshe Zeidner (2004, p. 192)

Daniel Goleman's books sit on the coffee tables of many executives. His audiotapes are under their car seats. His work has become enormously popular in the world of coaching and organizational development. *EI* or *EQ* (emotional intelligence) or *ESI* (emotional-social intelligence), and *SEI* (social–emotional intelligence) are buzzwords in training circles. Emotional intelligence joins the crowd of other intelligences such as practical intelligence, social intelligence, and the multiple intelligences of Howard Gardner. Because of EI's popularity and Goleman's claim that emotional intelligence can be more important than IQ, no modern book on executive coaching would be complete without a thorough discussion of this topic. It is clear that "EI appears to have a strong following in the business world" (Schmitt, 2006, p. 231).

This chapter will explain emotional intelligence, its history and development, discuss important controversies, and describe some ways that coaches can effectively use the ideas that Goleman and others have promoted. Although it is essential for coaches to understand the limitations and pitfalls associated with emotional intelligence, the EI phenomenon has potential to open doors and provides a powerful framework and vehicle for coaching.

History

Allusions to emotional and social intelligence have been made all the way back to Darwin (Bar-On, 2006), and the first mention of social intelligence in psychological literature can be found a century ago in the writings of John Dewey, the educational philosopher, where he defined social intelligence as "the power of observing and comprehending social situations" (1909, p. 43)

Edward Thorndike called attention to social intelligence in *Harper's* magazine in 1920. In that essay Thorndike, an educational psychology professor at Columbia University, made the following observation (p. 228):

> The facts of everyday life, when inspected critically, indicate that a man has not some one amount of one kind of intelligence, but varying amounts of different intelligences. ... No man is equally intelligent for all sorts of problems.

Thorndike goes on to recommend that intelligence be measured in three domains: mechanical, social, and abstract. He describes social intelligence as "the ability to understand and manage men and women, boys and girls—to act wisely in human relations" (1920, p. 228). He notes the difficulty in measuring such intelligence and seems to equate social intelligence with empathy and niceness or "character." He also recommends that work assignments be matched to type of intelligence and provides the example of the superior technical worker who is promoted to a management position only to fail for lack of social skills (p. 234).

David Wechsler, the creator of several mainstream IQ tests such as the WAIS (Wechsler Adult Intelligence Scales) and WISC (children's version), defined intelligence as "the aggregate or global capacity of the individual to act purposefully, to think rationally and to deal effectively with his environment" (1958, p. 7).

This basic, well-accepted definition does not exclude factors that are emotional, social, or noncognitive. In fact, one of Wechsler's most important contributions to intelligence testing was his addition of a set of scales that tapped nonverbal skills using block designs and mazes (1981). His picture arrangement subtest measures a person's ability to understand common social situations. Shortly after releasing his first major IQ test he began to publish a series of essays about "non-intellective" components of intelligence (1939). Wechsler was very aware of the limitations of cognitive intelligence. "Dealing effectively with one's environment" requires more than just information and logic. In describing and defining intelligence he went on to write, "so far as general intelligence is concerned, intellectual ability, per se, merely enters as a necessary minimum" (Wechsler, 1958, p. 7). He foreshadowed modern advocates of EI by writing that "every reader will be able to recall persons of high intellectual ability in some particular field whom they would unhesitatingly characterize as below average in general intelligence" (1958, p. 7). In 1981 Wechsler wrote:

> Intelligence is a function of the personality as a whole and is responsive to other factors besides those included under the concept of cognitive

abilities. Evidence … strongly implies the influence of personality traits and other nonintellective components, such as anxiety, persistence, goal awareness, and other conative dispositions. (p. 8)

It appears that the first actual use of the term *emotional intelligence* was by a German psychiatrist named Hanscarl Leuner, better known for his advocacy of the drug LSD (lysergic acid diethylamide) in psychotherapy. He published an essay in 1966 about women who did not accept certain aspects of gender role, coming to the conclusion that they had low emotional intelligence.

During this same period psychologists were studying people who did not seem to respond well to psychodynamic psychotherapy. In particular, they were concerned about patients who were not good at introspection or intrapersonal insight, and who possessed little emotional self-awareness. Some were diagnosed with psychosomatic illnesses (physical problems thought to have a psychological or emotional basis), and could not put words to their feelings. Clinicians called this condition *alexithymia*, and contrasted it against something called *psychological-mindedness*, the capacity to notice and work with internal emotional states (McCallum & Piper, 2000; Taylor & Bagboy, 2000).

Social intelligence was an important topic in psychology until interest withered in about 1970. Several formal tests were developed and tested, such as the George Washington Test of Social Intelligence developed by F. A. Moss in 1928 at George Washington University (Landy, 2006). The test had six components:

1. Judgment in Social Situations
2. Memory for Names and Faces
3. Recognition of Mental States from Facial Expression
4. Observation of Human Behavior
5. Social Information
6. Recognition of Mental States behind Words

In spite of how attractive these components appear, research using this instrument showed that people with high IQ tended to score high on the test, ostensibly because successful performance on the test depended on the use of language, "the ability to understand and work with words." This meant that the test was not measuring anything much different from existing cognitive and abstract intelligence tests. Landy's (2006) review of the history of social intelligence concluded that although the concept was very attractive, wishful thinking could not prevail in the face of "an unwillingness to practice the arduous exercises of the scientific enterprise." He went on to say that "it is tempting to come to much the same conclusion regarding current research on emotional intelligence" (Landy, 2006, p. 117).

In 1983, Howard Gardner offered seven types of intelligence in his theory of multiple intelligences. He was struck by the fact that people continued to adhere to the assumption that there is a single, general capacity of intelligence that every human being possesses to a greater or lesser extent (Gardner, 1993, p. x). His set of intelligences included:

Linguistic Intelligence—The ability to understand and manipulate written and spoken words.

Musical Intelligence—The complex capacities to understand, appreciate, and make music.

Logical–Mathematical Intelligence—The ability to understand and manipulate numbers to solve numerical problems.

Spatial Intelligence—The ability to perceive a form or object and manipulate it in space. This intelligence is needed to read a map, find a store in a shopping mall, or create a piece of sculpture.

Bodily–Kinesthetic Intelligence—The ability to understand and manipulate one's physical body to accomplish everyday tasks, to dance, and play sports.

Gardner describes two personal intelligences that are distinctly human. They are of particular importance in a discussion of emotional intelligence, because they are so similar to the essence of EI:

Intrapersonal Intelligence—The ability to access and make use of one's own feelings.

Interpersonal Intelligence—The ability to notice and make distinctions about the moods, temperaments, motivations, and intentions of other people.

The first American use of the term *EI* can be found in the unpublished doctoral dissertation of Wayne Payne in 1985 titled "A Study of Emotion: Developing Emotional Intelligence." This document asserted that (Hein, 2005):

> mass suppression of emotion throughout the civilized world has stifled our growth emotionally, leading us down a path of emotional ignorance. ... We've done this because we have had the wrong idea altogether about the nature of emotion and the important function it serves in our lives.

Payne advocated formal education in the effective use of emotions in everyday life. His dissertation did not seem to stir much interest at that time.

John Mayer, a professor at the University of New Hampshire, and Peter Salovey at Yale, were the first to make a serious academic inquiry of emotional intelligence. Their concern that intellect and emotion were generally seen as incompatible opposites motivated them to write an article in 1990 titled "Emotional Intelligence." Their efforts led them to develop one of the most important current models of EI (to be described later in this chapter). They were the first to take a serious look at the *construct* of emotional intelligence (its working definition) and to conduct serious scientific research. They focused attention on a set of *abilities* or *capacities* rather than traits. These abilities will be described later.

Emotional intelligence made its debut into the popular business and consulting world in 1995 with Goleman's publication of his book *Emotional Intelligence*. He had previously written two books, one on meditation and the other on self-deception, and had been writing a regular column for lay readers of psychology at the *New York Times*. Goleman knew of Mayer and Salovey's work and asked their permission to borrow the model and use the name *emotional intelligence* (Paul, 1999). The book was a commercial smash, selling millions of copies and becoming one of the most successful ever for that publisher. *Time* magazine (Gibbs, 1995) put emotional intelligence on its cover in huge red letters along with the words "emotional intelligence may be the best predictor of success in life, redefining what it means to be smart." Goleman followed the initial commercial success in 1998 with *Working with Emotional Intelligence* and again in 2002 with *Primal Leadership* (with coauthors Boyatzis and McKee). His latest effort is titled *Social Intelligence* (2006), and all four books are available on audio media. He recently collaborated on a book describing ways to develop EI in children (Lantieri & Goleman, 2008).

Beginning in 1997, Reuven Bar-On made a series of contributions that added a third model of EI along with an instrument to measure it. Over the next decade he and his colleagues produced a body of evaluative research that attempted to validate his model and his instrument. Bar-On's work is described later in this chapter.

Popularity

There are conflicts in the American psyche and business culture that help explain the attractiveness of emotional intelligence. First, there is palpable resentment toward the concept of IQ and toward those who possess too much of it. One reviewer (Brody, 2006) even asserts that we "hate *g*" (*g* is psychological notation for a person's total overall intelligence). Intelligence or IQ can be intimidating, especially to anyone who was not on the fast track in school. Brainy types are not universally respected or trusted in the mainstream American cultural view. Current emphasis on test scores such as the SAT and ACT in college admissions as well as IQ tests for entrance to private elementary schools have left many with a bad taste in their mouth regarding intelligence and related forms of testing. Some (Mathews, Zeidner, & Roberts, 2002, p. 5) have even observed an "antipathy to people with high IQs in Western society." Goleman (1995) has a chapter in his first book devoted to the ways that people with high IQ can do socially inept things (Chapter 3, "When Smart Is Dumb") and Robert Sternberg, arguably the modern dean of intelligence theory, edited a book in 2002 entitled *Why Smart People Can Be So Stupid*. Several observers (Mathews et. al, 2002; Mayer, Salovey, & Caruso, 2000; Paul, 1999) note that emotional intelligence serves as a counterbalance to a book titled *The Bell Curve* (Herrnstein & Murray, 1994) published in the year prior to Goleman's first best-seller. *The Bell Curve* was a polemic; it asserted that intelligence is normally distributed and immutable. Intelligence, it reported, was an important reason for the existence of social class, unequal distribution of wealth, and of poverty. It implied that people were successful because they were born with a high IQ, and there is little that can be done after that. This was "a rather pessimistic message for an egalitarian society and offered little hope for the future of those destined to be born into lower-class families or those coming from ethnic-minority backgrounds" (Mathews et al., 2002, p. 7). Some still had the 1984 movie *Revenge of the Nerds* in their consciousness, and everyone knew a technological whiz who could not manage or lead others.

EI was attractive, partly because it diminished the importance of IQ and symbolically opened the door to those who did not possess it. It more than leveled the playing field, and Goleman suggested that it could be taught and learned.

Second, emotional intelligence is popular because of the historic conflict between emotion and reason in Western culture, combined with the tendency of American businesses to distrust or devalue feeling when compared to rational thinking and statistical analysis. Salovey and Mayer (1990, p. 185) describe the Western view of emotions as "disorganized interruptions of mental activity, so potentially disruptive that they must be controlled." Business trends including *Six Sigma*, *Theory of Constraints* (TOC), *Total Quality Management* (TQM), and *Kaizen* (continuous process improvement) emphasized rational methods of progress and constant measurement of explicit goals or metrics. Business schools embraced these methods in the 1990s. Feeling and emotion were squeezed out of decision making. Then, emotional intelligence came along in 1995 and provided plausible support for those who consulted feelings along with logic and reason.

Emotional intelligence also offers a pathway toward integration of rational thinking and emotion, making it attractive to both sides of the argument. *Descartes' Error* by Antonio Damasio (1994) reported that decisions made in the absence of emotion are likely to be faulty, if not tragic. Damasio's research suggests that "without feelings, the decisions we make may not be in our best interest" (Grewal & Salovey, 2005, p. 332). Emotional intelligence argues that emotions should inform reasoning and decision making, a suggestion that is difficult to fault.

Furnham (2006) also notes that EI is popular because it is simple and supposedly learnable. Goleman's books in particular use positive anecdotes and success stories to make their points. Little about EI is counterintuitive; it all makes sense, even to people uninterested in deep examination of workplace and personal problems. Furnham also notes that since EI focuses on individuals, it does not require that organizations change their ways. Emotional intelligence is about feelings, and it feels good.

Models of Emotional Intelligence (EI)

There are at least three distinct models of emotional intelligence in the literature. Consultants can provide an important service to clients by understanding those models and implementing the most defensible aspects in consistent and useful ways. Executive coaches need to be able to articulate the most valuable concepts and components of EI in ways that make sense to clients. Executives who scan one of Goleman's popular books (or listen to it in their car) will not derive much practical value without a coach. At best, they may perceive that emotional intelligence is just another way to emphasize "soft skills" in the workplace; at worst they may feel confused or at a loss to define the value of EI.

This section describes the three most important models of emotional intelligence along with a fourth possibility. The first is an ability-based method; the second and third are mixed models (consisting of a combination of traits, abilities, and personality characteristics). The models are presented in rough historical order.

Model 1: Mayer and Salovey's Four-Branch Model

Mayer and Salovey were the first to conceptualize EI in a comprehensive way, beginning with the idea of *emotional information processing.* They first defined emotional intelligence as "the ability to monitor one's own and others' feelings and emotions, to discriminate among them and to use this information to guide one's thinking and action" (Salovey & Mayer, 1990, p. 189). They refined their definition years later to mean "the capacity to reason about emotions, and of emotions to enhance thinking. It includes the abilities to accurately perceive emotions, to access and generate emotions so as to assist thought, to understand emotions and emotional knowledge, and to reflectively regulate emotions so as to promote emotional and intellectual growth" (Mayer, Salovey, & Caruso, 2004, p. 197). The basic idea is that emotional intelligence involves the ability to perceive, assimilate, understand, and regulate emotions. In their view, emotions are "internal events that coordinate many psychological subsystems including physiological responses, cognitions, and conscious awareness" (Mayer, Caruso, & Salovey, 2000, p. 267). Emotions are enmeshed with thoughts; the ability to understand and use them to help think and behave is essential. Emotional information is seen as necessary and useful. Mayer and Salovey's view is that "emotional intelligence is a set of interrelated skills that allow people to process emotionally relevant information efficiently and accurately" (Salovey & Grewal, 2005, p. 282). Mayer has also described EI as "the capacity to reason with emotions" (1999).

Their working model describes *skills* or *abilities* in a hierarchy of four areas they call branches:

Branch 1: Perception, identification, appraisal, and expression of emotion—This is the nonverbal ability to notice and read emotions in oneself and in others and to express them effectively. It also includes the ability to distinguish between emotions that are similar and between honest, sincere emotions and false ones. This first branch is the building block for the rest of emotional intelligence. It involves reading emotional clues in oneself and others.

Branch 2: Using emotion to facilitate thinking—This is the ability to integrate emotions into the thought process. Emotions can help thinking in the following ways: they can direct one's attention to a specific line of thought, change perspective from pessimistic to optimistic, cause a change in priorities (from mundane to important or urgent or vice versa), cause one to understand things from a different perspective, or motivate one to look at something in a different or more focused way.

Branch 3: Understanding and comprehending emotions—This is the ability to understand emotions and apply emotional knowledge, to label emotions accurately, to interpret emotional meaning, to understand complex emotional nuance and reactions, and to discern the transition from one emotion to another, such as the transition from feeling hurt to expressing anger. Emotions can represent complex combinations and summaries of conscious and unconscious thoughts. Emotions convey important information.

Branch 4: Reflective regulation and management of emotion—This branch refers to the ability to remain open to feelings and be comfortable with the positive and negative feelings of others, to monitor emotional states, and to manage expression of emotion without repressing too much feeling. It is the ability to control emotions effectively in oneself and to work with and manage the emotions of others.

Lower-numbered branches must be mastered first in order to use the subsequent branches. For example, one must learn to accurately perceive emotions before he or she can use them to understand thinking. We must understand emotions before we can learn to regulate them effectively.

Mayer and Salovey's ability-based model has generated the most research and the most respect in the academic world. Its constructs and theoretical basis allow for empirical study, making it attractive to researchers and academics, if not consultants.

Model 2: Goleman's EI

Goleman's EI is the best-known model, especially in the popular press. Nearly everyone in business has heard of the term *emotional intelligence*, and most of them have heard of Goleman. They probably do not know of the other models and thought leaders. One text (Mathews et al., 2002) notes that Goleman's impact on the field "has assumed epic proportions" (p. 11). In effect, Goleman is responsible for coaches being interested in emotional intelligence at all.

In his first book, *Emotional Intelligence*, Goleman began by claiming that new brain research demonstrates the importance of managing fight-or-flight responses. He highlighted the human capacity to "harmonize emotion and thought." He appears to use brain studies to assert that frontal cortex control of the more primitive limbic system is an important component of success in life, and the book couched emotional self-control in the language of neuroscience. He pointed out that people with high IQs can make serious errors when they do not understand and harness their own emotional reactions. He asserted that IQ does not explain much of why some people succeed and others do not, especially in the universities he attended (Amherst and Harvard) and in corporate America, where the vast majority have a high IQ. At each level in an organization, everyone has about the same IQ (researches call this *range restriction*), so differences in success must be explained by factors other than IQ. For example, in medical school, there is probably little difference in IQ scores or GRE scores between students. They all have a high IQ. Goleman presents emotional intelligence as the thing that explains differential success.

A reader is hard-pressed to find a concise definition of emotional intelligence in Goleman's books. In a 2002 chapter he offers that EI "refers to the ability to recognize and regulate emotions in ourselves and in others" (p. 14). Goleman sees himself as a "synthesizer" who "brings together a broad array of findings and theories in psychology and integrates them into the emotional intelligence framework" (Goleman, 2002, p. 18). His model is built on four domains of emotional intelligence (Goleman et al., 2002). They are:

1. *Self-Awareness*—Perception and accurate understanding of one's own emotional states.

2. *Self-Management*—Emotional self-control, effective intrapersonal reactions to feelings.

3. *Social Awareness*—Awareness of relationship surroundings, empathy, understanding of the emotions of others, understanding how organizations work.

4. *Relationship Management*—Working effectively in the social arena, accomplishing goals with and through others, collaborating with teams and organizations.

The first two domains are about self; the last two about others. Self-awareness and social awareness focus on recognizing and knowing; self-management and relationship management focus on action and accomplishment. So, the model advocates awareness and management of personal feelings along with recognition and management of the feelings of others. In chart form, the model looks like Figure 11.1 (Cherniss & Goleman, 2002, p. 28).

Boyatzis, Goleman, and Rhee (2000) define EI in the following way:

> Emotional intelligence is observed when a person demonstrates the competencies that constitute self-awareness, self-management, social awareness, and social skills at appropriate times and ways in sufficient frequency to be effective in the situation. (p. 344)

They go on to describe 25 competencies in 5 clusters to flesh out their model, defining a competency in the following way: A "learned capability based on emotional intelligence that results in outstanding performance at work" (p. 344).

The technical manual for the ECI, Goleman and Boyatzis's assessment instrument, provides the following definition (Wolff, 2005):

> Emotional intelligence is the capacity for recognizing our own feelings and those of others, for motivating ourselves and for managing emotions effectively in ourselves and others. An emotional competence is a learned capacity based on emotional intelligence that contributes to effective performance at work. (p. 10)

	Self (Personal Competence)	Other (Social Competence)
Recognition	**Self-Awareness** • Emotional self-awareness • Accurate self-assessment • Self-confidence	**Social Awareness** • Empathy • Service orientation • Organizational awareness
Regulation	**Self-Management** • Emotional self-control • Trustworthiness • Conscientiousness • Adaptability • Achievement drive • Initiative	**Relationship Management** • Developing others • Influence • Communication • Conflict management • Visionary leadership • Catalyzing change • Building bonds • Teamwork and collaboration

Figure 11.1 A framework of emotional competencies.

Although this definition seems somewhat circular, Goleman sets out the following competencies in the popular 1998 (pp. 25–27) Goleman book *Working with Emotional Intelligence*:

Self-Awareness Cluster
> Emotional Self-Awareness (recognizing one's emotions and their effects)
> Accurate Self-Assessment (knowing one's own strengths and limitations)
> Self-Confidence (strong sense of self-worth and capability)

Self-Regulation Cluster
> Self-Control (keeping disruptive emotions and impulses in check)
> Trustworthiness (maintaining standards of honesty and integrity)
> Conscientiousness (taking responsibility for personal performance)
> Adaptability (flexibility in handling change)
> Innovation (comfortable with new ideas, approaches, and information)

Self-Motivation Cluster
> Achievement Orientation (striving to improve and excel)
> Commitment (aligning personal goals with organizational goals)
> Initiative (readiness to act on opportunities)
> Optimism (persistence in pursuing goals despite obstacles and setbacks)

Empathy Cluster
> Understanding Others (sensing, being interested in others' feelings, perspectives)
> Developing Others (sensing needs and bolstering the ability of others)
> Service Orientation (anticipating, recognizing, meeting customers' needs)
> Leveraging Diversity (cultivating opportunities with different kinds of people)
> Political Awareness (reading a group's emotional currents, power relationships)

Social Skills Cluster
> Influence (wielding effective tactics for persuasion)
> Communication (listening openly, sending convincing messages)
> Conflict Management (negotiating, resolving disagreements)
> Leadership (inspiring, guiding individuals and groups)
> Change Catalyst (initiating and managing change)

Building Bonds (nurturing instrumental relationships)
Collaboration and Cooperation (working with others toward shared
goals)

Team Capabilities (creating group synergy toward collective goals)

The background for each of these competencies is described in *Working with Emotional Intelligence*, mostly through anecdotes and success stories. The list varies slightly from publication to publication. The model is hierarchical, meaning that precursors are essential to development of later competencies on the list. Goleman claims that the competencies are independent from one another, although it is difficult to see how "sending convincing messages" is independent from "wielding effective tactics for persuasion" or how "bolstering the ability of others" is that much different from "nurturing instrumental relationships." However, the competencies are said to be interdependent as well. They are necessary abilities, but not sufficient to guarantee success. Finally, Goleman notes that the list is indeed generic, so that some of the competencies apply to some conditions and not necessarily to all jobs or organizations.

Model 3: Bar-On's Emotional-Social Intelligence (ESI)

Bar-On claims to have begun the exploration of emotional intelligence in an unpublished dissertation in South Africa in the 1980s, and that would make him a pioneer. He observed that there are important interpersonal as well as intrapersonal components of the construct and therefore favors the term *emotional-social intelligence* or *ESI* (Bar-On, 2006). He defines ESI as (Bar-On, 2007)

> a cross-section of interrelated emotional and social competencies, skills and facilitators that determine how well we understand and express ourselves, understand others and relate with them, and cope with daily demands, challenges and pressures.

The model is typically thought to be a mixed model comprised of various personality traits, qualities, mental abilities, and skills (Mathews et al., 2002; Mayer et al., 2000).

There are two components to Bar-On's model: the *conceptual* model and the *psychometric* model expressed in his assessment instrument, the Emotional Quotient Inventory (EQ-i). The broad conceptual model consists of five key components or "metafactors" (Bar-On, 2007):

1. *Intrapersonal*—The ability to understand emotions as well as express our feelings and ourselves.

2. *Interpersonal*—The ability to understand others' feelings and relate with people.

3. *Stress Management*—The ability to manage and control our emotions.

4. *Adaptability*—The ability to manage change and solve problems of an intrapersonal and interpersonal nature.

5. *General Mood*—The ability to generate a positive mood and be self-motivated.

There are 15 closely related "competencies, skills, and facilitators." They are:

Intrapersonal (Understanding One's Own Emotions)
> Self-Regard (being aware of, understanding, and accepting ourselves)
> Emotional Self-Awareness (being aware of and understanding our emotions)
> Assertiveness (expressing our feelings and ourselves nondestructively)
> Independence (being self-reliant and free of emotional dependency on others)
> Self-Actualization (setting and achieving goals to actualize our potential)

Interpersonal (Social Awareness and Interaction)
> Empathy (being aware of and understanding how others feel)
> Social Responsibility (identifying with and feeling part of our social groups)
> Interpersonal Relationship (establishing mutually satisfying relationships)

Stress Management (Emotional Management and Control)
> Stress Tolerance (effectively and constructively managing our emotions)
> Impulse Control (effectively and constructively controlling our emotions)

Adaptability (Change Management)
> Reality Testing (validating our feelings and thinking with external reality)
> Flexibility (coping with and adapting to change in our daily life)
> Problem Solving (generating effective solutions to problems of an intrapersonal and interpersonal nature)

General Mood (Self-Motivation)
> Optimism (having a positive outlook and looking at the brighter side of life)

Happiness (Feeling Content with Ourselves, Others, and Life in General)

Bar-On created a test to measure ESI, and he uses this instrument to simultaneously assess clients and to adjust the model. He reports that this instrument, the EQ-i, played an "instrumental role in developing the model" (Bar-On, 2006, p. 13). The instrument is an operational version of the conceptual model, and it will be described later.

Bar-On claims that social-emotional intelligence contributes to overall intelligence and is a significant contributor to overall success in life. He asserts, as does Goleman, that the skills, abilities, and traits in his model can be taught and learned.

A Possible Fourth Model: Trait Emotional Intelligence

British psychologists Petrides, Furnham, and Frederickson (2004) point out that emotional factors are not cognitive abilities, and therefore should not be considered to be "intelligence." Their effort to sort out methodological problems with EI led them to the conclusion that emotional intelligence is best understood and measured as a *trait*. Difficulties involved in trying to measure emotional abilities led them to focus on traits, which they claim are appropriately measured with self-report instruments. Emotional experience is inherently subjective, therefore viewing and measuring it as ability does not make sense. Abilities can be observed and measured by others. Traits (especially emotional ones) are self-perceived, meaning that they can only be perceived by the one experiencing them. They see intelligence as an ability and emotional activities as traits. Traits refer to the future, a tendency to do something (or not) or to do it in a certain way. They actually prefer the term *emotional self-efficacy* rather than emotional intelligence, although they retain the EI terminology to stay connected to the emotional intelligence literature. Their definition of the construct is (Petrides & Furnham, 2001; Petrides, Pita, & Kokkinaki, 2007): a constellation of emotion-related dispositions, behavioral tendencies, and self-perceived abilities that represents a compound personality structure.

Petrides and Furnham (2006, p. 554) go on to note that "the precise composition of these self-perceptions and dispositions tends to vary across different conceptualizations, some of which are broader than others." They also note that "trait EI theory is unrelated to what lay people understand by 'emotional intelligence' or 'EQ' and incompatible with other models of the construct" (London Psychometric Laboratory, 2001–2008).

People with high trait EI believe that they are "in touch" with their emotions and that they can regulate emotions in a way that promotes well-being. Petrides and colleagues believe that such people are likely to enjoy higher levels of happiness. They go on to say that "we believe that the future of EI lies in its conceptualization as a personality trait (i.e., trait EI)" (Petrides et al., 2004, p. 577). The specific facets of this model and their definitions (Petrides, Sangareau, Furnham, & Frederickson, 2006) are shown in Table 11.1.

Trait EI researchers such as Petrides and his colleagues have produced a body of innovative research that attempts to verify their point of view and

Table 11.1 Commonly Accepted Components of Emotional Intelligence

Facet	High Scorers Perceive Themselves As
Adaptability	Flexible and willing to adapt to new conditions
Assertiveness	Forthright, frank, and willing to stand up for their rights
Emotion Perception	Clear about their own and other people's feelings
Emotion Expression	Capable of communicating their feelings to others
Emotion Management	Capable of influencing other people's feelings
Emotion Regulation	Capable of controlling their emotions
Impulsiveness (low)	Reflective and less likely to give in to their urges
Relationships	Capable of maintaining fulfilling personal relationships
Self-Esteem	Successful and self-confident
Self-Motivation	Driven and unlikely to give up in the face of adversity
Social Awareness	Accomplished networkers with superior social skills
Stress Management	Capable of withstanding pressure and regulating stress
Trait Empathy	Capable of taking someone else's perspective
Trait Happiness	Cheerful and satisfied with their lives
Trait Optimism	Confident and likely to look on the bright side of life

validate trait constructs. They conclude that trait EI represents a distinct, compound psychological trait distinct from ability EI and of great future value.

Assessment of Emotional Intelligence

All of the creators of emotional intelligence models have developed formal instruments to assess EI from their point of view. They differ in that some (most) are self-report measures, whereas others attempt to measure abilities using an objectively scored test. Assessment activities typically influence subsequent theory development and refinement. There are serious psychometric challenges involved in this process, the most formidable being the problem of construct validity. Given that there is widespread disagreement about the basic definition of emotional intelligence and its essential components, it should come as no surprise that EI is difficult to measure. There are numerous other psychometric challenges in addition to the construct problem (Mathews et al., 2002, pp. 32–46 and chapter 5). Even so, there are literally hundreds of instruments that claim to assess EI, the vast majority of them rather unscientific. It is probably wise to avoid using any of these tests for selection, hiring, or promotion decisions. It makes little sense to make important decisions using instruments that may not be valid, and it would be difficult to defend their use if challenged in court. A Google search for "test of emotional intelligence" reveals 863,000 sites, many of which contain a quick or free test of EI or EQ. The best-known and well-accepted measures are described and evaluated next, in the same order that the respective theories were described previously. Table 11.2 provides a

Table 11.2 Major Formal Instruments for Assessment of Emotional Intelligence

Test	EI Model Tested	Time to Test	Approximate Cost (2008)	Scoring Method and Reports	User Qualifications Level	Ordering
MSCEIT	Mayer–Salovey (abilities)	141 items 25–45 minutes 8th grade reading level	$40 per report in addition to setup costs	Consensus, expert; online Personal summary report 15 scores (total score, area scores, branch scores, task scores)	B[a]	MHS (Multi-Health Systems, Inc.) http://www.mhs.com/mhs/ (800) 456-3003
ECI-ECSI	Goleman (mixed)	72 items 30–60 minutes (360-degree multirater instrument involves self, peers, manager, direct-reports)	$3,000 accreditation fee $150 each after setup	Online, available for consultants to use through Hay Group once accredited	"A good level of experience in delivering feedback" plus 2-day accreditation course	Hay Group http://www.haygroup.com/TL
EQ-i, Bar-On EQ 360	Bar-On	133 items 40 minutes for 6th grade reading level Youth, short, interview, and 360-degree versions available	$80–$120 per report after set up costs	Self-report, online computer 5 composite scales and 15 subscales Development Report, Individual Summary, Resource Report, Business Report, Group Report, Leadership Report	B	MHS (Multi-Health Systems, Inc.) http://www.mhs.com/mhs/ (800) 456-3003

| TEIQue (several forms and versions) | Petrides (trait EI) | Long form, 153 items; short form, 30 items 7–10 minutes | Free for academic research. About $30 otherwise. | Self-report. 15 facets, 4 factors Global trait EI Scoring key only available to members of ISSID[b] | Researcher | Long form: k.petrides@ioe.ac.uk Short form: http://www.ioe.ac.uk/schools/phd/kpetrides/The%20TEIQue-SF.pdf or http://www.psychometriclab.com/admins/files/TEIQue%20v.1.50.pdf |

[a] B-level administrator: Can be administered and scored by professionals with advanced training in psychological assessment and professionals from related disciplines that adhere to relevant assessment standards. Individuals without formal psychological training and professional affiliations need to be trained and certified to use the MSCEIT by the MHS Organizational Effectiveness Group. MSCEIT is classified as a B-level instrument, which requires that, as a minimum, the user has completed courses in tests and measurement at a university and/or has completed the MSCEIT Certification Workshop.

[b] ISSID: International Society for the Study of Individual Differences (http://www.issid.org/).

quick summary of the four standard instruments used to assess emotional intelligence.

The Multifactor Emotional Intelligence Scale (MEIS) and
Mayer–Salovey–Caruso Emotional Intelligence Test (MSCEIT)

MEIS and MSCEIT were created to measure EI from the ability model of Mayer and Salovey. The MEIS was developed in 1998 and was followed by a revised and improved version, the MSCEIT in 2002. Recall that the Mayer–Salovey model consists of four branches (emotional perception, facilitation, understanding, and management). The MSCEIT (version 2.0) uses 141 questions to test two areas in each of the four branches (Grewal & Salovey, 2005). In Branch 1, participants are asked to rate facial photos (along with landscapes and graphic designs) for the presences and degree of anger, sadness, happiness, disgust, fear, surprise, and excitement. In Branch 2 they are asked to compare emotional states with various tactile and sensory stimuli and to indicate how certain emotions might impact their performance (for example, Would boredom help with the task of planning a birthday party?) In Branch 3 participants are asked to complete sentences that test their understanding of the vocabulary of emotions as well as the ways that emotions tend to heighten, attenuate, and evolve from one to another. They are also asked to identify the emotions involved in a blended affective state. Branch 4 is tested with real-life scenarios. Participants are asked to devise a strategy to manage an emotionally laden hypothetical situation. They are also asked how they might handle the emotional reactions of others to accomplish a goal. Grading the test is difficult, and users without formal psychometric training are urged to take a certification program sponsored by the test publisher.

Mayer and Salovey were unwilling to use self-report methods, and much subjectivity is involved in the emotional world. The test uses two types of scoring methods, a consensual mode and an expert mode. In the consensus method they compare the participants' responses to those of 5,000 subjects in a diverse, worldwide sample group. In the expert scoring they compared participants' answers to those of 21 experts selected from the International Society for Research on the Emotions. Correlations between these two sets of scores are high, signaling to Mayer and Salovey that the combined score represents a convergence of "emotionally intelligent answers." They conclude that the MSCEIT has good reliability and that it represents something distinct from personality and from standard IQ. Although others point to serious problems with this instrument (Mathews et al., 2002, pp. 197–202), there is general agreement that, because it is *not* based upon self-report, the test is important. It is thought to hold promise, but requires psychometric attention. This is indeed a difficult area of human behavior to measure, and several authors note that this is a potentially rich arena for ambitious doctoral students in search of a dissertation topic.

The O. K. Buros review in *Mental Measurements Yearbook* reports that MSCEIT results indicate that women generally score higher than men and Whites scored higher than other ethnic groups on 14 of the 15 scales. The Buros report is cautious but generally positive about the instrument (Leung, 2005).

Goleman's ECI and ESCI

Goleman and Richard Boyatzis developed the original version of the Emotional Competence Inventory (ECI) in 1998 starting with Boyatzis's Self-Assessment Questionnaire (SAQ) and emotional competencies clustered by Boyatzis, Goleman, and Rhee (2000). Goleman and Boyatzis began with five clusters and eventually grouped Goleman's 25 competencies into four clusters. They were: self-awareness, self-management, social awareness, and relationship management. The original instrument had 110 items and took about half an hour to complete. *Tipping points* indicate where a subject was expected to be tipped over into superior performance on job competency (Gowing, 2001). Eventually, the Hay/McBer research team collaborated, and the ECI was replaced with the Emotional and Social Competence Inventory (ESCI). The ESCI is a 72-item, self-report inventory that uses a multirater methodology so that peers, managers, and direct-reports contribute to the self-report data. Coaches must complete a $3,000, 2-day accreditation program prior to administering the test.

Goleman claims the "ECI is the only instrument that incorporates the full depth of my research and that of my colleagues. Other instruments use the words 'Emotional Intelligence' but the ECI is the genuine article" (Hay/McBer, 2008).

Others are not so enthusiastic. Jensen and colleagues note that "of all the major measures of Emotional Intelligence, the least psychometric information is available for the ECI" and "little data is available for the ESCI" and "it is disappointing that better information was not gathered before the publication of the technical manual, or at least set as a priority for research following its publication" (Jensen, Kohn, Rilea, Hannon, & Howells, 2007, p. 18). Mathews and colleagues (2002, pp. 217–218) write "in truth, because it may be used for high-stakes decision-making, the reliability of the self-report subscales is marginal" and " an actual evaluation of the validity of the ECI is difficult" and "reliability is a cause for concern." They go on to conclude: "In sum, it is difficult not to be cynical of this measure, given the lack of publicly accessible data supplied by its creators and the constellation of old concepts packaged under its new label." The Buros review (Watson, 2007, p. 305) of the ECI was unenthusiastic, reporting that test materials were confusing. Its report states: "The ECI may be a reliable instrument. Currently, little empirical evidence has been offered to support this property. Validity too is questionable, given the many limiting factors of the studies reported in the test manual." (This was prior to the ECI version 2.0.)

Bar-On's EQ-i

Bar-On constructed the Emotional Quotient Inventory (EQ-i) in the early 1980s as an experimental instrument to explore components of emotional and social functioning (Bar-On, 2000). It was formally published in 1997 and was the first EI test to be included in Buros's *Mental Measurements Yearbook*. It was also the first such test to be sold by a commercial test publisher, Multi-Health Systems or MHS (Gowing, 2001). Bar-On describes it as "a self-report measure of emotionally and socially competent behavior that provides an estimate of one's emotional and social intelligence" (Bar-On, 2000, p. 364). He intentionally structured the instrument so that it resembles the format of standard IQ tests. The mean overall EQ score is 100 with a standard deviation of 15. It has been translated into 30 languages and normed internationally against large sample groups (Bar-On, 2006). It takes about 30 minutes to complete and requires a 6th grade reading level.

The test consists of five metafactors and fifteen subfactors. The five global factors are intrapersonal, interpersonal, adaptability/stress management, and general mood, the same ones listed earlier in this chapter as key components or metafactors in Bar-On's model of emotional intelligence. The test's fifteen subfactors are the same ones described earlier as competencies, skills, and facilitators. Hence, the instrument tests the model and the model is defined by the test. A comprehensive description of the subfactors can be found in Bar-On (2000).

The test uses Likert-type scales and contains four validity indicators (Omission Rate, Inconsistency Index, Positive Impression, and Negative Impression), and computer scoring automatically factors positive and negative impression scores into the total.

Bar-On (2000) claims that high scores on his instrument predict general success in life and makes numerous specific claims that derive from 20 predictive validity studies conducted on 22,971 participants in 7 countries (Bar-On, 2006, p. 18). He claims moderate to clear prediction of physical health, psychological well-being, performance at school, performance in the workplace, and self-actualization. He also recommends "encouraging continued empirical work in this area is the best way to discourage the proliferation of ungrounded 'theorizing' that abets misconceptions and false claims of what emotional intelligence is and is not" (2000, p. 386).

EQ-i scores indicate that emotional intelligence (or whatever the instrument actually tests) increases with age up to about 50, implying that older workers are more emotionally intelligent than younger ones. The test has also produced some small but intriguing gender findings. It appears that women score higher in some of the interpersonal areas including empathy and awareness of emotions, and social responsibility (Bar-On, 2000). Men seem to have higher self-regard, are more adaptable, and have better stress management. These effects were, as mentioned earlier, small.

A Buros review (Cox, 2001) points out the obvious problems in construct validity (disagreement and difficulty in defining emotional intelligence in the first place), and notes that Bar-On makes assertions without supportive data, but generally gives the EQ-i favorable ratings.

Mathews et al. (2002), on the other hand, are less positive. They observe that some of the subscales are empirically indefensible, and that the EQ-i is actually a measure of self-esteem, empathy, and impulse control. They point out that few of the evaluations of the test have been independent. They suspect that the EQ-i shows considerable overlap with personality tests, especially the *Big Five* personality factors (openness, conscientiousness, extraversion, agreeableness, and neuroticism). They also note that the EQ-i does not show convergence with the MSCEIT, meaning that they may not be testing the same construct.

Petrides's Trait Emotional Intelligence Questionnaire (TEIQue)

As previously mentioned, there are many available self-report measures of trait EI. Petrides points out that since emotional perception is subjective, self-report is the appropriate way to measure it. In 2003, he and his colleagues produced such an instrument, the *TEIQue*. The questionnaire is currently open access, and there is a free version available to academics wishing to study the construct and components. The instrument tests four factors: well-being, self-control, emotionality, and sociability. There are 15 subscales within those 4 main factors, the ones called facets in the earlier description of the Petrides model of trait EI. There are currently eight versions of the test in 12 languages, including a 360-degree version. The standard form has 153 questions using a 7-point Likert-type scale. A technical manual is currently in preparation. Petrides asserts that the "TEIQue is specifically developed and updated to provide a gateway to trait EI theory and it should not be seen as an alternative to the proliferating, and generally invalid 'EQ tests'" (London Psychometric Laboratory, 2001–2008, p. 11).

A Belgian study showed promising psychometric results along with observations similar to those of other tests of EI; that is, that women score higher on emotionality and men higher on self-control (Mikolajczak, Luminet, Leroy, & Roy, 2007).

Some of the other more substantial instruments available to measure EI include:

- Schutte Self-Report Inventory (SSRI)
- Emotional Accuracy Research Scale (EARS)
- Levels of Emotional Awareness Scale (LEAS)
- Emotional Control Questionnaire
- Swinburne University Emotional Intelligence Test (SUEIT)
- The Trait Meta-Mood Scale (TMMS)

- The Wong and Law Emotional Intelligence Scale (WLEIS)
- The Workgroup Emotional Intelligence Profile (WEIP)

Most of the information describing each of the tests is written by the authors of the instrument, and they tend to have a self-promotional tone. A recent impartial review done by the psychology department at the University of the Pacific concluded (Jensen et al., 2007, p. 24):

> Given the lack of research with EI measures in a university context, it is difficult to recommend the use of one specific measure over the others. Even within the business field, no measure has distinguished itself as the superior alternative. The available reviews ... suggest that the MSCEIT shows the most promise based on the fact that it does not overlap as much with personality factors and its more clearly defined theory and relationship to accepted definitions of intelligence. ... it is the most distinct measure of EI, being the only non self-report measure of EI.

Criticisms, Issues, and Challenges

Emotional intelligence is controversial. There is widespread disagreement about EI in academic, consulting, and organizational development (OD) circles. The most skeptical critics are to be found in academia, where standards for new approaches and accompanying psychometrics tend to be high. Business consultants tend to be the least critical, as they are always looking for new ways to make a difference and to create opportunities for new or innovative work. As there are many problems with emotional intelligence, it is important for coaches to understand that although EI can be useful, several concerns are quite serious. If coaches are to use EI—and they probably should—they must take care to avoid certain problem areas and to take the best and leave the rest. It may also be important for coaches to understand the most significant problem areas associated with EI so that they can respond cogently when challenged. The four most significant areas of criticism are:

1. The Construct (Basic Definition) of EI
2. Old Wine in New Bottles
3. Lack of Empirical (Research) Support
4. Commercialization and Overpromotion of the Concept

Construct Problems

There is no single, well-accepted definition of emotional intelligence. Current definitions are too broad, and existing definitions are something of a moving target, although new definitions pop up all the time. One respected business professor came to the conclusion that emotional intelligence is "defined so broadly and inclusively that it has no intelligible meaning" (Locke, 2005, p. 425). Mathews et al. (2002) conclude that EI is too generalized a construct to be useful. Mathews, Roberts, and Zeidner (2004, p. 180) conclude that "examination of the literature suggests that there is no clear, consensual definition of EI, and the multitude of qualities covered by the concept appears at times overwhelming."

Mayer and Salovey's definition is the one that seems to have garnered the most respect. Recall that they define emotional intelligence as "the ability to perceive emotion, integrate emotion to facilitate thought, understand emotions, and to regulate emotions to promote personal growth" (1997, p. 5). Note that this definition is a revision of their original definition from 7 years earlier (something of a moving target).

Goleman's work receives the most negative, even scathing criticism, as his characterization of emotional intelligence is so vast. As previously mentioned, after reading Goleman it is not entirely clear that he has actually provided a concise definition. His descriptions are so broad that virtually any positive psychological attribute could be included under the umbrella term of emotional intelligence. For example, Goleman variously includes self-confidence, moral character, adaptability, optimism, trustworthiness, conscientiousness, commitment, empathy, initiative, persistence, the ability to handle relationships smoothly, the capacity to hope, initiating change, listening openly, and a sense of humor in his long list of components of EI (1995, 1998, 2002). He eventually concludes that "some might call it *character*" (1995, p. 36).

Some EI constructs are ability based, whereas others are personality or trait based. Others are a mishmash of abilities, qualities, skills, and characteristics.

This construct confusion causes many problems, not the least of which is the difficulty in knowing what someone means when they advocate for emotional intelligence. What, exactly, are they seeking or talking about? Another problematic result is an inability to measure EI or to know when it exists, when it is high or low, and when it is not present at all. How do you know if you have something if you do not know its definition? How do you establish a training program to promote something that you cannot define? The construct problem also makes empirical research difficult if not impossible.

Old Wine in New Bottles

Attempts to demonstrate that EI represents something new or something different from familiar aspects of personality have not been fruitful. It appears that much of emotional intelligence overlaps or recycles what we already know to be core components of personality. Mathews et al. (2002, p. 529) report much of what self-report EI scales measure "constitutes standard personality traits" and that "for the most part, the scales are redundant." Much work has already been done in mainstream psychology on personality traits, and it appears that emotional intelligence rehashes that work, but in a less careful way.

Consultants, and business leaders and followers for that matter, have long known the importance of social and relationship factors. The notion that emotions and relationships matter is hardly news. The trick is to add something useful to the mix.

Lack of Empirical (Research) Support

Research psychologists and business consultants live in different worlds and have different standards. In academia, the empirical standards of science rule the roost. For concepts to be valuable they must make their way through the gauntlet of statistical significance and research design. It is different in the business arena where an idea must yield a practical benefit to be of value. Value can be added even when methods do not match the standards required by science. This seems to be the case with EI. Although the originators of the concept of emotional intelligence (Mayer and Salovey) continue to work in the academic arena, the majority of practitioners apply EI in an unscientific way.

Many of the claims of enthusiasts have not done well when tested systematically. Mathews et al. (2002) report that "Goleman appears willing to make strong claims with little (or scant) empirical backing" (p. 13) and that he "represents a journalist distilling scientific information for the consumption of the populist, rather than a legitimate scientific theory" (p. 14). Paul (1999) noted that "Mayer and Salovey ... concluded that Goleman was indeed playing fast and loose with the research." In a review of EI training, Clarke (2006, p. 437) comes to the following conclusion: "Despite the growth in training programs that purport to influence EI there remains little empirical support regarding their effectiveness." Another review (Conte, 2005, p. 438) found that "broad claims that EI is a more important predictor than general mental ability (e.g., Goleman, 1995, 1998) are unfounded and unsubstantiated."

Commercialization and Overpromotion

The most important thing about emotional intelligence may be its promotion, and in that arena Goleman has been a smash. Goleman's books and tapes have become enormously popular. Emotional intelligence has put soft skills back into the corporate spotlight, and from a coach's perspective, this is a good thing, indeed. Hundreds of companies and schools have incorporated EI principles and methods in their training programs (Paul, 1999).

But there is danger in overpromotion, and some of the claims made on behalf of EI seem overstated and superficial, if not preposterous. For example, Goleman variously contends that:

- EI accounts for 80% of life success (1995).
- Emotional competencies account for 80% to 100% of leadership success in outstanding performers (1998, p. 187).

- Emotional aptitude is a meta-ability that all other human skills depend upon (1995, p. 36).
- Great leadership works through the emotions (Goleman, Boyatzis, & McKee, 2002).

Whether such an overextension of reality will be harmful remains to be seen, but there is danger that emotional intelligence could devolve into just another fad. Skeptics are wary, and it is possible that emotional intelligence could become one more self-help craze in a long line of management consultant jokes. Locke, an influential business professor, warns, "With respect to the concept of EI ... we are more in need of rational guardians than ever" (2005, p. 430).

Claims that emotional intelligence is a panacea, that emotional intelligence (whatever it is) may be the best predictor of success in life, that it can be effectively taught and learned, that it can level the playing field between those with high IQ and the rest of us, along with claims that character can be measured and developed through emotional intelligence have the potential to raise unrealistic hopes.

What Is a Coach to Do?

Given the widespread notoriety of emotional intelligence, its following in the business community, and the fact that it is difficult to define and oversold, the answer is simple: Take the best and leave the rest. Throw out the bathwater, but save the baby. It makes good sense for coaches to take advantage of the opportunity that EI offers without further overpromotion.

First, coaches can study the available models and make decisions about what is valuable and what is not. Clients will expect coaches to know EI and will rely on them to sort things out. Coaches can provide a valuable service by promoting a realistic view. Coaches certainly need to define EI for themselves, and it seems that a reasonable definition of the construct ought to include the following:

1. *Recognition of internal emotional states*—It is indisputably better to know how you are feeling and to be able to label and study those emotional states immediately or soon after feeling them. It is also essential for clients to be able to accept and live with a variety of real-life emotions rather than to ignore or deny them.

2. *Use of emotional information*—Feelings can motivate; they can help us understand our real values, they can caution us, and they can help focus attention on things that may otherwise seem unimportant. They can cause us to feel and express empathy and to make prosocial decisions. They are a source of essential information that may not be otherwise available. Feelings are essential to introspection and reflection, two activities of enormous importance in the EI literature.

3. *Modulate emotional behavior appropriately*—If a client is too emotionally expressive or not expressive enough, connect rational decision making with felt emotions so that feelings are expressed well. Coaches can be extremely helpful in providing feedback and guidance in this area. Clients can learn to be smart about their feelings and emotional expression.

4. *Pay attention to the affect of others*—In psychology the term *emotion* typically refers to a felt feeling state. The term *affect* refers to the way that emotions are generally expressed by someone, usually as viewed by others. Most clients benefit from enhanced efforts to notice and learn about the affect of people around them. This is especially true for clients who seem to possess little interest in the nature of other people. Many hard-charging executives are waylaid because they have no idea about the feelings of colleagues, superiors, or direct-reports.

5. *Use EI to enhance relationships*—Emotional intelligence provides an opportunity and format for relationship development. Help clients assess the quality of their work relationships and use emotional intelligence concepts to create a plan for improvement. Most executives would benefit from relationship enhancements.

6. *Consider the fit*—Explore the match between a client's level of social and emotional abilities and current job requirements as well as the skills associated with his or her career goals.

Other Uses of EI

In spite of the problems cited, emotional intelligence is a perfect vehicle for the smuggling of more interpersonal and intrapersonal skills into the workplace. It can legitimize important so-called soft-skill training and coaching. Chosen carefully, EI can be an ideal package for the transmission of crucial but undervalued enhancements. Consultants can use EI as an umbrella to offer a wide range of topics. These soft or interpersonal skills can be of enormous value when working with clients who lack solid social skills.

Emotional intelligence and some of the EI measures could potentially be used to match people with tasks and environments. If an executive has weak interpersonal or emotional skills, there are two options: (1) improve those skills or (2) place that person in a work environment conducive to his or her skill set and personality.

Summary

The idea that emotional or social factors play an important role in success is an old and enticing notion. The likelihood that there is an important set of skills independent of "intelligence" is especially attractive. Goleman popularized this idea by publishing several books and audio versions for the popular market, and his view of emotional intelligence is extremely broad. Although Goleman's work is criticized in the academic literature, emotional intelligence creates an opportunity for coaches to develop programs to assess and enhance the intrapersonal, social, and interaction skills of clients. Such work has the potential to create significant benefit for individual clients and for organizations as well. The importance of self-understanding, introspection and reflection, empathy, and effective social interaction skills is indisputable, and can often be enhanced through coaching.

1. Coaches should invest time in the EI literature (and in this chapter) to decide what emotional intelligence should reasonably include. They must come up with a personal working definition of the construct for use in their consulting and must be able to articulate that definition as necessary.

2. There is nearly universal agreement that emotional and social factors are extremely important mediators of work success. Evaluate clients along these dimensions. Provide feedback to them and work together to establish a plan for development, enhancement, or remediation.

3. Personal reflection and introspection are important components of any reasonable view of EI. Promote and reinforce these activities in clients and organizations. Use the popularity and credibility of EI to do so.

4. Be wary of EI measurement instruments. Avoid using them for hiring, selection, or promotion. If you decide to use such tools, use them informally to acquire data for coaching.

5. Help clients notice intrapersonal events such as feelings, hunches, discomfort, wariness, anxiety, hostility, yearnings, or joy. The coaching relationship is an ideal and unique vehicle for overt discussion of these internal events, as they cannot often be discussed elsewhere.

6. Work with clients to improve their ability to read other people, especially aspects that are not obvious. Challenge them appropriately to get outside of their own point of view and to develop an interest in what others are thinking and feeling. Help them nurture their empathy.

References

Bar-On, R. (2000). Emotional and social intelligence: Insights from the emotional quotient inventory. In R. Bar-On & J. D. A. Parker (Eds.), *The handbook of emotional intelligence* (pp. 363–388). San Francisco: Jossey-Bass.

Bar-On, R. (2006). The Bar-On model of emotional–social intelligence (ESI). *Psicothema, 18*, 13–25.

Bar-On, R. (2007). *A broad definition of emotional-social intelligence according to the Bar-On model.* Retrieved January 25, 2009, from: http://www.reuvenbaron.org/bar-on-model/essay.php?i=2.

Boyatzis, R., Goleman, D., & Rhee, K. S. (2000). Clustering competence in emotional intelligence. In R. Bar-On & J. D. A. Parker (Eds.), *The handbook of emotional intelligence* (pp. 343–362). San Francisco: Jossey-Bass.

Brody, N. (2006). Beyond *g.* In K. R. Murphy (Ed.), *A critique of emotional intelligence* (pp. 161–185). New York: Lawrence Erlbaum Associates.

Cherniss, C., & Goleman, D. (Eds.). (2002). *The emotionally intelligent workplace.* San Francisco: Jossey-Bass.

Clarke, N. S. (2006). Emotional intelligence training: A case of caveat emptor. *Human Resource Development Review, 5*(4), 422–441.

Conte, J. M. (2005). A review and critique of emotional intelligence measures. *Journal of Organizational Behavior, 26,* 433–440.

Cox, A. (2001). Test review of the EQ-i. In B. S. Plake & J. C. Impara (Eds.), *The fourteenth mental measurements yearbook* [Electronic version]. Retrieved June 24, 2008, from the Buros Institute's Test Reviews Online Web site: http://www.unl.edu/buros.

Damasio, A. (1994). *Descartes' error: Emotion, reason, and the human brain.* New York: G. P. Putnam's Sons.

Dewey, J. (1909). Moral principles in education. New York: Houghton Mifflin.

Furnham, A. (2006). Explaining the popularity of emotional intelligence. In K. R. Murphy (Ed.), *A critique of emotional intelligence* (pp. 141–160). New York: Lawrence Erlbaum Associates.

Gardner, H. (1993). *Frames of mind: The theory of multiple intelligences* (10th ed.). New York: Basic Books.

Gibbs, N. (1995, October 2). The EQ factor. *Time.* Retrieved January 25, 2009, from: http://www.time.com/time/magazine/article/0,9171,983503,00.html.

Goleman, D. (1995). *Emotional intelligence: Why it can matter more than IQ.* New York: Bantam Books.

Goleman, D. (1998). *Working with emotional intelligence.* New York: Bantam Books.

Goleman, D. (2002). Emotional intelligence: Issues in paradigm building. In C. Cherniss & D. Goleman (Eds.), *The emotionally intelligent workplace* (pp. 13–26). San Francisco: Jossey-Bass.

Goleman, D. (2006). *Social intelligence: The new science of social relationships.* New York: Bantam Books.

Goleman, D., Boyatzis, R., & McKee, A. (2002). *Primal leadership: Realizing the power of emotional intelligence.* Boston: Harvard Business School Press.

Gowing, M. K. (2001). Measurement of individual emotional competence. In C. Cherniss & D. Goleman (Eds.), *The emotionally intelligent workplace* (pp. 83–131). San Francisco: Jossey-Bass.

Grewal, D., & Salovey, P. (2005). Feeling smart: The science of emotional intelligence. *American Scientist, 93,* 330–339.

Hay/McBer. (2008). *Emotional Competence Inventory (ECI).* Retrieved January 25, 2009, from: http://www.bostonsearchgroup.com/pdf/ECI_overview.pdf.

Hein, S. (2005). *Wayne Payne's 1985 doctoral paper on emotions and emotional intelligence.* Retrieved January 25, 2009, from: http://eqi.org/payne.htm#The%20original%20abstract.

Herrnstein, R., & Murray, C. (1994). *The bell curve: Intelligence and class structure in American life.* New York: Simon & Schuster.

Jensen, S., Kohn, C., Rilea, S., Hannon, R., & Howells, G. (2007). *Emotional intelligence; A literature review.* Unpublished manuscript, University of the Pacific, Stockton, California.

Landy, F. L. (2006). The long, frustrating, and fruitless search for social intelligence: A cautionary tale. In K. R. Murphy (Ed.), *A critique of emotional intelligence* (pp. 81–124). New York: Lawrence Erlbaum Associates.

Lantieri, L., & Goleman, D. (2008). *Building emotional intelligence: Techniques to cultivate inner strength in children.* Boulder, CO: Sounds True, Inc.

Leuner, B. (1966). Emotional intelligence and emancipation. *Praxis der Kinderpsychologie und Kinderpsychiatrie, 15,* 193–203.

Leung, S. (2005). Test review of the MSCEIT. In R. A. Spies & B. S. Plake (Eds.), *The sixteenth mental measurements yearbook.* Retrieved June 24, 2008, from the Buros Institute's Test Reviews Online Web site: http://www.unl.edu/buros.

Locke, E. A. (2005). Why emotional intelligence is an invalid concept. *Journal of Organizational Behavior, 26,* 425–431.

London Psychometric Laboratory. (2001–2008). Retrieved January 25, 2009, from: http://www.psychometriclab.com/Default.aspx?Content=Page&id=11.

Mathews, G., Zeidner, M., & Roberts, R. D. (2002). *Emotional intelligence, science and myth.* Cambridge, MA: MIT Press.

Mathews, G., Roberts, R. D., & Zeidner, M. (2004). Seven myths about emotional intelligence. *Psychological Inquiry, 15*(3), 179–196.

Mayer, J. D. (1999). Emotional intelligence: Popular or scientific psychology? *American Psychological Association Monitor, 30*(8). Retrieved from: http://www.apa.org/monitor/sep99/sp.html.

Mayer, J. D., Caruso, D. R., & Salovey, P. (2000). Emotional intelligence meets traditional standards for an intelligence. *Intelligence, 27*(4), 267–298.

Mayer, J. D., & Salovey, P. (1997). What is emotional intelligence? In P. Salovey & D. Sluyter (Eds.), *Emotional development and emotional intelligence: Educational applications* (pp. 3–31). New York: Basic Books.

Mayer, J. D., Salovey, P., & Caruso, D. R. (2000). Emotional intelligence as zeitgeist, as personality, and as a mental ability. In R. Bar-On & J. D. A. Parker (Eds.), *The handbook of emotional intelligence* (pp. 92–117). San Francisco: Jossey-Bass.

Mayer, J. D., Salovey, P., & Caruso, D. R. (2004). Emotional intelligence: Theory, findings, and implications. *Psychological Inquiry, 15*(3), 197–215.

McCallum, M., & Piper, W. E. (2000). Psychological mindedness and emotional intelligence. In R. Bar-On & J. D. A. Parker (Eds.), *The handbook of emotional intelligence* (pp. 118–135). San Francisco: Jossey-Bass.

Mikolajczak, M., Luminet, O., Leroy, C., & Roy, E. (2007). Psychometric properties of the trait emotional intelligence questionnaire: Factor structure, reliability, construct, and incremental validity in a French-speaking population. *Journal of Personality Assessment, 88*(3), 338–353.

Paul, A. M. (1999, June 28). *Promotional intelligence.* Retrieved January 25, 2009, from http://www.salon.com/books/it/1999/06/28/emotional/index.html

Petrides, K. V., & Furnham, A. (2001). Trait emotional intelligence: Psychometric investigation with reference to established trait taxonomies. *European Journal of Personality, 15,* 425–448.

Petrides, K. V., & Furnham, A. (2006). The role of trait emotional intelligence in a gender-specific model of organizational variables. *Journal of Applied Social Psychology, 36*(2), 552–569.

Petrides, K. V., Furnham, A., & Frederickson, N. (2004, October). Emotional intelligence. *The Psychologist, 17*(10), 574–577. Retrieved January 25, 2009, from http://www.ioe.ac.uk/schools/phd/kpetrides/Reprints/Psychologist%20-%20T_EI%20(2004).pdf

Petrides, K. V., Pita, R., & Kokkinaki, F. (2007). The location of trait emotional intelligence in personality factor space. *British Journal of Psychology, 98*, 273–289.

Petrides, K. V., Sangareau, Y., Furnham, A., & Frederickson, N. (2006). Trait emotional intelligence and children's peer relations at school. *Social Development, 15*, 537–547.

Salovey, P., & Grewal, D. (2005). The science of emotional intelligence. *Current Directions in Psychological Science, 14*(6), 281–285. Retrieved January 25, 2009, from http://research.yale.edu/heblab/pub_pdf/pub68_SaloveyGrewal2005_scienceofEI.pdf

Salovey, P., & Mayer, J. D. (1990). Emotional intelligence. *Imagination, Cognition, and Personality, 9*, 185–211.

Schmitt, A. J. (2006). EI in the business world. In K. R. Murphy (Ed.), *A critique of emotional intelligence* (pp. 211–234). New York: Lawrence Erlbaum Associates.

Sternberg, R. (Ed.). (2002). *Why smart people can be so stupid.* New Haven, CT: Yale University Press.

Taylor, G. J., & Bagboy, R. M. (2000). An overview of the alexithymia construct. In R. Bar-On & J. D. A. Parker (Eds.), *The handbook of emotional intelligence* (pp. 40–67). San Francisco: Jossey-Bass.

Thorndike, E. L. (1920, January). Intelligence and its uses. *Harper's Monthly Magazine,* 227–235.

Watson, T. (2007). Test review of the Emotional Competence Inventory. In K. F. Geisinger, R. A. Spies, J. F. Carlson, & B. S. Plake (Eds.), *The 17th mental measurements yearbook* (pp. 304–305). Lincoln, NE: University of Nebraska Press.

Wechsler, D. (1939). *The measurement of adult intelligence.* Baltimore, MD: Williams & Wilkins.

Wechsler, D. (1958). *The measurement and appraisal of adult intelligence* (4th ed.). Baltimore: Williams & Wilkins.

Wechsler, D. (1981). *WAIS-R manual: Wechsler Adult Intelligence Scale–Revised.* Cleveland, OH: The Psychological Corporation.

Wolff, S. B. (2005). *Emotional Competence Inventory (ECI) technical manual.* Retrieved January 25, 2009, from http://www.eiconsortium.org/pdf/ECI_2_0_Technical_Manual_v2.pdf

Recommended Readings

Bar-On, R., & Parker, J. D. A. (Eds.). (2000). *The handbook of emotional intelligence.* San Francisco: Jossey-Bass.

Mathews, G., Zeidner, M., & Roberts, R. D. (2002). *Emotional intelligence, science and myth.* Cambridge, MA: MIT Press.

Murphy, K. R. (Ed.). (2006). *A critique of emotional intelligence: What are the problems and how can they be fixed?* New York: Lawrence Erlbaum Associates.

12
Lessons from Athletic Coaches

Everybody's a coach in some aspect of life, and that means you. So grab your whistle and clipboard, and let's get in the game.

—Ken Blanchard and Don Shula (1995, p. 15)

Executive coaching has its roots in athletic and performance coaching, and there is a gaggle of books written by famous coaches to be found in the business section of every bookstore. Therefore, it makes sense to check the sports literature to see what nuggets lay there. Your clients have bought some of these books and might have even read a few.

One reason that coaching is called *coaching* and not executive counseling or workplace psychotherapy is that many hard-charging corporate types, especially men, are likely to favor a coach, but may be unwilling to enter therapy. Most identify with sports and would love to see themselves as athletes or, at least, as high performers. Most grew up on sports, following their favorite team and imitating their favorite athlete. Counseling is associated with trouble, weakness, and inadequacy, whereas coaching is identified with successful sports figures and winning teams. Great teams have great coaches, and Tiger Woods apparently visits his swing coach regularly.

Attempts to apply formal psychological methods to athletic coaching in the United States date to the 1920s, when Coleman Griffith, an academic psychologist at the University of Illinois, joined the Chicago Cubs baseball team in an ill-fated effort to try to improve coaching and performance (Green, 2003). He wrote the first text on psychology and coaching in 1926, called *The Psychology of Coaching: A Study of Coaching Methods from the Point of Psychology*. A surprisingly small number of serious scientific books were published after that. In about 1990, however, there was an explosion of books about successful coaching and its application to the business world. Famous coaches and athletes hired ghostwriters to describe the best ideas and the motivational techniques responsible for their success.

These books have relevance. Books by athletic coaches are interesting sources for executive coaches because team sports at the highest levels, especially football, have become corporate in nature. The San Francisco 49ers have an executive vice president for football "operations." Players are referred to as "personnel" and the teams are now "organizations." Former 49ers head coach Bill Walsh's book, *Finding the Winning Edge*, is essentially a large, detailed corporate organizational operations manual. The premier coaches insist on total control. Walsh wrote, "It was agreed that if I was going to be coach, I would be in charge of all football operations" (Walsh, Billick, & Peterson, 1998, p. 9).

Rather than cope with limited authority and meddling owners, athletic coaches now serve as "executives" of large, complex organizations. Much of what they do has significant relevance to the corporate executive. Most of these books make at least some reference to the business world, and Walsh published an extended series of management articles in *Forbes* magazine between 1993 and 1997 (Walsh et al., 1998). There is significant content overlap between the football coach and the executive coach.

Ninety percent of the game is half mental. (Berra, 1998, p. 96)

The reading of books by marquee coaches can be mind numbing. They all contain more than their share of clichés ("Failing to prepare is preparing to fail") and well-worn (worn-out) motivational mantras ("When the going gets tough, the tough get going"). To make matters worse, many of these books brim with quotes from famous military figures such as George Patton, Sun Tzu, and even Erwin Rommel (the Nazi Panzer commander).

In the real world, athletes tire of these clichés, having heard them year after year, and they simply turn them off. Even one of University of California, Los Angeles (UCLA) basketball coach John Wooden's stars reported that he never paid much attention to Wooden's famous Pyramid of Success while he was at UCLA. In tribute to Wooden, however, he admitted that the pyramid was meaningful to him later on as a professional player (Walton, 1992, p. 52).

Frank Deford (Jones, 1998) notes that "some incredibly stupid coaches have beaten some demonstrably brilliant coaches," so we have to be careful about giving too much credit where it is not necessarily due. He remembers that long-time Boston Celtics coach Red Auerbach's theories were brilliant as long as Bill Russell played on his teams. But some of these coaches have produced highly successful records over long periods, and star athletes and luck simply cannot account for all of their success. Some of what they have done has been masterful.

These busy winners probably do not actually "write" much of what is in their books themselves, and that is a good thing, for they did not attain success on the basis of their writing skills. It is also likely that the majority of coach books rest forever unopened on coffee tables and nightstands. There is a certain charm about these books, though, and each contains one or two real nuggets mixed in with all of the success speak and the examples from games won or lost along the way. Most coach books stress the obvious, such as hard work, teamwork, attention to detail, good communication, and positive attitude. This chapter synthesizes the less obvious lessons common to sports coach books (as well as a few nuggets) that are sure to be useful to the corporate coach.

Existential novelist and philosopher Albert Camus was once asked which he preferred, football or the theater. Camus is said to have replied, "Football, without hesitation. After many years during which I saw many things, what I know most surely about morality and the duty of man I owe to sport" (Albert Camus Society UK, n.d.).

Common Themes

There is a striking consistency to books by athletic coaches and, perhaps, to the philosophies of the successful ones. If that is the case, there may be some serious truths to be found there.

Theme 1: Drive

There is one quality that nearly all successful athletes and coaches have in common. This quality actually *diminishes* the usefulness of athletic lessons to the executive coach. Highly successful coaches and athletes are focused and driven to the extreme. Most normal humans do not possess their brand of single-mindedness. Regular people might not even possess the capacity.

> What I have learned about myself is that I am an animal when it comes to achievement and wanting success. There is never enough success for me. (Gary Player, as quoted in Jones, 1998, p. 56)
>
> I hate to say it because I don't think it's the best thing for developing a person, but the single-mindedness—just concentrating in that one area—that's what it takes to be a champion. (Chris Evert, as quoted in Jones, 1998, p. 83)

Virtually all of the popular sports or coaching books found in the bookstore say the same thing: Highly successful people are driven, focused, and single-minded in their dedication to their craft. They work much harder than normal people and do not have balanced lives.

Most of these books stress the importance of *dreaming* and *setting goals*. It seems that drive and dreams are related, and it would do well for executive coaches to help clients decipher their dreams or lack of them. Certainly, we cannot expect executive clients to be working in the job of their dreams like basketball players or golfers often seem to do. But it is a coach's job to help a client figure out where passions reside and whether those passions are too distant from the real-life workplace. If dreams and drive can be harnessed and ridden like a fine steed, all the better. That makes the task simple. Align everything directly, and go for it. But when a client is working at a career with great ambivalence, that is a different matter. It is also different when clients feel that their work is secondary to other aspects of life, such as family or triathlons or Girl Scouts. Coach books stress the importance of balance in life, especially with regard to family. But, in some cases, coaches go on to say that they did not do a very good job with their own familial responsibilities, and others quietly got a divorce sometime after their book was published. One coach's book is dedicated to his father: "I never got to say goodbye or tell you that I loved you."

This can be a starting point in executive coaching: Where does work fit into your life and your dreams? How driven are you now and how driven do you want to be? Would you feel confused if your larger priorities limited your career success? Similarly, would you be ashamed if your career strivings produced family pathology or spousal resentment? Perhaps an intense career drive was feasible early in one's career, but incongruent later? Success in important leadership roles often requires a massive commitment of time and energy. Is your client certain that this is what they want to do with their life? Would the commitment be temporary or permanent? Is it part of their character structure to be committed and to work 18 hours per day? If they are part of a family or intimate relationship, are partners clear about the commitment, rules, and agreements?

None of this is meant to demean drive. It is central to excellence in anything, and positive mental health and self-esteem are greatly enhanced when a person is excellent at something. But that "something" does not necessarily have to be career; nor is it reasonable to expect obsessive drive in most clients.

If a client intends great success at work, single-mindedness should be considered, though. Coaches can help clients develop drive, once focus has been defined and established. But I say: consciously choose one or the other (single-mindedness or a balanced life) and remember that you made the choice. Take joy in the outcome, but do not make one choice and expect the fruits of the other. Each path has its benefits and its liabilities. As a coach, help clients clear this up, as it can be confusing and even demoralizing. Organizations often advocate work–life balance, but they rarely reward it. It is the coach's job to stimulate clarity.

> Everyone has noted the astonishing sources of energy that seem available to those who enjoy what they are doing, who find meaning in what they are doing. The self-renewing man knows that if he has no great conviction about what he is doing, he had better find something that he can have great conviction about. (John Gardner, as quoted in Robinson, 1996, p. 31)

Theme 2: Teach the Fundamentals

If you keep too busy learning the tricks of the trade, you may never learn the trade.

—John Wooden (Walton, 1992, p. 46)

Coach Wooden is famous for starting each new season with a lesson on how to properly put on sweat socks. All of the coaching books stress fundamentals, the teaching and learning of the basics of the game that is being played. Famous coaches typically view themselves as teachers, first and foremost. Several felt that it was their teaching skills that separated them from less successful coaches. They stressed redundant coverage of the fundamental skills, even to highly talented players with huge egos. They repeated and repeated these lessons until the skills were second nature, so that they could be executed under the extreme pressures of white-hot competition at the national level. These coaches simply refused to accept an athlete's reluctance to go over and over the basics. They forced the issue, using their best teaching skills.

Executive coaches can do the same thing. With your client, establish a taxonomy of the basic skills and competencies. Your clients may lack basic listening skills (many people do), they might not send thank you notes, they might be poor time managers and show up late for meetings, or maybe they don't return phone calls or e-mails promptly. Perhaps they do not know how to make an excellent oral presentation (most people do not). Maybe they cannot write an effective memo or proposal. Some people do not know how to behave at a meeting. Some do not know how to dress. Do they know how to delegate? Conduct an in-depth assessment of the relevant basics, and then go to work on them. Coaches need not be reticent about this. If you do not raise these issues, who will? Break jobs down into component skills and offer a few new ones. Teach these skills using your best teaching. Read pertinent corporate manuals and review them for your clients. Assign readings and go over them step by step. Practice the skills off-line where there is no risk or pressure. Model them for your clients. Problem solve when your clients get stuck. Sell the basics, especially when your clients think they seem simple or when it seems embarrassing to admit they are missing a skill. Some clients have been able to avoid confronting a skill deficit for years, but now it has finally caught up with them.

Teaching, first, requires an agreement between teacher and student. Each must agree to take on the appropriate role, along with its attitudes and behaviors. The teacher must first set the scene and create a learning atmosphere. He or she must then make a clear presentation, give examples, answer questions, and give guiding feedback. Sometimes the teacher exhorts, sometimes the teacher praises. Teachers also respond to feedback about their own effectiveness, making adjustments as they go.

Theme 3: Use Individual Approaches, Flexibility, and Ingenuity

Psychologists sometimes get stuck in their primary theoretical point of view. This is professionally acceptable in the practice of psychotherapy, in part because it is a function of theoretical integrity. But such a stance is counterproductive in executive coaching. Unlike many psychotherapy patients, coaching clients will quit the relationship when they are not getting results.

> A teacher needs to find the trigger inside each student that will release his or her best work. Some students need to be pushed; others need space. (Tara VanDerveer, Women's Basketball Coach, Stanford University, as quoted in Walsh et al., 1998, p. 34)

Virtually all of the sports books emphasize flexibility in human relations. Don Shula refers to this as being "audible-ready" (Blanchard & Shula, 1995). (An audible is a change made in a football play at the absolute last moment—well after you have committed to a different plan.) Each coaching book stresses that absolute rules are counterproductive because athletes must be treated as individuals. Some people learn one way, some another. A coach with a limited or inflexible repertoire will not succeed. Even the athletic coaches with the most rigid reputations recognized this facet of their work, before the appearance of the free-spirited or "modern" self-centered athlete. Cookbook approaches are doomed, and executive clients will sniff them out and run for the door. Most executives have paid their dues in seminars and leadership classes. They have tried cookbook approaches, or they have bought the book but neglected to read it or have forgotten what it said. Coaches are hired and paid to bring a wide-ranging, creative, individually designed and compelling repertoire to the effort.

> If something isn't working, we innovate. We try anything that will help. In coaching, we never give up. Never! (Jim Valvano, as quoted in Krzyzewski & Phillips, 2000, p. 250)

It is best to treat each new client as a unique adventure. Versatility is essential in executive coaching. There is no need to stick with one theory or one approach as a psychotherapist might do. There are really no theoretical constraints in coaching. Be ready to try any innovative approach that has promise. Even if it does not work, both coach and client can learn from the trial. Communicate a sense that the coaching process is an adventure, and that it will be tailored for that specific client. Seek innovative ways to work with each client, and when something is not paying off, move quickly to a different method.

Theme 4: Play against Yourself

> One of the most intriguing aspects of sports is that at the end of a contest (not unlike the end of a business day) you can look up and see exactly how you did. There's always a large scoreboard, and it tells you (and the world) whether you won or lost.
>
> **—Charlie Jones (1998, p. 10)**

Most coach books do not buy this harsh point of view, that the final score is all that matters. Although some of these books stress winning—often at enormous cost—the majority focus on playing against yourself; that is, striving to better your own best performance. They advocate setting goals relevant to your own progress and measuring performance against those, rather than against an opponent or scoreboard. They value a worthy opponent, as such an adversary offers the best test, but they do not vest much self-esteem in the outcome. One successful coach makes the point that if all the coaches in America choose the national championship as their goal, 99% of them will have to label their season a failure at the end of every year. Wooden is the most steadfast advocate of this view (and is arguably the most successful basketball coach of all time). Wooden even emphasized the *processes* of preparing and playing as more important than the outcome—the journey over the destination. Wooden made it a point of saying (when in public) that his team scored more points than the opponent, not that they beat them. "He never challenged us to win the game. He always challenged us to do the best we could do" (Walt Hazzard, as quoted in Walton, 1992, p. 65).

With so much at stake it seems implausible that big-time coaches would embrace this perspective, but apparently coaches believe it. For college teams, alumni are all over them to "produce" (read: win), and large amounts of money are involved. These books are quite convincing, though, and their coach-authors make a consistent case for the validity of unrelenting self-improvement with an emphasis on excellence. Most of these coaches stress goal setting, but the goals derive from an effort to improve relative to one's own gifts and previous accomplishments, not to the performance of others.

> If you're always striving to achieve success that is defined by someone else, you'll always be frustrated. Define your own success. (Krzyzewski & Phillips, 2000, p. 64)

This lesson is of value to the executive coach and client. Rather than relying on the scoreboard of institutional personnel decisions, why not set your own personal learning and competence goals and then measure yourself against them? This is a much saner approach. You cannot control the decisions that an organization makes about you, but you can control your expectations, goals, and effort. In this way, you can take some control of your own destiny. You choose the goals, you choose the standards, and you decide how well you are doing and how to respond. When you get passed over or downsized or offered an attractive opportunity, evaluate the situation based on how it fits into your own personal plan. Then decide how to feel and react. Coaches can teach this point of view to clients and the advice of celebrity athletic coaches will provide support.

Theme 5: Visualize

Virtually all successful athletic coaches use covert imagery rehearsal, or visualization, as they call it. This technique has truly made it from cognitive psychology into the arena of big-time sports performance. Athletes go through their entire performance ahead of time in their mind, step by step. John Robinson, the former University of Southern California (USC) football coach, calls this "rehearsal vision" and notes that diver Greg Louganis mentally rehearsed his dives 40 times prior to the actual event (Robinson, 1996, p. 24). Athletes who have used visualization say that when they actually played, they had the feeling that they had done it all before and that it was now second nature. One professional basketball coach described how he engaged in 45 minutes of visualization at home prior to each game "to prepare my mind and come up with last minute adjustments" (Jackson & Delehanty, 1995, p. 121).

Guided imagery literature is available to executive coaches, and covert rehearsal is an essential tool in the coach's kit. Virtually anything can be rehearsed in the mind prior to execution. If coaches need a refresher in covert rehearsal, sources are included at the end of this chapter (Bry, 1978; Lazarus, 1977). Assign these readings to willing clients. Coaches can teach and demonstrate covert rehearsal in client meetings and advocate its use at home and at work.

Theme 6: Video Feedback

Successful athletic coaches make extensive and creative use of video feedback to teach and support their lessons. Video provides us with information that is unavailable any other way, and it does so powerfully. No talk is necessary, and the feedback can be provided without much verbal criticism. Verbal feedback must be offered skillfully, lest the receiver experience it as criticism. The tape is not critical, and it does not lie. Certain things simply cannot be communicated adequately with words, and sometimes a picture really *is* worth a thousand words. Athletic coaches would not think of coaching without video. Big-time college and professional programs rely on video to understand what they are doing and what they need to change, even during contests, while the action is taking place on the field. Most use video to understand technical elements, but some creatively use it to change a player's attitude or to reward good performance or loyalty. For example, basketball coach Mike Krzyzewski once used it this way:

> So one day I had a five-minute videotape compiled of nothing but shots of Hurley's facial expressions during games. Then I sat him down in private and showed him how he looked to me and to everyone else on the court. He saw himself pouting, whining, pointing fingers, dropping his head, and losing his temper. When the tape finished, I leaned over

to him and quietly said: "Bobby, is that the message you want to send to your teammates?" (Krzyzewski & Phillips, 2000, pp. 92–93)

On another occasion Krzyzewski spliced together a segment of the awful plays that a star had made during one bad performance and played it in front of the entire team. This seems risky, but perhaps this player needed a serious wake-up call. On the other hand, Krzyzewski presents each senior with a video of the highlights of his best efforts each spring as a graduation gift to celebrate his career.

Walsh once produced a video with a series of brief clips of stirring moments from several sports, focusing on the athletes' eyes and the way that they focused their concentration. He used it to motivate a complacent team (Walsh et al., 1998, p. 330).

Most psychologists and mental health practitioners underutilize video. The Harvard survey of experienced executive coaches revealed that coaches do not think very highly of video feedback in practice. Only 25% reported that video is a "particularly valuable" tool, whereas 18% felt that video has little or no value in coaching (Kauffman & Coutu, 2009, p. 16). In my view, video feedback has enormous potential for executive coaches and should be used with virtually every client. Younger clients grew up with YouTube and are comfortable around cameras, webcams, and screenings. The equipment is inexpensive and convenient. Nonetheless, some measure of creativity is necessary, and some clients will be reluctant at first. But the benefits are clearly worth it. Show clients how they look, how they act, and how they speak and sound. Record meetings and evaluate them later. Practice new skills on tape and review them. Audio recordings can be a powerful tool. With your clients' permission, record messages that your clients send. Listen and practice them until they are perfect. It is much easier to learn how to leave an effective voice message when you can hear yourself and get a coach's feedback than it is to read about it in a book. Rehearse important conversations and interactions prior to execution. For example, audio-video rehearsal is useful when a client must deliver a difficult message to a partner or employee, when a client must sell something, and when a client must change a troublesome mannerism. Video is of particular value when an analyst or manager strives to become a partner. A significant job promotion often requires a shift in identity and style, and this is very hard to communicate without visual input. A recent *Harvard Business Review* essay makes the point that aspiring partners must "forge a new identity," but all the help they get is "snippets of vague advice" such as "If you want to be a partner, start acting like one" (Ibarra, 2000). This is easier said than done, but video feedback closes the loop between a comment like that and real learning. When you see how partners behave and then compare it to how you appear on a video screen, the changes are tangible. This way, the coach does not have to be the bearer of bad news. Just let the video do the talking.

Theme 7: Learning from Defeat

Virtually every coach's and athlete's book makes reference to the importance of adversity and one's response to it. They credit losses with great learning.

> To win, you have to lose and then get pissed off. (Joe Namath, as quoted in Jones, 1998, p. 43)

Some of these books refer to personal tragedies such as the loss of a loved one or a hurricane as having been motivational. Duke's basketball coach, Krzyzewski, calls failure a part of success (Krzyzewski & Phillips, 2000, p. 44). Former NBA coach Pat Riley even has a name for sudden adversity or losses: He calls them "thunderbolts." Such a thunderbolt can occur when a star athlete suddenly goes down with a major injury. These books make a great deal of how important it is to learn from negative events and to grow stronger from them.

This is of relevance to the executive coach, especially when called in to help a client who has suffered a major career setback. There is a lot to be learned when you are passed over for a promotion or a prized assignment. A coach can help reframe the loss, while being careful not to trivialize it. First, empathize with how significant and disappointing the loss seems and feels. Next, figure out how your client views it. Then find a way to introduce the possibility that the experience can be a turning point or learning point. What is there to learn from the event? What weaknesses does it expose? Does the loss imply that this client needs to move in a different direction or strengthen a skill or learn a new skill? The response of some people to a setback is to tell themselves that they simply must work harder. This is rarely effective, because they risk doing even more of the things that were not working in the first place. It is more likely true that they need to sift through the wreckage and find ways to change, to do some things differently, to view other things differently, or to learn something completely new.

Pain and disappointment can generate energy, and the coach can help direct that energy toward a productive change rather than allow it to be squandered or used to further damage client self-esteem. Coaches must be there to remind clients that things cannot possibly go your way 100% of the time. Setbacks are normal and expectable. Sports books are unanimous and clear about this. Everyone suffers setbacks, and the key is to take advantage of them, just as you take advantage of vitamins or the wind at your back.

Most of these books stress flexibility. One must be able to adjust to changes to succeed. When an opponent throws something your way that is new or unexpected you must be able to shift your thinking, make exceptions to the rules, and take a different approach. Although many famous athletic coaches come across as steely taskmasters, their books typically contain examples of how they broke their own rules from time to time with good results. Often these exceptions were on behalf of a player who made a mistake, and were made on the basis of the coach's intuition rather than published rules.

Theme 8: Communication, Trust, and Integrity

Sports coaching books stress the importance of communication, but then, so does everyone. The trick is to figure out what they mean. In some cases it is possible that these big-time coaches have no idea what they mean and are, in fact, terrible communicators much of the time. Sometimes they simply mean that you should use clear language and a direct approach when you talk to an athlete.

"Coach K will always tell you the truth" (Steve Wojciechowski, Duke athlete, as quoted in Krzyzewski & Phillips, 2000, p. 221). Several coach books emphasize the importance of direct, frank, and honest interaction. They point out that this may create difficult moments, but that benefits clearly outweigh the negatives. Krzyzewski even goes so far as to recommend that you "make the truth the basis of all you do." This would be hard to swallow from most big-time, big-program coaches, but Krzyzewski is a West Pointer, and you get the impression that he really means it.

Most of these coaches connect communication with trust, and trust with honesty. For several of these coaches, communication means looking the other person in the eye when you talk and listen, so that you fully understand his or her intention. They talk about clarity and checking assumptions, giving examples of what has happened when they failed to do so. They advocate confrontation of problems quickly and directly. Basketball coach Rick Pitino (Pitino & Reynolds, 1997, p. 136) makes the recommendation that, in interpersonal confrontations "the goal is to connect, not defeat." This is an important insight because of the natural competitive dynamics that tend to lurk in male-to-male coaching or mentoring situations.

High-level communication skills are the primary set of tools for the executive coach. This means that you are able to model them as well as teach them. Directness, excellent active listening skills, and a commitment to the truth are as important to the executive coach as they are to the football coach. If you need a refresher in active listening, get one. Reread Chapter 5 of this book. If you need to listen to yourself speak, record some meetings and study how you sound. Upgrade the quality of your speaking and listening. Make it a point to read the latest on communication in business. Executive coaches are expected to know what the gurus are saying, and it is best if you can teach what they advocate (if you agree with it) or teach something better in response.

Executive coaches often find themselves in the role of consultant, and a lot of baggage accompanies that role. For many, the first reaction to a consultant is cynicism and distrust. Clients have had experiences with consultants that left a bad taste in their mouth, often because consultants overpromised and underdelivered. After that, they disappeared or were let go. Consider absolute honesty and frankness to be core business skills. As the old expression goes, honesty shocks people. Serious, high integrity, communicated directly, enables you to stand out in the crowd, especially over the long haul, assuming that you are not obnoxious or dogmatic about it. This is a tough standard, but it is absolutely worth it. Any embarrassment or loss of work or money over the short run will eventually pay off, even if the payoff is only in the realm of your own sense of self. Your integrity is liable to be tested at least once with every client in some small or large way. Make sure that you pass the test the first time.

Nuggets

Aside from the important themes common to the genre of books by coaches, many contain small and unique nuggets of advice for executive coaches. Here are a few that can be useful.

Nugget 1: Innocence

This is a very intriguing concept introduced by professional basketball coach Pat Riley. Although Riley's book (Riley, 1993) is never completely clear about his philosophy, it advocates an innocence regarding the basic tension between the human urge to take and to give. He recommends that his players take a chance on one another, giving—on the assumption that the gift will be reciprocated, resulting in a win–win outcome. Therapists sometimes call this "opening your heart." Without this attitude of innocence, cooperation cannot flourish.

Executive coaches would do well to experiment with such innocence. Begin with a commitment to integrity and assume that you can count on the same from others. Sometimes the results will disappoint. But without an innocent premise, long-term trust is unlikely.

Nugget 2: Clear Contract

Michael Jordan, Shaquille O'Neal, and Kobe Bryant's coach, Phil Jackson, advocates a "clear set of agreed-upon principles" because they reduce conflict and "depersonalize criticism" (Jackson & Delehanty, 1995). Riley advocates a "core covenant," and although his book is not exactly clear about what he means, he advocates the establishment of some form of central agreement between team members and coach—an agreement that all would hold sacred so that everyone could count on it (Riley, 1993).

This is excellent advice for the executive coach who is sometimes called into situations typified by their singular lack of clarity. Something is wrong or someone needs to be changed, but it is not exactly clear what that is, and you may not be assigned to the right person to fix the problem. The effort required to make a clear pact and to agree on principles is well worth the time. It allows you to learn about your client at the same time you communicate and model the importance of clarity. Plus, as Jackson says, if you have agreement on principles, restrictions do not need to be personal. If your client has to miss a coaching meeting, you have already agreed on how it will be handled. There is no reason for either party to take it personally. The agreement is in place, so you just stick with it.

Nugget 3: Goal Setting Is Overrated

This nugget comes from Don Shula's book (Blanchard & Shula, 1995). Shula is old school, and a dean of American football coaching. His view is that goals can get in the way of present-moment living, of making the most of the opportunities and energy we have today. He feels that goal setting is important, but it is the follow-up and attention to details on a day-to-day basis that make things work. He also advocates that goals, when set, should be small, clear, and well monitored, and that they should not get in the way of immediate awareness.

He is right. Together with your client, choose discrete, doable goals that are tracked. When you accomplish those, congratulate yourselves and move on to new ones with a sense of self-efficacy. Do not let them blind you to what is happening in the here and now. And do not pick goals that are global and difficult to accomplish or measure. They tend to hang over everyone's head and pollute the atmosphere when they are not accomplished and will not quite go away.

Nugget 4: Curiosity and Confusion

Swimming coach James "Doc" Counsilman points out that curiosity is the first step in the learning process. He figures that curiosity must be present for learning to occur. Confusion follows when the learner is confronted with a situation that does not make sense using the current knowledge available to the student. This is followed by a "quest for knowledge" (Walton, 1992, p. 78).

These factors are important to the executive coach who is often confronted with a client who is not necessarily curious about skills to be learned but is confused by what has happened. Instead of sorting out the confusion and helping clients to feel better immediately, it is probably a good idea to exploit these feelings of confusion to motivate the learner's curiosity. Reframe the situation so that it is perceived as an opportunity. Leverage the confusion to nourish curiosity.

Nugget 5: Perpetual Change

"The older we get, the more we must change." Rick Pitino, the basketball coach, makes this interesting point in his book *Success Is a Choice: Ten Steps to Overachieving in Business and Life* (Pitino & Reynolds, 1997). He writes that change becomes more important as we age, because it keeps us fresh and energized and young. This is often the opposite of how humans behave in real life, as we get older and more stuck in the same old dependable ruts. Pitino points out how quickly the business environment changes and how important it is to be ahead of the changes, or at least excited to move along with them. Mental health practitioners certainly must be willing to take heed and change with the times. This might mean a reexamination of important ideas, values, and techniques for the sake of surviving and thriving.

Nugget 6: Patience Is Not a Virtue

Although few of the marquee coaches seem to be patient human beings, Walsh is explicit about it: "In reality, patience is not always a virtue" (Walsh et al., 1998, p. 355). He goes on to say that a proactive approach is better than giving the impression that things will work out in the end.

Executive coaches must pay attention to this factor and make difficult decisions about pushiness. How accepting should they be about the client's timeline and progress? Most business people expect to change and to grow faster than most psychotherapy patients. And they do. It is always possible that the pushy coach could alienate his client or foster resistance, but pushiness is more likely to be welcomed, especially when the fees are high. This can be difficult for former psychotherapists to learn and do, after years of patients and patience. Plus, it tends to run against the Rogerian stance advocated in Chapter 5 of this book.

Nugget 7: Love, Fun, and Work

The master in the art of living makes little distinction between his work and his play, his labor and his leisure, his mind and his body, his information and his recreation, his love and his religion. He hardly knows which is which. He simply pursues his vision of excellence at whatever he does, leaving others to decide whether he is working or playing. To him, he's always doing both.

—James Michener (Blanchard & Shula, 1995, p. 67)

Most coaching books make this point in some fashion. Several point out the importance of fun—of having a good time while you work. John Robinson uses fun as a barometer: "Pay attention when you are not having fun," as this is an indicator that something is wrong (Robinson, 1996). Robinson's successor at USC, Pete Carroll, is the epitome of a successful person who has fun at work.

Executive coaching is the same way. Keep track of the level of humor and fun along the way, as well as the level of optimism and excitement. Use these qualities to measure the process. Add your style and the personality of your client to the mix. (Some people are very uncomfortable with mirth in the workplace, especially at first.) Enjoyment does not necessarily mean laughter or jokes. It can simply be an attitude that everything has an amusing or joyful element to it. Find an appropriate way to mix fun with the work. Make it a priority.

Nugget 8: Awareness Is Everything

> *Being aware is more important than being smart.*

> **—Phil Jackson (Jackson & Delehanty, 1995, p. 113)**

One coach book stands out from the crowd of others, in that it takes a distinctly "Eastern" perspective on big-time basketball. This is Los Angeles Lakers' coach Phil Jackson's book *Sacred Hoops* (Jackson & Delehanty, 1995). Jackson mixes the Pentecostal religion of his youth with Lakota Sioux culture and Zen koans and Buddhist practice. The result is an intriguing take on how to align and motivate athletic megastars to win championships. One of the several valuable points he makes is that awareness is central to all that he teaches. You must be open to what is happening now—in the present moment, right here.

This is just as important to the executive coach as it is to the athletic coach. It is a fine idea to go into client meetings armed with extensive tools and tentative plans. But it is a mistake to allow those plans to interfere with observation and present-moment awareness. Take a posture of readiness—see what is going on and react. Notice.

Consider the following example. As an executive coach, you go to a session with a client, and you have clear ideas about what that client needs to do. But, as you pay attention to his physical movement and voice, you notice that he is fidgety and seems tense. Something about him tells you that he is not focused on what you are planning. So you stop what you are doing and ask questions. You inquire about his attention—what is on his mind? He tells you that he is facing a deadline. He has two days before his annual self-assessment is due, and he is immobilized. He does not know what to write or how to get started. So you shift gears (radically) and use the meeting to help him think about and write that document. You invite him to open up his laptop and you start to draft the assessment together. As part of the effort, you help him explore the issues you had originally intended to work on in the meeting. It is all related, and your client is highly interested and focused, because you are attending to the matter that is of highest priority to him at the present moment.

Prepare, and then be aware.

Summary

1. Hundreds of sports books and famous coachs' books flood the market these days. They are littered with clichés and well-meaning but simple motivational ideas. There is a sameness about them, but there are a few core ideas of great usefulness to the executive coach. Among these are:

   - Take the high road. Create honest relationships and protect your integrity.

- Establish a clear working contract with your client and stick to it.
- Learn, teach, and practice to perfection the basic, fundamental building block skills required for success in the business world, even with "high-level" players.
- Treat each client uniquely. Adjust quickly when things are not working.
- Consider the use of audio and video feedback with every client.
- Pay attention to your own drive and single-mindedness. See if you can find a way to do your work that really gets your juices flowing. Then watch your balance.
- Pay attention to the level of excitement and fun. If it is not there, find out why. Integrate humor into everything, even if it is just a smiling attitude.
- Remain aware. Bring a tentative plan, but stay present. Do not let your plan get in the way. Notice what is happening in the here and now, and be ready to adjust.

2. Sample the genre of sports motivation books. Find a few that you like and consider assigning them to clients for reading and discussion. Several are listed in the References and Recommended Readings sections that follow.

References

Albert Camus Society UK. (n.d.). *Albert Camus and football.* Retrieved January 3, 2009, from: http://www.camus-society.com/camus-football.htm.

Berra, Y. (1998). *The Yogi book (I really didn't say everything I said).* New York: Workman.

Blanchard, K., & Shula, D. (1995). *Everyone's a coach: Five business secrets for high-performance coaching.* New York: Harper Business Books.

Bry, A. (1978). *Visualization: Directing the movies of your mind.* New York: Harper & Rowe.

Green, C. D. (2003). Psychology strikes out: Coleman R. Griffith and the Chicago Cubs. *History of Psychology, 6*(3), 267–283.

Griffith, C. R. (1926). *The psychology of coaching: A study of coaching methods from the point of psychology.* New York: Scribner's.

Ibarra, H. (2000, March–April). Making partner: A mentor's guide to the psychological journey. *Harvard Business Review, 78*(2), 147–155.

Jackson, P., & Delehanty, H. (1995). *Sacred hoops.* New York: Hyperion.

Jones, C. (1998). *What makes winners win: Thoughts and reflections from successful athletes.* New York: Broadway Books.

Kauffman, C., & Coutu, D. (2009). *HBR research report: The realities of executive coaching.* Available at: coachingreport.hbr.org

Krzyzewski, M., & Phillips, D. T. (2000). *Leading with the heart: Coach K's successful strategies for basketball, business, and life.* New York: Warner Books.

Lazarus, A. (1977). *In the mind's eye: The power of imagery for personal enrichment.* New York: The Guilford Press.

Pitino, R., & Reynolds, B. (1997). *Success is a choice: Ten steps to overachieving in business and life*. New York: Broadway Books.

Riley, P. (1993). *The winner within*. New York: Berkley Books.

Robinson, J. (1996). *Coach to coach: Business lessons from the locker room*. San Diego, CA: Pfeiffer & Company.

Walsh, B., Billick, B., & Peterson, J. A. (1998). *Finding the winning edge*. Champaign, IL: Sports Publishing.

Walton, G. M. (1992). *Beyond winning: The timeless wisdom of great philosopher coaches*. Champaign, IL: Leisure Press.

Recommended Readings

Bradley, B. (1998). *Values of the game*. New York: Broadway Books.

Carril, P., & White, D. (1997). *The smart take from the strong: The basketball philosophy of Pete Carril*. New York: Simon & Schuster.

Cousy, B., and Power, F. (1970). *Basketball: Concepts and techniques*. Boston: Allyn & Bacon.

Chu, D. (1982). *Dimensions of sports studies*. New York: Wiley.

Davis, J. (1999). *Talkin' tuna: The wit and wisdom of coach Bill Parcells*. Toronto, Ontario: Evangelicals Concerned Western Regional Publishers.

Didinger, R. (Ed.), & Sheedy, B. (1996). *Game plans for success: Winning strategies for business and life from ten top NFL head coaches*. Chicago: NTC/Contemporary Publishing.

Gallwey, W. T. (1974). *The inner game of tennis*. New York: Random House.

Gopnik, A. (1999, September 20). America's coach (Vince Lombardi). *The New Yorker*, pp. 124–133.

Hill, B. (1999). *Basketball: Coaching for success*. Champaign, IL: Sagamore Publishing.

Holtz, L. (1998). *Winning every day*. New York: Harper Business Books.

Lombardi, V. (1963). *Run to daylight*. New York: Prentice Hall.

Lombardi, V. (1995). *Coaching for teamwork: Winning concepts for business in the 21st century*. Bellevue, WA: Reinforcement Press.

Martens, R. (1987). *Coaches guide to sport psychology*. Champaign, IL: Human Kinetics Publishers.

Penick, H., & Schrake, B. (1992). *Harvey Penick's little red book: Lessons and teaching from a lifetime in golf*. New York: Simon & Schuster.

Penick, H., & Schrake, B. (1993). *And if you play golf, you're my friend: Further reflections of a grown caddy*. New York: Simon & Schuster.

Selleck, G. (1999). *Court sense: The invisible edge in basketball and life*. South Bend, IN: Diamond Communications.

Suinn, R. (1980). *Psychology in sports*. Minneapolis: Burgess Publishing Company.

Walsh, B. (1993, June 7). How to manage superstars. *Forbes ASAP*.

Walsh, B., & Dickey, G. (1990). *Building a champion*. New York: St. Martin's.

Wooden, J., & Jamison, S. (1997). *Wooden: A lifetime of observations and reflections on and off the court*. Chicago: NTC/Contemporary Publishing.

13
Coaching Women

It is absurd to put a woman down for having the very qualities that would send a man to the top.

—Felice N. Schwartz (1989, p. 69)

Although much has changed since publication of the first edition of this book in 2001, there are still four good reasons to consider the coaching of women as a special case. It must be stated at the onset of a chapter such as this that generalizing and stereotyping are dangerous—and as likely as not to be wrong in an individual case. There is no standard woman or typical man. There are men who think more like women and women who think more like men. Men and women who neatly fit the stereotypes are actually quite rare, and few, if any of us, are prototypes of our gender. Although there is serious risk of stereotyping in such a discussion, the conversation is worth having, as an appreciation of gender has potential to produce more good than harm. It seems indisputable that many, if not most, men are significantly different (in important ways) from many, if not most, women. Here is one map useful to understand gender differences:

- We are all alike because we are all human. We have that in common.
- We are all unique. There is no one on the planet who is just like you.
- We all possess some characteristics that are associated with our gender.

These three things are simultaneously true.

The first reason for a coaching-women chapter is that gender-based differences between men and women are often real and significant. Although this observation can be discomforting, it is undeniable. Recent observations from neurobiology point to brain differences between men and women (Gurian & Annis, 2008), and differential social enculturation continues to be a powerful force.

Second, women and men do not fare the same way in the workplace. Organizations undeniably perceive and treat men and women differently. There are structural, cultural, social, intra- and interpersonal explanations for this, and coaches can be instrumental in helping men, women, and organizations evolve.

Third, there are clear, plausible, empirical data demonstrating that companies with greater gender diversity perform better; specifically that companies with three or more women in top leadership positions have better return on investment (ROI), better earnings (EBIT), and greater stock price growth (Desvaux, Devillard-Hoellinger, & Baumgarten, 2007). Female executives represent an untapped asset and potential competitive advantage.

Fourth, women do not have the same access to informal sources of mentoring at work. Coaches can help fill this gap. Women are more likely to welcome the help of a coach, as men tend to be notorious help-rejecters. Men may even see the acceptance of help as a sign of weakness, plus they often have access to important informal mentors, and they know it. Women are far more likely to grasp the value of a coach—someone outside of the organization who knows the ropes, someone who can make observations, give clear feedback, and someone who will listen to things that cannot always be spoken in public.

The problems of gender are not new. Thoughtful insights have been available in the literature for years if not centuries. Take, for example, the work of Simone de Beauvoir (1952). She wrote half a century ago about the role confusion that women experience when they enter the workforce. These confusions are shifting, and as culture evolves, gender relations evolve. But these difficulties cannot be ignored, and it is unwise to pretend that the differences between men and women are insignificant.

This chapter is divided into three sections: (1) what coaches need to learn to effectively coach women; (2) ways coaches can enhance the careers and effectiveness of women; and (3) what organizations can do to take greater advantage of female potential.

What Coaches Need to Know

Regarding the Workplace

Glass Ceilings and Walls

A review of longitudinal studies reveals several areas in which a sharp upward trend in the 1970s and 1980s has been followed by a slowing and flattening in recent years (for instance, in the percentage of managers who are women). The pause is also evident in some attitudinal data— like the percentage of people who approve of female bosses and who believe that women are at least as well suited as men for politics.

—**Alice H. Eagly and Linda L. Carli (2007, p. 67)**

To start, coaches need to understand the current situation of women in the workplace, especially regarding women in leadership. Women have arrived in all arenas of the workplace, and they are not about to go back home as they did after World War II. There are clear signs that women are major players in the current economy, and although the pipeline to the top of large corporations is 20 years long, a few women have already made their way into powerful leadership positions. But women have simply not made their way into these higher leadership positions in organizations at statistically expectable levels. The glass ceiling is real. Women are entering higher education at rates equal to or greater than men. Females outnumber males at American medical schools and the same is nearly true at traditionally male dental schools. This trend does not seem to be true for business schools, where females represent less than 35% of recent MBA graduates (Alsop, 2007). Data from a 2009 Catalyst census indicates the following:

- Women represent 46% of the American work force. This number has been stable for the past decade.

- The percentage of women in managerial and professional positions in the American workforce increased steadily until about 1999 when it leveled off at 50%.

- The percentage of corporate officer positions held by women in Fortune 500 companies increased steadily until about 2002 when it leveled off at about 15%.

- The percentage of corporate board positions held by women in Fortune 500 companies increased steadily until about 2003 when it leveled off at about 14%.

- Women now represent just 6% of Fortune 500 top earners and 3% of CEOs.

It appears that the rise of women to the top of American corporations has stagnated or even declined. There is also evidence at all levels that women are still paid less than men for the same work and are promoted more slowly, even when competing explanatory factors are held constant (Eagly & Carli, 2007).

In addition to the glass ceiling, there are also "glass walls" in business organizations. Women still tend to be clustered in a small number of areas including human resources and marketing, the "pink collar" jobs where they are occupationally segregated. Although this is certainly changing, not as many women tend to make it into information technology (IT) or operations, which are still typically male dominated. The reasons are complex, and the choices and behavior of male managers and female workers both contribute to the problem, as does the workplace culture.

A Labyrinth of Challenges   Eagly and Carli (2007) make the point that the glass ceiling metaphor is too simple, too discouraging, and that it wrongly implies that women do well until they reach a certain limiting level, high in the organization. Instead, they point out that limitations are consistent throughout the workplace and the absence of women at the highest levels represents an accumulation of restricting forces throughout a woman's career. These forces include lingering gender prejudices, resistance to female leadership, differential male and female responses to the demands of family, and differences in the ways that men and women participate in work activities that take place outside of the office time and setting.

Male-Centric Culture Business organizations are typically male led, and they are dominated by masculine culture and assumptions. Men invented the current rules. Even the office furniture is built for men (Evans, 2000, p. 128), as is the decor. American corporations tend to reward a competitive approach to things, a direct, in-your-face mentality and communication style that puts measurable performance and self-promotion ahead of relationships. Here's a *Wall Street Journal* headline from August 8, 2000, that exemplifies this attitude: "Competitive Drive: Palm Puts Up Its Fists as Microsoft Attacks Hand-Held PC Market." It is widely prevalent in the business milieu.

Metaphors of war are common in the current competitive American business environment. Men play fighting games as children. They keep score, and there are clear winners and losers. The object of these games is to beat the other team or person, and then go on to the next game and do it again. Girls often play games for very different reasons: to develop, study, and cement relationships, or to nurture all involved. After years of athletic coaching, Kathleen DeBoer (2004, p. 34) came to the conclusion that men and women typically compete quite differently: "Men struggle first, expecting acceptance only after they perform. Females seek acceptance before they will commit to struggle." Felice Schwartz observed that "women who compete like men are considered unfeminine. Women who emphasize family are considered uncommitted" (1989, p. 67).

Aggressive verbal behavior is rewarded in male culture, and the stress is modulated with jokes about sports or sex or the ineptness of a colleague. The metaphors are often sports based, and it is sometimes difficult to understand them if you do not know baseball or football (touch base, hit a home run, or I think we should punt are three of a thousand such examples). Team building is done on the golf course or at sporting events, and a season ticket is a legitimate business expense in the eyes of the IRS. Eagly and Carli (2007) report about an executive retreat at Sam Walton's ranch that included quail hunting and visits to strip clubs and Hooters. Many women love baseball and some enjoy quail hunting, but going to strip clubs and Hooters to succeed in your career?

Women are often left out of the formal and informal communication loops in the male organization. This is often an inadvertent or structural omission, and women are not always aware that it is happening. Sometimes women spend too much time diligently attending to the details of a project rather than attending meetings that do not appear to be important. To them, it does not seem like much gets done at such meetings. Men, on the other hand, attend those meetings to stay connected with key players, stay visible and promote their interests, and develop trusting relationships. This is part of the game.

These days, women are increasingly involved with team sports at a young age. But it is less natural for women to think and behave in these typically "male ways" to compete, and there is an adaptation or accommodation required to succeed in male-led organizations. When women interact in an all-female setting, the topics and behavior patterns are typically quite different. DeBoer (2004) insists that women compete as hard as or harder than men. They just do it differently, and this is not well understood by men. It takes extra energy for many women to succeed in a male culture. Some women resent this adaptation and would rather not have to bother with it in order to succeed. It represents an additional layer of barriers.

There is still an "anytime, anywhere" mentality in many work settings. People desiring the best and most challenging assignments are expected to be willing to put in unlimited time and to travel as much and as often as necessary. Any sign of reluctance is subtly or overtly punished. This attitude is not always necessary or productive, and it probably hurts women more than men.

Prejudice, Stereotypes, and Misconceptions   Women face complex and powerful stereotypes in the business world, including these described by Reardon (1995, p. 77):

- Women are not sufficiently committed to their work and career. They have conflicted motives (work vs. home) and are likely to leave the job to raise a family.
- Women do not work well with other women.
- Women generally lack sports experience, so they cannot be expected to understand teamwork.
- Women do not make compelling leaders.
- Women are too emotional (and insufficiently rational).
- Assertive women are difficult and demanding.
- Women are not good at technical matters.
- Men resent female bosses.
- Women lack the killer instinct necessary for a successful business in a competitive climate.

Other recent speculations in the literature include the notion that women are not as ambitious as men (Fels, 2004), and that women lack the capacity to provide corporate vision (Ibarra & Obodaru, 2009). There's still a widespread perception that women cannot do math or lack interest in technology. Although these stereotypes are not often openly discussed or acknowledged, they still exert a powerful influence on workplace perceptions and decision making.

A recent McKinsey study indicated that 27% of women and only 7% of men perceived that they had been discriminated against in their career (Desvaux et al., 2007). Some leaders are likely to perceive an unspoken risk when it comes to promoting a promising female executive. Women are less likely to get second chances. There is a smaller tolerance for error or experimentation in the learning process. There are still officers in large organizations (and customers, too) who wonder whether women belong. After the first error or mediocre performance, the woman is effectively out the door, figuratively, if not literally.

Mentors and Role Models   There are fewer successful role models for women looking up the hierarchy. There is sometimes no one to observe to see how a successful woman behaves in an organization. When there is only one woman in a leadership role it is hard to know whether she is a good model for other women there. There is also a dearth of mentors and patrons for women. Male organizations and corporations use a complex and unspoken set of codes to transmit meaning and rules and values. Women need mentors and colleagues to help them interpret and understand how the rules work. Even when mentors can be found, gender-based relationship dynamics can make things more complex. As Barsh, Craske, and Cranston (2008, p. 45) observed: "awkward sexual politics, real or perceived, between senior men and younger women, make it harder for women to find sponsors." Male mentors are not likely to treat female protégés in the same familiar way that they treat other men. They are not likely to have the same off-site, after-work experiences that they might with other males.

Regarding Gender and Women

Some qualities associated with women are worth mentioning. They may not be true in every case, but they are widely shared and described in the business literature. Their impact is complicated and it is not clear how it all works, but coaches must be aware of these issues if they intend to work effectively with women.

Women and Nurturing

The feminine mode of ethical decision-making is based upon the maintenance of relationships, upon the importance of cooperation, connection, and concern for others. ... Responsibility to meet the needs of others lies at the core of the feminine perspective.

—Anneka Davidson (1994, p. 415)

Women are widely thought to be more nurturing and compassionate than men. A similar perception is that women are more relationship oriented and process oriented than task oriented, and that women tend to work more collaboratively than men. Eagly and Carli (2007) refer to these qualities as *communal* as opposed to the *agentic* tendencies of men, who are thought to be more self-reliant, aggressive, dominant, and independent. It is the agentic qualities that most people currently associate with effective leadership. As a result, women find themselves in a bind. If they act "naturally" and compassionately, working collaboratively in a network of teammates, they may not be perceived to be leader-like. If they conform to male leadership norms, they can be perceived to be difficult or pushy or not a team player (or worse). Soccer coach Anson Dorrance (n.d.) makes a similar observation after struggling to figure out how to best to coach women:

> Women relate through an interconnected web of personal connections, as opposed to the male hierarchical style. ... [and coaches] are forced to develop a connective leadership style that is much richer and more satisfying than the hierarchical style that pervades so much of male leadership.

Self-Promotion

They know what a good job I'm doing. Why don't they just reward me for it?

> —**Gail Evans (2000, p. 8)**

Many observers note that women are much less likely to feel comfortable taking credit for accomplishments and "blowing their own horn" (Smith, 2000; Tannen, 1994). In meetings, men in business often jump into a discussion, making their certainty and expertise explicit. They can sound quite positive, as they have been taught to do, whereas women can be more comfortable expressing doubts and uncertainty. Successful male leaders model self-promotion that is borderline boastful, and executives are expected to let people know about the important contributions that they have made.

Rosabeth Moss Kanter makes this observation ("A Vote of Confidence," 2005) about her MBA students at Harvard:

> There sometimes is a difference between the men and women in willingness to claim air time in class. The men seem to feel that they can start talking and eventually they'll have a point to make. ... The women are just as likely to have wonderful things to say, but there's a self-censorship going on.

Women are more likely to be polite to avoid seeming egotistical or presumptuous. Sometimes women allow themselves to be interrupted or ignored at meetings while men are elbowing each other for airtime. Women, according to

Tannen and others, do not want to seem as if they are putting themselves "above" others. Soccer coach Dorrance (n.d.) makes the following observation:

> Men love public praise. But if you praise a young woman publicly, every woman in the room now hates her with a passion, and every woman in the room also hates you, because you have not praised her. To top it off, the young woman you've praised hates you for embarrassing her in front of her teammates.

Women tend to seek interpersonal balance or, at least, the impression of it. Whereas men feel that they must regularly assert their achievements to be taken seriously as a person with a future in the organization, women sometimes hang back, uncomfortable with this male posturing. Men and women even "boast" differently, with men playing a "mine-is-bigger-than-yours" kind of game, whereas women tend to promote themselves in a more understated way (Miller, Cooke, Tsang, & Morgan, 1992).

> When guys brag, it reminds them of being on a team. When women brag, men and women hear rudeness and pushiness. (Evans, 2000, p. 76)

Eagly and Carli (2007) point out that "male" behavior can be problematic when exhibited by females. Self-promotion is not communal, and modesty is still expected from women. When they behave like a male stereotype, they create discomfort and confusion and resistance.

Sometimes women aspire to success by working behind the scenes. This stance may be comfortable for them, but it is unlikely to produce greatness or success beyond a circumscribed limit or glass ceiling.

Serious career effectiveness requires visibility. Once again, the key is in the interpretation or perception. In certain male environments, when modesty is interpreted as inadequacy, the woman is the loser. The challenge for women is to figure out how to promote themselves without alienation from self and others. Not surprisingly, research indicates that some women react to negative stereotyping by "disappearing" (Goffee & Jones, 2000). They wear clothes that disguise their femininity or hide their unique flair, or they try to blend in by behaving like men. This reduces their chance of being seen as leader material, and it diminishes the likelihood that the unique qualities women bring to the workplace will be appreciated. Inauthenticity is rarely a good long-term strategy.

Communication Style   Women and men communicate differently in the workplace. Significant differences are described in Tannen's (1986, 1990, 1994) three volumes of work on male and female conversation. They are essential reading for the executive coach. Tannen is a sociolinguist who has spent considerable time observing communication in business settings and comes to the following general conclusions: Men and women tend to use different conversational styles, and when styles clash or are misunderstood, the problems they cause are mislabeled as bad intentions, lack of ability, poor character, or some other negative intrapersonal quality. The problem for women in the workplace is that, as Tannen puts it (1990, p. 15): "The male is seen as normative, the female as departing from the norm. … Furthermore, if women's and men's styles are shown to be different, it is usually women who are told to change." She notes that women are judged negatively because of their conversational style, a style learned early by many girls as a part of normal female development.

Here are several of the prominent themes that Tannen describes. The reader is urged to consult the original sources.

1. Women are inclined to make requests or suggestions rather than make a direct injunction (e.g., "Would you mind taking a look at the Bull's-Eye account if you get a chance?" instead of "Please audit the Bull's-Eye account and let me know how it looks by Tuesday"). Frankel (2004) calls this "couching statements as questions." This tactic can feel safer, but can be confusing to men or women who do not understand what the request actually means (Tannen, 1994, pp. 78–94). Some people appreciate this style while others actually do not understand it. Here's an example from everyday life (courtesy of Tracey Pomeroy):

Jane: Where would you like to go for lunch? (Thinking, "Let's talk about it. I care about you and am trying to politely engage you in a friendly negotiation, so that we can agree on a place.")

John: Let's go to Chevy's. (Thinking, "You asked a simple, direct question and I gave you a clear answer. This is polite, because it lets you know what I want, plus it doesn't waste a lot of time haggling. I just want to eat, and Chevy's sounds good right now.")

Jane: What about Tortolla's? (Thinking, "He's being a little rude and pushy. Why didn't he ask me what I wanted to do? Doesn't he care at all about me and what I think?")

John: Tortolla's might be crowded at this time of day. (Thinking, "If she wanted to go to Tortolla's, why didn't she just say so in the first place, instead of tricking me by asking what I wanted to do, and then ignoring my answer? What's going on here?")

This is an example of how different communication styles can get in the way of two well-meaning people and create confusion and bad feelings. Neither style is right or wrong. They are just different, and they strive to get to the same place by a different route.

2. Some women apologize compulsively and unnecessarily (Tannen, 1994, pp. 43–51). This is a social convention, a kind of politeness, much like the greeting "How are you?" (No one really expects a direct, explicit answer to *that* question.) When women apologize (e.g., "Sorry I didn't get back to you yesterday"), men often see it as a sign of deference or even of weakness. Women simply use apologies to keep relationships balanced and to show respect. "When a guy hears *sorry*, he infers that you've made a mistake" (Evans, 2000, p. 147).

3. In this same way, women say thank you to sustain positive feelings in a relationship, not necessarily because something must be thanked (Tannen, 1994, pp. 54–57). This is sometimes confusing to men, who may figure that they must have done something to deserve gratitude. For men, thanking can put the thanker in a one-down position. In the competitive games of life, for men, thanking someone can mean that they have just lost a round.

4. Women sometimes ask for an opinion as a way to show consideration for another person, even when they do not intend to actually use that opinion (Tannen, 1994, pp. 61–63). For women, a request for an opinion can simply be a tactic to show respect or to open a discussion. This can be confusing to men if they render an opinion but it is not used. Males may interpret such opinion-seeking as manipulative or as a sign of weakness or indecisiveness or disrespect.

5. Men and women might use praise and criticism differently. Tannen describes the intrinsic trickiness in these behaviors, as people interpret and desire feedback in very different ways, depending on their personality and background (Tannen, 1994, pp. 66–70). Some people interpret praise as manipulative or prying, whereas others are embarrassed by it. Others think they are performing poorly when no praise is given. Some bosses do not say anything to solid performers, because "everything is OK." Conversely, many men have had a coach or a father who told them not to worry when they are being yelled at or corrected. "Worry when I stop yelling at you, for that means I've lost interest in your development," they say. Tannen speculates that "many men feel women don't tell them directly enough when they are doing something wrong, and many women feel that men don't tell them directly enough if they are doing well" (1994, p. 68). Dorrance (n.d.) observed that:

> If you make a general criticism of a men's team, they all think you are talking about someone else. Videotape is proof of the guilty party. You don't need that proof with a woman. In fact, if

you make a general criticism of women, everyone in the room thinks you are talking about her. If you tell a woman she made a mistake, she'll believe you. Seeing it on tape often only makes it worse. However, because I have found that a lot of women do not have the confidence to feel they are as good as they actually are, we use our videos as highlight reels to build their confidence.

6. Women use *trouble talk* as a rapport builder (Evans, 2000, p. 23; Tannen, 1994, pp. 71–72). They share difficulties as a way to connect with others. Men sometimes do not know what to make of such talk, and they often feel compelled to solve the problem presented in the talking. The female participant interprets this as a lack of empathy, an inability to listen and care. Many men view such trouble talk as complaining or whining. In their view, real team players focus on the positives. They roll up their sleeves and get to work. For men, talk is more likely to be seen as the simple transmission of information, whereas women use talk to maintain relationship, support, and interaction. Evans (2000, p. 31) notes that you never heard *Dragnet* Sergeant Joe Friday say "Just the facts, *sir.*"

7. Women (and some men) communicate indirectly, and the indirectness is confusing to others (Tannen, 1994, pp. 78–95). Traditional male leaders, especially those who played on athletic teams or served in the military, are used to giving and receiving direct statements at work. Tannen gives several examples of women and men who hint around at important information instead of providing direct speech (including a transcript of a hypothetical airline crash that might have been avoided: "What do you think about that ice on the wings …"). Indirectness is not the same as weakness, but it can be interpreted that way in some cultures. Once again, women do this as a way to sustain relationships. It comes across as caring and respectful (e.g., "Would you mind getting the Anderson file when you get a chance, please?").

Dysfunctional Communication Patterns In her book *They Just Don't Get It, Do They?*, Kathleen Reardon describes five ways that male–female communication patterns damage women in the workplace. She refers to these dysfunctional communication patterns as DCPs. They are:

- *Dismissive DCPs*—This is the most common pattern. It happens when men interrupt, talk over, or simply ignore what women say. Women are put in the difficult position of having to reassert their point, sometimes against resistance. In this situation it can be easier to relent and be silent, which perpetuates the problem. The trick is to find a way to create a culture that does not value this pattern or allow it to continue. Calling attention to the pattern off-line (later on and behind closed doors) and commenting about it when it happens are two ways to start.

- *Retaliatory DCPs*—Sometimes men communicate with women in a manner that retaliates for all of the perceived slights that they have received at the hands of women in their lives. Sometimes they limit conversation as a way to avoid being bested by a woman, which many men find humiliating and unacceptable. When a woman has a bright idea they abruptly find fault, and then criticize in a way that mystifies that woman. All of this happens without comment on the process.

- *Patronizing DCPs*—This problem derives from the traditional roles that women are perceived to play (mothers, wives, or daughters). Some men communicate with women as if they were communicating with their mother or wife or daughter, and sometimes women respond in kind. Men find it hard to view a woman as a colleague, so they diffuse the role discomfort by flirting or trivializing the conversation. Women then have to make the difficult decision about whether to go along with the role problem or confront and dispute it.

- *Exclusionary DCPs*—Reardon makes the point that men (like women) often have two communication modes: one for use in an all-male situation and one for when women are present. This becomes clear when a man says something at a meeting and then apologizes to a woman who is present. This implies that certain things just cannot be said in front of women, an exclusionary sign, when you think about it. This also happens when critical information is passed along at informal, all-male gatherings, of which women are well aware. Once again, the question arises: Should I confront this situation? If so, when and how? If not, what are the consequences for myself and other women (and men) in the company?

- *Undermining DCPs*—These are observations made about women that are disparaging or even devastating to a career. They are subtle and found in media reports that give organizations reason to sustain stereotyped responses to women in the workforce. Examples include the evolution of the "Mommy track" for women who were not assumed to be fully committed to their careers, and the highlighting of women who criticize other women in the workplace. It can be exhausting to have to deal with these subtly undermining influences in the media and the corporate culture.

Unless both parties are on the same song sheet, misunderstandings are likely. The best communication happens when both parties naturally understand what things mean (which is unlikely) or when they have ongoing discussions about conversational style, make allowances, and get used to each other.

Speaking Up   This is a difficult gender area, and another in which differential perceptions hurt ambitious females. Males are taught to stand up and speak up. Plebes at West Point are made to stand on the bank of the Hudson River and give commands that can be heard on the opposite shore. Many have trouble at first, but eventually all cadets learn how to do it. Women often learn the opposite: to hang back and let others take the floor, to speak quietly and modestly, and avoid sticking out in a crowd. When women do speak out, they run the risk of seeming boorish or obnoxious or pushy.

Occasionally, men can even yell at work and get away with it. Such an outburst might be seen as a "great leadership moment." But when a woman raises her voice, she runs the risk of being seen as out of control: "She's lost it. You know how women are ..."

Even looking men directly in the eye can be risky for women. When men do it, it is seen as an act of good communication, even honesty. Straightforward men in White American culture reach out and offer a firm handshake and look you right in the eye. When women look men right in the eye, men do not always know how to interpret things. They get uncomfortable. It is confusing.

Many women have the experience of speaking but not being heard. To succeed in the present business environment, women must find an assertive voice and find a way to navigate through these narrow waters. Too cautious and you are seen as inadequate; too loud and you are viewed as pushy. But modern business moves quickly, and there's no time to wait for others to politely draw you out.

> It's very easy for them to ignore what you have to say. You have to be willing to speak up and occasionally make a fuss or they won't pay attention to you. (Shirley Peterson, Northrup Vice President, as quoted in Reardon, 1995, p. 5)

Leadership Style   There is substantial research evidence to indicate that women tend to lead differently than men, and this is no surprise, given the different ways that boys and girls are raised and socialized. Evidence implies that women are typically more inclusive and participatory in their leadership efforts. They are inclined to seek consensus and participation, and a case can be made that those qualities are truly modern and can be more effective in a creative, entrepreneurial economy with today's workers. Women are also more likely to share knowledge and to solicit information before they act. They are less likely to value domination or hierarchy, and tend to behave as someone in the center of a web of human resources. One female chief executive officer (CEO) calls her style "empathic enabling" (Betsey Cohen in Smith, 2000, p. 3).

This is a far cry from the descriptions of leadership that male athletic coaches provide in Chapter 12 of this book. Several sources of research on leadership styles associated with women are listed in the "References" section (Carr-Rufino, 1993; Gilligan, 1982; Helgesen, 1990; Rosener, 1990; Smith, 2000).

Transformational and transactional leadership models are described in Chapter 15. Transformational leaders are viewed as powerful role models who gain trust and empower followers to reach common goals. They influence by communicating positive values and optimistic excitement. Transactional leaders understand leadership as an exchange between leader and follower, a give and take that appeals to the self-interest of both parties. They overtly reward and punish desired and unacceptable behavior with money and assignments. Eagly, Johannesen-Schmidt, and van Engen (2003) describe empirical evidence that women tend to be more transformational in style, and there is a widespread perception in the leadership literature that such a style, especially when it is warm in tone, is effective in the current business environment.

Multitasking   There is evidence that women are more comfortable doing several things at once, whereas men are thought to prefer sequential tasking. This observation has some early support from functional MRI studies of brain activity (Gurian & Annis, 2008), but much of the evidence derives from observations of the harried mother who effectively manages several children, the demands of a household, aging parents, and school board meetings all at the same time.

Response to Role Pressures   It is clear that, on average, women spend more time and energy on family matters than men, and that they pay a price. In the McKinsey study (Desvaux et al., p. 15), men and women reported that family was perceived to be important at about equal levels, but that women pay a higher price. Hewlett paints a depressing picture in her *Harvard Business Review* report (2002), noting that as women climb higher in the corporate world they tend to have fewer children, while the reverse is true for men.

> There is a secret out there—a painful, well-kept secret: At midlife, between a third and a half of all successful career women in the United States do not have children. ... that figure rises to 42% in corporate America. These women have not chosen to remain childless. The vast majority, in fact, yearn for children. (Hewlett, 2002, p. 66)

Hewlett goes on to point out that "the persistent wage gap between men and women is due mainly to the penalties that women incur when they interrupt their careers to have children" (2002, p. 69). Men and women do not respond in the same way to perceptions of familial responsibilities, and men cannot bear children. Since the workplace favors continuity and commitment to long hours, women lose out. As an example, older dentists have been known to decline to hire a younger female associate because they are worried that she will settle in to their practice, establish important relationships with a patient base, and then leave to have children and start a family.

Familial responsibilities also make it hard to participate fully in social activities outside of work, and such participation is crucial to advancement. It is impossible to get ahead in 40 hours per week. There is much to be done outside of the workplace at receptions, dinners, meetings, outings, and charity events. Everyone knows this, but that does not change the fact that there are also soccer games, orthodontic appointments, and family crises that cannot be calendared.

How Coaches Can Help

Coaches must first sort out a challenging conceptual and practical matter: How and where do you focus attention? If you believe that powerful workplace forces inhibit female success, why would you work with individual female clients to change their personal behavior? This can imply that there is something wrong or inadequate about them, and that is why they are not being promoted. Although this diagnosis could certainly be accurate, women face multiple, complicated forces of resistance in the workplace. The environment is not always helpful or fair. Trend data indicate that the progress of women in corporate life has stalled or is even headed south. The trick for coaches is to provide help with personal change in an unaccommodating environment without blaming the victim. The concept of blaming the victim made it into the social change literature with Ryan's 1971 book of the same name. It cautioned against blaming people for their responses to systemic discrimination by insisting that they should change. In this model, widespread poverty, especially in one ethnic group, is blamed on personal sloth. This is a variation of the *fundamental attribution error* described in Chapter 9 ("Social Psychology and Coaching"). Context is the most powerful force, but negative outcomes are attributed to individual behavior and personal characteristics. Coaches have to figure out how to establish collaborative relationships with female clients such that they can help women respond to workplace challenges without implying pathology, inadequacy, or blame. There are ways to do this.

> First, there is reason to believe that many women are somewhat unsure of themselves in the male business world, especially at first. Often, women are unnecessarily hard on themselves. When a man cuts himself, he throws away the razor. When a woman cuts herself, she blames herself. (Gail Koff, as quoted in Smith, 2000, p. 263)

Women face difficult decisions about whether to go along with or challenge the prevailing culture and trends. Women clearly cannot sit back and hope that things will improve or that they will somehow succeed by chance.

Coaches can help them find ways to learn about the work culture, get feedback about their own performance, and make necessary changes to respond to difficult workplace challenges.

First, study the gender literature. It is well developed and extremely interesting. No coach, male or female, should work with a female executive without exposure to this body of literature. Recommended readings are listed at the end of this chapter. The books by athletic coaches are surprisingly relevant and compelling. Most men will be enlightened by what they read.

Work on relationship development with your client. Establish a solid, unique bond with each new client. Find out from your client what she wants to accomplish and assess her personal goals.

A coach can provide a calibrating influence. Help your female clients notice how they feel and how they want to feel, then work toward getting there. Sometimes just having a supportive confidant is enough to solve this problem; sometimes a change project must be implemented.

In many ways, the coach's job is to help clients assess and push their comfort levels. Often, a serious career upgrade requires a visit to the outside of one's comfort zone. Along those lines, a coach can often help a female client figure out how to become more visible in an organization without feeling too uncomfortable. Women cannot expect promotion to the highest levels of organizations if they have spent their entire career below the radar or in places most comfortable for women. It is important to have experience in marketing and, perhaps, human resources. But it is at least as important to demonstrate success and expertise in operations or finance or IT or strategic planning, and it may not be easy getting there.

Coaches can help female clients communicate their career aspirations to those who "count" in their organization. Sometimes, because a woman has been "hanging back," key people in the organization misjudge her ambition or goals. This perception can often be corrected when an executive makes her desires explicit. This can be as simple as sitting down with a leader and expressing those aspirations. Occasionally this must be done repeatedly with several key people in the organization. Women cannot expect others to read their minds or guess accurately at their career goals, because others will often get them wrong. Along those lines, a coach can help clients devise and suggest alternative ways for performance evaluation. Present methods may be based upon male norms and may be wholly inappropriate for a woman and her goals.

A wise and experienced coach can sometimes serve as a "gender translator." If that coach has been around organizations and has been observant, he or she may be able to translate rules, mores, codes, and the behavior of others for an executive client. Work can be viewed as a "game" that must be played. Games have rules, and you need a thorough understanding of the rules to succeed. Coaches can also serve as an ersatz mentor, even though he or she is outside of the organizational culture.

In some ways women actually have an advantage in this area. As traditional outsiders to the male corporate world they often understand men better than men understand women. This is a result of historic power dynamics. Women have been in a position that required them to pay attention, and men have not. Sometimes men have no idea about gender-related aspects of everyday life, and this causes them to seem clueless.

Coaching Women for Leadership

Judith Blanton (2009) and colleagues (RHR International) have produced a model that centers on the idea of authenticity. They interviewed 65 female executives and 35 other stakeholders and came to the conclusion that women lead best when operating from an authentic place, expressing their true self as experienced from within. They focused on five forces that can provide a useful map for assessment and for change:

1. *The Sphere of Authenticity*—This is the critical component and it consists of the internal consistency between values and overt behavior as well as the external perception by others that the leader is expressing real values and is genuine and trustworthy. Internal consistency comes first, and it requires that female executives explore and understand their own values and priorities.

2. *Women Leader Climate*—The climate for female leadership must be carefully assessed and acknowledged. Ultimately the authentic leader has a role in shaping this climate. Organizational cultures vary widely along this dimension. Expression of authentic leadership is easier in more accepting corporate cultures.

3. *Individual Psychology and Interpersonal Resources*—These are thought to be strengths for most women in the workplace. Internal individual resources include emotional intelligence, motivational and cognitive traits, and the skills and knowledge accumulated along the way. External interpersonal resources include mentors, networks, and a variety of social skills.

4. *Leader Expectations*—This is the organization's existing view of good leadership. It consists of things like style, method, and appearance. It is often based upon traditional male ways of leading. It is what the organization expects from good leaders. These views can make it harder or easier for women to lead authentically, depending on their quality.

5. *External Commitments*—These are the obligations that women face outside of the work setting, including family responsibilities and community interests. They are typically perceived to be more pressing by women than men.

In this model, the organization and the female executive influence each other, and a win–win situation is possible. "Successful women lead authentically; pushing the envelope of institutional norms with power and credibility" (Blanton, p. 10). The organization grows and women thrive. It is hard to imagine sustained success for female executives if they are not able to lead with authenticity, but authentic leadership is likely to challenge, and perhaps, threaten traditionally male cultures.

Centered Leadership

Barsh et al. (2008), as a part of a McKinsey Leadership Project, interviewed 85 successful female leaders and combined their views with academic literature to devise a leadership model for women. It presupposes the following conditions: intelligence, tolerance for change, desire to lead, and communication skills.

- The model begins with a focus on *meaning*. Leaders must figure out what they care for and find a way to work toward a purpose. The work must be personally meaningful, as in following one's heart. When this is not possible because of organizational culture or market forces, (and it is not feasible to relocate) it may be possible to find meaning in the job that is actually available.

- To be successful as a leader, one must *manage energy* effectively. Since most successful people work long hours, and since women come home to work a "second shift," it is imperative to carefully observe and manage personal energy without squandering it or giving it away needlessly.

- One must learn to use *positive framing* to succeed (see Chapter 6 of this book on cognitive therapy). This involves learned optimism and accurate, mostly positive thinking. Some people are better at this than others, but it is essential to successful leadership.

- Women who want to lead and succeed must *connect*. In spite of the systemic challenges, networks must be established and mentors recruited. Positive personal relationships with senior colleagues are crucial. Sponsors can help women highlight their successes and potential to the organization. Women also have to get better at reciprocity, the give-and-take interactions that are central to the transactional leadership style often favored by men.

- Women must take risks and *engage*. McKinsey found that people who took calculated risks were happier. It seems clear that women cannot sit by and wait for things to change.

Specific Feedback about Client Behavior

A coach can sometimes be of enormous help by observing and giving feedback about small, but important things that a client does. These are behaviors that are under that client's control and can be changed rather quickly and sometimes painlessly, with powerful results. There are many books now on the market to provide examples of this kind of feedback. One example, Lois Frankel's *Nice Girls Don't Get the Corner Office* (2004), is mandatory reading for coaches, and it includes a treasure chest of hard-hitting, specific suggestions for coaching consideration. Her list of 101 mistakes that women make in the workplace includes:

- Pretending it isn't a game
- Doing the work of others
- Needing to be liked
- Acting like a man
- Decorating your office like your living room
- Using only your nickname or first name
- Waiting to be noticed
- Giving away your ideas
- Being invisible
- Couching statements as questions
- Asking permission
- Using touchy-feely language
- Smiling inappropriately
- Tilting your head
- Grooming in public
- Wearing glasses around your neck
- Internalizing messages
- Accepting the *fait accompli*
- Being the last to speak

This kind of direct feedback can be tricky to deliver and to receive. It implies that a woman is willing to take risks in order to move ahead. There *is* risk (mentioned earlier in this chapter), and risks should be discussed, negotiated, and agreed upon between coach and client. Sometimes a coach and client can get buy-in for changes from the organization, so that new client behavior is understood in a positive frame. Some clients expect this kind of feedback and direct advice from coaches and will not feel coached until they get it.

Coaches can help female executives become more comfortable with power and more creative in gaining and managing it. Many women would benefit from experimentation with how they present themselves. Coaches can observe, assess, and provide feedback to clients about their communication and behavioral style. This can be crucial. People cannot accurately judge their own style or impact, and a coach can be essential to this process. Watch your client on the job. Get real-time data and information. Synthesize it and communicate it to your clients in a way that energizes them and motivates them to make small but important changes. Create a change project with target behaviors. Monitor the changes and adjust the plan. Get more feedback and do it again.

Help your client with the family *balance question,* if it is relevant. This is an important challenge for most women, and it probably ought to be for most men. A neutral person—someone outside of job and home—can be very useful in this process. It can be gut wrenching, because success in some jobs precludes a healthy family life. Hard choices have to be made.

> You can't have it all. As a CEO, my work came first, my daughter second, and my husband third. Sometimes you don't feel very good about that. (Ann Spector Lief, as quoted in Smith, 2000, p. 254)

Requirements for Coaching

Not every coach will be able to be useful to every client. Some men and some women may not be comfortable confronting the issue of gender as a coach. Some clients demonstrate no interest in gender issues, and others consider them to be irrelevant, offensive, or a distraction. Some are exquisitely aware of the dangers related to gender politics in a male-dominated corporation or market, and they steer a wide course around these dangers. Many business people, including women, view attention to gender as a "liberal" or "feminist" agenda, and a distraction from the real matters at hand. Others seem to possess a macho attitude, dismissive of gender bias or problems. Some women detest any potential association with the victim role. In the business press, it is common to read newspaper articles containing quotes from successful women (and these are actual quotes), such as, "I never found myself disadvantaged based upon being a woman," "Do what you love. If you do, other things will take care of themselves," and "When I encounter stereotypes, I put my head down and execute." Some women fear the prospect of bringing gender questions into the workplace, and there is often good reason for that fear.

Assess your clients along this dimension. See how they view gender and the role that it plays. If there is a good match between your readiness and skill with the interests and needs of your client, proceed to study the gender question, head-on. If not, consider packaging gender issues in other, more acceptable ways. The same feedback and the same behavior changes can be viewed as an individual matter, leaving the abstraction of gender out of the picture entirely.

Effective coaching for women certainly requires a coach's awareness of these issues, as well as an interest in them. Gender is a central aspect of our identity, and it is extremely interesting. As Tannen notes (1994, pp. 13–14), "Few elements of our identities come as close to our sense of who we are as gender. When you spot a person walking down the street toward you, you immediately and automatically identify that person as male or female." You could misjudge someone's racial or ethnic identity or not care about it (which is not to diminish the serious relevance of ethnicity). But it is virtually impossible to miss gender. It simply cannot be ignored.

The effective coach surely must study the gender-in-business literature to prepare for the role of coaching women. It is a complex landscape, and nearly everyone has a powerfully felt opinion. Several books in the References and Recommended Readings sections are important enough to be considered required reading. Of special note are Coughlin, Wingard, and Hollihan (2005), Harragan (1976), Helgesen (1990), Tannen (1994), Reardon (1995), Smith (2000), and Evans (2000).

What Organizations Can Do

It is in the best interest of companies and organizations to increase diversity. Executive coaches often have access to the highest levels of leadership. This presents an opportunity for them to weigh in on organizational factors that might be limiting the company and preventing it from taking full competitive advantage of their female resources.

Coaches must bring a positive outlook to the leadership table. Not much will happen if organizational leaders feel that they must try to diversify because they are being told to do so or forced to do so or because they must be perceived as politically correct. It is the job of corporate officers to make a profit. They must create and sustain competitive advantage. Coaches have the best chance of making a difference if they are able to convince leadership that greater gender diversity results in better company output. Accumulate empirical data and case studies to make your point (do it in a condensed format, of course). Help your individual clients do the same.

The McKinsey report (Desvaux et al., 2007, pp. 19–21) recommends four specific ways to enhance gender diversity:

1. Create and maintain gender diversity indicators without creating quotas. The company should establish an ongoing data-collection system to track how women fare in the organization. Segregation by gender within the organization (glass walls) should be monitored.

2. Implement flexible working arrangements for everyone (males and females). This would include flexible hours, mobile offices, and technological ways that minimize the impact of geography and rigid time schedules. Norms related to long hours and heavy travel should be reexamined and adjusted. This has to be done in ways that increase productivity in the long run. Younger employees and managers are

likely to have a strong preference for time and location flexibility. The problem to be solved is the old notion that more hours are better and that people need to be sitting at their desks from 9 to 5 or, preferably, much later.

Explore and develop nonlinear career paths (for women and men) to include breaks in service. Maternity leaves should be carefully structured to maintain contact between the employee and the organization during periods of absence.

3. Adapt the human resources process to make recruiting, appraisal, and career-management systems more women-friendly.

4. Help women master the dominant codes and nurture their ambition. Coaching, mentoring, and female networking fit in here.

The McKinsey report makes the point that leadership at the highest levels, including the CEO, must be involved and committed to this process. The Catalyst guide to corporate best practices (*Advancing Women in Business*, 1998) is listed in the "References" section.

Summary

1. Remember that men and women often see things differently. They have different impulses, different views of how to get things done, and different ideas on what is most important. At the same time, remember that stereotyping and generalizing are quite dangerous. There is no prototype "typical female" or "typical male" in real life. If there are, they are small in number. In fact, some women think and act more like stereotypical males than females, and you can not tell that by looking at them. Appearances are deceptive sometimes. Most of us possess aspects of both genders. Study this question and help clients evaluate themselves. The key is to ask, listen, and watch. Encourage active discussion of the ways that gender influences things. Put gender on the table. Organizations that are male-run tend to favor male mores, although some men lead in a "female" style. Even in "male" organizations, however, a "female" style can flourish. In some cases, it can have a transformative impact on the organization. This generally requires buy-in from leadership, and changes probably cannot be sold as "female."

2. Help female clients decide what to do about the gender problem on a case-by-case basis. Help them think through the rules and decide how they want to handle things. There are usually several options. Do not try to force people to behave in ways which they do not agree with or find objectionable. It is best for clients to take advantage of their own style rather than to try to make a radical change.

Small adaptations are usually possible, and wholesale gender style changes are ill advised. Success has many faces and there are multiple paths.

An option that often makes sense is to help a female client enter into discussions with key colleagues and leaders to clear things up. "What do you think I mean when I say …?" is an example of the kind of discussion that can clarify and strengthen work relationships between the genders. "Why do we do things this way or that?" is another. The key is to establish a culture that welcomes open gender talk, even when disagreement is involved. Most people find it intriguing when presented in the right way.

A gender-based 360-degree evaluation is a creative way to discover some of the gender trends and "mores"of the organization.

3. Avoid the impulse to blame and scapegoat. Do not blame the person and do not blame the organization. It is a waste of time and energy, and it tends to create costly negative emotions. If changes can be made in the organization, work on those changes. But, be willing to help your coaching clients accept the organization just as it is, without self-pity and perhaps without anger. Help them become savvy about gender politics and relations. It is unwise to take these things too personally. If the organization will not change and your client cannot accept this fact, explore the feasibility of a job change.

4. Help female clients figure out the unwritten rules and gender codes. Do a research project. Ask others in the organization about these rules. Most people have their own take on them and are happy to reveal this to a coach or a coworker.

5. Encourage your client to find an informal mentor within or outside the organization. This is nearly essential to career progress and development. Coaches may have to challenge the sponsoring organization to cooperate with this need.

6. Create a career plan or succession plan with your client. If this is not possible, at least open a discussion about where she is headed. Be careful about glass walls—invisible barriers that keep women in career ghettos. A successful rise to the top of a hierarchical organization usually requires time in key organizational positions (revenue generators, decision making, make-or-break jobs).

7. Coaches would be wise to support female executives at times when they become discouraged or demoralized by the prospect of swimming upstream in a male-dominated organization. The day-to-day toll can be exhausting, and it helps to have someone in your corner.

Finally, there are gender advantages available to women in the workplace these days, some small and some significant. Coaches can help women find them. "It is a common perception that women will steadily gain greater access to leadership roles. ... But social change does not proceed without struggle and conflict" (Eagly & Carli, 2007, p. 67).

Note

The author wishes to acknowledge the contributions of Ana Maria Irueste-Montes to the chapter that appeared in the first edition of this book, as well as the gracious help of Judith Blanton of RHR International and Rebecca Turner of Alliant University in San Francisco.

References

Advancing women in business—The Catalyst guide: Best practices from the corporate leaders. (1998). San Francisco: Jossey-Bass.

Alsop, R. (2007, July 17). How to raise female MBA enrollment. *Wall Street Journal.* Retrieved January, 31, 2009, from: http://online.wsj.com/article/SB11846288896 6268184.html.

Barsh, J., Craske, R. A., & Cranston, S. (2008, September). Centered leadership: How talented women thrive. *McKinsey Quarterly.* Available at: http://www.mckinsey-quarterly.com/Centered_leadership_How_talented_women_thrive_2193.

Blanton, J. S. (2009). Women and authentic leadership. *The California Psychologist, 42*(1), 6–10.

Carr-Rufino, N. (1993). *The promotable woman: Advancing through leadership skills.* Belmont, CA: Wadsworth.

Catalyst. (2009). *Women in leadership.* Available at: http://www.catalyst.org/.

Competitive drive: Palm puts up its fists as Microsoft attacks hand-held PC market. (2000, August 8). *Wall Street Journal,* p. A1.

Coughlin, L., Wingard, E., & Hollihan, K. (Eds.). (2005). *Enlightened power: How women are transforming the practice of leadership.* San Francisco: Jossey-Bass.

Davidson, A. (1994). Gender differences in administrative ethics. In T. Cooper (Ed.), *Handbook of administrative ethics* (pp. 415–434). New York: Marcel Dekker.

de Beauvoir, S. (1952). *The second sex.* New York: Vintage Books.

DeBoer, K. (2004). *Gender and competition.* Monterey, CA: Coaches Choice.

Desvaux, G., Devillard-Hoellinger, S., & Baumgarten, P. (2007). *Women matter: Gender diversity, a corporate performance driver.* Available at: http://www.mckinsey.com/locations/paris/home/womenmatter/pdfs/Women_matter_oct2007_english.pdf.

Dorrance, A. (n.d.). *Coaching women: Going against the instinct of my gender.* Retrieved February 1, 2009, from: www.spartan.org/resources/coachingwomen.doc.

Eagly, A. H., & Carli, L. L. (2007). Women and the labyrinth of leadership. *Harvard Business Review, 85*(9), 63–71.

Eagly, A. H., Johannesen-Schmidt, M. C., & van Engen, M. L. (2003). Transformational, transactional, and laissez-faire leadership styles: A meta-analysis comparing women and men. *Psychological Bulletin, 129*(4), 569–591.

Evans, G. (2000). *Play like a man, win like a woman.* New York: Broadway Books.

Fels, A. (2004). Do women lack ambition? *Harvard Business Review, 82*(4), 50–60.

Frankel, L. P. (2004). *Nice girls don't get the corner office.* New York: Warner Business Books.

Gilligan, C. (1982). *In a different voice.* Cambridge, MA: Harvard University Press.

Goffee, R., & Jones, G. (2000, September–October). Why should anyone be led by you? *Harvard Business Review,* 63–70.

Gurian, M., & Annis, B. (2008). *Leadership and the sexes.* San Francisco: Jossey-Bass.

Harragan, B. (1976). *Games mother never taught you.* New York: Warner Books.

Helgesen, S. (1990). *The female advantage: Women's ways of leading.* Garden City, NY: Doubleday.

Hewlett, S. A. (2002, April). Executive women and the myth of having it all. *Harvard Business Review, 80*(4), 66–73.

Ibarra, H., & Obodaru, O. (2009, January). Women and the vision thing. *Harvard Business Review.* Available at http://hbr.harvardbusiness.org/2009/01/women-and-the-vision-thing/ar/1

Miller, L., Cooke, L., Tsang, J., & Morgan, F. (1992, March). Should I brag? Nature and impact of positive and boastful disclosures for women and men. *Human Communication Research,* 364–399.

Reardon, K. (1995). *They just don't get it, do they?* Boston: Little, Brown.

Rosener, J. (1990, November/December). Ways women lead. *Harvard Business Review,* 119–125.

Ryan, W. (1971). *Blaming the victim.* New York: Vintage Books.

Schwartz, F. (1989, January–February). Management women and the new facts of life. *Harvard Business Review,* 65–76.

Smith, D. (2000). *Women at work: Leadership for the next century.* Upper Saddle River, NJ: Prentice Hall.

Tannen, D. (1986). *That's not what I meant! How conversational style makes or breaks relationships.* New York: Ballantine.

Tannen, D. (1990). *You just don't understand: Women and men in conversation.* New York: Ballantine.

Tannen, D. (1994). *Talking from 9 to 5: How women's and men's conversational styles affect who gets heard, who gets credit, and what gets done at work.* New York: William Morrow and Company.

A vote of confidence. (2005, November 14). *Newsweek,* p. 62.

Recommended Readings

Blum, D. (1997). *Sex on the brain: The biological differences between men and women.* New York: Penguin Books.

Book, E. W. (200). *Why the best man for the job is a woman.* New York: HarperCollins Books.

Davidson, M. J., & Cooper, C. L. (1992). *Shattering the glass ceiling.* London: Paul Chapman.

Gray, J. (1992). *Men are from Mars, women are from Venus: A practical guide for improving communication and getting what you want from your relationships.* New York: Harper Collins.

Henning, M., & Jardim, A. (1977). *The managerial woman.* New York: Pocket Books.

Morrison, A. M., White, R. P., & Van Velsor, E. (1992). *Breaking the glass ceiling.* Cambridge, MA: Perseus.

Swiss, D. J. (1996). *Women breaking through.* Princeton, NJ: Peterson's/Pacesetter Books.

Tavris, C. (1992). *The mismeasure of woman.* New York: Simon & Schuster.

Willen, S. (1993). *The new woman manager: 50 fast and savvy solutions for executive excellence.* Lower Lake, CA: Asian Publishing.

14

Psychopathology and Coaching

About half of Americans will meet the criteria for a DSM-IV disorder sometime in their life, with first onset usually in childhood or adolescence.

—National Comorbidity Survey Replication (Kessler et al., 2005, p. 593)

Coaches are not expected to function as psychologists or psychotherapists. It is a mistake for a coach to try to conduct therapy in the workplace, as there are practical and ethical prohibitions. Challenges in this area are described in the "Introduction" of this book, where a chart is provided to differentiate between coaching and therapy. Related issues are also discussed in Chapter 18, "Making the Transition."

Although it is essential for coaches to understand their personal and professional limitations, it is also true that there is an abundance of psychopathology in the workplace. Although accurate epidemiological statistics are uncommon, reliable estimates imply that nearly half of us will experience significant mental illness in our lifetime. The implications of such an estimate are stunning really, as this surely means that we will all encounter problems related to psychopathology in the workplace. Many of the disorders described in epidemiology data describe disorders of childhood, and many afflicted with those disorders will never actually enter the workplace. Even so, this still leaves large numbers of generally competent people who will have to cope with a wide variety of disorders while still managing to survive or thrive in the workplace. The fact that employers often assign coaches to employees who are struggling adds to the likelihood that a coach will be confronted with client psychopathology from time to time.

This chapter describes the numerous kinds of mental disorders that coaches are likely to encounter along with the traits, patterns, and behaviors that characterize these disorders. There are more than 400 officially defined mental disorders in various medical and psychological nosologies. This chapter covers a small number of the most relevant ones. It differentiates between traits and actual disorders, and it offers advice about how to proceed when the coach is confronted with actual client psychopathology.

Traits versus Pathology

It is important to begin by noting the difference between *traits* and *disorder* or between personality patterns and psychopathology. We all have personalities—complex patterns of thinking, feeling, and behaving that characterize us. Many of these traits are healthy and effective, whereas other traits are the opposite: they hurt us, they set us back, or they cause pain, discomfort, or inconvenience. In short, they are self-defeating. It is impossible to imagine a person lacking in any or all negative personality qualities. The trick in coaching is to discover those traits quickly and to discern whether any are "bad" enough to warrant the label of pathology or disorder. Theoretically, this is not especially difficult to do, as there are detailed formal standards available in the *Diagnostic and Statistical Manual of Mental Disorders* (4th ed., text rev.; American Psychiatric Association [APA], 2000), psychiatry's bible of psychopathology. This hefty document is available at any large bookstore, and coaches trained in a mental health discipline are well aware of it. The *DSM* contains all of the nearly 400 diagnostic categories of disorders currently known to the psychological professions. There are detailed lists of signs and symptoms, written in a relatively jargon-free vocabulary, so that the material is more or less accessible to the lay public. The essential distinction between pathology and trait is ostensibly clear in the *DSM*, and it all boils down to the extent of *distress and disability*. If the behaviors or characteristics of a person cause significant distress or disability, they qualify for the formal diagnosis of a mental disorder. If not, that person has *traits*. In this model, *distress* refers to subjective discomfort or pain. If the emotional or psychological pain is significant, especially if it is chronic or long lasting, then one probably has a *disorder*. More important, if the signs and symptoms actually cause *disability* (an inability to do things that one previously was able to do, or an inability to do things that most other people can do, or the inability to do things required of a person in the conduct of their life), then that person has a disorder.

The concept of disorder—and the diagnostic process—can have several useful purposes. First, the naming of a set of behaviors, signs, or symptoms as a disorder might actually lead to an effective treatment. Second, a diagnosis may allow a clinician to file for health plan reimbursement to pay for therapy. Finally, many people find comfort in a diagnosis, as some of the mystery disappears and they "finally know what they've got." They feel relief in that there is a name for what has been happening to them and with that name comes a sense of control and hope.

But coaches do not diagnose mental disorders. It is not their job and they are unlikely to be qualified to do so, anyway. Most coaches are not especially interested in diagnosis and find the concept counterproductive to the task at hand. Recall that coaching can be *remedial* (focused on "fixing" a problem or deficit) or *developmental* (enhancing and growing a valued employee), and a positively focused developmental coaching process has no interest in chasing after disorders. Nonetheless, coaches inevitably encounter mild, moderate, or even serious pathology in the workplace, and it would be difficult to make a case for simply bypassing these issues. Personality pathology is important because it has a way of undermining organizations and careers. It cannot be ignored.

It should be noted that most of the disorders described in this chapter affect just 1% to 2% of the general population, and the impact of symptoms often keeps sufferers out of the workplace or executive boardroom. Although 1% may not sound like a large number, such prevalence would mean that a community of 100,000 would include 1,000 such people. A business with 800 employees might include 8 to 16 people with a significant mental disorder and several others with minor, less disturbing psychopathologies. These figures might include high performers.

Coaches are likely to try to sidestep subtle or even obvious pathology if they are self-conscious or nervous about their lack of psychology skills. This reaction is completely understandable, as mental illness and abnormal behavior tend to be frightening anyway. But coaches must be able to stand up to this kind of situation and respond appropriately, partly because they may have been hired to coach precisely because of a perception that something is "wrong" with the client. Even in the best-case scenario, in the absence of disorder, negative pathological traits may be the "problem."

There is stigma attached to mental disorders, and this creates another level of complexity and difficulty for both the inexperienced and the psychologically minded coach. People generally hide their flaws, and they specifically hide their mental health issues in the workplace. For example, those suffering from substance abuse and eating disorders are notoriously secretive and deliberately deceptive. It is wise that coaches never assume they know everything of importance about a client. We all have secrets.

It must be noted that very little of importance can be known about someone based upon his or her appearance or the way that they come across at first. You must get to know them to understand them very well, so be careful about first or second impressions. Soak up these impressions, note them and log them, but do not rely upon them. At the same time, be wary of your intuition. Although most people have an affectionate attachment to their own intuition, research is not so kind. Intuition is notoriously unreliable. Sometimes your intuition is correct and sometimes it is not. Which is it this time? There is no way to know for certain.

The Mentally Healthy Person

It may help to begin the search for psychopathology with a description of its opposite: mental health. If we can define what is healthy, we can compare behavior against that standard. Although clear-cut norms do not exist, most psychologists and others generally agree about a few things. First, the mentally healthy person understands and lives in consensual reality. This is called *reality testing*, and it implies that the person perceives things in generally accepted ways. This is a gross standard, meaning, for example, that the person does not see hallucinations, illusions, and is not bothered by delusional thinking. There are no (literal) space monsters in the bedroom (or the boardroom, for that matter). They do not hear voices or suffer paranoid or grand ideas that could not possibly be true. This standard is not conformist. It does not mean that people must be average or politically centrist or religious in the ways that most people tend to be. Mentally healthy people may think differently or even idiosyncratically, but they do not distort reality.

When reality testing goes awry, terrible things happen. However, it is uncommon to encounter clinically "crazy" people in the workplace. This is good news for the workplace and bad news for those with schizophrenia or a debilitating bipolar disorder. Although recent improvements in treatment and medications have made life and work far better for those with serious mental disorders, it is still difficult (if not impossible) to have a highly productive or satisfying career if you suffer from one of the psychotic conditions. Nonetheless, it is possible for a previously healthy and productive person to experience a break with reality. With schizophrenia this typically happens to people when they are in their late teens or early 20s; however, there is a similar disorder called a delusional disorder that tends to appear at the age of 40 or 50. However, these kinds of illnesses are uncommon (1% of the general population), but they certainly exist and have been known to derail a previously successful person.

A second essential quality of the mentally healthy person is *positive energy*, both physical and psychological. Mentally healthy people tend to take a positive point of view and an optimistic slant on things. If not naturally disposed toward optimism, they are able to move themselves toward a neutral or positive perspective without too much difficulty. Energy seems highly correlated to business success, and a lack of physical or psychic energy can be associated with depression. People with great physical energy have a natural advantage, as they can get more done, go to more meetings, meet more people, read more, require less sleep, and maintain a more positive attitude for longer periods. Often, they make things seem easy. It is difficult to succeed without ample energy. Although physical and psychological energies seem connected, there are often medical reasons for diminished energy. Those reasons must be investigated so that hidden maladies such as anemia, thyroid deficiency, or low blood sugar are not labeled as depression or low self-esteem.

Closely associated with energy is the capacity for *engagement*. Healthy people are engaged. They are busy with activities and projects and ideas that compel them. They do not sit around with nothing to do. They care about things, and they are passionate about a few of those things. They dig in and get involved. They are capable of deep concentration, and they can and do focus on tasks for extended periods, typically seeing them through to completion. They have developed a complex set of skills that require commitment and time. They apply themselves and find satisfaction in the process.

Mentally healthy people are capable of *empathy*, the ability to discern what others might be thinking and feeling and to care about them. This quality assumes an interest in others. The actual amount of interest can vary widely, as there are many successful people who work in relative isolation. But mental health requires the capacity for empathy when one works with other humans. Some, perhaps as many as 3% or 4% of the general population, simply do not possess this capacity (Grant et al., 2004). Others possess it in varied amounts. High empathy is required for success in some jobs, whereas other careers require little empathic capacity. The worst problems associated with a lack of empathy are described later in this chapter.

Accurate self-awareness is also associated with mental health. A healthy person is aware of what is going on inside himself or herself, and can evaluate his or her own thoughts, feelings, and reactions and respond appropriately. This self-awareness allows them to understand things more deeply and effectively and to make adjustments as a result. Emotional and social self-management is then possible. This issue is associated with psychological-mindedness and is discussed at greater length in Chapter 11 ("Emotional Intelligence").

There are *social skills* required of the mentally healthy person as well, and these include the usual day-to-day interaction skills, applied in the right amount. Mentally healthy people are capable of appropriate intimacy, and they are capable of maintaining effective interpersonal boundaries. They know how to say "yes" in a superficial and deep way, and they know how to say "no" as well. They know where they start and end, and do not take responsibility for the ways that others feel. As a result, they are difficult to manipulate.

Similarly, mentally healthy people act in alignment with their own values and goals. In this way, it can be said that they possess *integrity*. They walk their talk; they do the things that they have decided are important. Important decisions come from within rather than from outside sources of authority.

Healthy people are *flexible*. They do not get "stuck" or bogged down by rigid thinking or compulsions. They are open to new ideas and are capable of change when appropriate. They are also *resilient*. Bad things happen to all of us, and the healthy ones bounce back as required, over and over again.

Although there are many other qualities associated with the mentally healthy person, the last (but certainly not least) on this list is the capacity for *humor*. Healthy people are able to see the world in funny ways, and they laugh a lot. They realize that everything in life is temporary and much of it ridiculous. They do not take everything seriously because they have acquired a sense of perspective. They know what really matters and what does not, and they do not mix up those areas. Consequently, they tend to find a healthy work–life balance and are able to manage stress comfortably.

Pathologies

Before describing the various important mental disorders, there are two factors that coaches must understand. First, all psychopathologies wax and wane, meaning that they get better and worse on a continual basis. Even people with the most disabling disorders experience periods of relative remission when things seem OKAY. There is an old saying in psychology that "nobody's crazy all the time." This means that it may be difficult to spot a disorder if you only observe a person for a short period. Those who have more experience with the person are likely to have a more accurate view.

Second, stress makes everything worse. People are often able to "maintain" for long periods and do very well. Then something stressful happens and their mental health deteriorates as a result. Stress is capable of causing any underlying psychopathology to emerge, to become florid, obvious, and disabling.

Most of the psychological disorders described in this chapter run in families. Sometimes the familial correlations are not strong ones, but often those with a disorder have parents or close relatives who have experienced a similar disorder in the past.

The Most Disabling Mental Disorders

Although any psychopathology can be disabling, depending upon its nature, severity, and the demands faced by a person, there are three that tend to be the most disabling. The first is *schizophrenia*. It is the disorder most commonly associated with the term *crazy*, as people with this disorder can seem quite strange. People with schizophrenia suffer from "psychotic" symptoms including hallucinations, delusions, and illusions that are often bizarre in nature. They see things that are not there, hear voices, misinterpret stimuli, and hold beliefs that could not possibly be true. Many homeless people are psychotic, medicating themselves with alcohol. The hallucinations are often frightening and disorienting, and they cause people to reside in a world of their own, trying with all of their might to solve the riddles of their symptoms. Schizophrenia typically afflicts a person when they are in their late teens or early twenties. It often begins with prodromal indicators, odd behavior that is not itself disabling or terribly distinctive. People often do not take notice, especially when the afflicted is a teenager. When the disorder becomes full blown, others are shocked and terribly dismayed. The person whom they knew disappears forever, replaced by a stranger who now lives in a different and incomprehensible world. Medication is available, and it can be relatively effective. But antipsychotic medications typically bring side effects that are troublesome and disabling themselves. Sometimes the medication does not work very well, and all too often, the psychotic person is unwilling to start or continue to take medication. Schizophrenia is a lifelong disorder and no one has a definitive explanation of its cause or a comprehensive understanding of the biochemical mechanisms. Roughly 1% of the world's population is thought to suffer from schizophrenia.

Bipolar disorder is a second, highly disabling disease, and it is often called manic-depressive illness. Although onset can occur at any age, it often begins at the age of 20 or so. The onset is usually disruptive and damaging. It is a recurrent disorder, as it comes and goes, characterized by periods of mania and/or depression. The *DSM–IV–TR* (APA, 2000) describes manic episodes in the following way: "a distinct period during which there is an abnormally and persistently elevated, expansive, or irritable mood." That mood is accompanied by grandiosity, decreased need for sleep, pressured (intensely forced) speech, flight of ideas (thoughts that seem to race through the mind without control), and increased energy to be devoted to tasks that often do not make sense to others. Bad (terrible) judgment is usually a problem, as the person acts on decisions that are extremely risky or even ridiculous. Families of people with bipolar disorder have sad stories of how the afflicted person impulsively refinanced the house to bet on a horse or a new invention, only to quickly lose all of the money. People in a manic phase stay up all night and drive others crazy. They are very difficult to be around. They can be a danger to themselves, and suicide or reckless physical behavior, including risky sexual activity, is always a possibility. Depression is often present, and some people with bipolar disorder only experience hypomanic episodes or no mania at all. Hypomania is a milder, less dramatic form of mania that is not nearly as bad. Medication is likely to be the only remedy for a bipolar disorder. Even so, the available medications are not yet highly effective, and they all come with unattractive side effects such as dry mouth, stomach upset, and acne. Lithium, a traditional medication for bipolar disorder, is so toxic that treatment requires ongoing blood testing to make sure that dosages are safe. Although gentler, more effective medications are increasingly available, people with this disorder typically do not continue taking medication until they learn—through difficult trial and error—that they simply must. This process can take years.

The third highly disabling mental disorder is *dementia*, a sudden or gradual loss of mental abilities. There are many kinds and causes of dementia, and people lose the ability to remember things, to name things, to order things, even to make sense out of daily life. For example, people with dementia might not recall the name of common items such as keys or coffee cups. They might not be able to remember the names of familiar people. They might not recognize family members. They might leave the house with their underwear on the outside of their clothing. They get lost in familiar places and have to be escorted home by the police. They cannot balance their checkbook or do their taxes. They might forget to turn off the gas burner on the stove.

When the onset of dementia is sudden, it is usually the result of a physically traumatic injury (such as a car crash or a mugging) or a stroke (when a blood vessel in the brain is clogged or bursts). Such sudden dementias can be massive or small; they can be permanent or temporary. When the onset is slow, it is sometimes the result of a series of tiny strokes, called multi-infarct dementia, or the result of a disease process such as Alzheimer's disease or AIDS or alcoholism. Medications can prolong memory capacity, but none can "cure" the underlying problem or the loss of function. Experts predict an epidemic of new Alzheimer's cases in the next couple of decades.

Although dementia is associated with older people, it is, for the most part, not a natural function of the aging process. When dementia is present, it signals a pathology (something is "wrong"). A small loss of cognitive function is typical in many healthy older people, but dementia is not. All of us know someone who is quite old and has not lost a step. It is important for coaches to know that dementia is not limited to older people. Several of the various causes can occur in youth, such as car crashes, fights, ski accidents, and even strokes. Strokes can be quite silent and undramatic, leaving the victim with a vague sense of disorientation and a mild, mysterious, perceptible loss of function.

The Most Common Psychopathologies

There are four disorders commonly found in the workplace. First, and foremost, is *anxiety*. There are a number of anxiety-based diagnoses, and taken together they form the most common set of disorders in the general population. These include generalized anxiety, panic disorders, agoraphobia, social and specific phobias, posttraumatic stress disorder (PTSD), acute stress disorders, and obsessive-compulsive disorder. Anxiety is defined by apprehension, fearfulness, uneasiness, distress, worry, and tension. Fears are typically irrational and unresponsive to rational, corrective input. Anxious people cannot be talked out of their worries. Some anxieties make sense to others, as they derived from traumatic experiences. Others are mysterious and inexplicable in their origin. Since there can be physical causes such as hyperthyroidism, mitral valve prolapse, and food allergies, medical conditions must be ruled out early on. Sometimes people are anxious because their parents raised them to be afraid, sometimes people are anxious because they think in frightening ways, and sometimes people suffer because they are perpetually tense and stressed, with a nervous system that is continuously on fight-or-flight.

There is an important distinction between the stress of a workplace and the stress that people feel. One is a condition of the external work setting, the other is an internal perception. These terms are mixed and used synonymously, but some people are sensitively reactive to the stress of the workplace and others are not. Some are overwhelmed by it. Some bring anxiety disorders into the workplace and try as hard as they can to hide them. It can be difficult to succeed when troubled by the symptoms of anxiety such as disordered sleep, mental distraction, specific phobias and generalized fears, stomach upset, and constant muscle tension. Whereas some people suffer from a generalized anxiety disorder and feel nervous and troubled all the time, others experience unpredictable and immobilizing panic attacks. Anyone who has ever had a panic attack will tell you that it is one of the most horrible experiences imaginable. Emergency rooms and cardiologists often are the first to diagnose panic attacks, as people truly believe that they are dying. These sudden attacks can include heart palpitations, a feeling that you are choking or smothering, chest pain, dizziness or body tingling, derealization (a sense that things are not real), a fear of losing control or losing your mind, and a profound impression that death is imminent. Frequently, repeated panic attacks turn into a panic disorder and can even lead to agoraphobia, when a person attempts to avoid future attacks by avoiding situations that are associated with previous attacks. The lifetime prevalence rate for panic disorders is about 2% of the general population.

Anxiety disorders can be extremely disabling, but most are amenable to a combination of medication and psychological treatment. The side effects of modern medications are not typically disruptive or sedating, and many people are able to function at high levels of productivity while taking medications for anxiety disorders. Cognitive therapy, described in Chapter 6, involves training in thought management and is often quite helpful to people with chronic anxiety.

The second common disorder in the workplace and general population is *depression*, and it is sometimes difficult to distinguish from anxiety, as many people suffer from some vague combination of anxiety and depression. When the condition is seriously disabling it is called major depression; when it is milder and less disabling it is called *dysthymia*. The dysthymic person is the chronic worrywart, the person who generally sees things from a negative and gloomy point of view, has low energy, and experiences little joy. Many fully functioning workers and executives suffer from dysthymia, and they suck it up, work hard, and make the best of it, never really enjoying the ride but discharging their responsibilities fully.

Major depression is another matter, and it is significant. The lifetime prevalence rate (the percentage of people in the general population who will experience depression during the course of their lifetime) is figured to be 5% to 12% for men and 10% to 25% for women. A major depressive disorder is quite disabling, and some people are actually bedridden by it. People with major depression cannot think clearly or focus adequately to work. They suffer from anhedonia, the inability to experience joy. They distort things in the most negative possible ways and cannot be talked out of their negative thinking. They eat poorly and sleep inadequately. Sometimes they drink to try to find relief, and the alcohol makes everything worse. They become irritable and annoy people who are close to them. They are difficult to be around. They need to exercise, but simply cannot find the energy.

Some people respond well to the right medication, and side effects are often minimal or tolerable, especially relative to the unpleasantness of the depression. It may require a lengthy period of medical experimentation to arrive at an optimal pharmacological regimen, but medication in combination with cognitive therapy can be quite effective to many (but not all) depressive people.

The fourth disorder common to the workplace is *ADHD*, attention deficit/hyperactivity disorder. Although ADHD is traditionally considered a childhood disorder, clinicians have recently noted that many suffer from symptoms well into adulthood. The disorder can include either inattention (attention deficit), or hyperactivity and impulsivity, or both. The disorder is often associated with specific learning problems, especially with reading. Signs and symptoms of inattention include distractibility and difficulty in maintaining attention or focus, forgetfulness, disorganization, trouble following through with tasks to completion, and difficulty with attention to detail. People with inattention often do not seem to be listening when you speak to them, as their mind may actually be wandering or they may be focusing on several things at once. Symptoms of hyperactivity include difficulty in sitting still for extended periods, excessive talking, fidgety motor activity, and feelings of restlessness. People with impulsivity often blurt out answers before questions have been completed and they tend to interrupt speakers and have difficulty waiting to speak or waiting their turn. They sometimes seem insensitive and can be unpopular with peers. Although children with ADHD often do poorly in school, symptoms usually abate as they get older. As a result, a person may not be left with a full-blown disorder but may still suffer from the difficulties that these symptoms create. ADHD affects about 2% of males in the general population and a smaller percentage of females. Effective medication is available, typically in the form of a mild speed such as Ritalin or Aderall. Side effects are often mild and tolerable.

Personality Disorders

Personality disorders is a family of difficult and problematic disorders that tend to be lifelong. They are called "personality" disorders because they represent a structural problem in the organization of a person's basic, distinctive character. Personality is best understood as the pattern of thinking, feeling, behaving, and coping that characterizes or defines someone (Millon, 1981). In many ways, you essentially *are* your personality. Personality is a pervasive, comprehensive set of qualities that are present across all aspects of one's life. It is present during morning, noon, and night, and when you are with others. Your personality is present when you are at home, and it goes with you to work. Everyone notices it and must deal with it. Millon points out that people with personality disorders tend to think and behave in ways that are inflexible. They find it difficult to adapt to new interpersonal situations and have a limited number of alternative strategies. Their thinking tends to be rigid, and stress is hard on them. They often organize their lives in ways that enable them to avoid new or challenging situations. They tend to think and behave in vicious circles. Narrow and distorted thinking constrains them and causes them to repeat their mistakes, even when it should be obvious that they are not getting anywhere. They tend to experience the same difficulties over and over without insight. They are fragile and lack resilience. When things get difficult or when their dysfunctional coping mechanisms fail, they tend to distort reality to try to cope.

Again, it must be said that all of us have personalities and personality characteristics. The difference between characteristics and a disorder has to do with the extent of distress and disability present. With some personality disorders (specifically those in Cluster B, see following list) it is often other people who experience the distress rather than the person with the disorder. The level of distress and disability must be significant in order to diagnose a disorder rather than just a set of traits, and they must have an impact in two of the following areas: thinking, feeling, impulse control, and interpersonal functioning. Presently available medication does not seem to be of much help with these disorders.

The *DSM–IV–TR* (APA, 2000) lists 10 personality disorders organized into three categories or clusters:

Cluster A
  Paranoid
  Schizoid
  Schizotypal

Cluster B
  Antisocial
  Histrionic
  Borderline
  Narcissistic

Cluster C
  Avoidant
  Dependent
  Obsessive-Compulsive

Cluster A People with disorders in Cluster A tend not to do well with other people and tend not to enter the workplace or last very long there. *Paranoids* are characteristically distrustful without justification. They are suspicious without warrant and they fear exploitation. As the old saying goes, they think that "everyone's out to get them." They are preoccupied with unjustified suspicion about the motives and behaviors of others. They personalize everything.

People with a *schizoid* personality disorder have little or no interest in other people. They have no interpersonal relationships and infrequent interactions. They are interpersonally cold and engage in solitary activities.

People with a *schizotypal* personality disorders are extremely eccentric and odd. They have very unusual thoughts and behaviors, but not so different that they qualify as bizarre. Their disorder is likely to exclude them from the everyday workplace.

Cluster B   Cluster B contains personality disorders that haunt the workplace and make life difficult for everyone. They are of significant relevance to the coach and the business organization. Coaches will encounter people with significant traits, if not the full-blown personality disorders found in this cluster. They tend to share narcissism, a dysfunctional self-centeredness as a central dynamic, and they tend to be highly manipulative of others. They are all about themselves, fragile, and resistant to change or influence. They lack empathy and are interested in other people only insofar as those others can help them get what they want. They are difficult to be around for very long, and they do not have deep or enduring friendships. They feel empty, but hide their real feelings behind charm and superficial extraversion.

The defining characteristic of the *antisocial* personality disorder is chronic disregard for other people and their property. The term *sociopath* is synonymous with antisocial personality. People with this disorder do not conform to social norms of honesty, fidelity, and integrity. They tend to be charming, dishonest, and unreliable. They were probably in chronic trouble as a child. Their charm gets them into organizations, and when they are clever, they are able to sustain a career, especially if that career rewards the personality characteristics that they possess. They can be finaglers and hustlers. Successful politicians and operatives often have antisocial traits, as do some salespeople. They are good at doing whatever it takes to get ahead, especially in the short term. Progress and career success are limited by their lack of integrity and absence of empathy. Although people find them highly attractive at first, most eventually figure them out for what they are: an exploiter. Those with antisocial personality disorder may actually engage in illegal activities to get what they want. Millon (1981, p. 474) estimates that 75% of those in prison have this disorder, whereas only 3% of American males have it. They are unstable and unreliable and have poor behavioral self-control. Coaches are likely to be recruited to help them, and they will superficially engage with a helpful coach at first, doing whatever seems necessary to get out of the immediate trouble. People with personality disorders are unlikely to change very quickly or very much. People sometimes "grow out" of these disorders to some extent over long periods, but this takes too long to satisfy an organization, bosses, or colleagues. The prognosis is poor. Sociopaths tend to do better in situations with a clear, forceful structure (such as military service) if they can tolerate it.

People with a *histrionic* personality are excessively emotional and always on stage. They are gregarious and dramatic but vapid. They are constantly on the search for attention, craving it, and deeply and frantically afraid that they might not get it. They are uncomfortable when they are not the center of attention, for when they are not, they fear that they might just collapse into a deep caldron of nothingness or simply disappear. They require constant social approval. They seem full of life and charm, and are often seductive. They are the life of the party. They might use sexual evocativeness to inappropriately commandeer attention. They dress and groom carefully and deliberately to attract attention, and they speak in dramatic, excessive ways, full of flair. They are likely to be highly influenced by the latest trends or fads and are extremely sensitive to the moods of others. Their emotions are expressed emphatically, often to the puzzlement or embarrassment of others, and emotions seem to be turned on and off quickly. They are likely to overestimate and overstate the quality or intensity of their personal relationships, assuming that their relationships have a depth that others do not share. Paradoxically and sadly, they are interpersonally shallow. They are wary of real interpersonal close-ness, as such closeness might allow others to discover the truly fraudulent nature of their personality, as this is how they perceive themselves. Histrionic people are not prone to introspection. Inactivity can be threatening because such periods can allow awareness of the deep emptiness.

The *borderline* personality disorder is notorious in clinical psychology. The term *borderline* is a somewhat unfortunate label, as it does not accurately describe this disorder. The term seems to have evolved as earlier clinicians viewed people with this disorder as being on the boundary or border between neurosis (chronically self-defeating) and psychosis (out of touch with consen-sual reality). The term was also used when doctors were uncertain about a diagnosis that did not seem severe enough to be viewed as definitively psy-chotic. Millon (1981), in his important text on personality disorders, notes that labels such as "erratic" or "unstable" or "cycloid" or "labile" would have been a preferable choice, but his recommendations did not prevail.

Clinicians have been known to dread meetings with "borderlines," as they can be extremely difficult to deal with. These clients have a fragile sense of self and an unstable identity that is papered over with a false grandiosity. They feel empty inside and seek to use others to fill the void. As a result, they are exquisitely sensitive to rejection, which they experience as a deeply primal sense of abandonment. The *DSM–IV–TR* (APA, 2000) refers to this phenom-enon as "frantic efforts to avoid real or imagined abandonment." The thought of being alone can be terrifying. The sense of who they are shifts suddenly and unpredictably. They can quickly shift the focus of hostility from self to others and back again. Their relationships are unstable as they jet back and forth between idolization of another person (who shows potential to fill them up) and hostile rejection of that same person if shown the slightest sign of disagreement. Others experience them as oddly flattering, suddenly hostile, and overtly angry. Clinicians use the term *splitting* to describe this characteristic black-to-white thinking and behavior. People with a borderline personality disorder sometimes cut or mutilate themselves, either for attention or as a distraction to fill the emptiness and prove to themselves that they are "real."

Coaches are unlikely to encounter people with this disorder in the workplace, but they almost certainly will run into those with borderline traits. Even when relatively mild, such traits are typically problematic and difficult to understand or change.

The *narcissistic* personality disorder is closely associated with the borderline, as it shares qualities to some extent. Narcissism is interesting and important to any discussion of coaching because of the prominence of narcissism in many powerful and successful business leaders. Narcissism has been the focus of several highly regarded studies of American corporate and entrepreneurial leadership (Maccoby, 2000; Rosenthal & Pittinsky, 2006).

The narcissistic personality disorder is defined by the *DSM* in the following ways. The essential quality is a grandiose sense of self-importance complicated by a fragile self-concept that is constantly in need of support. Narcissists are preoccupied with powerful fantasies of unlimited success but are at the same time burdened by deep feelings of inadequacy. They sense that they might actually be a fraud, and their response to this possibility is to seek constant and excessive confirmation from their apparent successes and admiration from those around them. They are hypersensitive to the tiniest criticism. In spite of their sensitivity to their own feelings, they are ignorant of the feelings of others, essentially unable to accurately guess at what others might experience. In fact, they are not all that interested in others, unless that other person can add to their feelings of grandiosity and entitlement. They lack empathy. They are manipulative users who need others to support their fantasies of personal superiority and power. They can be quite charming, as necessary, but punitive when someone threatens them by daring to disagree. They are typically poor listeners, and can be paranoid and downright hostile when they feel threatened. They do not make deep friendships, and others eventually see through their charm and grow to fear and avoid them. People with this disorder are typically male, and they are present in the general population at the rate of about 1%.

The rate of narcissists in the population of charismatic and entrepreneurial corporate leaders is probably much higher, however. Maccoby (2000) and Rosenthal and Pittinsky (2006) have argued that narcissism is a double-edged sword, and that narcissistic qualities are rather frequently found in important and successful leaders. They point out that narcissists are charming, charismatic risk takers, driven in part by fantasies of grand success. They are hypercompetitive, with big ideas, and they can mobilize others especially in times of fear or stress. They step into the breach and seem fearless when others are more wary. They are highly motivated to achieve personal power, success, and the accompanying admiration. They make excellent first impressions and can inspire confidence in their organizations, at least temporarily. Narcissists typically thrive in chaos but do not do well in times of organizational stability.

The critical issue is whether a narcissist has a full-blown disorder or just narcissistic traits. All of us need some narcissism to leave the house in the morning. We need to feel important enough to assert ourselves and to ask for things that we want. The distinction between healthy self-confidence and narcissism is crucial. Rosenthal and Pittinsky (2006) point out that healthy narcissists have some insight into their own self-centeredness. They are aware of their own tendencies and able to step back, monitor, and manage it all, often with a gentle sense of self-deprecating humor. They are stable rather than unstable, and they do not insist on uniformly fawning feedback from others. Even though it might not be natural or easy to do, they find ways to get outside of themselves and pay genuine attention to others.

Deeply narcissistic leaders face two insurmountable problems. First, they inevitably alienate those who have to work with them. Rather than cultivating loyalty and admiration (which they desperately seek), they end up with followers who silently dislike and distrust them. Their arrogance and egocentricity create inauthentic relationships. Those followers who can no longer tolerate such a personality find a way to leave when they can. Those forced to remain become bitter and careful. Second, the ambition of the narcissist's fantasy eventually outruns market reality. They risk too much, and refuse to listen to those who caution them, taking the organization too far, often causing great harm to the company and its employees. They then move on, unable or unwilling to incorporate negative results into their internal concept of self. They blame others and learn nothing from the experience.

As much as narcissists could benefit from coaching, they are insulated and interpersonally isolated; not all that interested in coaching, especially if the enterprise is to include honest or critical feedback. They are liable to feel threatened by a coach who might be able to see through their fragile and fraudulent sense of self-esteem. They are also likely to be suspicious of a coach. Should they submit to coaching, the coach–client relationship is likely to be challenging, typified by disruptions that could derail the process at any moment. A coach should expect to be tested and rejected at the slightest hint of disagreement. Even then, it would be the rare narcissist who seeks and embraces help, and as Rosenthal and Pittinsky (2006, p. 626) note about the activities of a coach, "It is far from clear that they are the types of practices to which any narcissist would be amenable." Nonetheless, Rosenthal and Pittinsky speculate the possibility that "without such ego-driven leaders, we would live in a world relatively devoid of bold innovation and social change" (p. 630).

Cluster C   Cluster C includes people who are pathologically anxious, tense, and controlling. People with an *avoidant* personality disorder crave interpersonal, interactional interaction and relationships, but are too frightened to do anything social. They are extremely hypersensitive and dread criticism. They take almost no social risk, feeling deeply inferior. People with this disorder are likely to avoid any work situation that might involve contact with people or the possibility of social error, disapproval, embarrassment, or rejection. They are occasionally able to form interpersonal relationships, but only when they feel safe, and usually under conditions of "assurance of uncritical acceptance" (APA, 2000, p. 718). For the most part, they remain socially invisible.

The *dependent* personality disorder is typified by extreme passivity and interpersonal dependence. These people desperately fear separation and are pathologically submissive and clinging. They are unable to tolerate aloneness or independence. They need constant reassurance, and are unwilling to take responsibility for much of anything. They will go to great lengths to secure support and strongly prefer to be told what to do rather than to initiate action. They are unlikely to start projects or to carry them out without consistent supervision and reassurance. They are typically indecisive.

There are two disorders that include obsessions and compulsions, obsessive-compulsive disorder, and obsessive-compulsive personality disorder. *Obsessions* are thoughts; persistent, recurrent ideas that cannot be controlled. These thoughts are intrusive and inappropriate and irrational, and they tend to dominate one's thinking. *Compulsions* are repetitive actions or behaviors carried out in an attempt to reduce anxiety or anticipated distress.

When obsessions and compulsions are prominent, a diagnosis of *obsessive-compulsive disorder* (OCD) is appropriate. OCD is an anxiety disorder that is relatively common (2.5% lifetime prevalence) and can be quite disabling. Compulsions can be complicated and can profoundly interfere with essential life activities. It might take hours to complete regular daily functions such as meal preparation and eating. Obsessions commonly focus on fear of contamination, loss of order or control, and doubts (for example, "Did I leave the stove on?" or "Did I leave a light on?" or even "Did I run someone over with my car on the way home tonight?"). This disorder can actually get worse as one gets older, and prevalence rates are thought to be greater in those with higher IQ or social class (Morrison, 2001).

Rigid perfectionism is the hallmark of the obsessive-compulsive personality disorder. People with this disorder do not suffer from actual obsessions or compulsions, but their personality is organized in an obsessively, compulsively overcontrolled way. They are preoccupied with order and completely inflexible. Control is the central theme of their character structure. They may be devoted to work and to efficiency, but they overdo it and cause more harm than good by excessive attention to unnecessary detail and by driving everyone around them crazy. They can also be indecisive, unable to commit unless and until all conditions are perfect. They can turn any activity into a tedious, odious task. They cannot relax. As expected, they do not delegate well, as others do not have the requisite level of high standards. They may be stingy or miserly, and they may turn into packrats, accumulating too much clutter. They are poor team players and do not appreciate having to carry out someone else's plan, and if they express affection, it is in a controlled, conventional style.

Intermittent Explosive Disorder

Intermittent explosive disorder might fit several general categories, as it involves impulse control, anger, and aggression. It is often associated with substance abuse as well. Some feel that this disorder is not actually a discrete disorder but merely a sign of other disorders such as an antisocial personality (Morrison, 2001). Coaches may encounter this problem and should be aware of it in any case. It is characterized by repetitive, uncontrolled, sudden outbreaks of explosive aggression. This is a person with unpredictable, frightening temper tantrums, a reaction grossly out of proportion to the events at hand. The disorder has not been well studied, but is more common in men than in women. The episodes are felt to be uncontrolled by the person manifesting them, and they are extremely distressing to all involved. The disorder has been known to cause job loss, school suspension, divorce, hospitalization, legal problems, and career derailment. Those with this disorder are amenable to treatment, but the treatment process can be quite difficult and frustrating. They are likely to be motivated for treatment after experiencing several devastating and embarrassing incidents.

Somatoform Disorders

The word *somatic* means "body-based." There are several challenging disorders in the somatoform category. People with these disorders seem to have physical or medical problems that cause significant distress or disability, but medical consultation cannot fully explain things.

With *somatization disorder* people experience at least eight physical symptoms in various parts of the body prior to the age of 30, and at least one of the symptoms must be sexual in nature. Patients with this disorder are more likely to be female than male, and it tends to run in families. Physicians become frustrated, as they are not able to provide comprehensive or effective treatment.

When chronic pain is disabling and psychological factors are thought to play an important role in the onset, maintenance, or worsening of the pain, a *pain disorder* is diagnosed. This happens to women more often than men, and it can follow an accident or previous medical condition. This disorder is known to cause significant career impairment and can be quite disabling, physically and emotionally.

When emotional conflicts or problems are converted into physical conditions, the diagnosis is *conversion disorder*. The conversion process and conversion symptoms are common. As much as one third of the general population has experienced a physical symptom resulting from an emotional or psychological problem. Who has not gotten a stress headache or felt a stomachache when faced with a frightening situation? People break out with rashes, they get acne, and they suffer tightness in their chest. Their mouth gets dry. But when these symptoms convert into actual medical conditions that a doctor cannot explain, a conversion disorder may be the cause.

When a person systematically misinterprets physical signs or symptoms to mean that they have a serious illness that does not exist, they may be experiencing *hypochondriasis*. This is a disorder characterized by preoccupation with the fear that one has a serious or life-threatening medical disease. Medical consultation and reassurance do not help and do not change the sufferer's mind. Their belief is irrational and refractory to evidence.

One last somatoform disorder that might be encountered by the coach is *body dysmorphic disorder*, a peculiar form of self-focused obsession. People with this disorder are powerfully preoccupied with an imagined deficit in appearance, most often in the face, hair, breasts, or genitals. This problem can be devastating, especially when people with the disorder can find cooperative plastic surgeons. The lore and literature of psychotherapy is littered with stories of people who ruined their facial appearance with multiple redundant cosmetic surgeries (Tignol, Biraben-Gotzamanis, Martin-Guehl, Grabot, & Aouizerate, 2007). People with this disorder commit suicide at significantly higher rates than the general population (Phillips & Menard, 2006). Sufferers spend significant time inspecting their imagined flaws, grooming, and compensating. They are likely to avoid activities that would expose others to their perceived ugliness. This disorder can severely impact any career that requires frequent contact and interaction with others.

Traumatic Events

Nearly everyone is exposed to the harshness of unexpected pain or loss. Few escape at least a modest amount of trauma. After a difficult life event, such as a divorce or the loss of a loved one or a serious career or financial setback, it takes time for humans to return to previous levels of happiness and functionality. This is normal. When a person does not "bounce back," when they continue to be depressed or listless or when they do not reengage in life's activities, there is a diagnostic label for them. If the trauma was severe, such as in war or earthquake, fire, kidnapping, or serious sexual abuse, some people are left with *PTSD* (posttraumatic stress disorder). When this happens, they may experience recurrent and intrusive memories or dreams of the event, they may become phobic about traveling to places that remind them of the event; they may become numb, detached, and estranged; and they may have difficulty sleeping and concentrating. They may have persistent anxiety and an exaggerated startle response. This disorder requires significant professional help.

When a person suffers from exposure to an extreme trauma and the symptoms resolve within 1 month or so, the diagnosis of *acute stress disorder* is appropriate. If those signs and symptoms linger, PTSD is the more accurate diagnosis, and PTSD can last for years, perhaps even a lifetime.

On the other hand, when someone is subjected to a less traumatic event, such as a divorce or job loss or other significant setback, they may experience emotional or behavior symptoms such as depression, anxiety, odd behavior, or substance abuse. When this reaction is in excess of what would generally be anticipated, a diagnosis of *adjustment disorder* may be appropriate. In this disorder the symptoms are expected to resolve within 6 months of the time that the original stressor ended.

Habit Disorders and Addictive Behavior

Another important and common set of problems is that of addiction. Taken together, the number of people in the workplace who are addicted or dependent overwhelms all of the other psychological problems described so far (APA, 2000; National Center for Health Statistics, 2007). Tobacco, alcohol, marijuana, and prescription drugs are an undeniable feature of the modern workplace. The so-called War on Drugs has been a colossal failure, and American professionals and workers use and abuse drugs at high rates (National Center for Health Statistics, 2007; Tracey, 2008; Walter, 2008). *The Economist* recently reported this astonishing fact: Marijuana is now by far California's most valuable agricultural crop ("Home Grown," 2007). Coaches are certain to have to deal with clients who are either addicted or struggling with excessive or counterproductive alcohol or other substance use. Recent research on the typology of alcoholism (Moss, Chen, & Yi, 2007, p. 155) describes a "functional subtype" comprised of "generally middle-aged, working adults who tend to have stable relationships, more education, and higher incomes than other alcoholics. They tend to drink every other day, often consuming five or more drinks on drinking days." This group makes up about 20% of all alcoholics.

Shame and embarrassment are commonly associated with alcohol and drug use, and most heavy users keep their habits to themselves. Much of the addictive behavior found in or around the workplace is secretive, but it can still be the cause of significant disruption, dysfunction, and loss of efficiency. Consumption of alcohol and other substances on the job is an obvious problem. Issues related to substance abuse after work are less obvious but just as important. Addicted people typically deny or minimize difficulties and are often unaware of the losses they suffer. This adds a level of difficulty to the coaching challenge. It is entirely possible for a coach to completely miss the fact that a client is addicted, and that the addictive behavior (or its consequences) is an important part of the overall picture. Unless there is a very special rapport along with a clear promise of confidentiality, clients are unlikely to share this important information with a coach. The unknown addiction can result in a mysterious spinning of wheels as nothing changes and no one can discern underlying causes for the inertia.

Addiction can be to an astonishing variety of substances and experiences. The following definition is useful here: *Addiction is a compulsive and pathological relationship to a mood altering experience that has life-damaging consequences* (Peele, 1985).

In this view, it is easy to see that coaches will encounter clients who are addicted to experiences such as work, gambling, sex, food, caffeine, exercise, Internet porn, and others too numerous to mention. They will also suffer from obsessions (constantly repeating thoughts they cannot shake) along with compulsions (irresistible urges toward repetitive behaviors designed to reduce anxiety or stress). They will, most likely, disguise and hide these thoughts, urges, and behaviors to avoid seeming weird to those around them. Some clients will be troubled by a compulsive need to do things perfectly and, perhaps to demand that quality of behavior from others. Others will be bulimic, eating compulsively and then secretly "purging."

The good news is that treatment for addictions is widely available and can be inexpensive. The bad news is that addicts typically "bottom out" or suffer terrible consequences prior to entering treatment. Coaching would be of enormous value if it could help a client avoid tragedy by entering treatment before disaster strikes.

What Is a Coach to Do?

It bears repeating that coaches are not psychotherapists or doctors. They are not usually trained in these areas, and therapy is not their job. The differences between coaches and therapists are described in detail earlier in this book and depicted in the "Introduction" in Table I.1. The coach has a performance focus rather than a therapeutic orientation. It is not the coach's job to help fix personality problems. That task is outside the scope of coaching. Coaches must resist any temptation to attempt therapy.

Nonetheless, it is essential for coaches to be familiar with the traits and disorders described in this chapter. They should not be too surprised or caught (too much) off guard when confronted with psychopathology. Coaches can potentially be of great help to clients and organizations when they recognize traits and disorders, label them in an appropriate way, and help clients decide what to do. "What to do" might include a referral for a more definitive diagnosis or a recommendation for effective therapeutic help. It might include discussions about how to minimize the impact of traits in the workplace and career.

It is also possible that coaches may encounter clients who have psychological disorders and are already engaged in professional treatment. Many successful people have acknowledged psychological issues and gotten treatment. Many are taking psychotropic medications with a good effect. There are large numbers of people in the American workforce who are in a successful, ongoing recovery from substance abuse problems. In those cases it may be important for coaches to be able to understand relevant disorders and coordinate coaching with therapy. Coaches should take care to discern whether psychotherapeutic treatment is "public" or confidential from the point of view of their client.

Coaches ought to wonder about hidden psychopathology when things do not "add up." If there is mystery, if something does not quite make sense, or if it seems that the coach is "missing something," it is a good time to wonder about the possibility that addiction, depression, disordered thinking, dementia, an eating disorder, or some other secret problem lurks. Recall that psychopathologies wax and wane, meaning that they get better and worse periodically. You may have met your client during a "good" phase and did not notice symptoms at first. He or she may later phase into a more difficult period. His or her colleagues have seen this person in several phases and are likely to have a more comprehensive view. It is a coach's job to effectively and accurately integrate third-party information into the assessment, and this can be a challenge. One must be careful not to allow a global positive impression to cause a coach to distort reality. It is entirely possible for a coach with good client rapport to discount negative data points or observations when it makes a favored client look or seem "bad" or "sick." Also, recall that stress tends to bring out pathology and to make self-defeating traits worse. When stress builds, observe clients to see the impact.

Remember that many people succeed by effectively managing negative traits or psychological disorders. Modern medication, when properly prescribed and taken can work miracles, especially when combined with consistent, appropriate psychotherapy. Psychotropic medications represent a profit center for drug companies and are constantly improving. It is reasonable to anticipate that clients with a serious psychological disorder could—with help—manage or transcend their difficulties and continue to thrive.

It seems important that coaches consider who is the client when psychopathology appears. Is the sponsoring organization the client or is the client the client? Is it appropriate to hide pathology from an organization that is paying a coach? Is it necessary to reveal pathology to that organization, and if so, under what circumstances? To whom does the coach owe which obligations? These can be difficult questions indeed.

Finally, it is important for coaches to "step up," notice, and address psychopathology when it is present. The temptation to ignore a problem, to politely sidestep it, or to minimize it will be attractive. Psychological disorders are disruptive, confusing, embarrassing, and frightening. Coaches can potentially add enormous value by responding courageously and appropriately when pathology emerges.

References

American Psychiatric Association (APA). (2000). *Diagnostic and statistical manual of mental disorders* (4th ed., text rev.). Washington, DC: Author.

Grant, B. F., Hasin, D. S., Stinson, F. S., Dawson, D. A., Chou, S. P., Ruan, W. J., et al. (2004). Prevalence, correlates, and disability of personality disorders in the United States: Results from the National Epidemiologic Survey on Alcohol and Related Conditions. *Journal of Clinical Psychiatry, 65*, 948–958.

Home grown: Forget wine—California's biggest crop is bright green and funny-smelling. (2007, October 18). *The Economist*. Retrieved January 24, 2009, from: http://www.economist.com/world/na/PrinterFriendly.cfm?story_id=10000884.

Kessler, R. C., Berglund, P., Demler, O., Jin, R., Merikangas, K. R., & Walters, E. E. (2005). Lifetime prevalence and age-of-onset distributions of *DSM-IV* disorders in the National Comorbidity Survey Replication. *Archives of General Psychiatry, 62*, 593–602.

Maccoby, M. (2000, January–February). Narcissistic leaders: The incredible pros, the inevitable cons. *Harvard Business Review*.

Millon, T. (1981). Disorders *of personality*. New York: John Wiley & Sons.

Morrison, J. (2001). *DSM-IV made easy: The clinician's guide to diagnosis*. New York: Guilford Press.

Moss, H. B., Chen, C. M., & Yi, H. (2007, December). Subtypes of alcohol dependence in a nationally representative sample. *Drug and Alcohol Dependence, 91*, 149–158.

National Center for Health Statistics. (2007). *Health, United States, 2007: With chartbook on trends in the health of Americans*. Retrieved January 24, 2009, from: http://www.cdc.gov/nchs/data/hus/hus07.pdf#068.

Peele, S. (1985). *The meaning of addiction: Compulsive experience and its interpretation*. Lexington, MA: Lexington Books.

Phillips, K. A., & Menard, W. (2006). Suicidality in body dysmorphic disorder: A prospective study. *The American Journal of Psychiatry, 163*, 1280–1282.

Rosenthal, S. A., & Pittinsky, T. L. (2006). Narcissistic leadership. *The Leadership Quarterly, 17*, 617–633.

Tignol, J., Biraben-Gotzamanis, L., Martin-Guehl, C., Grabot, D., & Aouizerate, B. (2007). Body dysmorphic disorder and cosmetic surgery: Evolution of 24 subjects with a minimal defect in appearance 5 years after their request for cosmetic surgery. *European Psychiatry: The Journal of the Association of European Psychiatrists, 22*(8), 520–524.

Tracey, J. (2008). The mind of the alcoholic. *Journal of the American College of Dentists, 74*(4), 18–23.

Walter, J. (2008). Dentistry: Risks for addictive disease. *Journal of the American College of Dentists, 74*(4), 24–27.

Recommended Readings

Babiak, P., & Hare, R. D. (2006). *Snakes in suits*. New York: HarperCollins.

Buckley, A., & Buckley, C. (2006). *A guide to coaching and mental health: The recognition and management of psychological issues*. London: Routledge.

Jourard, S. M., & Landsman, T. (1980). *Healthy personality*. New York: Macmillan.

Kilburg, R. (1986). *Professionals in distress: Issues, syndromes, and solutions in psychology*. Washington, DC: American Psychological Association.

Kohut, H. (1966). Forms and transformations of narcissism. *Journal of the American Psychoanalytic Association, 14*, 243–272.

Masterson, J. (1981). *The narcissistic and borderline disorders: An integrated developmental approach*. New York: Routledge.

15
Leadership

In the best of times, we tend to forget how urgent the study of leadership is. But leadership always matters, and it has never mattered more than it does now.

—Warren Bennis (2007, p. 2)

Leadership is a lot like love. Everyone thinks it is special, but hardly anyone agrees on a definition. Warren Bennis (a student of the subject for six decades) put it this way: "It is almost a cliché of the leadership literature that a single definition of leadership is lacking" (2007, p. 2). In an earlier review (Bennis & Nanus, 1985, p. 4) he noted that

> no clear and unequivocal understanding exists as to what distinguishes leaders from nonleaders, and perhaps more important, what distinguishes effective leaders from ineffective leaders.

and

> leadership is an endless subject and endlessly interesting, because you can never get your conceptual arms fully around it. (Syrett & Hogg, 1992, p. xix)

In addition to the confusion about the subject, experts decry a lack of leadership in civic and corporate life. The revered Harvard Business School expert John Kotter noted (1999):

> After conducting fourteen formal studies and more than a thousand interviews, directly observing dozens of executives in action, and compiling innumerable surveys, I am completely convinced that most organizations today lack the leadership they need. And the shortfall is often large. ...
>
> The confusion around some of these points (regarding definitions of leadership) occasionally strikes me as staggering. ... I have witnessed this cluttered thinking endless times in intelligent people. When capable individuals make such remarks, we have a clear indication of the need for a better understanding of what leaders really do. (pp. 1, 4)

Since leadership is of undisputed importance, and since high quality leadership is relatively rare, leader development is often the focus of executive coaching. Coaches are expected to know about these things and to provide needed help. Effective coaches must be intimately familiar with the leadership literature, leadership theory, and prominent models. This chapter is an overview and explanation of the most important theories of leadership and the research that supports them, both historical and modern. The term *theories* here refers to the formal structural models that exist to explain good or bad leadership, its characteristics, and its development. The leadership literature found in business texts and psychological research is complex. This chapter is an attempt to summarize and simplify complicated concepts for practical use by executive coaches. Clients and their organizations will raise the issue of leadership, but they are unlikely to possess a clear or coherent view. Coaches are advised to develop a set of solid concepts and frameworks for leader assessment and development, so that they can present them to clients and use these tools in practice. Coaches must be familiar with traditional models of leadership and be able to articulate important conceptual foundations.

Overview and Various Starting Points

Leadership has ancient roots, and its students have included Plato, Socrates, Confucius, and Shakespeare. Leadership is a topic of interest in the Old and New Testaments of the Bible and in the Koran as well. Vast amounts have been written about leadership both in academic and popular literature, and the literature is diverse enough to cause vertigo. One observer notes:

> The field of leadership is a conundrum of theories, definitions, measurements, descriptions, prescriptions, and philosophies. ... The literature is dense and widespread, and the true grit and meat of leadership research is neither easily found nor readily discernable. ... As a result, leadership research has taken on several, often competing directions, yielding a literature that appears more haphazard in nature than deliberate. (Kroek, Lowe, & Brown, 2004, p. 72)

Academic texts tend to come from business schools and schools of education, as leadership has not been a topic of interest to academic psychology until fairly recently. Much of the formal literature is filled with esoteric diagrams full of circles and arrows that are only of interest to insiders, and they tend to produce headaches in practitioners. The pop literature, on the other hand, is enchanting and inspirational, but empty of intellectual substance and unlikely to be of much serious help to a professional coach. One leadership book refers to pop literature as the "Troubadour Tradition" and describes it as "score-settling reminiscences of countless former CEOs" (Dotlich & Cairo, 2003, p. xiii). Coaching clients have already skimmed the popular literature and need more substantial help. There are many varieties and models of leadership, and they differ significantly from one another. Some focus on action or behavior, some focus on the personal qualities of the leader, some focus on the situation at hand, some focus on the leader–context match. *There is no single, overarching model of leadership that is universally embraced.*

Leadership theory has suffered a similar fate to that of psychotherapy theory in that new theoretical frameworks tend to replace older ones rather than build on them. In other words, there is chaos out there and many difficult, unanswered questions.

First, is the ancient question of whether leaders are born or bred (Conger, 1992). If leadership is a quality that is born in some people, then resources should be spent on effective recruitment and selection rather than training. If leadership is a skill that can be learned, then training should be emphasized. (The smart money is always on the interaction between nature and nurture.)

There is the important question of whether *anyone* in an organization can be a leader. Does leadership imply a position, and does all viable leadership behavior have to come from those in formal leadership positions? If not, then who qualifies as a leader, and what behavior constitutes leadership under what circumstances? This is sometimes referred to as the *leadership of versus leadership in* question.

There is a question of enthusiasm in the leadership literature. Must followers gladly and voluntarily follow someone, or does leadership exist when people comply with rules or obey with reluctance? Are tyrants leaders? Is coercion a leadership skill?

The biographies of famous or prominent successful leaders (e.g., Lincoln, Churchill, or the latest prominent CEO) was pretty much the exclusive focus of early leadership studies (Bennis, 2007), but that approach has fallen out of favor in university circles. Instead, leadership is generally viewed as a "property of a social system" wherein leadership functions are shared by many in an organization (Yukl, 1994).

Does the leader's intention or motivation matter? Is it still leadership if a person in the leadership role is predominantly interested in self-promotion and personal greed? Do we call it leadership if the person in charge builds an organization only for personal gain? Was it leadership if they subsequently walked away and left a mess? It seems that there are two central vectors of good or bad leadership. Leaders can be good or bad in the sense that they are competent and effective. They can also be good or bad in the quality of their intentions. So, a leader could be well intentioned but incompetent, and another leader could be highly competent but malevolent. How do we evaluate leadership in those situations?

Leadership literature in the United States shows a distinctly North American–European cultural bias, and it has a clear masculine tone. All descriptions of leadership contain biases, and American views tend to favor individualism and personal autonomy. Leaders are expected to be direct, clear, and assertive—even bold in communication. Confrontation is generally seen as positive, if done according to certain rules. Emotional openness and direct expression are common and accepted. Competition is valued and expected, and aggressive leaders are admired. Acquisition is a well-accepted goal. Western theories assume and value rationality. Business leaders in the United States are unlikely to reveal that intuition is favored over empiricism in decision making. Incentives and rewards tend to be provided for individual effort rather than for those of a group or team. Although family gets much lip service, few organizations actually behave in ways that honor familial obligations. Cultural variation in leadership is complex and important enough to merit its own chapter in any comprehensive book on leadership.

There is even a skeptic *school* of leadership that asserts that leadership really does not matter. People are thrust into leadership positions and events take their course. What the leader does or does not do makes little difference, and that person is thought to be a great leader when things work out well and a poor leader when they do not. Leadership is simply one of the ways that people explain why an organization did well or did poorly, especially when the true underlying reasons are too complex to know or understand. When organizations do well, followers and others give their leaders high marks; when organizations do poorly, the opposite is usually true. In this view, it is a chicken-or-an-egg problem, where causation is difficult to locate. In fact, in large organizations, there is such a distance between executives and those who produce products or services that it may be difficult to show any real connection between the two. This means that large organizations with good leaders might perform poorly (because line workers perform poorly or out of alignment with goals set by executives). The opposite might also be true. Poor leaders are sometimes credited with the success of their organization, especially when their leadership does not get in the way.

Measurement or assessment of leadership effectiveness is equally difficult (no surprise) given that there is no clear or accepted definition of the quality that is to be assessed. The most common measure of leader effectiveness is whether the organization achieved its goals and to what extent.

Finally, researchers and scholars report that progress is being made in these areas. Knowledge is being accumulated in the study of leaders and leadership. They are optimistic. But there is much to be learned.

Some Definitions of Leadership

As a reference point, here is a sampling of several commonly held views of what defines leadership:

> *The process of social influence in which one person is able to enlist the aid and support of others in the accomplishment of a common task* (Chemers, 1997, p. 1).

... an ethical act of influencing others toward effecting positive change through the accomplishment of a common goal (University of the Pacific, 2009, p. 2).

Leadership is the art of getting someone else to do something you want done because he wants to do it (Dwight Eisenhower in Brown, Scott, & Lewis, 2004, p. 126).

... a process of motivating people to work together collaboratively to accomplish great things (Vroom & Jago, 2007, p. 18).

A process of giving purpose (meaningful direction) to collective effort, and causing willing effort to be expended to achieve purpose (Jacobs & Jaques, 1990, p. 281).

Influencing others by establishing a direction for collective effort and managing, shaping, and developing the collective activities in accordance with this direction (Zaccaro, 2007, p. 9).

Leadership is an influence relationship between leaders and followers who intend real changes that reflect their mutual purposes (Ciulla, 2004, p. 306).

Leadership concerns the capacity to build and maintain a high-performing team, and leadership should be evaluated in terms of the performance of the team (Hogan in Dotlich & Cairo, 2003, p. xiv).

Leadership over human beings is exercised when persons with certain motives and purposes mobilize, in competition or conflict with others, institutional, political, psychological, and other resources so as to arouse, engage, and satisfy the motives of followers (Burns, 1978, p. 18).

Influence processes affecting the interpretation of events for followers, the choice of objectives for the group or organization, the organization of work activities to accomplish the objectives, the motivation of followers to achieve the objectives, the maintenance of cooperative relationships and teamwork, and the enlistment of support and cooperation from people outside the group or organization (Yukl, 1994, p. 5).

The definition of leadership depends upon the theory chosen and its focus. The differences between theories are significant. For example, a trait-focused leadership theory is most interested in characteristics (intelligence, personality, values, and habits) of the person who is leading. Situational theories focus on the qualities of the context and its challenges. Contingency theories focus on the interaction (fit and match) between characteristics of the leader and the situation. Behavioral theories attend to the actions of leaders. Most of the currently accepted definitions of leadership, independent of theoretical basis, involve *influence* and *change*.

Classic Historical Leadership Studies

There are three well-known lines of research that all coaches should know about, even though they are not much in use these days. Most business students have read them, and they have had a powerful influence on the theories that followed. They are leadership style, Theory X–Y, and the managerial grid.

Leadership Style

Early research efforts in psychology focused on the style of the leader. Kurt Lewin and two colleagues (Lewin, Lippitt, & White, 1939) published one of the earliest empirical efforts in the formal study of leadership at the beginning of World War II. The world was reeling from the powerful influence of three especially toxic leaders—Hitler, Mussolini, and Stalin—and social psychologists were curious about how such strange tyrants could prevail. Lewin conducted a study of young boys by providing three kinds of leaders and videotaping subsequent behavior. An *authoritarian-autocratic* leader gave clear and explicit orders and the boys had no input to the goals or methods to be used. There was a clear hierarchy and formal distinction between leader and follower. A *democratic* leader sought input from followers about goals and how to proceed, then guided followers without providing much external structure. Followers had a say in decision making. A *laissez-faire* leader offered little clear guidance, took a hands-off approach, and left decision making completely in the hands of the boys. Extensive reviews of the tapes led the researchers to conclude that each of the three leadership styles produced a different quality of follower response and output. The researchers made the following observations:

> *Autocratic Leader Style*—Productivity in this group tended to be higher, but less creative in quality. Followers often devolved into two types; an aggressive type and an apathetic type. The boys tended to work hard while the autocratic leader was present, but goofed off and worked less when the leader was not physically present. An autocratic leadership style may be preferable when quick, decisive action is required but less preferable when creative or sustained efforts are desired.

> *Democratic Leader Style*—Followers in this group tended to be more self-motivated, and they continued to work on task when the leader was not physically present. This group was less productive, but the quality of work was higher and more creative. Morale was higher and members were more congenial toward one another.

Laissez-Faire Leader Style—This was the least productive group of the three. The boys were unable to work independently, tended not to cooperate, and their work efforts tended to be disorganized.

There is also evidence that people prefer democratic or participative leadership during times of low stress, but favor a more autocratic style during crises (Dixon, 1992). Events surrounding and immediately following the attacks of September 11 seem to support such an assertion.

Although style has been an important topic of interest to writers and researchers over the past 50 years, it is not synonymous with leadership. It is a *way* to lead or a *quality* of the ways that leaders behave. Kotter (1999, p. 2) asserts that

> style is not the key leadership issue. Substance is. It is about core behavior on the job, not surface detail and tactics, a core that changes little over time, across different cultures, or in different industries.

Theory X and Theory Y

In 1960, Douglas McGregor proposed a format for categorizing two basic types of human motivation and effective leadership responses. In the Theory X view, people are inherently lazy, they possess a natural dislike for work, and will avoid it whenever possible. People do not tend to be motivated to achieve without external pressures, as they strive essentially toward security. They avoid responsibility and work solely for the money. Therefore, it is management's job to find ways to motivate and control them. In Theory X, these ways include authoritarian coercion, punishment, and tight control. Leaders might use threats or ultimatums, and they are not inclined to seek input from workers. They do not trust workers. When something goes wrong, leaders blame followers rather than the system or business conditions.

Theory Y differs, as it views humans much more positively. In this view, people are not lazy. They appreciate work, perhaps as much as they enjoy play, and there is not so much of a fine distinction between the two activities. People tend naturally to seek and accept responsibility and enjoy accomplishment. Theory Y management is collaborative and participatory, and it believes in the untapped potential of the worker. It tends to reward rather than punish, and to empower and enable followers. McGregor's ideas derived, in part, from Maslow's hierarchy of needs, where Theory X people were striving to meet basic, lower level survival needs (money, food, safety, housing), and Theory Y workers felt secure in those basic needs and were reaching up Maslow's hierarchy toward a sense of achievement, self-respect, and respect from others. Organizations in this model were evaluated based upon how closely their practices fit into Theory X or Y.

In 1981 William Ouchi proposed a Theory Z, which came to be known as the Japanese management style at that time. Ouchi and Japanese leaders had been exposed to W. Edwards Deming's ideas and his powerful "14 Points" (Deming, 1986). Ouchi recommended leadership that encouraged and rewarded long-term worker loyalty. This was done by shared responsibility, collective decision making, and respect for the total person and their family.

The Managerial Grid

In about 1964, Robert Blake and Jane Mouton formulated a grid that described five categories of leadership style based on relative concern for production versus people. Their grid was a response to McGregor's work and an attempt to synthesize Theory X and Theory Y behavior. The grid requires that leaders ask themselves the question: How much do I value the needs of my people, their concerns, their ideas, their interests, and their development? On the other hand, how much am I concerned about specific, concrete objectives, productivity, efficiency, and task accomplishment? The dichotomy is famously referred to as *task orientation* versus *people orientation*. Leaders can plot their orientation on a grid that Blake and Mouton developed. It is reproduced in Figure 15.1. The five resulting styles are:

1. *Country Club Style* (high people, low production orientation)— This style assumes that if people are happy, work goals will be met, and the organization will succeed. Success is likely to depend upon the kind and quality of followers. Some workers respond very well

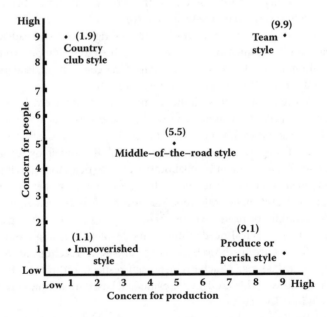

Figure 15.1 The Blake–Mouton grid.

to this kind of culture under certain circumstances, others take advantage of it.

2. *Team Style* (high people, high production orientation)—This is an optimal style, likely to produce great outcomes and happy organizations. It is, however, rare to find an organization that can operate this way over extended periods. Nonetheless, this situation is highly desirable in Blake and Mouton's view.

3. *Produce or Perish Style* (low people, high production orientation)— This is the Theory X culture, where the bottom line is all that matters. Nobody is very happy in this scenario, and people take a hard-nosed view of business: Get it done or go away.

4. *Impoverished Style* (low people, low production orientation)—This is the worst-case scenario, where people are miserable and little is accomplished.

5. *Middle-of-the-Road Style* (moderate people, moderate production orientation)—The literature tends to view this position as "weak," a compromise seen as the best that one can do without pushing things or alienating people. Still, such a culture is probably better than the worst ones in the grid.

Modern Leadership Theories

The remainder of this chapter will explain in the simplest terms several of the most important and widely studied current leadership models.

Charisma and Trait Theory

Much leader research has historically focused on leader attributes and behavior, or what is sometimes called great man theory. This focus seems to have intellectual roots in the work of Thomas Carlyle (2007), the Scottish philosopher who described six categories of leaders in 1840 and wrote: "For, as I take it, Universal History, the history of what man has accomplished in this world, is at bottom the History of the Great Men who have worked here."

The big idea in this view is that successful leaders possess exceptional qualities that influence others and result in great organizational success. Much popular leadership literature still seems to have hero worship as its focus, and the biographies of charismatic historical leaders such as Gandhi, King, Lincoln, Churchill, and Mandela are well worth reading. On the other hand, the books of many celebrity CEOs and sports coaches are brimming with illogical, self-serving pap, and your client has probably read some of it. That said, there is still much to be learned by studying the behavior of the leaders of successful organizations or cultures.

In addition to biographies, there is a large body of ongoing and important empirical research in the area of leader traits and behaviors. The trend is to carefully search for universal qualities or behaviors associated with leader success so that these traits can be shared, taught, and learned.

Charismatic views in the research literature have come and gone and come again. In the 1970s and 1980s there was a resurgence of charismatic interest in the form of something called transformational leadership. The transformational figure is one who, through personal leadership, is able to cause major change in an organization or even a country or culture. The notion that a powerful leader can transform an organization is the basis for outlandish, gaudy executive pay where a leader is paid 250 times that of the average worker. Famous college football and basketball coaches are paid millions of dollars a year—often more than the president of the university—to try to work their transformative magic (they rarely deliver). In fact, the football coach at the U.S. Military Academy almost certainly made more money than the President of the United States in 2007, although his salary was kept secret according to the Army's freedom of information officer (Upton, 2007). That coach was later fired after two unsuccessful seasons (Associated Press, 2008).

The work of sociologist Max Weber (1947) established a framework for study based on the observation that charismatic leaders emerge during periods of social crisis, when potential followers feel threatened by forces they cannot control. Weber thought that heroic leaders were born with extraordinary gifts and solved a crisis with a radical idea. Charismatic leaders offer solutions through a bold vision founded on the needs and values of followers. Follower needs are often communicated through expression of values that are transcendent or beyond self-interest (Jacobsen & House, 1999). Much current thinking on this subject is reflected in Robert House's 1976 theory of charismatic leadership (1977; House & Shamir, 1993), which has subsequently been subjected to an impressive amount of empirical research. In this view "charismatic leaders engage follower self-concepts and cause followers to link valued aspects of their self-concepts to their involvement in the leader's vision and mission" (House & Shamir, 1993, p. 82). This idea is reflected in Martin Luther King's 1961 observation that

> People are often led to causes and often become committed to great ideas through persons who personify these ideas. They have to find embodiment of the idea in flesh and blood in order to commit themselves to it. (Phillips, 1998, p. 1).

There is even research indicating that charismatic leaders tend to relieve followers' subjective feelings of stress and alienation, transform their organization, and motivate followers to transcend their own self-interest to better their organization. To do these things, charismatic leaders must have the following characteristics:

- A strong need for power and social influence.
- A bold vision that differs from the status quo.
- Relentless optimism, energy, and determination.
- High self-confidence and general sense of self-worth.
- A strong conviction in their own beliefs and ideals.
- An ability to articulate their vision in a compelling way.

Charismatic leaders typically:

- Communicate a bold vision, couched in positive moral values, but challenging current convention.
- Convince others that the vision is realistic and attainable.
- Communicate high performance expectations and arouse motivation.
- Build and maintain a positive personal image consistent with the vision.
- Set an example as a role model for change and for high values.
- Create empowering opportunities for others (to connect their destiny to the vision) and express confidence in followers.
- Take risks and make personal sacrifices for the mission.

The Negative Sides of Charisma   Charismatic leadership is not for everyone, nor is it always optimal for an organization. It is also clear that, from a moral standpoint, some charismatic leaders are better than others. There can be no denying that Adolf Hitler met all the criteria for charismatic leadership. He just had a monstrous vision and took the world in a disastrous direction. Charismatic leaders are not always the most stable characters, either. The person who communicates a bold new vision is not always the kind of person best suited to shepherd an organization over the long haul. A central problem with charismatic leadership is that organizational benefits depend upon a single person. When that person departs, it is usually difficult, if not impossible, to control or maintain the positive impact of an inspiring leader.

Trait Theory

Charisma aside, there is a set of theories and a body of research that focus on the general qualities associated with leadership, including personal, interpersonal, and even intrapersonal (within the person) qualities. Among these are intellect, personality, skills, knowledge, temperament, values, and motivation. A *trait*, in this view, is any personal quality or characteristic that accompanies the leader wherever he or she may go. It is observable across a variety of work situations or settings, and independent of any organizational culture or job description. Traits are uniform across situations.

The earliest modern trait research focused on intelligence. Although a certain level of intellect is required for leadership, cognitive ability itself does not predict leader success. In fact, evidence indicates that too much traditional IQ may actually work against a leader, as people tend to favor those with an intelligence that seems about the same as their own (Turner, 2007). Sometimes people resent those with obvious intellectual genius, and occasionally those who are extremely "smart" have trouble understanding, relating, and identifying with the rest of us. Other kinds of intelligence, such as emotional or social intelligence, are increasingly thought to be important and are discussed in Chapter 11. Sternberg (2007) points out that successful intelligence includes academic and practical components, but that *wisdom* is much more important.

The best known leadership trait researcher of the 20th century was Ralph Stogdill, a professor at Ohio State University. He conducted two major reviews of trait studies (1948, 1974) and came to two kinds of conclusions. First, he identified a rather long list of traits and skills that characterized successful leaders. They included qualities such as: a strong desire to influence others, ambitious and achievement-oriented, persuasive; energetic, self-confident, decisive, diplomatic, assertive, adaptable, dependable, and creative (Stogdill, 1974). It is difficult to imagine that such a vague, all-encompassing list of obviously positive qualities could be of much real value to a coach or aspiring leader. His second conclusion was that "the relative importance of each trait depends on the situation" (Yukl, 1994, p. 255) and that characteristics of effective leaders are related to the characteristics and goals of followers (Stogdill, 1948, p. 64). Eventually, Stogdill came to the conclusion that the search for a discrete set of universal, individual leadership traits was fruitless.

Recent interest on personality traits has focused on the "Big Five" personality factors (Turner, 2007). The Big Five are the result of extensive factor analysis where many personality descriptors are statistically grouped and reduced into the five most distinct ones. A 2002 meta-analysis of 73 studies (Judge, Bono, Ilies, & Gerhardt, 2002) revealed the ways that these five factors influenced leadership effectiveness. They are listed in the traditional *OCEAN* order.

> **O***penness to experience (curious, interested in a variety of things)*—This quality was highly correlated to leadership effectiveness.

> **C***onscientiousness (self-disciplined, well-regulated, reliable)*—Also highly correlated to good leadership.

> **E***xtraversion (outgoingness, enthusiasm with others)*—This was the personality quality most consistently associated with good leadership,

and it was especially correlated with leader emergence (who becomes a leader and who does not).

Agreeableness (cooperative, willing to compromise, optimistic about others)—For reasons difficult to understand, this quality was *not* highly correlated to good leadership in the studies reviewed.

Neuroticism (emotional instability and self-defeating intrapersonal processes)—Effective leaders were low in this area and had fewer neurotic or unstable personality characteristics.

Yukl (1994) and others have surveyed the research on leader traits and concluded that there are a relatively small number of widely supported characteristics:

High Energy—Successful leaders typically have a lot of physical and mental energy and stamina.

Good Stress Tolerance—They can handle relentless pressure, hectic pace, and unending demands without panicking, withdrawing, or blaming others.

Self-Confidence—This includes self-esteem (having an accurately high opinion of one's self) and self-efficacy (believing that you can successfully accomplish difficult tasks that you may not have done before). These qualities allow a person to take risks and to convince others that his or her vision is worth pursuing. In successful leaders, this self-confidence is not excessive or unjustified.

Internal Locus of Control—They believe that what happens is a result of their own efforts, not fate or chance or others. They know that if something is going to happen, they need to take action to make it happen. They are also able to accurately take credit or blame and do not blame outside forces or conditions.

Emotional Maturity—They are well adjusted, emotionally stable with self-control, care about others and capable of empathy, open and not defensive, and manage anger and use it productively. Many of these qualities are associated with emotional intelligence.

Integrity—They walk their talk. Their actual behavior (public and private) is aligned with their espoused values. They are not especially deceptive or secretive, and as a result, are perceived to be trustworthy. They keep their promises and commitments. They are discrete and can keep information confidential. They take responsibility for their decisions and the related outcomes.

Power Motivation—They seek power and positions of authority and seek to influence others. They appreciate organizational politics and are not intimidated or turned off by them. Research indicates that they have a socialized power orientation rather than a personalized orientation. This means that they are interested in power because it can accomplish positive goals for others. Those with a personalized power orientation seek to dominate others for reasons related to their own ego satisfaction. Their behavior resembles that of the bully or the boss with a huge ego. They are selfish and do not share power.

Achievement Orientation—They have a strong drive to excel and to accomplish real goals. The research in this area is complicated, and Yukl reports that a moderate level of achievement orientation may be optimal, because a super-high achiever can create organizational problems, especially when ego drives achievement needs. Fast-rising, high-achieving stars can fall when others perceive that success is driven by narcissism rather than a shared interest in the larger goals of the organization and its people. In any case, everyone agrees that low achievement orientation is not associated with successful leadership.

Need for Affiliation—This is another complicated area, where a moderate level of need for affiliation is probably best. Those with a high need to be liked and accepted by others are not likely to be able to make unpopular decisions. Those with a high need for affiliation tend to avoid conflict and strive to keep relationships smooth. At the other end of the spectrum, good leaders are rarely loners. Good leaders work well with others, but are able to put the mission first.

Technical Skills—The importance of specific, technical skills is variable. Leaders need some familiarity with the body of content knowledge required to accomplish an organization's goals. They must know the vocabulary of the field and have some notion of the embedded challenges and the tacit difficulties faced by followers. Extensive industry-specific skills are desirable except when a leader tends toward micromanagement. There is also a set of leadership-specific skills that are crucial, such as the ability to skillfully delegate, to lead meetings, to formulate strategy, to understand a complex budget, and to understand environmental and market forces. These skills are likely to be in development throughout one's career.

Interpersonal Skills—If influence is an essential component of our definition of leadership, then the need for social skills is a given. Some of these skills seem to be born in a person as part of temperament. Others can be learned and cultivated. These qualities include listening skills, interaction skills across cultures, the ability to work a room with a glass in one's hand, the ability to manage different kinds of personalities and difficult people in a hierarchy (including board members and key customers), the ability to deliver difficult or negative messages, and the ability to mentor others and develop them. It is a wise leader who understands his or her strengths and weaknesses and works continuously on interpersonal skill development. These skills are not to be taken for granted, even as one rises in power and prestige.

Conceptual and Tacit Skills—There is a need for high levels of complex mental skills such as the ability to reason, to problem solve, to use logic, to make sense out of ambiguity and confusion, the ability to prioritize competing goals, and to adjust to changing times. There are also tacit skills that one develops along the way that are essential but nearly impossible to identify and measure.

In a formal study of successful managing directors, Cox and Cooper (1988) endorsed most of the traits listed by Yukl and added a few more. Their subjects demonstrated determination (many had been forced into early independence in life), learned from adversity, had a well-integrated value system based upon integrity, and had a well-organized life where work took precedence over home life. Difficult early life experiences are also associated with development of authentic leadership style (George, Gergen, & Sims, 2007).

With all that said, it is clear that a trait-only view of leadership is inadequate. In spite of the intuitive importance of leader traits, the popular appeal of a charismatic view, and the historic and current focus on character in the popular business press, actual research reveals a more complicated picture. George, Sims, McLean, and Mayer (2007, p. 130) conducted in-depth interviews with 125 established leaders in their work on authentic leadership and wrote:

After interviewing these individuals, we believe we understand why more than 1,000 studies have not produced a profile of an ideal leader. Analyzing 3,000 pages of transcripts, our team was startled to see that these people did not identify any universal characteristics, traits, skills, or styles that led to their success.

Yukl (1994, p. 256) noted: "The premise that some leader traits are absolutely necessary for effective leadership has not been substantiated in several decades of trait research."

And finally:

Despite the long history of the trait-based approach and its recent resurgence, a consensus about the role of leader traits, the magnitude and mechanisms of their influence, and the determining role of leadership situations have remained elusive. (Zaccaro, 2007, p. 14)

Situational Leadership

Researchers frustrated with the inadequacy of trait theories and trait heritage turned their attention to contextual factors that influenced leadership. These factors included the nature of the organizational task, the characteristics of followers, the organizational culture and norms, the formal level or position of the leader in the organization, the size of the organization and number of subordinates, the independence of the leader, the stability of the organization (or whether it is in crisis), and the developmental stage of the company (is it a start-up or well established).

As mentioned in Chapter 9 on social psychology, the power of the situation is often underestimated. Situations exert a powerful influence on how we all behave, and leaders are no exception to this rule. Situational leadership reminds us that without followers there is no leader. This approach views leadership as a process rather than a property of a person (Vroom & Jago, 2007), and asserts that trait and charisma theories have been largely discredited by research. The situational view sees leader behavior as a function of the situation. Vroom and Jago (2007) point out that leaders have less real power in most organizations than commonly thought, that complicated and comprehensive hiring practices tend to screen out any leader truly different from the norm (so that there is little difference between leaders), and that any remaining differences will be washed out by the power of situational demands. Pure-situation theory notes that organizational success is dictated by factors generally not under leader control. They also point out that contextual forces also shape leader behavior and that outcomes are first and foremost a function of context rather than leader behavior.

The term *situational leadership* is also the name of a proprietary model developed by Paul Hersey and popular management guru Kenneth Blanchard in the 1960s (Hersey, Blanchard, & Johnson, 2008). It advocated the matching of leadership behavior (supporting, coaching, delegating, or directing) with the developmental level of followers based on worker level of competence and commitment. Task-oriented leaders are better when followers are less mature, less able, or less willing to do the job required. Although Hersey and Blanchard's approach is called *situational leadership*, it is probably better characterized as one of the contingency theories described later in this chapter.

Transactional and Exchange Theories

A series of complex models attempt to explain leadership from the viewpoint of the transactions that take place between leaders and followers. They extend the focus from leader → follower to the *interaction* between the two. Their conceptual basis is in human motivation toward self-interest. Humans tend to maximize personal gain and minimize loss or cost. Life consists of transactions with other humans, each attempting to make his or her own best deal. Leader–follower interactions are seen as a subset of this type of exchange, and the quality of the exchanges or transactions determine the effectiveness of leadership. When both parties—leaders and followers—perceive that the exchanges are beneficial or valuable (based on their perception of cost–benefit ratios), then transactions will continue and both parties will feel good. When the opposite is true, or when one party feels that the exchange is unjust, the system falls apart. Leadership depends upon the perception by followers that transactions are just and worth making. Good leadership is built on high levels of mutual respect and trust, shared interest in the outcomes, reasoned appeals and arguments, clear rules and interactions, and a perception that transactions are entered into freely (Chemers, 1997).

Contingency Models

When the inadequacies of trait models became clear and the importance of the situation acknowledged, theories that match leaders with followers or circumstances began to emerge. Fred Fiedler's research (1967) on task-oriented versus relationship-oriented leaders broke ground in the 1960s. In earlier work he had shown that some psychotherapists rated their least favorite patients lower than other psychotherapists rated theirs, and that the ones who rated patients lower were less effective therapists, as they were thought to be more distant from patients. His leadership research began by looking for traits of leaders based upon their task or relationship motivation. He developed an instrument called the *least preferred coworker* (LPC) scale and used it to segregate leaders into two groups. Leaders were asked to rate their least favorite coworker. Those who rated coworkers lower were called *low LPC leaders*. Those who rated their least favorite coworker higher were called *high LPC leaders*, and it was thought that they tended to be more relationship oriented. Fielder hypothesized that since business leaders are rewarded primarily for results (as athletic coaches are rewarded for winning), those who were task oriented would be better leaders. Earlier research had implied that more distant leaders were more effective. Fiedler's first results with steel workers and B-29 bombers seemed to support his hypothesis that favored low LPC leaders (those who were more task oriented and distant), but as soon as he published his findings, other studies began to contradict his research. Reports from farm collectives, lab groups working on complex ambiguous or creative tasks, and groups working under great stress seemed to perform better with high LPC leaders (Chemers, 1997, p. 29). Most important was the variability between reports from differing kinds of work settings and situations. As an example, he noted that task-oriented leaders were better in crises or dangerous situations (like war), but that such leadership fell flat under other circumstances. Fiedler concluded that his original formulation was too simplistic and that there was a missing moderator. He reported that the relationship between leader traits and group performance was *contingent* upon some other factor or factors. Hence the name contingency theory.

Fiedler eventually formulated a contingency model that included three categories of situational favorability. Since leadership involves influence, the quality of the social aspects of the situation was considered key. He proposed three situational aspects and rated them good–poor and weak–strong. The components were:

1. *Leader–Member Relations*—This was a measure of the quality of interpersonal interactions and feelings between leaders and others. If rapport is good, it is easier for a leader to influence followers.

2. *Position Power*—How much authority did the leader have by virtue of his or her formal position in the organization? How much capacity does the leader have to reward and punish followers?

3. *Task Structure*—How clear are the job, the task, and the goals? When those things are clearer, with more structure, it is easier to exercise effective leadership.

Successful leadership, in this model, derives from the interaction of leadership style (a trait) and situational favorability. Fiedler's work was influential and controversial. Many found fault in his views, but as a result, leadership research had finally differentiated itself from trait theories.

This led to sustained interest in the concept of "fit." The basic idea is that there is no "one best way" to lead organizations. Instead, it is best to match organizations with optimal leadership, optimal followers, optimal structure, and optimal goals and methods, given the circumstances involved. Circumstances might include the business environment, the nature of competitors, available resources, and the history of the organization to date. An organization and its leadership might work very well in one situation and poorly in a different one. The most obvious evidence for the wisdom of this point of view again comes from the world of sports. Famous coaches often move from one optimal situation (where they were fabulously successful) to a new situation where they flop. This is a common and expensive scenario. The same thing no doubt happens in the corporate world where flops are a bit less public and somewhat less obvious to outsiders.

Path–Goal Theory

Fiedler's model only goes so far, as it does not get around to explaining how leaders should behave. How does a good leader interact with followers and motivate them? What are the specific tasks involved? What is expected of followers?

Path–goal theory attempts to fill that gap by describing and testing possible contingent leader actions. The theory is based on the premise that leadership is most effective when it helps followers understand how to maximize personal benefit and satisfaction through their work. It is founded on *expectancy theory*, which asserts that workers use a rational decision process to decide how much effort to put forth on a moment-to-moment basis. Maximum effort occurs when workers perceive that "a valued outcome can be attained only by making a serious effort and they believe that such an effort will succeed" (Yukl, 1994, p. 286). In this view, the leader's primary task is to effectively influence workers' perceptions of expectancies.

Path–goal theory began by studying the effect of two types of leadership: directive and supportive (House, 1971). *Directive* leaders are task oriented, and they provide structure and manipulate clear formal incentives, including rewards. They clarify the task, and provide schedules and specific goals. *Supportive* leaders (often called *consideration leadership*) help people feel at ease, provide encouragement and psychosocial support, reduce boredom and anxiety, and try to enhance worker self-esteem. Researchers later added two other leadership types, participative and achievement oriented. The task of the leader is to apply the most appropriate and effective leadership by matching it to the nature of followers and work tasks. They found that when a task is stressful, dangerous, tedious, unfulfilling, or boring, supportive leadership tends to increase worker effort and satisfaction by diminishing negative psychological factors such as anxiety, boredom, and frustration. Encouragement in these conditions helps enhance worker perception that efforts are likely to lead to success. When a task is intrinsically interesting or enjoyable to workers, supportive leadership has little or no positive effect. On the other hand, when tasks are ambiguous or complex and workers are inexperienced or not highly capable, directive leadership is more likely to enhance worker productivity and satisfaction. When workers are confused about their work they are unlikely to expect success, and directive leadership can help by providing clarity. This clarity then leads to higher worker expectations of success, which then leads to enhanced work efforts and greater satisfaction. On the other hand, when the task is well structured and workers are competent, directive leadership does not help. In fact, such leadership might annoy workers and have a negative impact on work output and worker satisfaction. Although path–goal theory has its detractors, there is substantial empirical support for its core ideas and the model provides a solid theoretical basis for the notion that leader–situation–follower match (or fit) is worthy of serious attention. There are many questions left to be answered, especially regarding the role of follower characteristics.

Substitutes for Leadership

A subsequent line of research in this area focuses on the missing elements in the worker's job environment. In the *substitutes for leadership* approach, leaders must evaluate the work situation and discover what is missing or needed by followers (Kerr & Jermier, 1978; Podsakoff, Niehoff, MacKenzie, & Williams, 1993). It is the leader's job to then supply what is missing or lacking (for example, structure when the task is unclear or praise for competent workers who do not need direction). Kerr and Jermier (1978) developed a taxonomy of 14 situational contingencies divided into three classes: characteristics of subordinates, the nature of subordinate tasks, and characteristics of the organization (Ayman, 2004). The larger point of all this is that leader behavior does not have a consistent, universal effect on organizational outcomes. It is the interaction between leader characteristics/behavior, characteristics of followers, and the situation or environmental context that determines outcomes. No universal leadership style or approach is best for all situations.

Normative Decision Theory

Vroom and colleagues (Vroom & Jago, 1988; Vroom & Yetton, 1973) researched executive decision making and learned that leadership decisions depend on an interaction with the context or situation. They studied conditions and contingencies of leader decision making and proposed a set of normative (prescriptive) principles to guide effective leader decision making based on the premise that "one of a leader's important prerogatives is controlling the process by which decisions are made" (Chemers, 1997, p. 49). They began by identifying five categories of decision making based upon whether the leader was autocratic, consultative, or democratic, and they evaluated processes based upon whether they (1) produced a good decision; (2) improved worker involvement; (3) reduced time; or (4) developed subordinates. Situational parameters included factors such as: whether subordinates had adequate information to effectively influence the process; whether followers were likely to support the decision and commit to execution; and the degree of conflict among workers regarding the decision. They found that leader style (autocratic, consultative, or democratic) should vary according to which of the four aforementioned concerns was most important. For example, if time is of the essence, a consultative or democratic process is ruled out. If worker buy-in is essential, a democratic process is recommended. Decision method is matched to the situational needs and demands.

Vroom and Jago (1988) and Vroom and Yetton (1973) describe five categories of leader decision style, including:

1. *Autocratic I*—The leader makes the decision alone using information at hand.

2. *Autocratic II*—The leader solicits information from subordinates and then makes the decision.

3. *Consultative I*—The leader shares information with each key subordinate separately, seeks information and advice, and makes the decision. No group meeting is involved.

4. *Consultative II*—The leader shares information and seeks advice from key subordinates in a group setting, then makes the decision alone.

5. *Group II*—The leader discusses the problem with followers in a group setting and invites them to share equally in the decision making. The group makes the final decision.

Chemers (1997, p. 50) reduced the Vroom team's extensive findings to six decision-making principles for leaders (paraphrased here):

1. Check to make sure that you have enough high-quality information. If not, get it from somewhere.
2. Make sure that the situation is structured clearly enough and that you understand it. If not, get clarification.
3. If you need buy-in and commitment from followers, use a more participatory process. Match participation with follower characteristics.
4. If followers are not committed to the goals involved in the decision, they cannot be allowed to make the decision, even though their input should be sought and considered.
5. If followers are in conflict about the matter, they must be allowed to air opinions together before a decision is made.
6. Followers must be represented, and their input sought and heard, before decisions are made that will impact them.

Normative decision theory is another example of a contingency theory of leadership in that it advocates a match between decision-making method (an important leadership behavior) and contingencies of followers and the situation.

Authentic Leadership

There is renewed interest in leadership theory that focuses on authenticity. This may be the result of a perception that numerous high-profile corporate executives and political figures have lacked integrity recently, causing many others to pay a heavy price for their greed and mendacity.

> Over the past five years, people have developed a deep distrust of leaders. (George et al., 2007, p. 129)

> People want to be led by someone "real." … We all suspect that we're being duped. (Goffee & Jones, 2005, p. 87)

Authenticity's origin as a topic of interest dates back to the humanism movement in psychology, the "third force." This school, led by Abraham Maslow, Carl Rogers, Fritz Perls, and Rollo May, emphasized self-actualization, positive growth, individual autonomy, and authenticity. People were encouraged to live from within rather than in response to external forces. Judith Blanton (2009, p. 8), in describing a model she helped develop at RHR International, distinguishes "internal authenticity" from "external authenticity" and asserts that internal consistency was of special importance to emerging female leaders. Authenticity is often defined as a condition where internal values and external behavior are aligned.

Harvard professor William George has written several books (2003, 2007) on the subject and essentially made authentic leadership into something of a brand. In his view, authentic leadership involves alignment of leader behavior with an internal compass as well as with high-quality ethical principles. George's research included a series of 125 interviews with successful leaders who are perceived to be authentic. Many seem to have benefitted from an evolution out of early trauma. "Crucible" experiences such as poverty, death of a parent or loved one, job loss, or a series of personal failures were important developmental forces. The process of surviving and resolving early life difficulties is thought to be essential to authentic leader development. George and his researchers (2007) conclude that leadership derives from a person's life story, and that leaders must "work hard at understanding and developing themselves" (p. 130). The role of a good executive coach seems clear in this context. George's work is interesting because it contains so many references to simple human qualities such as kindness, empathy, caring about others, and behaviors that create positive feelings. George's interviewees were extremely hard workers, but his observations invariably emphasize soft skills and common sense.

Goffee and Jones (2005) offer several practical bits of advice for leaders who want to be perceived as authentic, focusing on the paradox of trying to become something that is usually defined as being who you naturally are. In the Goffee and Jones view, authenticity only matters in a business sense when others *perceive* you to be authentic. There are things you have to do to be viewed as authentic. First, you must make sure that your words match your deeds, that you "walk the talk." This is a pretty good definition of integrity. Goffee and Jones observed that integrity and authenticity are easier to achieve when organizational goals are aligned with a leader's own personal values. Second, you must find common ground with followers so that they can relate to you on a personal basis. This requires an interest in others as well as an appropriate amount of self-disclosure. Too much disclosure is seen as narcissistic, whereas too little is associated with detachment, distance, or disinterest. Leaders must develop what Goffee and Jones call *discernment skills*, the ability to figure out what qualities followers desire in their leader. Authentic leaders demonstrate pride in their roots, but again, in just the right amount. Too much pride is boorish. Leaders must also decide how much to conform to organizational norms and how much to lead or change them. Too much or too little conformity are both deadly, but all leaders must conform to gain acceptance at first. Goffee and Jones conclude that a reputation of authenticity must be "painstakingly earned" and "carefully managed." They point out that the recent American president perceived to be the most authentic was, in fact, a professional actor prior to entering politics.

Personal Drive and Successful Leadership

Research at the Hay Group by Spreier, Fontaine, and Malloy (2006) indicates that high achievement drive is not always a good thing in a leader. They studied a large number of managers and leaders at IBM and identified six primary leadership styles (p. 80):

1. *Directive*—A command and control style that sometimes employs coercion. It can be effective during crises and when dealing with poor performers. It tends to stifle creativity and initiative, but is favored by high achievers when stressed.

2. *Visionary*—Workers are challenged by larger organizational goals and directions, which tends to energize them.

3. *Affiliative*—A style that focuses on relationships and on employee needs and emotions. Seldom effective alone, it must be combined with one or more of the other styles. It is useful when followers are stressed or in crisis.

4. *Participative*—Collaborative and democratic. This style engages others in decision making to build trust and consensus. Requires high-functioning employees.

5. *Pacesetting*—Leadership by example and personal heroics. Leaders insist that their high standards be met, even when they have to do the work themselves. This style is favored by high achievers and can demoralize others.

6. *Coaching*—Emphasizes mentoring and development of the long-term careers of followers. Powerful and underused.

Spreier et al. reported that the best leaders were competent at all six of the styles, using each as appropriate to the situation. They found that most people have a default leadership style that they favor or employ under stress. A high-achievement motivation and pacesetting style were associated with managers who created the least preferred work climates.

Developmental Action Logic

Rooke and Torbert (2005) used a sentence completion survey called the Leadership Development Profile to assess the "internal action logic" of leaders when their power or safety was perceived to be challenged. Internal action logic refers to the ways that leaders interpret their surroundings and react under perceived negative stress. They created a hierarchy of "ways of leading" and concluded that a leader can evolve deliberately if he or she is willing to carefully assess their own style and work hard to grow. The stages are:

1. *Opportunist* (5% of leaders in study)—These are leaders who believe that "might makes right." They are manipulative, deceptive, and self-oriented. They may have a short-term advantage in sales opportunities and emergencies—until people figure them out.

2. *Diplomat* (12%)—This person avoids conflict and tries extra hard to fit in and please others. Rarely rocks the boat and serves the important function of keeping people together. Great in a support role. Strategy works well in more junior positions, but not so well at higher levels when this leader avoids or ignores conflict.

3. *Expert* (38%)—These leaders are high on content knowledge and they use data to drive decision making. They do not value emotional intelligence and tend to be poor at collaboration. They make excellent individual contributions.

4. *Achiever* (30%)—Tends to understand how to create collaborations that achieve strategic goals. This leader does a good job of juggling relationships and action. Tends to make a good manager.

5. *Individualist* (10%)—Highly productive but tends to be a wild card or loose cannon, causing larger organizational problems resulting from creative and innovative solutions on individual projects. Effective in venture and consulting roles.

6. *Strategist* (4%)—Excellent vision and takes a strategic point of view. Understands the big picture and figures out how to change things. Transformational leader.

7. *Alchemist* (1%)—Able to integrate big ideas and motivate others to engage in transformation. Rare and extremely valuable. Excellent at many levels at the same time. Nelson Mandela is presented as an example.

Rooke and Torbert (2005) report that their research led them to believe that leaders can actively and deliberately evolve from one stage to the next if they receive enough accurate feedback in a planned and structured effort. This research implies that executive coaches could make a significant difference when armed with this model.

Developmental Stages of Leaders

Bennis (2004b) offers a developmental map of leadership patterned after Shakespeare's seven ages of man described in his play *As You Like It.* There are expected issues and crises to be resolved in each stage:

1. *The Infant Executive*—The key to success at this early stage is to recruit able mentors. It can be lonely in this first leadership position, and young leaders should not go it alone. Coaches are essential here.

2. *The Schoolboy, with shining face*—It is still essential to learn from others at this stage, especially those who report to you. Leaders must learn which follower assessments are accurate and worth attending to and which should be ignored. Getting accurate feedback and input from your surroundings is the key.

3. *The Lover, with a woeful ballad*—This stage involves the task of learning how to navigate waters that are more negative, that of dealing with former peers who now report to you and with employees who must be eliminated from the organization. One must learn to execute these unpleasant duties with skill and humanity.

4. *The Bearded Soldier*—Leaders must now learn to understand the impact they have on followers, as relationships tend to become less open and authentic. They cannot become too comfortable because they are being observed at all times, and the things they say and do have a big impact on those around them. They must also watch out for professional jealousies, their own and that of others.

5. *The General, full of wise saws*—The leader at this stage is cautioned to listen and pay attention to the context. Once a person reaches this stage they have a demonstrated and successful track record, and the temptation is to think that they know too much. Success here requires wisdom in discerning how to navigate the existing culture.

6. *The Statesman, with spectacles on nose*—A leader's power may begin to wane at this stage and Bennis observes that wonderful opportunities may arise where this leader can inject a lifetime of experience into helping others with difficult leadership challenges. Leaders at this stage have leverage because they are financially and psychologically secure.

7. *The Sage, second childishness*—Leaders at this stage can derive great benefit from mentoring others if willing. The benefits of mentoring go

both ways, and older leaders are able to stay plugged in and relevant by connecting with younger leaders who need them.

Good and Bad Leadership

The point of all this is to try to figure out what constitutes good leadership and how to identify, promote, and develop it. Although the questions seem relatively simple, answers are certainly not.

Toxic Leadership

One way to identify characteristics of good leadership is to first describe important qualities of bad leaders, use a process of elimination, and evaluate what is left. There exists a significant body of literature that describes the various ways that leaders crash and burn.

From a trait perspective of leadership, there are personality types and behavioral styles that will doom any person in a leadership position. Most people have been exposed to these problematic kinds of leaders. It is a good idea to avoid becoming one, to avoid hiring one, and to avoid working for one when possible.

The first, and most prominent, is the narcissistic leader, made famous in the literature by Maccoby in an essay in the *Harvard Business Review* in 2000. Narcissism as a personality disorder is described in detail in Chapter 14 ("Psychopathology and Counseling"). People with full-blown personality disorders are unlikely to make it to significant leadership positions, although this certainly happens from time to time. But narcissism in small to moderate amounts is commonly found in those with enough self-confidence to assume command of significant leadership positions. The line between great self-confidence and grandiosity is a fine line indeed, and it can be challenging to distinguish the difference.

Babiak and Hare write in the preface of their book *Snakes in Suits* (2006, p. xiv) that

> psychopaths do work in modern organizations; they often are successful by most standard measures of career success; and their destructive personality characteristics are invisible to most of the people with whom they interact.

They go on to describe the abusive behaviors, manipulation, sense of entitlement, charm, and lack of personal insight that characterize the psychopath. They speculate that narcissists are not uncommon in leadership positions for several reasons. First, the negative qualities—for short periods—can seem attractive and tend to mirror a simplistic, stereotyped view of the charismatic leader. Second, recent business trends tend to favor a fast-moving, aggressive, highly optimistic, expansive, change-oriented style of leadership, and psychopaths can seem attractive in that context, at least at first. Maccoby noted:

> Given the large number of narcissists at the helm of corporations today, the challenge facing organizations is to ensure that such leaders do not self-destruct or lead the company to disaster. ... employees must learn to recognize—and work around—narcissistic bosses. (2000, p. 71)

Problems Associated with Charisma

Charisma can be a double-edged sword with clear advantages and a few not-so-clear drawbacks. The first such drawback has to do with what Yukl (1994) calls the *routinization of charisma*. Charisma is necessarily associated with one single person, and when that leader moves on or dies, it is extremely difficult to sustain the atmosphere and advantages associated with that person. There is no telling what then happens in the absence of excellent succession planning, and charismatic leaders are not generally known for succession planning. As Yukl notes, "a smooth transition rarely occurs" (p. 332). That said, even a *discussion* of succession can be difficult with a charismatic leader, especially if an organization's current success is tied directly to the image and identity of that leader.

A second challenge has to do with the extent to which charismatic leaders focus their followers' energy on the organization's goals and needs (positive charismatics) and how much they focus follower energy on themselves (negative charismatics). Those who personalize their power tend to have an overall negative impact on the organization, whereas leaders who socialize their power on behalf of organizational goals are more likely to have a positive impact over time.

There are several other potentially negative consequences of charismatic leadership. Frequently, charismatic leaders are weak administrators who loathe detail. Sometimes their organization suffers from their excessive or unwarranted self-confidence. The same boldness that got them into power and motivated the organization can result in poorly conceived or poorly researched decisions. Sometimes bright and driven subordinates get tired of the attention given to charismatic leaders and they either leave or undermine the boss. Occasionally, charismatic leaders lack long-term, high-quality interpersonal skills and, over time, others figure this out and become disenchanted. Occasionally charisma works in one market context but does not translate to other organizations or new strategic directions, resulting in a poor leader–situation fit.

Whicker (1996) explores toxic leadership in more detail and describes three categories of leadership: trustworthy, transitional, and toxic. Trustworthy leaders are a positive force for the organization and society. They possess many positive qualities including integrity and the ability to cultivate others. Transitional leaders suffer from egotistical self-absorption and they tend to keep their organization in a holding pattern. Their flaws are not immediately obvious to followers. This category includes *absentee leaders, busybodies,* and *controllers.* Toxic leaders are downright malevolent and Whicker describes three types: the *enforcer,* the *street fighter,* and the *bully.* Her descriptions of the impact of negative leadership on organizations and her conclusions are not encouraging.

Derailment

Leadership researchers have shown considerable interest in promising or successful leaders who suddenly fail or prematurely plateau. There is evidence that this happens with surprising frequency, and derailment rates between 30% to 50% can be found in the literature (Lombardo & Eichinger, 1989, p. 4).

In their book *Why CEOs Fail,* Dotlich and Cairo (2003) describe 11 behavior patterns or "derailers" associated with the downfall of previously successful leaders. They are: arrogance, melodrama, volatility, excessive caution, habitual distrust, aloofness, mischievousness, eccentricity, passive resistance, perfectionism, and eagerness to please. Coaches would do well to keep an eye out for these behavior patterns when working with clients interested in leadership.

The Center for Creative Leadership (Leslie & Van Velsor, 1996) conducted several large-scale evaluations of leaders who had fallen by the corporate wayside, using interviews and a group dynamics questionnaire in the United States and in six European countries. They compared results with previous derailment studies and identified four consistent or enduring derailment themes:

1. Problems with interpersonal relationships.
2. Failure to meet business objectives.
3. Inability to build and lead a team.
4. Inability to adapt during a transition.

The two enduring themes—*poor working relationships* and *inability to develop or adapt* (including inflexibility)—were mentioned by more than 50% of the participants. Other frequently cited qualities included authoritarianism and excessive ambition, insensitivity, aloofness, lack of follow-through, and inability to do strategic planning.

On the positive side, the Center for Creative Leadership (Leslie & Van Velsor, 1996) identified eight success themes that seem to have endured across time and culture. They are:

1. Ambitiousness (appropriate amount)
2. Establish strong relationships
3. Consistent high performance
4. Team-building skills
5. Intelligence
6. Willingness to take appropriate risks

7. Adaptability

8. Being a problem solver

The Center for Creative Leadership concluded that, again, leader "fit" is crucially important, in this case a fit with "evolving demand":

> Although the key use of derailment research in the past has been to understand the development needed (to prevent derailment) by people as they move up in an organization, at its core derailment really has to do with a failure of fit of the individual with the evolving demands of the job over time (often at successively higher organizational levels). (Leslie & Van Velsor, 1996, p. 36)

Finally, on the negative side, Goldsmith and Reiter (2007) present a list of 20 habits that hold people back in leadership positions in their book *What Got You Here Won't Get You There*. Their premise is that some qualities are extremely useful at one point in a career but become liabilities later. Their list includes:

- Winning too much (competing compulsively)
- Adding too much value (always adding your "two cents")
- Passing judgment (rating others and imposing your own standards)
- Making destructive comments (witty, cutting, sarcastic remarks)
- Negativity, starting with "no" or "but" or "however"
- Telling the world how smart you are
- Speaking when angry (emotional volatility)
- Withholding information (to try to gain an advantage)
- Failure to give credit, recognition, and gratitude
- Claiming undeserved credit
- Making excuses
- Clinging to the past
- Playing favorites
- Refusing to express regret
- Not listening
- Punishing the messenger
- Passing the buck
- Excessive "need to be me" (exalting faults as if they were virtues)

Goldsmith and Reiter offer prescriptive advice about how to fix those faults in their book.

Summary

Leadership and leader development is an important topic with a rich and complex literature that derives from two sources: popular business books and empirical (data-based) research. There is no single, adequate, or universally accepted definition of the concept itself. This makes leadership hard to research and difficult to teach or evaluate in any logical way. Often, leaders who are extremely successful in one context or organization are mediocre or fail in others. In any case, there is a small number of rather clear trends that can be wrung out of the leadership literature, both popular and academic. They are:

1. There are no universal traits that will ensure good leadership across the spectrum of organizational contexts. That said, there are two lists of traits that are attractive and worth mention. The first is a relatively short list, including those qualities that seem to rise to the top of most of the research on leader traits. These seem to be the most important personal qualities of anyone hoping to lead successfully. Since most definitions of leadership involve the intentional movement of groups of people effectively to accomplish new goals, the nature of leadership necessarily involves social influence.

   - An ability to establish strong collaborative relationships
   - Integrity and the ability to create a climate of trust
   - High practical intelligence (more is better, to a point)
   - Strong motivation to lead other people
   - Self-confidence and a sense of independence
   - Capacity for vision
   - Ability to articulate a vision and influence others
   - Adaptive flexibility
   - Extraversion and outgoingness
   - High energy, capacity to work a lot
   - Emotional maturity, emotional intelligence (ability to notice and manage emotions and reactions)

   There are numerous other qualities that have been the focus of research attention including stress tolerance, optimism, listening skills, resilience, empowerment and respect for others, strategic thinking, and skills in various aspects of leadership such as the ability to negotiate, to delegate, to run effective meetings, and to work cocktail parties. It is important to be able to take effective risk and to take responsibility for the outcomes of decisions made. Good leaders are not control freaks and they do not snap at other people or intentionally intimidate them. Coaches can use this list and other lists in the literature as a tool to evaluate clients, give constructive feedback, and craft a short- and long-term plan for leadership development.

2. Leader–situation "fit" is key. Since there is no universal set of leader qualities that will be optimal in all settings, one must carefully assess

the leadership demands of the specific organizational context and match them. This probably means that all organizations or positions are not suitable for all leaders. Organizations and leaders must take care to make winning matches. Coaches can potentially help organizations with leader selection. The popular literature is filled with tales of woe, situations where an organization hired a charismatic leader with a disastrous outcome, the result of a poor fit. Organizations should be extremely careful in hiring a previously successful executive from a business sector or organizational context different from their own.

3. Not everyone is well-suited for leadership. There are a few core characteristics required of leaders, and everyone does not possess them. There is a certain kind of motivation to lead other people that is relatively rare but essential. Not everyone is all that interested in being in front, providing the vision, the energy, and taking the risks involved in good leadership. Few have the required energy. Many people do not wish to have others depend upon them relentlessly, and few are eager to work most or all of the time. Not everyone enjoys the task of spending hours at social events with a work agenda in mind. Followers do not always communicate authentically with leaders, and they are careful with what they say. Not everyone wishes to put himself or herself in the position where it is difficult to get the "unvarnished" truth from people on a regular basis.

Steven Sample's observation from *The Contrarian's Guide to Leadership* (2002, p. 190) is instructive here: "Many people want to *be* leader, but few want to *do* leader; if you're not in the latter group you should stay away from the leader business altogether."

Although leaders are highly valued, as they should be, organizations should also value those who choose not to lead in a formal or informal way. Good leaders require good followers, and plenty of them.

Bennis (2007) recently summarized his decades of interest in leadership by proposing six essential competencies. They are written in the form of universal leader tasks:

    a. Create a sense of mission.
    b. Motivate others to join you.
    c. Create an adaptive social architecture.
    d. Generate trust and optimism.
    e. Develop other leaders.
    f. Get results.

The list is a challenging one, indeed.

Finally, as Bennis points out, the question of leadership—who leads whom in what direction and in what ways—is crucial (2004a,

p. 331): "It is important to remember that the quality of our lives is dependent on the quality of our leadership. Only when we understand leaders will we be able to control them."

References

Associated Press. (2008). Army coach Stan Brock fired. *Washington Post*. Retrieved December 21, 2008, from: http://www.washingtonpost.com/wp-dyn/content/article/2008/12/12/AR2008121201414.html?tid=informbox.

Ayman, R. (2004). Situational and contingency approaches to leadership. In J. Antonakis, A. T. Cianciolo, & R. J. Sternberg (Eds.), *The nature of leadership* (pp. 148–170). Thousand Oaks, CA: Sage.

Babiak, P., & Hare, R. (2006). *Snakes in suits: When psychopaths go to work*. New York: HarperCollins.

Bennis, W. (2004a). The crucibles of authentic leadership. In J. Antonakis, A. T. Cianciolo, & R. J. Sternberg (Eds.), *The nature of leadership* (pp. 331–342). Thousand Oaks, CA: Sage.

Bennis, W. (2004b). The seven ages of the leader. *Harvard Business Review, 82*(1), 46–53.

Bennis, W. (2007). The challenges of leadership in the modern world. *American Psychologist, 62*(1), 2–5.

Bennis, W., & Nanus, B. (1985). *Leaders: The strategies for taking charge*. New York: Harper.

Blake, R. R., & Mouton, J. S. (1964). *The managerial grid*. Houston, TX: Gulf.

Blanton, J. S. (2009, January/February). Women and authentic leadership. *The California Psychologist*, 6–10.

Brown, D. J., Scott, K. A., & Lewis, H. (2004). Information processing and leadership. In J. Antonakis, A. T. Cianciolo, & R. J. Sternberg (Eds.), *The nature of leadership* (pp. 125–147). Thousand Oaks, CA: Sage.

Burns, J. M. (1978). *Leadership*. NY: Harper & Row.

Carlyle, T. (2007). *On heroes, hero-worship and the heroic in history*. Teddington, UK: Echo Library.

Chemers, M. M. (1997). *An integrative theory of leadership*. Mahwah, NJ: Lawrence Erlbaum Associates.

Ciulla, J. B. (2004). Ethics and leadership effectiveness. In J. Antonakis, A. T. Cianciolo, & R. J. Sternberg (Eds.), *The nature of leadership* (pp. 302–327). Thousand Oaks, CA: Sage.

Conger, J. A. (1992). Leaders: Born or bred? In M. Syrett & C. Hogg (Eds.), *Frontiers of leadership* (pp. 361–369). UK: Blackwell.

Cox, C. J., & Cooper, C. L. (1988). *High flyers: An anatomy of managerial success*. Oxford, UK: Blackwell.

Deming, W. E. (1986). *Out of the crisis*. Cambridge, MA: MIT Press.

Dixon, N. F. (1992). Leaders of men. In M. Syrett & C. Hogg (Eds.), *Frontiers of leadership* (pp. 51–58). Oxford, UK: Blackwell.

Dotlich, D. L., & Cairo, P. C. (2003). *Why CEOs fail*. San Francisco: Jossey-Bass.

Fiedler, F. E. (1967). *A theory of leadership effectiveness*. New York: McGraw-Hill.

George, W. (2003). *Authentic leadership: Rediscovering the secrets to creating lasting value*. San Francisco: Jossey-Bass.

George, W., Gergen, D., & Sims, P. (2007). *True north: Discover your authentic leadership*. San Francisco: Jossey-Bass.

George, W., Sims, P., McLean, A. N., & Mayer, D. (2007) Discovering your authentic leadership. *Harvard Business Review, 85*(2), 129–138.

Goffee, R., & Jones, G. (2005). Managing authenticity: The paradox of great leadership. *Harvard Business Review, 83*(12), 87–94.

Goldsmith, M., & Reiter, M. (2007). *What got you here won't get you there.* New York: Hyperion.

Hersey, P., Blanchard, K., & Johnson, D. (2008). *Management of organizational behavior: Leading human resources* (9th ed.). Upper Saddle River, NJ: Pearson Education.

House, R. J. (1971). A path-goal theory of leadership. *Administrative Science Quarterly, 16,* 321–338.

House, R. J. (1977). A 1976 theory of charismatic leadership. In J. G. Hunt & L. L. Larson (Eds.), *Leadership: The cutting edge* (pp. 189–207). Carbondale, IL: Southern Illinois University Press.

House, R. J., & Shamir, B. (1993). Toward the integration of transformational, charismatic, and visionary theories. In M. M. Chemers & R. Ayman (Eds.), *Leadership theory and research* (pp. 81–107). New York: Academic Press.

Jacobs, T. O., & Jaques, E. (1990). Military executive leadership. In K. E. Clark & M. B. Clark (Eds.), *Measures of leadership* (pp. 281–295). West Orange, NJ: Leadership Library of America.

Jacobsen, C., & House, R. (1999). *The rise and decline of charismatic leadership.* Retrieved January 25, 2009, from the Wharton Center for Leadership and Change Management Web site: http://leadership.wharton.upenn.edu/l_change/publications/house.shtml.

Judge, T. A., Bono, J. E., Ilies, R., & Gerhardt, M. W. (2002). Personality and leadership: A qualitative and quantitative review. *Journal of Applied Psychology, 87*(4), 765–780.

Kerr, S., & Jermier, J. M. (1978). Substitutes for leadership: Their meaning and measurement. *Organizational Behavior and Human Performance, 22,* 275–403.

Kotter, J. (1999). *John P. Kotter on what leaders really do.* Cambridge, MA: Harvard Business Review Book.

Kroek, K. G., Lowe, K. B., & Brown, K. W. (2004). The assessment of leadership. In J. Antonakis, A.T. Cianciolo, & R. J. Sternberg (Eds.), *The nature of leadership* (pp. 71–98). Thousand Oaks, CA: Sage.

Leslie, J. B., & Van Velsor, E. (1996). *A look at derailment today: North America and Europe* (Stock no. 169). Greensboro, NC: Center for Creative Leadership.

Lewin, K., Lippitt, R., & White, R. K. (1939). Patterns of aggressive behavior in experimentally created social climates. *Journal of Social Psychology, 10,* 271–301.

Lombardo, M. M., & Eichinger, R. W. (1989). *Preventing derailment: What to do before it's too late* (Stock no. 138). Greensboro, NC: Center for Creative Leadership.

Maccoby, M. (2000, January–February). Narcissistic leaders. The incredible pros, the inevitable cons. *Harvard Business Review,* 69–77.

McGregor, D. (1960) *The human side of enterprise.* New York: McGraw-Hill.

Ouchi, W. G. (1981). *Theory Z: How American business can meet the Japanese challenge.* New York: Addison-Wesley.

Phillips, D. T. (1998). *Martin Luther King, Jr. on leadership.* New York: Warner Books.

Podsakoff, P. M., Niehoff, B. P., MacKenzie, S. B., & Williams, M. L. (1993). Do substitutes for leadership really substitute for leadership? An empirical examination of Kerr and Jermier's situational leadership model. *Organizational Behavior and Human Decision Processes, 54,* 1–44.

Rooke, D., & Torbert, W. R. (2005, April). Transformations of leadership. *Harvard Business Review, 83*(4), 67–76.

Sample, S. (2002). *The contrarian's guide to leadership.* San Francisco: Jossey-Bass.

Spreier, S. W., Fontaine, M. H., & Malloy, R. L. (2006, June). Leadership run amok: The destructive potential of overachievers. *Harvard Business Review,* 71–82.

Sternberg, R. J. (2007). A systems model of leadership. *American Psychologist, 62*(1), 34–42.

Stogdill, R. M. (1948). Personal factors associated with leadership: A survey of the literature. *Journal of Psychology, 25,* 35–71.

Stogdill, R. M. (1974). *Handbook of leadership: A survey of the literature.* New York: Free Press.

Syrett, M., & Hogg, C. (Eds.). (1992). *Frontiers of leadership.* Oxford, UK: Blackwell.

Turner, R. A. (2007, September/October). Leadership success: Does personality matter? *The California Psychologist,* 10–14.

University of the Pacific. (2009, March 3). *Leadership development at the Pacific.* Retrieved June 13, 2009, from: http://web.pacific.edu/Documents/provost/acrobat/Leadership%20definition%20final%203%203%202009%20_2_.pdf.

Upton, J. (2007). West Point keeps coach's pay secret. *USA Today.* Retrieved December 21, 2008, from: http://www.usatoday.com/sports/college/football/2007-12-05-army-pay_N.htm.

Vroom, V. H., & Jago, A. G. (1988). *The new leadership: Managing participation in organizations.* Englewood Cliffs, NJ: Prentice-Hall.

Vroom, V. H., & Jago, A. G. (2007). The role of situation in leadership. *American Psychologist, 62*(1), 17–24.

Vroom, V. H., & Yetton, P. W. (1973). *Leadership and decision-making.* Pittsburgh, PA: University of Pittsburgh Press.

Weber, M. (1947). *The theory of social and economic organization* (A. M. Henderson & T. Parsons (Trans. & Eds.). New York: Free Press. (Originally work published in 1924)

Whicker, M. L. (1996). *Toxic leaders: When organizations go bad.* Westport, CT: Quorum Books.

Yukl, G. (1994). *Leadership in organizations.* Englewood Cliffs, NJ: Prentice-Hall.

Zaccaro, S. J. (2007). Trait-based perspectives of leadership. *American Psychologist, 62*(1), 6–16.

Recommended Readings

Antonakis, J., Cianciolo, A. T., & Sternberg, R. J. (2004). *The nature of leadership.* Thousand Oaks, CA: Sage.

Bjerke, B. (1999). *Business leadership and culture.* Northampton, MA: Edward Elger.

Fuqua, D. R., & Newman, J. L. (2004). Moving beyond the great leader model. *Consulting Psychology Journal: Practice and Research, 56*(3), 146–153.

Harvard Business Review on leadership. (1998). Boston: Harvard Business School Publishing.

Inside the mind of the leader [Special issue]. (2004, January). *Harvard Business Review, 82*(1).

McCauley, C., Moxley, R. S., & Van Velsor, E. (Eds.). (1998). T*he Center for Creative Leadership handbook of leadership development.* San Francisco: Jossey-Bass.

Winum, P. C. (2003). Developing leadership: What is distinctive about what psychologists can offer? *Consulting Psychology Journal: Practice and Research, 55*(1), 41–46.

16
Workers, Managers, and Leaders

Leadership is different from management, but not for the reasons most people think.

—**John P. Kotter (1990, p. 103)**

People generally do not understand the essential differences between leaders and others. Much of what they do know is wrong and problematic. Because coaches are often called upon to help line workers make the transition from follower to manager and to help managers move into leadership, it is essential that coaches clearly understand the different sets of skills and behaviors required at each level. Many executives have not thought much about the distinctions between leadership and management. The old industrial paradigm sees leadership as simply excellent management or management that is particularly popular or effective or even charismatic.

The skills and the differences between leadership and management are not generally taught in school, and people are supposed to pick them up, somehow, as they move through their career. This is impossible to accomplish without independent study, partly because of myths related to the leadership function, myths like the following:

Myth: Leaders are born, not raised.

Myth: Leadership skills develop naturally as one moves up an organization and takes on more responsibility.

Myth: You must thoroughly understand (and preferably master) the content skills of those you lead.

Myth: Before you become a leader, you must learn how to be an excellent follower.

Myth: Managers must be leaders.

Myth: What we really need is more leadership and less management.

Myth: Real leadership cannot be taught.

Myth: There is no unique set of leadership skills. It is common sense, and for the most part, consists of good personal and work habits combined with some natural charisma.

Myth: Managers and leaders do about the same thing in an organization, just at different levels (and for different compensation).

These myths create problems for organizations, as they inhibit good leadership as well as good management. It is clear that leadership skills can be learned by motivated learners. It is also clear that, as John Kotter (1990, p. 109) puts it, "the on-the-job experiences of most people actually seem to *undermine* the development of attributes needed for leadership." There is little evidence that good followers make good leaders. The required skill sets seem to be nearly independent of each other. Some great leaders have been notably poor followers (George Patton being the paradigm example). In today's business culture, there is virtually no way that leaders can possess the technical skills of those they lead. The requisite skills change too quickly. Do you suppose that Bill Gates or Steve Jobs can still write useful computer programming code? Can the CEOs of video gaming companies skillfully play the games their companies produce? Can deans of dental schools still perform complex procedures such as root canals or the new skills required to place implants? Leaders and managers perform uniquely different functions using different sets of skills, and both are crucial to organizational success.

The last myth on the list—that managing and leading are essentially the same—is the one that coaches must thoroughly debunk. Coaches are often called upon to help a bright, promising executive move from worker to manager and from manager to leader. They must be able to teach clients the important differences and help them develop leadership skills that will enable them to excel. In fact, the skills that make for a great line worker might actually get in the way of someone in the manager's role, and the skills and personality of a terrific manager can be counterproductive when that same person is thrust into the leadership role. Sometimes content skills distract a leader who should be focused on strategy and the future. Other times terrific managers can make a mess by micromanaging rather than delegating. The following section outlines some important distinctions between workers, managers, and leaders in a typical hierarchical organization. Table 16.1 summarizes these differences.

Differences among Workers, Managers, and Leaders

The Line Worker or Professional Worker

A review of the essential skills required by workers at the entry level is called for. There are extensive sets of personal habits and behaviors that ought to be in place before a competent worker shows up for work. This is not always the case, and coaches can certainly help workers identify and develop the necessary skill set. For example, most people are not born with all of the skills required of a successful salesperson, even though they might possess excellent prerequisites. Certain other skills, such as project management skills, are

Table 16.1 Differences among Workers, Managers, and Leaders

Worker/Professional	Manager	Leader
Performs basic tasks	Controls things	Creates things
Performs repetitive tasks	Keeps track of things	Changes things
Needs and uses resources	Budgets, makes ends meet	Finds resources
Develops specific-task expertise	Plans	Gets the mission defined
Finds new business	Organizes	Creates an environment
Creates product/provides service	Solves problems	Shakes things up
In contact with customers	Copes with complexity	Sets the direction and tone
Enlists new clients, customers	Staffs jobs and tasks; external locus of control; conservative and cautious	Aligns people; internal locus of control; creative risk taker
Follows rules	Rule-oriented, system-based	Imagination-based
Needs managers (and leaders)	Needs leaders (and workers)	Needs managers (and workers)
Interacts with outsiders	Interacts internally; keeps people in line with systems	Interacts with outsiders; inspires people
Responsible for own effort, production, and sales	Responsible for performance of organization	Responsible for overall outcome
Works independently	Deductive process	Inductive process
Lacks overarching viewpoint	Creates structure; risk averse	Creates mandates; risk taker
Takes direction from others	Uses authority and rules; gives direction; keeps everybody lined up	Uses influence; convinces; shows the direction
Provides feedback to organization	Monitors organizational culture	Monitors outside culture

essential because they are the fundamental basis for the organization's success. New customers and new clients must come in, and work must go out. Employees must possess energy to get things done, and they need basic communications skills, basic content skills, and basic computer skills. They must be well organized and reliable. Some jobs require extraordinarily complex skills and a strong drive to succeed. Some jobs require workers to develop a serious special expertise. Employees must be adequately loyal to the organization and its goals, even when they do not agree with current tactics. Leadership requires competent followers. They need to be willing to be told what to do, and to "follow orders" sometimes when the orders do not make sense or when they disagree with the instructions. They need a positive attitude to be able to see things in a good light and to behave pleasantly. Increasingly, workers must be able to make a good impression with customers through a service orientation and the willingness to go the extra mile to provide exceptional customer service. They also need to be able to provide feedback to the organization when something is amiss or is being done poorly. They need to be reasonably well organized and able to cope with paperwork efficiently. They have to be able to learn new tasks as demand arises. They must avoid the destructive behavioral traps of substance abuse, sexual harassment, overwhelming stress, and entangling office romance. They must be able to effectively manipulate the written word and use the latest technology. And they need to be able to get things done and see projects through to their completion. These are all basic worker skills required in the 21st century.

The Manager

> Managers seek order and control, and are almost compulsively addicted to disposing of problems even before they understand their potential significance.

> **—Abraham Zaleznik (1992, p. 131)**

Managers, as Abraham Zaleznik wrote in the *Harvard Business Review* (1998, p. 61), "ensure that an organization's day to day business gets done." Managers are about *control*. They create order out of potential chaos and translate the leadership's vision into productive reality. They tame complexity. They direct people, reinforce desired behavior, and punish that which does not conform. They are the gatekeepers and often say "no" when an idea is out of conformity with the system. They limit things and they dislike disorder. They make sure that the organization has "the right products in the right places at the right time and in the right quantity" (Sloan, 1964, p. 440). They regulate and safeguard the company's resources, and pay close attention to what is happening in the present moment. They know where everything is, and they work hard to meet established goals. They set goals that are aligned with organizational strategy as they understand it. Much of what they do and think is data based these days, and they rely on spreadsheets and the details found on them. They are highly interested in what leadership is thinking and are likely to be involved in bureaucratic politics and intrigue. They know where the bodies are buried. When something works, they keep doing it, and they can be hostile to change, for change is unpredictable and it causes them problems. They have systems in place that have worked well, and changes force them to adjust their systems.

The managerial personality is best when it is calm, rational, and analytical. Managers are tolerant but demanding. They are on the lookout for problems, for shortages, and for deviation from the system. The successful ones are diplomatic. They are sensible and reliable. They tend to be realists, and they do not like risk (nor should they). Managers are focused on *how* and *whether* things get done rather than why or even what. Tell them what needs to be done and they will find a way to get their system and people to do it.

None of this is meant to disparage managers or managing. Excellent management is essential for organizational success; it is rare and difficult to do. Recent business literature and training have given the impression that leadership is a good thing and that management a something of a bad thing (Bennis & Nanus, 1985). In this view managers are associated with bureaucracy, and that is seen as bad. Leaders save the day by cutting through red tape and creating action. Good management, however, creates systems that work, and people rarely complain about those. Nor do managers get much credit. Management is not as glamorous as leadership, that's for sure, but is exceptionally important. If you have a great idea and hard-working employees but you cannot get a product to market, you fail. If you have a great product but you cannot get it delivered on time, what is the point? If your resources are squandered through laxness, how could your organization possibly succeed? Leadership can motivate people to try harder, but a good system is required. What good is a mayor who charismatically urges good public transportation if there is no one in place who knows how to get such a complex system started and managed?

Although good management is not as rare as good leadership, it is not common. Managers organize and coordinate complex systems that are essential to our well-being. Disorganization and poor coordination drive people crazy, damaging morale and running customers off. Organizations need effective management to survive and succeed.

People hate to work for dictators, and the set of personal and functional skills required by effective managers is extremely valuable. Humane efficiency is worth its weight in gold, yet it is often taken for granted.

> Effective managers are a joy to behold and a pleasure to work with in any organization. People love to work for well-organized managers who facilitate getting the job done by coordinating the work of various people, and they hate to work for managers who are ineffective, uncoordinated, or incompetent. (Rost, 1991, p. 106)

Managers certainly exhibit leadership behaviors (such as interpersonal influence), but those behaviors are not necessarily found in their job description nor are the behaviors essential to their function. Those behaviors are often helpful but sometimes counterproductive. Although a manager might be charismatic, and his or her charisma might be helpful, it is not an essential component of effective management performance. Sometimes the charisma of a manager can get in the way, causing jealousy and resentment from above. Managers might be visionaries, but that is not an essential management quality. Although it is often best to influence subordinates, a manager influences people to conform to a system that is in place, not to change the basic arrangements. When a manager influences people to work harder or to do things in a new way, he or she is using leadership skills, but this is not a leadership function. When everyone in an organization exercises leadership, the resulting changes must still be coordinated and managed.

> Of course, leadership from many sources does not necessarily converge. To the contrary, it can easily conflict. For multiple leadership roles to work together, people's actions must be carefully coordinated ... by strong networks of informal relationships. (Kotter, 1990, p. 109)

Leaders, hopefully, have established a culture with overarching mores and formal and informal relationships for followers. Too much leadership behavior (in the wrong places) can create the very chaos that managers are paid to control.

The Leader

> Leadership is not equivalent to office-holding or high prestige or authority or decision-making. It is not helpful to identify leadership with whatever is done by people in high places.
>
> **—Joseph C. Rost (1991, p. 98)**

In addition to the information in the previous chapter, here are some observations about leadership that will help differentiate it from managing. Leaders are responsible for the overall outcome, and they determine the overall direction for the company. They create the organization's vision, and they align people and things to realize that vision. They create a process by which the social order of the organization is formed or shifted (Rost, 1991). Their focus is usually on change. They sometimes create chaos that managers then have to clear up. Leaders influence the reality and direction of an organization. Although management can coerce you, you must volunteer to be led.

Classic leader behaviors include breaking paradigms, motivating people to see things in a new way, causing others to shift priorities, and disrupting the status quo. Good leaders are not always comfortable to be around or to hear. They can disturb and frighten. They upset things; they point out faults in the way things are. They *intend real changes* (Rost, 1991). They do not always make everyone happy.

Although there may be times when minimal leadership is required, in the present modern environment, where change seems rapid and normal, leadership takes on an essential role. It is a rare organization that can survive by simply doing something well for long periods in the same ways. Other companies catch up or find a better way. Frequently, market dynamics change. Stagnant organizations get left behind in a hurry these days.

Leaders tend to be restless as a personality style. They love change and hate mundane, repetitive work. They like to use their imagination and they trust their own intuition. They enjoy being alone and like to reflect on things. They are comfortable with risk and understand its role and importance. They tend to be competitive by nature, and this translates into a desire to be "the best," to be on top of the heap. Competition gets their juices flowing. Sometimes they act without thinking things through. They do not always realize that they must follow all of the same rules as everyone else. Their work life and workplace might even be disorganized, so they hire someone to organize them.

Although it is a plus when leaders are also good managers, it is not essential. If real leaders are rare, then real leaders with good management skills are even more rare. An organization simply cannot wait around for such a person to evolve, so it hires a leader (or follows an emergent one) who lacks management skills. (A common alternative is to choose an excellent manager on the assumption that he or she will turn out to be a good leader. This works well in some cases, not so well in others.) It is then essential to hire excellent managers to complement and administer the leader's vision. In many cases, great leaders could never put their ideas into practice (or if they could, it would not be for long), and great managers could never think up the ideas that they are now managing. Leaders and managers need each other.

Leaders communicate with organizational outsiders. They present the vision and image of the organization to stockholders, funding sources, government agents, board members, industry leaders, and the public. They pay attention to the interests of those parties and bring feedback to the organization so that adjustments can be made. They manage boards. They establish life-or-death interpersonal relationships with important outsiders. Effective leaders are able to create trusting relationships that become resources in times of trouble.

Leaders do one more thing that is not typically associated with the management function: They think. They reflect, they synthesize, they develop and use their imagination. They take in information from wide-ranging sources (including newspapers, the Internet, colleagues from other companies and industries, and best-selling books). They integrate new ideas into the organization they lead. Managers have no time to think. They are paid to be on top of the details, resources, and deadlines. They do not have much time, and they are not paid to take time. Leaders, in contrast, are paid to reflect.

Please refer to Chapter 15 for a detailed review of the general literature on leadership and the conclusions that can be drawn from it.

The "Modern" View

There are alternatives to the traditional view of the hierarchical organization. Newer versions of business organizations stress a flatter, more matrixed structure, with shared responsibility for leadership throughout the organization. Each member of the company team is responsible for providing vision, motivation, and direction. Such a structure can be enormously effective in some markets and environments. But it is probably not suitable for all business situations, and it often does not survive as a company matures.

Similarly, many managers find it important to serve as leaders of those who report to them. Certainly they must motivate and find creative ways to accomplish their tasks. Nonetheless, most of the critical leader functions are still most appropriate for those in leadership positions.

The Coach's Opportunity

Leadership coaches are hired for two reasons. They are either paid to help "fix" problem people (or remediate deficits) or they are brought in to help a person make the transition from one career step to another. Sometimes they are hired for the specific purpose of helping a promising leader to emerge successfully.

Coaches thrive most when they are seen as an essential component in the developmental process of the organization's leadership. If you (as an individual) have a coach, the organization sees you as having promise and is willing to invest in your transition from worker to manager and from manager to partner or leader. The distinctions between these roles offer an important opportunity for the coach.

Most organizations are poor teachers of leadership, and few are organized to grow real leaders. Many actually punish those with real leadership inclinations. The leadership literature points out that people desiring leadership development cannot learn their skills in school or at institutes or by reading leadership books (although these activities certainly help). They need to have guided leadership experiences and they need help to learn from their own inevitable mistakes. They need to be able to grow as a result of their developmental difficulties. They require challenging assignments early in their career, and they can use extensive mentoring and time for reflection. They need good, hard-hitting feedback, delivered in a way that helps and does not hurt. A coach can be of enormous help in this ongoing process, especially when in-house mentors are not available.

The Roles That Coaches Play

In 1997, Witherspoon and White wrote a defining booklet on executive coaching at the Center for Creative Leadership (*Four Essential Ways That Coaching Can Help Executives*). They describe the following four essential roles that coaches can play. These roles should be contemplated and discussed with clients early in the coaching relationship.

Coaching for Skills

Witherspoon and White (1997) recommend skills coaching when workers (and occasionally managers or leaders) need quick help to learn an important skill. This process can start from the basis of a self-perceived deficit or as the result of an assessment. Examples of such skills include public speaking, listening, personal organization and time management, presentation of self (appearance or behavior), teaching how to cold-call, and even providing an in-depth understanding of the product or service that the organization offers. Sometimes a professional becomes aware that he or she is not "coming across" effectively. Coaches can perform an assessment, present the results, collaborate in the creation of a learning plan, and help the client put his or her learning into effect. This aspect of coaching tends to be brief and circumscribed. When the executive learns the skill, the coaching is finished.

Coaching for Effect

Coaching for effect focuses on the executive's current job and his or her performance in it. Such coaching is appropriate for managers who face difficult obstacles. Clients often do not know what is wrong or lacking, but they have reason to believe that they need to improve what they do. This form of coaching is more comprehensive, and it, too, begins with an assessment, but this assessment is likely to seek input from a wide range of sources. A 360-degree evaluation is often useful. It tends to be intermediate in time span, lasting over several months or as long as a year. It has specific goals, and the goals are organizational in nature. For example, the coach and client will know that they are successful when specified organizational outputs improve. Coaching might focus on analytical skills or tasks, problem-solving measures, team building, organizational architecture, or operations management problems. Such a coach must possess expertise in the arena of focus or at least be able to locate someone with task-specific skills for consultation.

Coaching for Development

Coaching for development is appropriate for workers, managers, and leaders alike. It strives to prepare a person to move to the next level. It involves an analysis of the essential skills required for the future, an evaluation of skills in place, and a comparison of the two. The coach and client work together to develop those necessary skills and the experiences required to gain them. As Witherspoon and White (1997) point out, it may even involve the unlearning of a behavior that was once useful but will be a liability in the future. The goals may be less clear and more personal in nature, and they might even involve an examination of where the client wants to go with a nascent career. It might call for a clear-eyed look at client goals to determine whether they are realistic and attainable.

Coaching for the Executive's Agenda

Coaching for the executive's agenda is most closely related to the leader function. A coach can be used by a leader to help that leader develop and to help him or her evolve the organization. This role is likely to be ongoing, with ambiguous and ambitious goals. The coach may be available regularly or on an as-needed basis. He or she may help the leader to think things through, to reflect, to make decisions, and to provide support when problems get difficult or the process gets lonely. The coach can act as a sounding board and reality test. For a detailed explanation how to do this, along with a discussion of expectable challenges, see Nadler's (2005) essay in the *Harvard Business Review*.

Summary

1. Management and leadership are different, and the relationship between the two is widely misunderstood. Coaches can bring useful clarity to an organization, even in modern "flat" organizations.

2. Coaches can help clients move from one level to another. It is nearly impossible to learn adequate management and leadership skills without mentoring and challenging growth experiences. You cannot learn to ride a bicycle without getting on and falling off a few times. Most organizations do not provide effective mentoring from within. Mistakes will be made, and coaches can serve as important mentors and teachers in this process.

3. Coaches must help clients accurately determine the appropriate purpose for coaching and then apply the right interventions. Significantly different interventions are useful in different circumstances. Coaching for leadership is different from coaching for management or coaching for sales skills. One coach cannot possibly fit all of these situations.

4. The role of coach as developmental mentor is important (to the coach), for it removes him or her from the negative role of remediator of "losers" or people the organization will eventually shed. Coaching can be a resource for "fast-track" people.

5. Most organizations do not breed leaders. Coaches can help them create a leadership development culture.

6. Not everyone is suited to be a leader, and many people are not willing to do the things that leaders do. Excellent managers should think twice before taking a leadership position (even if the money is attractive).

References

Bennis, W. G., & Nanus, B. (1985). *Leaders: The strategy for taking charge*. New York: Harper & Row.

Kotter, J. P. (1990, May–June). What leaders really do. *Harvard Business Review, 68*(3), 103–111.

Nadler, D. A. (2005, September). Confessions of a trusted advisor. *Harvard Business Review, 83*(9), 68–77.

Rost, J. C. (1991). Leadership and management. In G. R. Hickman (Ed.), *Leading organizations* (pp. 97–114). Thousand Oaks, CA: Sage.

Sloan, A. P. (1964). *My years with General Motors.* New York: Doubleday.

Witherspoon, R., & White, R. (1997). *Four essential ways that coaching can help executives.* Greensboro, NC: Center for Creative Leadership.

Zaleznik, A. (1992, March–April). Managers and leaders: Are they different? *Harvard Business Review,* 126–135.

Zaleznik, A. (1998). Managers and leaders: Are they different? In *Harvard Business Review on leadership* (pp. 61–88). Boston: Harvard Business School Publishing.

Recommended Readings

Bennis, W. G. (1977, March–April). Where have all the leaders gone? *Technological Review,* 3–12.

Bennis, W. G. (1989). *On becoming a leader.* Reading, MA: Addison-Wesley.

Bennis, W. G. (1989). *Why leaders can't lead.* San Francisco, CA: Jossey-Bass.

Goffee, R., & Jones, G. (2006). *Why should anyone be led by you?* Cambridge, MA: Harvard Business School Press.

Goleman, D. (1998, November–December). What makes a leader? *Harvard Business Review,* 93–102.

Harvard Business Review on leadership. (1998). Boston: Harvard Business School Publishing.

Mintzberg, H. (1990, March–April). The manager's job: Folklore and fact. *Harvard Business Review,* 163–176.

Phillips, D. T. (1998). *Martin Luther King, Jr. on leadership.* New York: Warner Books.

Syrett, M., & Hogg, C. (Eds.). (1992). *Frontiers of leadership, an essential reader.* Oxford, UK: Blackwell.

Weinstein, B. (2000, August 27). What a techie gives up to be a manager. *San Francisco Examiner and Chronicle,* p. CL 23.

17
Ethics in Coaching

The search for excellence, whatever it may be, begins with ethics.

—Robert Solomon (1997, p. xiii)

Clinicians are used to formal ethics codes and standards. Each subspecialty within psychology has a written code, and members of professional organizations are generally well aware of them. Therapists take required ethics courses in graduate school, and clinicians take mandatory continuing education in various ethical and legal topics as they evolve. Psychotherapists of various types are members of long-standing, established professions and these professions have rules, traditions, organizations, mores, and a culture. The American Psychological Association has been publishing ethical codes and standards since 1953. In psychotherapy, there is even a complex "standard of care," the unwritten normative behaviors expected of members of the professional community. Practitioners are held to those standards.

This is not so true in management consulting or executive coaching. Executive coaching is too new for long-standing, well-defined group norms or formal professional structures, so coaches must monitor themselves. Ethical standards are in the process of development, and most coach-training institutes have now developed and published formal codes of ethics. Some of these codes are listed at the end of this chapter. There is a great unevenness in these codes, and although some of them are exemplary, no single document prevails. The Code of Ethics published by the International Coach Federation (2009), a non-profit support and resource organization for coaches, is a solid, representative model of the kinds of codes that are available, and it mirrors much of the advice rendered by typical psychotherapy codes. The reader is also referred to Rodney Lowman's text *The Ethical Practice of Psychology in Organizations* (1998), a casebook that demonstrates how the American Psychological Association's Code of Conduct can be applied in business settings.

To a great extent, individual coaches are on their own to make difficult moral decisions, especially if they are not members of an organization that demands conformity to a pledge or code. There is no formal licensure process required of business coaches, and although clinical codes and standards are available as a reference point, they do not suffice. This chapter outlines areas where clinical and coaching ethics are similar or the same, along with several difficult areas where they differ. References and published guidelines are provided at the end of the chapter. As the practice of executive coaching continues to evolve, so will the need to clarify and codify ethical standards. For now, coaches must use thoughtful individual judgment and healthy doses of collegial consultation. In general, honesty and avoidance of exploitation are probably the best general guidelines for coaching practice. When unclear about an ethical issue or problem, a consultation with a mentor or trusted colleague is highly recommended.

Professionalism

Executive coaching is popular enough and mature enough to begin to ask the question: Is executive coaching a profession? If not, is it moving in that direction, should it move in that direction, and if so, how?

The concept of *professionalism* is an important one even though there is no widespread agreement on its definition. Practitioners in many fields strive to become professionals, but it is not exactly clear what this means. Older practitioners sometimes urge younger ones to "be professional" when they would like them to conform to norms or traditions, and this occasionally represents an unfortunate trivialization of an important ideal. If the concept of professionalism is to be of value, a set of consensus standards is required. The field of bioethics has produced some such standards that are worthy of scrutiny (Peltier, 2001). Here are components of professionalism found in the bioethics literature:

- Practitioners in a profession possess an *important* and *uncommon* expertise. They routinely do things for people that people cannot do for themselves. For example, you can color your own hair, but you cannot perform a root canal on yourself.

- Substantive and relevant *barriers to entry* exist. Such barriers typically include education, training, and certification designed to serve and protect the public. As a result, professionals often enjoy monopoly status in their area of expertise.

- Professionals are granted substantial *autonomy* in practice. They are trusted to do the right thing, to practice with excellence, and to look after the interests of clients without exploitation or incompetence. Patients or clients cannot effectively evaluate the recommendations or work of the professional. One can easily tell if they have gotten a good haircut, but they cannot evaluate a doctor's recommendation that he or she needs an urgent appendectomy. This results in a fiduciary relationship wherein clients and patients must trust their doctor or professional. Professionals effectively look after the interests of people who cannot do so for themselves. The public does not feel that members of a profession need to be micromanaged to ensure trustworthiness.

- Professionals are *formally organized* to ensure that members maintain their obligation to the public. Organized structure is typically codified in written documents. Such organizations have both a self-serving and public service orientation. Public service obligations derive from the privileges granted by the public in exchange for essential trustworthiness required by asymmetric knowledge (the professional knows so much more than the client about the matter at hand).

The recent Harvard survey of experienced coaches reported a majority opinion that executive coaching is in its "adolescence" as a profession (Kauffman & Coutu, 2009, p. 24). Many respondents felt that whereas the skills of coaches were highly developed, the profession is not. Many pointed out the problem posed by charlatans and dilettantes and the need for enhanced credentialing. This problem is associated with inadequate barriers to entry. Some training and credentialing paths into coaching are merely weekend seminars, and anyone willing to pay the tuition is welcome. Credentials are offered, but it is reasonable to doubt the credibility of such a process. As a legal and practical matter, there is no requirement that a new coach even partake of any training at all. If people want to call themselves "executive coaches" and organizations want to hire them, what's to prevent that? Who would stop Jack Welch or Steve Jobs or Carly Fiorina or Colin Powell from taking an assignment as an executive coach, even though none of them has special training or certification in coaching? Here are representative comments of coaches from the Harvard survey (Kauffman & Coutu, 2009, p. 25):

> *This is a business that needs a shakeout. More money is being made in coach education than in coaching, and the lack of entry barriers (other than marketing) is a problem.*

> *There are a lot of charlatans out there who give the profession a bad name. I expect it will become more professionalized over time.*

> *[There is a] need to standardize the profession without stifling it.*

> *The industry is maturing. We will see more coaches coming from university graduate programs as it becomes more of a recognized profession.*

It is encouraging to note the development of several rather new written instruments to codify coaching ethics, including the previously mentioned International Coach Federation's Code of Ethics. Several important coaching organizations recently produced and signed a "Statement of Shared Professional Values" in the United Kingdom (UK Coaching Round Table, 2008). This agreement lists one metaprinciple ("To continually enhance the competence and reputation of the coaching profession") and seven aspirational principles related to difficult coaching issues. The 2008 *Handbook of*

Coaching Psychology lists 10 major coaching associations or interest groups and four professional journals in its appendices (Palmer & Whybrow, 2008).

The fact that effectiveness is extremely difficult to gauge poses a second major obstacle to professionalism. It is difficult to actually describe what coaches do in concrete, measurable terms. How do coaches and others know if and when coaching is excellent or, on the other hand, worthless or harmful? If we do not know excellence, how do we agree on it or attain it in the field? Most of what we think about coaching is anecdotal, as little outcome research is currently available. Here is one more quote from the Harvard survey: "To be credible, coaching must codify its purpose, objectives, methodologies, and ethics and generate credible research that measures real impact" (Kauffman & Coutu, 2009, p. 25).

A third important professionalism question has to do with supervision. If the field is to monitor its members and conduct effective quality assurance, perhaps regular, ongoing supervision needs to become a systematic part of the executive coaching culture. Carroll (2008) explored this question in detail, noting that counseling psychology has a long-standing tradition of active, regular supervision and that this practice has produced significant benefit for clinicians and clients alike. He noted that much of the conceptual and practical spadework has been done, so that coaches could conveniently adopt those models for use in this young profession. Supervision offers so many clear benefits including the opportunity for reflection, training, development of new coaches, sharing of best practices, handling of difficult or complex cases, protection of clients, monitoring of weak coaches or those with poor judgment, enhanced referrals, and the stress relief that comes with sharing the burden with colleagues.

Scope of Practice

Scope of practice refers to limitations on the behaviors and practices of a professional in any field. It describes the areas that are within bounds or off limits, depending upon a person's license, the definition of that person's professional work area, personal training, competence, and expertise. There are two categories of scope of practice: *professional scope* defined by a profession or a license, and *personal scope* determined by a practitioner's own personal training and experience. For example, professional scope prohibits a psychologist from giving injections to a patient. Injections are within the scope of practice of physicians, but outside of the scope of practice of psychology and all psychologists, based upon the definition of their profession, the training of all psychologists, and legal limitations imposed by state boards. Some psychologists administer psychological testing and provide full psychological assessments and some do not. Such activities are within the legal scope of practice of the profession of psychology, but outside of the personal scope of practice of those psychologists lacking ample training and experience in testing and assessment themselves. In this case, individual psychologists are expected to use solid personal and professional judgment to determine whether to conduct psychological assessments.

There are at least two reasons why scope of practice is an important issue with regard to coaching and psychotherapy. First, there are areas of overlap in practice, and it is left to individual coaches to monitor themselves and manage their professional behavior. Who is to say when or whether it is appropriate, for example, for a coach to use the cognitive methods described in this book? What if their business client's career is suffering from that client's characteristically negative point of view? At what point does this constitute a mild depression or dysthymia, and does coaching then converge with psychotherapy? Should Jack Welch practice counseling or psychotherapy with executive clients? Although there are relatively clear clinical guidelines and benchmarks available to decide how to handle psychologically distressed clients, who actually makes this referral decision, and on what basis? Coaches are unlikely to be eager to refer business clients for psychotherapy when it means that they may lose a client, or when it implies that the coach thinks that their client is mentally ill, especially when that client is happy with the coaching and wants to continue. How do coaches decide whether their behavior constitutes coaching or personal/mental health counseling? Business clients or human resources personnel cannot be expected to have clear guidelines regarding this decision. The public must therefore depend on the professional ethics and personal judgment of each practicing coach. When these situations arise—as they no doubt will—coaches are strongly encouraged to get supervision or consultation or use a mentor. They must remember to keep the best interests of their client in mind; however, they define the term *client*.

Second, there are some who claim to be coaching when actually practicing psychotherapy without a license. This matter presents serious ethical challenges. Most states and countries have a system of regulation for psychotherapy, usually in the form of a state board. People desiring to practice psychotherapy or mental health counseling are required to complete a carefully prescribed course of formal studies culminating in a licensing exam. Licensees are required to then complete ongoing programs of continuing education for the rest of their careers, and the hours are monitored by the board. These boards have jurisdiction over those they license, but no authority over those not licensed. It has become virtually impossible to keep up with all of the people out there practicing life coaching and various other forms of "coaching," as there has been an explosion of interest in this kind of activity. There are now thousands of life coaches waiting in cyberspace to help people change and grow. These "coaches" have many letters after their names such as PCC, CUCG, CPCC, MCC, LMT, CEC, CPC, CLO, CLC, and NCGC (the list seems endless). They offer to help you "align your life, deal with harmful emotions, remove self-doubt, rekindle your relationships, transform your life, make more money, and achieve your greatest dreams." One Web site calls coaching "one of the fastest growing professions in the world." Coaches offer quick fixes and fast results. Training to become such a coach can also be fast, with some "institutes" offering an education program that lasts just one weekend. The situation has become mind boggling, and it is virtually impossible for the public to know what is of value, what is a harmless waste of time and money, and what is downright dangerous.

Although there have always been people standing by to help others improve their lives (for a fee), the situation causes problems for those calling themselves coaches, as they are likely to be viewed as part of this larger meshuga. There is no simple solution to this problem, as no one should necessarily stop those who want to help others (even when it is for a fee) and no one should reflexively try to stop people from seeking help from those willing to provide it. It seems incumbent upon good practitioners everywhere to ensure that they train themselves well and practice only that which they truly know how to do. Practitioners are also obligated to avoid making false or misleading public statements or advertisements as well.

Two Different Cultures

There is a cultural problem one encounters when making the transition from clinical counseling to management consulting or executive coaching. It has to do with primary value orientations in the two fields of mental health and business coaching. In business, there is a proprietary culture, one based upon a *competitive* market premise. Buyers and sellers compete for the best deal they can get. Each expects the other to compete. Buyers do not expect sellers to look out for them or for their interests. Caveat emptor prevails, and everyone knows it.

This is very different from the fiduciary culture of psychotherapy. Clinicians use an "ethic of care" to guide their work. In this model, doctors or therapists take care of patients or clients. They look after their clients' best interests. These interests are central to the arrangement, and the arrangement is *cooperative*. The clinical relationship includes essential fiduciary dynamics as a result of asymmetric information. Clients must trust therapists to look after their interests, and clients are not always in the best position to know whether this is actually being done. Therapy clients are often in a weakened or vulnerable position. Think about how competent you might be (as a client) just after your spouse has announced an intention to divorce, or when you seek counseling because your child has died, or because you find yourself seriously depressed and you cannot figure out why. If a psychiatrist prescribes a particular antidepressant medication, you are in no position to adequately evaluate that recommendation. You must decide whether to trust the doctor, and if you do, accept his or her advice.

Executive coaches must navigate between these two cultures. On the one hand, they are working in a business culture, where the profit motive rules. It would be considered unethical for a business, particularly a corporation (as a public entity), to place any value above that of delivering a healthy return to shareholders. That is the primary purpose of the corporation. Other purposes come second. This point of view is well understood by corporate officers and leaders. Coaches must understand it as well. On the other hand, executive coaches must apply some aspects of the fiduciary ethic of care to their individual clients. This balancing act can become tricky and confusing. Consider the circumstance where executives must cut costs to protect profit or to protect the survival of the company. Even though downsizing—the release of good people—is heartbreaking to the executive as well as to the person who will lose his job, it must be done. A coach must, therefore, be able to understand the point of view of the corporation and find a way to synthesize the *competitive* with the *cooperative* point of view. It can be downright inhumane to lay a person off from his or her job, but it must be done sometimes for a company to remain viable.

Areas of Similarity

There are numerous areas where clinical and coaching ethics overlap. The usual virtues of integrity, honesty, and responsibility are urged by consulting codes (Institute of Management Consultants, 2008; International Coach Federation, 2009) as well as clinical codes of ethics (American Association of Marriage and Family Therapists, 2001; American Counseling Association, 2005; American Psychological Association, 2002). Virtually all professions advocate such values. Among the paragraphs of these worthwhile normative values are three particular areas of similarity between the work of mental health professionals and the business of coaches that deserve special attention.

Similarity 1: Clear Agreements

Clear agreements between practitioners and clients are recommended, and they are required by ethics codes in both cultures. These make good sense and good practice. They do, however, require sophisticated communication skills and a solid professional self-esteem. Clients will appreciate such clarity and it is worth the effort. Clients in the business world are often used to clear agreements and written contracts, generally more so than most psychotherapists. In any case, the need for clarity at the beginning of the coaching relationship is quite real. When this seems difficult, colleagues or mentors can help. *The Complete Guide to Consulting Contracts* (Holtz, 1997) would also be helpful. Existing codes of ethics for coaches generally emphasize the need for clear agreements between coaches, clients, and sponsoring organizations. In the Harvard survey of experienced coaches, 88% reported that they establish an upfront timeframe for the coaching initiative (Kauffman & Coutu, 2009, p. 11) and most advocate clear agreements regarding progress reports.

Similarity 2: Whistle-Blowing

Both cultures, business consulting and clinical counseling, advocate whistle-blowing, particularly when colleagues behave poorly or are found to be incompetent. Both cultures recommend that someone step in and say something to a colleague or report unethical behavior to a professional organization or board, even though most practitioners are loath to actually do so when faced with this situation.

Similarity 3: Know Your Limits

Psychotherapists are taught to practice within their personal limits. They are urged to use specific counseling techniques only after adequate training and supervision. They learn which clients or patients to accept for treatment and which to refer, based upon their training, experience, and (their own) personality. No ethical psychotherapist would attempt to treat every patient who shows up for an appointment. The standard of care requires an intake interview to assess and evaluate the fit between professional and client. When the fit is suboptimal, a referral is made on behalf of the best interests of the client (and, from a longer-term, pragmatic point of view, the best interest of the clinician as well. Most seasoned psychotherapists recall the occasions when they took on a patient against their better judgment and suffered for it later). Many formal coaching codes of ethics prescribe appropriate referral when a client has needs that cannot be met by a current coach.

Business and consulting standards require that coaches decline work for which they are not qualified and that they represent their skills honestly to other people. Deceptive advertising is expressly prohibited, but business people are used to hyperbole when consultants hawk their services, and nearly everyone has been burned by a consultant who could not deliver that which had been promised. Even so, it may be difficult for coaches to accurately assess the limits of their own expertise. If you have never worked with a certain kind of client or have never worked in a particular industry, how are you to know if you have the expertise in advance? Do you err on the side of a conservative presentation of your skills or do you take a risk, present a confident front, and hope that you build your parachute on the way down, and figuring things out when you get on site? Since coaching is relatively new—both to coaches and clients—an aggressive approach seems defensible, especially since the mental health of a person in a fragile state is not typically at stake as is often the case in clinical psychology. A more aggressive, experimental tack is certainly more acceptable when the coach has a mentor or support group in the wings.

Areas That Are Unclear

There are many more areas of executive coaching where the ethics of clinical practice can be instructive but inadequate. Psychotherapists are likely to be naive about these business areas and without deliberate preparation could wade into an ethical minefield. As a result, they could end up harming clients or client organizations. Here are some of the minefields.

Who Is the Client?

Whom the client is is a practical as well as philosophical issue. It is similar, in some ways, to the problem that occurs in clinical practice when third-party payers (such as health insurance companies) become involved in treatment. Loyalties become stretched and twisted. When a company hires a coach to work with an individual executive, who is the client? Is it the sponsoring company, who hires and pays the coach to help with a business need? Or is it the individual executive, who is seeking to grow and move forward in his or her career? This question is easily answered when the executive personally pays the coach's fee. But, what about when the company pays the bill, as is more typical? In a 1999 doctoral dissertation, Macmillan posed this question to business consultants and found widespread uncertainty and disagreement. To whom does the coach owe loyalty? What happens when a client's interests or intended behavior are at odds with those of the company? For example, what if a client wants to focus on developing skills that the company clearly does not need, or skills that the client would like to use in her next job or as an entrepreneur? What happens when a client is angry and contemplating legal action against the company, or is plotting his next move to a new company? How does a coach work with such a client? These are difficult questions indeed. Along with the obvious challenges related to loyalties, confidentiality or discretion can also become tricky.

Clear contractual arrangements spelled out in advance are one antidote, especially when such problems can be anticipated at the onset. However, specific difficulties in these areas are often unforeseeable. A second guideline is to favor openness. Direct discussions between coaches and clients about such problems—at the beginning and continuously as they arise—can help enormously.

For example, a coach can raise the issue: "Jane, I'm concerned that what you and I are talking about may not be aligned with the company's goals. What you want to work on with me doesn't seem to be in the firm's best interest, yet it is the company that is funding our work together. What's your thinking about this? Does it seem fair to you? What should we do?"

Such a discussion might cause the focus of coaching to change. It might necessitate a discussion with the person in the company who authorized the coaching in order to seek "permission" to wander a bit. Results from the Harvard survey of coaches revealed that 132 of the 140 coaches found that the focus of coaching shifted frequently. Fifty-eight of the coaches reported that they eventually worked on "deeper goals" with clients (Kauffman & Coutu, 2009, p. 8). Some organizations would have no problem with coaching that serves to enhance the skills of a valued executive even when there is only a small chance that the effects will be immediately applicable to current business needs (although other organizations might). Some companies will figure that by providing coaching to a smart, effective executive, they will create goodwill and cement a long-term positive relationship—or smooth over a bad relationship prior to a parting of the ways.

There is also a chance that a discussion with your client about shifting goals might precipitate termination of the coaching. It is certainly difficult to justify a coaching process that is contrary to the best interests of the organization that is paying for the coaching. Coaches in that position should make a reasonable adjustment when this happens. Change the focus, rethink the content and purpose, and move in the direction of integrity. Ask the question: "How would I feel if I had to honestly describe what we are doing to the client's boss or to a group of senior managers?" If the answer to that question is uncomfortable, reconsider and realign. Occasional forays into tangential territory seem inevitable and acceptable, but when the focus is wrong, the work is wrong, especially when this is a secret.

Confidentiality

> Confidentiality has to be at the absolute highest level, and you (the coach) really only get one shot at that. If at any point I tell you something and somehow it leaks out and I find out, we're done … absolutely done … you don't get a second chance.
>
> **—Executive coaching client (Stevens, 2005, p. 280)**

There is another important ethical component of executive coaching that is unclear: To what extent is the relationship between coach and client confidential? In clinical practice, both the *fact* of the counseling relationship (contact confidentiality), and the *content* of the relationship are confidential, and the rules are clear. Psychotherapists do not even reveal the names of their clients. In clinical work there are a few rare exceptions (e.g., child and elder abuse, danger to third parties), and these can be discussed with clients ahead of time. But what about the coaching relationship? Many people in the company are aware that coaching is happening and with whom, but the rules for content confidentiality are essentially up for grabs. Coaches often tell clients that they will treat communication confidentially, but such a promise is not always realistic. The Harvard survey of experienced executive coaches reported that 70% of coaches kept the executive's manager informed of progress and 55% communicated with human resources personnel about their work (Kauffman & Coutu, 2009, p. 3). Coaches and clients must somehow define and establish working arrangements as they go along, and clients vary with regard to their interest in privacy. Some (naively) do not seem to care. Others are positively paranoid about it. Even when clear arrangements are struck at the onset, difficulties can arise. What do you do about information that you (the coach) wish the "boss" (of your client) or the sponsoring organization could have? What if the entire company culture could benefit from impressions or information you got from your individual client?

There is a second difficult aspect of confidentiality in executive coaching. To what extent does the coach owe the organization a confidential relationship? Coaches come across important information about the company, not just about the client. For example, how should coaches handle proprietary secrets and insider stock information? What about a merger in the wings? What about illegal activities proposed by your client or borderline activities by the company? Information or rumors about sexual harassment or problematic office romances? This is a swamp, and the coach must be thoughtful and careful. Adequate guidelines, specific to executive coaching, are not really available, and even where they do exist, individual coach maturity is essential.

There are two preliminary (and admittedly inadequate) answers to these confidentiality questions. The first is the "cure-all": direct, frank, explicit discussions at the onset of coaching. It is the coach's responsibility to bring up confidentiality and to do so in a way that does not unnecessarily alarm. Clients might not initiate such a discussion, because they do not want to give the impression that they have something to hide or that they are too private or not open enough. Others have not given the matter any thought, but would have concerns if they did. Many cannot anticipate the difficulties lurking around the corner, whereas a good coach certainly should. The most difficult ethical problems are often those that cannot be fully anticipated at the onset.

Therefore, a frank discussion about the demand for confidentiality (if demand exists or should exist) must be initiated by the coach, complete with examples. This discussion can start with the prospective client and include essential others, such as seniors, colleagues, and human resources personnel who might later inquire about progress. One way to head off problems is to offer regular progress reports to the organization, done collaboratively by the coach and client. The format can be devised at the beginning and based upon established goals. That way, if someone asks about coaching, the answer can be, "We'll have a written progress report for you in a couple of weeks." Face-to-face meetings with third parties should include your client whenever feasible.

It is often a good idea to encourage clients to be open about the fact that they are getting coached. Coaching can be framed as a positive—something that healthy, realistic, ambitious people do from time to time—and it is a compliment that the company is willing to fund it. There is a clear trend in the coaching world in this direction, as many see the fact that someone has a coach as a plus.

In reality, most people are happy to cooperate with the confidentiality arrangements that coaches and clients establish. They are generally aware that much is at stake, and few desire to do anything that might "gum up the works." Most others in the organization realize that they, too, have a vested interest in the positive development of the client.

The second "cure" for this problem requires that groups of coaches work together to establish consensus norms. These can be hammered out in professional meetings or through discussions in journals, but, in any case, written guidelines are sorely needed. Coaches with experience should continue to make their thinking about this matter public, and written codes for coaches now emphasize the importance of confidentiality as well as clear agreements between coaches, clients, and sponsors of coaching. The International Coach Federation (2009) describes practices for careful management of coaching records in its code. Principle number four of the UK Coaching Round Table "Statement of Shared Professional Values" (2008, p. 3) states:

> Every coach has a professional responsibility (beyond the terms of the contract with the client) to apply high standards in their service provision and behaviour. He/she needs to be open and frank about methods and techniques used in the coaching process, maintain only appropriate records and to respect the confidentiality a) of the work with their clients and b) of their representative body's member information.

Coach-training institutes should regularly upgrade their ethics codes. As the field or profession of coaching evolves and matures, codification of group norms regarding confidentiality will become clearer and more useful to practitioners.

Consent

In clinical practice, nothing is done without clear client consent. In business coaching, clients may participate in coaching without a clear consenting agreement, especially when told that they need coaching to advance their career, to make partner, or to simply survive with the company. What executive would decline such an "opportunity"? It is likely that clients sometimes participate in coaching with mixed motives and ambivalence, yet they are generally unwilling to reveal these motives to coaches. This is akin to mandated therapy when clients are referred to a clinician by a court or government body. The consent is not really voluntary in the strictest sense of the word, but it has to suffice.

Current coaching codes now mention the requirement for informed consent, and the International Coach Federation code (2009), for example, states that "I will carefully explain ... prior to or at the initial meeting ... the nature of coaching, the nature and limits of confidentiality, financial agreements, and any other terms of the coaching agreement or contract."

Coaches must remain alert for this mixed-motive scenario and confront it appropriately from the point of view of the client (rather than from the perspective of the company). Help clients figure out what to do. Such a discussion depends upon the level of trust established in the coaching relationship. Even without trust, a coach can offer a well-crafted statement to alert a client and open the "bidding." For example: "You know, sometimes it seems like you are not completely engaged in the coaching. I think about it a lot and wonder if you don't have some mixed feelings." One could add, "If I were in your position, I might have mixed feelings, too, given the current situation."

It may also be useful to develop a written consent form, appropriate to the corporate culture. This form could be used as a format for discussion of the important issues at the onset of the coaching relationship.

Boundaries

Since about 1980, the standard of practice in psychotherapy has moved toward increasingly rigid professional boundaries. This change evolved because a small number of therapists damaged clients by blurring or ignoring appropriate boundaries. Other professions such as dentistry and law have recently formalized prohibitions about romantic or sexual interaction with patients and clients. Psychotherapists since about 2000 have taken a more sophisticated and variegated point of view as clinicians realized that some dual relationships produce more good than harm, whereas others are unavoidable. That said, mental health clinicians generally avoid mixing therapeutic relationships with social or other kinds of additional relationships. In therapeutic settings, prudent practitioners generally avoid all other kinds of contact. You do not have dinner with clients, you do not play golf with them, you do not sell things to them or buy things from them, you do not ask them for stock tips, and you do not go to cocktail parties or receptions with them. There are legitimate theoretical and practical reasons for this policy. The therapeutic relationship and the process, as well as clients themselves, are often hurt when boundaries are crossed. The exemplary International Coach Federation code (2009) states the following (p. 3):

(17) I will be responsible for setting clear, appropriate, and culturally sensitive boundaries that govern any physical contact I may have with my clients or sponsors; and

(18) I will not become sexually intimate with any of my current clients or sponsors.

Nonetheless, things are different in business consulting and executive coaching. Consultants and coaches are *expected* to attend business or social events with clients and their companies. To miss these events would seem odd to businesspeople, and would isolate a coach from the company's culture and from other opportunities to observe the client in action. When a group of executives invites a coach to an event sponsored by the company, that coach needs to think twice about declining the offer. A no-show might be seen as unsupportive of the organization or unenthusiastic about the work. Plus, you might miss out on an excellent opportunity to assess your client in an important working situation. In other words, executive coaches must, after careful consideration, attend social events with clients and other important *players* in the organization. There are valid coaching and business reasons to do so.

This different set of expectations does not, however, indemnify the coach or client from some of the difficulties that can arise in such "dual-relationship" situations. They simply must be managed with sound judgment and a commitment to avoid any role exploitation. A coach must also learn to think on his or her feet when difficult or uncomfortable situations arise, as they surely will. Again, when things get weird, stall for time and get a consultation from someone you trust.

A preemptory discussion about these matters is generally a good idea. Psychotherapists bring a special expertise to this situation, as they have usually given more thought to the pitfalls of mixing one's settings. They have seen, firsthand, how problems of dual relationships can evolve, and many therapists have engaged in frank and open discussions with clients about them. They have learned about the potential for misunderstanding, resentment, and embarrassment. Most businesspeople do not have this experience and have no idea that problems can occur. Although consultants are generally welcome at corporate outings, it is certainly possible that a client may wish that his or her coach stay away. Check with your client. Ask for his or her preference, discuss what it means, and honor it.

It must be noted that executive clients are not as vulnerable as psychotherapy clients. They are not in the same position with respect to the coach as a patient is to a therapist, and hopefully not hurting or overwhelmed or depressed or paranoid. Their self-esteem is usually (but not always) intact and high. When tricky social events occur, they are in a better position to interpret things in a healthy way or to let something roll off their back or to even ignore a small embarrassment. Therapy patients are often uncomfortable when confronted with their therapist in settings outside of the consulting room, whereas executives are unlikely to feel the same way.

Beware, however, of letting your guard completely down. Remember—as businesspeople learn to do—that a social outing with the company is still work. It is not purely a social event, even if people act like it is, and mistakes can be made that can ruin a perfectly good business relationship. Consider the following example: You join your client at a golf outing. You are not a good golfer, although you enjoy the game from time to time. You and your client play a friendly match, and he sets up a wager with the other team. On the last hole, you play terribly, and you and your client lose a substantial amount of money. Conversely, imagine the same scenario in reverse. You are an excellent golfer, and your client plays poorly, causing your team to lose the wager. These events complicate your relationship. They might damage it, or they might deepen it or even create a learning experience.

Other Areas in Question

There are numerous other areas where psychotherapy guidelines might help, but do not neatly apply. Coaches must sort out the following areas in the future.

Record Keeping

What kind of records should executive coaches keep, and how should they be managed and protected? Certainly, notes can be important and useful to the coach, especially when a coach works with multiple clients simultaneously, or when an ex-client calls for additional coaching after a few years away. It is probably a good idea to apply the basic rules that therapists use for record keeping, although there is certainly no mandate for process notes, as there is in the practice of psychotherapy. Accurate financial records are essential, and assessment data, goals, and notes about observations should be maintained and safeguarded. Periodic reports will have to be rendered to sponsors. It is hoped that the need for notes and records will be driven by a coach's interest in his or her client, rather than a perceived need to protect oneself from criticism or future harm, as is sometimes the case in the healthcare arena. The usual questions of whether such information is subject to subpoena will have to be sorted out by the lawyers. Coaches who come from the world of psychotherapy know that they must be extremely careful when writing something in records that would embarrass them or their clients. Some coaching codes now recommend maintenance of records in ways that protect confidentiality and comply with local laws.

Termination of the Coaching Relationship

What is the best way to wrap things up when goals have not been met or when corporate money runs out? The Harvard survey indicated that the vast majority of coaching projects last from 2 to 18 months (Kauffman & Coutu, 2009, p. 10). Often companies are not willing to finance coaching that goes on and on without timely and demonstrable results. What do you do when progress stalls or is nonexistent? What happens when a coach or a client is reassigned or relocated? Sometimes nearly random events cause premature termination. Does a coach have any obligation to continue the coaching relationship after a client leaves the company? Is there ever an obligation to continue coaching at a reduced fee (if the client is struggling and must personally assume payment)? Certainly, a clear discussion of how and when coaching will end is appropriate material for initial discussions in the relationship.

Conflicts of Interest

Coaching codes discuss possible conflicts that psychotherapists encounter only occasionally. Some are related to the problem of client identification (who is the real client) and loyalty, and some do not. The International Coach Federation's 2009 code states the following (2009):

> (9) I will seek to avoid conflicts of interest and potential conflicts of interest and openly disclose any such conflicts. I will offer to remove myself when such a conflict arises.

> (10) I will disclose to my client and his or her sponsor all anticipated compensation from third parties that I may pay or receive for referrals of that client.

> (11) I will only barter for services, goods or other non-monetary remuneration when it will not impair the coaching relationship.

> (12) I will not knowingly take any personal, professional, or monetary advantage or benefit of the coach–client relationship, except by a form of compensation as agreed in the agreement or contract.

Assessment

What level of psychological testing skills must a coach possess before using instruments with coaching clients? Are the rules the same as for psychologists or master's-level counselors? There are hundreds of proprietary assessment instruments to be found on the Internet. At the same time, there are really no legal constraints because coaches typically use instruments that do not require the user to hold a clinical license. Some providers of testing tools may ask if the purchaser has a bachelor's or master's degree, but even that is unlikely. The general rule for clinicians is helpful here. Use an instrument only under the following circumstances:

1. The instrument has been shown to be valid, reliable, and appropriate for the purpose intended. Coaches must be wary, as there are many unvalidated instruments available to business consultants, and testing companies are only too willing to recommend them. Business clients are typically naive about issues of test validity and reliability, and they are often willing to accept whatever feedback they are given by a consultant.

2. The coach/user possesses adequate skills and experience (including supervision, when appropriate) to administer and interpret the specific instrument.

3. The testee is properly informed about the instrument ahead of time, and the results are provided in language that he or she comprehends. Results are tailored specifically for each client.

4. Norms are appropriate for the client being tested. This means that if your client's responses are to be compared to norms, the people in those norm groups are known and reasonably similar to that client. For example, if you are using a formal instrument to test a woman, were women included in the norm group when percentiles were established? Are you comparing a woman's scores to the scores of men? Under the circumstances, does that make a difference in how you would interpret the results?

Duty to Protect or Warn

Do coaches face the same obligations as clinicians when clients become a danger to self or others? Is there a duty to safeguard an executive from harm to himself or a duty to warn others to prevent danger? Some executive clients can become quite depressed when major downturns occur in their industry or personal career. Executives who are caught cheating can become humiliated and extremely irrational. Are there other duties in business coaching that clinicians cannot anticipate? Is it fair to hold coaches to the same legal standards to which clinicians are held, given that coaches often are not privy to the same depth of interpersonal information that therapists possess about their patients? None of the currently available coaching codes appear to address these questions in a specific or helpful way.

The guidelines used by clinicians in this area can be extremely useful in the very rare circumstance when a client is psychologically troubled. Such clients are lucky to be in the hands of a coach who has clinical training and experience. Generally accepted principles for clients who are a danger to self or others ought to be applied. Examples of workers who have exploded or assaulted someone after being terminated or slighted cannot be ignored. Sometimes business organizations specifically hire business coaches to help with difficult employees or disgruntled managers, and coaches must evaluate such clients for impulse control, emotional range, substance abuse, perception, and attribution.

Pro Bono Services

Shouldn't coaches, who command higher fees than clinicians, have an obligation to give back to the community? What community? Should coaches provide some services to nonprofit organizations at a reduced fee? Should they give back to the profession from whence they came?

Many ethical aspects of executive coaching are not clear, and the ethical principles and methods used by clinicians might be extremely useful, if not universally applicable. Significant areas for thoughtful discussion exist, and as coaching continues to become more widely accepted, professional standards must continue to be developed and disseminated. As professional coaching organizations evolve, it will become increasingly important that they revise and expand explicit standards and guidelines to express aspirations and to limit problem behavior or damage. These standards will enhance the prospect of long-term success and survival for coaches and the field of coaching. Current codes of ethics for coaching represent a good start, but they must be enhanced. In the meantime, coaches should use good judgment, consult with a trusted colleague or mentor, and take care.

Summary

1. Executive coaching is in a nascent stage of professionalism. Enhanced professional organization and structure are needed. This includes more serious credentialing processes, standardization of training, strengthened professional groups, enhanced written codes of conduct, and supervision. Charlatans currently threaten the credibility of the field.

2. Coaches and clinicians live in different ethical cultures, and this requires modest but significant adaptations by clinicians.

3. Codes, standards, and guidelines now exist for executive coaches, but they are in early stages of development and are relatively vague. Coaches must adapt existing standards as they go, applying some as-is and adjusting others to fit.

4. Clear initial agreements between coaches, clients, and the sponsoring organization are essential, and such agreements help to avoid many ethical problems.

5. Coach–client confidentiality, although not absolute, must be respected, discussed, and managed.

6. Boundary expectations are quite different in the corporate world, as executives often expect consultants to join them on company outings and social events. Coaching clients are typically less vulnerable than counseling clients.

7. Psychotherapists possess useful skills when it comes to record keeping and record management. Although clinical standards are more extensive and restrictive than might be necessary in the coaching world, it would be a good idea to keep them in mind when managing coaching notes and records.

8. Most of the assessment instruments used by coaches are less complex than those used by psychologists, but the same practical requirements apply. Coaches should only use instruments that they understand to be appropriate, valid, and reliable. There are many questionable questionnaires out there in the world of business consulting.

9. Psychotherapists possess sophisticated and useful skills for the rare occasion when an executive becomes a danger to self or to others. These skills should be applied in much the same way as they are in a clinical situation. Be careful about the potential embarrassment and weigh it against the potential danger.

References

American Association of Marriage and Family Therapists. (2001). *AAMFT Code of ethics*. Washington, DC: Author. Retrieved January 9, 2009, from: http://www.aamft.org/resources/lrm_plan/ethics/ethicscode2001.asp.

American Counseling Association. (2005). *Code of ethics and standards of practice*. Alexandria, VA: Author. Available online at: http://www.counseling.org/.

American Psychological Association. (2002). *Ethical principles of psychologists and code of conduct*. Washington, DC: Author. Retrieved January 9, 2009, from: http://www.apa.org/ethics/code2002.pdf.

Carroll, M. (2008). Coaching psychology supervision: Luxury or necessity? In S. Palmer & A. Whybrow (Eds.), *Handbook of coaching psychology* (pp. 431–448). London: Routledge.

Holtz, H. (1997). *The complete guide to consulting contracts* (2nd ed.). Chicago: Dearborn Financial Books.

Institute of Management Consultants. (2008). *Code of ethics*. New York: Author. Available online at: www.imc.org.au/.

International Coach Federation (2009). *Code of ethics*. Retrieved June 13, 2009, from: http://www.coachfederation.org/about-icf/ethics-&-regulation/icf-code-of-ethics/.

Kauffman, C., & Coutu, D. (2009). *HBR research report: The realities of executive coaching*. Available online at coachingreport.hbr.org

Lowman, R. (Ed.). (1998). *The ethical practice of psychology in organizations*. Washington, DC: American Psychological Association.

Macmillan, C. (1999). *The role of the organizational consultant: A model for clinicians*. Unpublished doctoral dissertation, Massachusetts School of Professional Psychology, Boston.

Palmer, S., & Whybrow, A. (Eds.). (2008). *Handbook of coaching psychology*. London: Routledge.

Peltier, B. (2001). The ethical responsibility of professional autonomy. *Journal of the California Dental Association, 29*(7), 522–525.

Solomon, R. (1997). *It's good business: Ethics and free enterprise for the new millennium*. Lanham, MD: Rowman & Littlefield.

Stevens, J. H. (2005). Executive coaching from the executive's perspective. *Consulting Psychology Journal: Practice and Research, 57*(4), 274–285.

UK Coaching Round Table. (2008, February). *Major breakthrough—UK coaching bodies roundtable produce the first UK agreed statement of shared professional values*. Retrieved January 17, 2009, from: http://www.associationforcoaching.com/news/M80221.pdf.

Recommended Readings

Bersoff, D. (Ed.). (1999). *Ethical conflicts in psychology*. Washington, DC: American Psychological Association.

Brotman, L., Liberi, W., & Wasylyshyn, K. (1998). Executive coaching: The need for standards of competence. *Consulting Psychology Journal: Practice and Research, 50*(1), 40–46.

Corey, G., Corey, M., & Callahan, P. (2006). *Issues and ethics in the helping professions* (7th ed.). Pacific Grove, CA: Brooks/Cole.

Devine, G. (1996). *Responses to 101 questions on business ethics*. Mahwah, NJ: Paulist Press.

Gorlin, R. (1999). *Codes of professional responsibility: Ethics standards in business, health, and law* (4th ed). Washington, DC: BNA Books (Bureau of National Affairs).

Keith-Spiegel, P., & Koocher, G. (2008). *Ethics in psychology and the mental health professions: Professional standards and cases* (3rd ed.). New York: Oxford University Press.

Messick, D., & Tenbrunsel, A. (1997) *Codes of conduct: Behavioral research into business ethics*. New York: Russell Sage Foundation.

Nagy, T. (2000). *Ethics in plain English: An illustrative casebook for psychologists*. Washington, DC: American Psychological Association.

Nash, D. (1994). A tension between two cultures … dentistry as a profession and dentistry as proprietary. *Journal of Dental Education, 58*(4), 301–306.

Peltier, B., & Dugoni, A. (1994). A four-part model to energize ethical conversation. *Journal of the California Dental Association, 22*(10), 23–26.

Rest, J., & Narvaez, D. (Eds.). (1994). *Moral development in the professions: Psychology and applied ethics*. Hillsdale, NJ: Erlbaum.

Snoeyenbos, M., Humber, J., & Almeder, R. (Eds.). (1992). *Business ethics: Corporate values and society*. New York: Prometheus Books.

Solomon, R. (1993). *Ethics and excellence: Cooperation and integrity in business*. New York: Oxford University Press.

18
Making the Transition

When you come to a fork in the road, take it.

—Yogi Berra (1998, p. 48)

In the 8 years since publication of the first edition of this book, it has become clear that coaching is here to stay. Several powerful trends support this statement. The workplace continues to change at an accelerating pace. It is a fast-moving, independent, creative, and more demanding place than ever. Job security, at every level, has disappeared, and the economy is uncertain at best. Diversity is finally coming of age. Women continue to crack and break through glass and pink constraints. Customers are more demanding. International markets are open, and the Internet is connecting us all. The world economy has gone through frightening changes, and effective, honest leadership is more important than ever. Executives and managers who want to make it in this economy will need every possible advantage. What remains to be seen in the current cycle is how executive coaching will fare when businesses and other organizations tighten their belts.

It has become clear that mental health practitioners have much to offer the business community, and it is time for some to make a transition from therapist to executive coach. You may want to stick a toe in the water first. Just because a new market has potential does not mean there is a good fit. Coaching might not suit you, because the business world is different from the psychotherapy world. There are some lovely aspects about working as a psychotherapist, and you just might miss them. Psychotherapists help people who are struggling and in pain. They heal wounds. They help people grow in the most important ways. They fill in gaps left by inadequate parents. They occasionally dissuade someone who is seriously suicidal. There are the smaller perks, too. Therapists have significant professional autonomy. They can call most of their own shots, choose their own hours, and wear comfortable clothes that express who they really are. They can occasionally provide their services gratis or at a low fee to someone who really needs it and is appreciative. They can use their work as a platform for their own personal development. Many careers tend to unbalance life. A career as a psychotherapist has the opposite effect. It presents an opportunity to think seriously and continuously about health, what it is, how to find it, and how to keep it.

One could certainly do some executive coaching on the side or on a part-time basis without making a total commitment to life in the consulting world. This might involve some measure of dissociation on your part, but it is a viable option. The consulting world includes two kinds of coaches: One is an employee or independent contractor for a large consulting firm. The firm finds and sells work and controls the action of the coach, while paying that coach some percentage of the total fees. The other kind of coach is the individual consultant, referred to by the large firms as the "boutique" operator. This person must find and sell his or her own work, and as a result, can keep all of the profits. They get to take all of the associated risk as well. Coaching fees tend to be substantial relative to those paid to psychotherapists, and there is no managed care broker or bothersome paperwork to contend (although the consulting world has its own forms of onerous paperwork to be sure).

The fact that many therapy skills are transferable to executive coaching should not encourage you to jump in willy-nilly or to take the dilettante's path. You can spot articles in the newspaper from time to time highlighting a therapist who has gleefully transformed her psychotherapy practice into a "coaching practice." Instead of struggling along with depressed, low-fee patients, she now does executive coaching from the comfort of her home, over the telephone! No more difficult people, no more managed care, no office hours. One such recent success story showed a photo of an ex-therapist doing phone coaching in Bermuda shorts and expensive sunglasses from the hull of her sailboat. She is gazing off over the water for inspiration and speaking to a client whom she has never met in person. One brochure depicts a coach sitting on a sandy beach, breeze blowing through his hair, telecoaching in the sun. One flyer calls coaching "The hottest market niche for the new millennium." Much of this kind of coaching is actually personal counseling framed as "life coaching," outside of the business world with clients who are mentally healthy but looking to get an edge or make a change. Such personal success coaching is a fine activity, but it is not executive coaching, and it is potentially damaging to the corporate coach's reputation (and focus) to mix them up.

Various types of coaching have evolved over the past decade, and some coaching activities are a cause for concern, especially when clients could be placed in harm's way. Coaching gets a bad name and business/executive coaches are hurt when life coaches, personal coaches, transformational coaches, and success coaches advertise and conduct themselves in ways that trivialize the real challenges people face. The ethical issues associated with this very real problem were addressed in Chapter 17 "Ethics in Coaching." Life coaching seems fine (when it is not psychotherapy without a license or training), especially if it is done effectively. But the risk associated with untrained, well-meaning people who somehow think that they have a special talent that enables them to fix others is real and significant. If you do plan to take a serious look at business or executive coaching there are transitions to be made.

Transition A: The Business Culture and the Profit Motive

Executive coaching requires considerable involvement in the business and corporate world. There are several areas that require attention and adjustment.

Money

The most important difference between the therapy world and corporate culture is fundamental, and it has to do with money. Simply stated, *the purpose of a corporation is to return value to stakeholders and stockholders.* That is typically accomplished by making a profit. In business school, students are taught that this is an *ethical* issue. Officers of a publicly held corporation must make decisions that are aligned with the interests of investors. To confuse the profit motive with other tasks or motives is to do a disservice to shareholders who are counting on you to use their money well. To place other functions ahead of profit is unethical. That is how important the bottom line is to a publicly held corporation. Small businesses are not held to this profit-oriented standard, but the motivation is still powerful. You have to pay your rent and your employees. You must make a profit or stop doing business, properly labeling what you do as a "hobby." The Internal Revenue Service (IRS) insists on this. If you do not make a profit after a certain period of time you cannot deduct expenses against revenues, because the government would then be underwriting your hobby. Small-business owners, in many ways, are even more serious about the importance of the bottom line. If they do not make money, they go out of business. Such risk tends to focus one's attention. The bottom-line profit orientation in the business world runs deep, it is powerful, and no one makes apologies for it.

In the therapy world, money is seen as a by-product of having provided a useful service and for caring. The health care service is central and the money is a happy bit of a "necessary evil." Few revel in it, and few therapists don't know how much money they make. It is not part of the culture. Therapists are uncomfortable with greed. Most would love to make more money, but they do not speak directly about this. Most psychotherapists probably chose their profession because of a desire to help people, to make a positive difference, or because they were fascinated with the theories and ideas. Money was secondary.

Businesspeople (always, but especially after about 1990) have no such pretensions about the role of money. It is the way to keep score. The money you take home tells you (and others) how you are doing. It is a clear and simple standard, and few apologize. That is just the way it is, and most think it is a pretty good way. Of course many businesspeople are doing work that is intended to improve the world, but the money is still how they keep score. Read Ayn Rand for the overarching perspective. Read the *Wall Street Journal* (called *The Journal* by business folks) to get the day-to-day point of view. Any psychotherapist making a transition into consulting must grasp this difference concerning money and accommodate it in some healthy, effective, realistic way.

Speed

The business world tends to move more quickly than the world of psychotherapy. "Getting directly from point A to point B" prevails over a therapist's "peeling the onion" metaphor. Although psychotherapists value contemplation and reflection, the business world insists on results—soon. Businesspeople tend to be action-oriented; they trust activity, often at the expense of reflection. They avoid the "paralysis of analysis." Psychotherapists work with abstractions; they reflect. Therapy constructs are difficult to quantify and measure, and that is OK. Businesspeople are taught to be goal oriented and to measure progress continuously. They like benchmarks and "metrics." They must present bottom-line results on a quarterly basis, and improvement is expected. As a result, they move as fast as they can. Thoughtfulness sometimes gets lost in the shuffle. There's no time.

Executive coaches must be able to swim in these waters. You do not have to agree with this point of view, but do not disparage it if you want to work in the business culture. Find a way to live with it. Find a way to let it energize you, too, without compromising the values you cherish. Indeed, coaches often represent a mandate for reflective activity. Reflection is powerful. There just is not enough of it in the day-to-day work world.

Transition B: Presentation of Self

Marketing consists of all activities by which a company adapts itself to its environment—creatively and profitably.

—Ray Corey (Kotler, 1997, p. 1)

You cannot go into business organizations and act, look, or speak like a psychotherapist. Therapists have patients, and businesspeople are reluctant to take on the qualities associated with the role of "patient." The two main areas of difference are appearance and speech.

Appearance and Culture

First, you must dress and behave like a businessperson to some reasonable extent. Initial impressions are powerful (remember social psychology), and you will make a poor impression if you dress like a stereotypical "bohemian" therapist. If you are serious about coaching and think that you need help in this area, get a clothing coach. It is entirely possible that you do not have good judgment about how to dress yourself. Perhaps you do not really care, as you do not value clothing and physical appearance much. However, if you understand that clothing is a mode of self-expression, take care to express business savvy in the business arena. If you view clothing as a tool, sharpen and focus it. You do not have to try to look like a banker, and there is ample room for self-expression, but your appearance must convey a sense of seriousness and substance, and, to some extent, conformity. Outliers frighten businesspeople. Happily, corporate dress codes are changing, and many firms are dumping ties and high heels. Find out how they dress at the places you want to consult and match them, especially when you intend to physically enter the workplace to coach or to "shadow" your client on-site. Businesspeople tend to respect those who know how to "dress sharp." Be cautious about dressing in sexually expressive ways, and keep your tattoos and piercings to yourself unless the organization values them.

Speech and Language

Second, you must change your vocabulary. Psychotherapy, like all professions, has its own jargon. This vocabulary is not obvious to nonpsychotherapists, as it seems normal, but its use can become a distinct "turnoff" in the business environment. Businesses and specific industries also have their own way of speaking, and you must learn that language. You do not need to speak it yourself (and attempts to do so can come across as phony), but you must be comfortable with the vocabulary of the industry. For example, if you consult or coach in a dental office, you need to learn what they mean by terms like *perio* or *restorative*, and you need to call patient files *charts*, and know the difference between hygienists and assistants. No one will expect you to know these things immediately, but you must learn quickly. Do not fake it, and be willing to ask lots of questions at first. Then do your homework.

Table 18.1 contains examples of generic business language changes to consider. For example, instead of saying "You have issues around performance under stress," you might say, "One of the challenges you face is how to take advantage of unanticipated opportunities." This business-speak can get a little ridiculous, and it typically involves positive sounding action words such as *solution-oriented*. But to an important extent, it is the coin of the realm. People do not take this kind of language completely seriously, but there is a game to be played here, and as an outsider you have to pay attention to the game. Be wary of jargon, though. Instead of saying, "I get a sense that you are feeling anxious," you might consider, "You seem nervous about this." Or "You look nervous. What was your reaction? What's your thinking?" You may want to consider the word *upset* when emotions are involved. Rather than inquiring about anger or hurt feelings or shame, as you might in a therapy setting, mention to clients that they seem "upset." At any rate, develop your own coaching vocabulary to bridge these two very different cultures.

Many psychotherapists have developed unfortunate vocal tics and tonal habits that will undermine their impact in the business world. These manners of speech

Table 18.1 Language Differences between Therapy and Coaching

Therapy Language to Avoid	Business Language to Learn
Issue ("What are your issues?")	Challenge, solution ("What challenges are you facing?"; "What solutions are required?")
Why ("Why is this happening?")	How ("How does it happen?")
Sessions (with clients)	Meetings
Way I work, way of working	Method or methodology
Sense ("I get a sense that …")	Idea ("Here's my idea"; "Here's what I think.")
Feeling ("What are you feeling?")	Reaction ("What is your reaction?")
Around ("I have feelings around this issue.")	About ("I am concerned about this.")
Tasks ("What do we need to do?")	Results and deliverables ("What are the deliverables?")

do not matter much in the therapy world, but they stand out in the corporate world. For example, if you use the word *like* more than once in each paragraph (or sentence) you will be perceived as "young" or not "so bright." If you tend to use "rising intonations" (raising the tone of your voice toward the end of sentences) even though you are not asking a question, you will confuse listeners. They will wonder if you are certain about your assertions or if you really know what you are talking about. Linguistic uncertainty makes sense in the world of science and psychotherapy (where we are never completely sure about anything), but it can sink you in the business world. Listen to yourself. Record yourself and listen to the audio. Enlist others to help you enhance your speaking skills and style.

Transition C: Marketing and Sales

Marketing's job is to convert societal needs into profitable opportunities.

—Philip Kotler (1997, p. 1)

You must learn to market and sell your services. Most people do not understand the difference between these two essential tasks. Marketing is not the same as advertising, and many psychotherapists hate the idea that they must sell something. They do not see themselves as able to do it, either. Marketing is an umbrella function, and it includes advertising and sales. But it involves much more, and it can be very interesting.

Marketing is so basic that is cannot be considered a separate function. It is the whole business seen from … the customer's point of view. (Peter Drucker, as quoted in Kotler, 1997, p. 1)

Marketing means that you must figure out what consumers need or want and what they are willing to buy, and then match those things with a product or service that you are willing and able to provide. It involves assessment of potential clients and an accurate understanding of what you can offer that might fit client needs. It includes an assessment of what the market lacks. This may sound simple, but it is not easy, for there are many out there trying to do the same thing, and they have already met a lot of known consumer need.

The evolution of customer demand requires constant adaptation. Executive coaching is an example of how mental health providers can fit evolving business needs, and most of the heavy lifting has already been done for you. The coaching market has already been developed. Corporations are now well aware of executive coaching and of their need for coaching, but coaches need to figure out how to make themselves useful and attractive in a down market. At the same time, employers do not want to lose their best and brightest and they do not intend to squander money on training and development. They know how much it costs to hire and train a good executive, and they do not like it when employees leave, taking their knowledge with them along with some negative feelings. They are generally aware of the havoc and damage a poor or inappropriate leader can wreak. They also know that they cannot simply promote an excellent analyst or software engineer and expect him or her to make a quick and easy transition to manager or partner.

There is work to be done in marketing, however. First you must figure out just what it is that you have to offer. Then add to it or adjust it to meet the needs of prospective customers. That might involve research about what customers want. It might involve serious introspection and self-assessment. It might even allow for creative development of new services that you could offer to clients (still close enough to your core competencies), once you have made them aware of a need that you can fill. You may want to offer new "products" or new ways to provide coaching. Or you may decide to offer coaching to a subset of potential clients that others have not considered (e.g., dentists or attorneys or accountants or printers or hardware store owners or hotel managers or family businesses). It really helps to enter a niche that you know or a content area where you have some experience.

The Core Competency

At the same time you must decide to focus on one or two core competencies. This is a central concept, as it defines what you do and keeps you pointed in the proper direction. A *core competency* (sometimes called a distinctive competency) is defined as the single thing that you do the best, and it distinguishes you from others. It is what you are all about, and it includes your unique strengths and qualities. It is your specialty, that which you have organized your efforts around for a long period of time. It is what you know best and do best. It includes your natural talents, your skills, and your resources, and it is difficult for others to imitate. Every successful business has one, whether acknowledged or not. (If they do not have one, they probably will not survive without some other significant advantage, such as a unique location or reputation.) Leverage that distinctive competency; do not spread your energy all over the place and become mediocre. Do not try to do everything or to be all things to all people, even though this impulse can be tempting. Focus on your core competency and become exceptional at it. This creates an interesting tension between evolving needs of the marketplace and the solid constancy of your core skills (the market might not be interested in what you would like to offer). Pay attention to this conflict. Trends come and go. The big idea is to create a *sustainable competitive advantage.*

Marketing traditionally includes the "Four Ps." Together they form the basis for comprehensive marketing planning. They are *product, place, price,* and *promotion.*

Product   Decide what it is that you want to offer. This can include a "product mix" of several services including tangible products such as books, DVDs, workshops, or Web materials.

It is especially important to be able to describe what you do in a clear and concise way. You must be able to define coaching, and you should choose a definition that is results-oriented. This is not an easy task, for the service that coaches provide is intangible by nature. Here are some thoughts to help you construct your definition. First, consider the *tasks* a coach can accomplish. A coach can enhance a client's:

- Listening skills
- Interpersonal skills
- Delegating
- Behavior in meetings, and ability to run meetings
- Public speaking
- Ability to give feedback
- Understanding of company politics
- Self-understanding
- Presentation of self
- Strategic thinking

Coaches must be able to also talk about what they offer in terms of client company *outcomes.* For example, coaching can:

- Enhance an executive's performance
- Help increase market share
- Enhance the company's image or reputation
- Increase customer satisfaction
- Decrease complaints
- Improve productivity
- Increase efficiency

- Retain high-performing executives
- Develop leaders

The main idea is that coaching must be explained to potential clients in terms of *what's in it for them.* What will be different (better) after you have done your coaching? Where's the benefit? Such outcomes need to be expressed in practical terms (increased profitability or employee retention) whenever feasible. Organizations are not likely to spend money to make employees feel better or happier.

Place   Figure out where you will operate and how customers and clients will find you. For example, decide whether you will operate as a consultant to a larger consulting firm, as an independent operator, or as an in-house consultant to the company whose employees you will coach. Create an effective Web site. Decide how much you are willing to travel. Business consultants sometimes travel extensively. Determine whether you are willing to live in a hotel room for days or weeks at a time when necessary.

Price   Determine how you will price your services. Consult with others in your geographic area and in your target industry. Consider a wide range of pricing alternatives including a daily rate, an annual rate, acceptance of stock options or other benefits instead of cash, and strongly consider value-based fees. A value-based approach sets a fee (one total number) based upon the total worth in specific and general outcomes to the client. Read Weiss (1998) for a detailed explanation of this approach to pricing. Be careful about locking yourself into an hourly fee. It can become too restrictive after you have established your reputation and value in the marketplace. Project pricing is the model most often used these days in management consulting, and businesses are quite used to paying consultants on this basis. One more thing about price: If you have something of value to organizations or corporations, do not be shy about your fees. Remember to factor in all of the costs involved in placing yourself in front of clients.

Promotion   Decide how you are going to inform and educate potential clients about your services and their value. You cannot expect clients to find you, and although self-promotion is anathema to many psychotherapists, it is an essential aspect of successful consulting. Think this one through. Find a way to understand the key idea: You have a valuable and important service— something that can make a very positive impact for the right client. (If you do not believe this, rethink what you are doing and why you are doing it. This has to be true—as a baseline requirement. If you do not think that you have something valuable to offer, develop or change what you offer or get out of the business.)

You have to connect with a potential new client. Promotion does not mean bragging or hustling people. It means that you match your services with client needs in a win–win paradigm. There really are many clients out there in the world who would benefit from excellent coaching. Remember that you have much to offer the business and corporate world. And do not limit your target to mainstream businesses. There are many businesses and organizations that can dearly use your services, including dental offices, physician practices, law offices, nonprofits, and family businesses. There are books available to help with this process, and some are listed in the "References" section of this chapter.

If you have decided to give coaching a shot, here's what you have to accomplish:

1. *Figure out what the market wants and needs*—You could do this by reading, taking coaching training, or interviewing businesspeople. The goal is to figure out where opportunities exist and how to assess the existing barriers. What forces or factors exist in the market environment that will make penetration difficult? Where is the opportunity greatest?

2. *Figure out what you have to offer*—Decide if you are willing to adapt or learn new skills to fit the need. Take a clear look at your strengths and weaknesses relative to the opportunities in the market. Some companies or businesses are likely to be more accessible than others, given your contacts and skill set. Match your skills and resources to the existing opportunities and barriers.

3. *Differentiate your services from psychotherapy and from the services of your competitors*—Decide about your distinctive competencies, the things that you are really good at. Be able to succinctly explain how you are different and what kind of situations you are best suited to handle. When you are not the optimal coach for a particular client or industry, be ready to recommend someone else. Take a service orientation, and help customers solve their problems, even when you are not going to get the current piece of work. Most businesspeople are wary of consultants who are trying to hustle business. Direct your efforts toward their success. They will remember your help and be more likely to come back when they need your skill or to recommend you to someone else in the future.

4. *Make your presence known*—Let companies know about the services you offer. Organizations need consultants. Consultants help them solve problems they do not know how to solve. Consultants save them money. Consultants provide expertise that the company does not have and does not want to develop. You can do it less expensively and more efficiently for them than they can do it for themselves.

5. *Constantly assess the value of your service*—Adjust as you go along. Work hard to match what you offer to what clients need. Help them discern their needs, as well. They probably have significant and unrecognized needs. Help them understand these needs and the fact that paying you to help will, in the long run, save them money and make them better. It must be a value proposition for them if it is to be sustainable for you. One way to do this is to develop and implement data-based outcome evaluations of everything you do. Produce and retain information that documents your impact and success. Your clients and future clients will be impressed and able to defend your practice to those who pay the bills. If you are not sure how to do this, hire someone who can help. Think about paying them on a contingency basis as a variable cost, then pass that cost on to your client.

6. *Spend time with businesspeople*—Do not spend most of your professional time with other psychotherapists. As Weiss (1998) notes, that is like trying to sell stamps to the post office. Skip meetings of therapist organizations, and start to attend meetings of management consultant organizations. Better yet, attend meetings of businesspeople. Seek out chambers of commerce or rotary clubs or human resource trainings. Let people know what you do, and let them help you structure your service. Rotary clubs are always looking for speakers at their lunch meetings, and businesspeople are well aware that one of the reasons for these organizations is to connect businesspeople to one another.

7. *Find a mentor*—Establish a relationship with someone who knows what you do not. Nourish the relationship and pay attention. (Be prepared to pay for this help.) A mentor can make all the difference.

What You Have to Offer

Although connections and reputation are the two main ways that you will get work as a business consultant, if you do not already have those, you must start somewhere. In the *Harvard Business Review* survey (Kauffman & Coutu, 2009, p. 20) experienced executive coaches recommended that organizations should look for the following (in rank order) when thinking about hiring a coach (percentages represent the number of coaches, out of 140 responding, who endorsed the criterion):

1. Coach has experience in a similar setting (65%)
2. Coach can articulate a clear methodology (61%)
3. Quality of the coach's client list (50%)
4. Coach has experience as a coachee (36%)
5. Coach has a background in organizational development (35%)
6. Ability to measure return on investment (32%)

7. Certification in a proven coaching method (29%)
8. Experience working in a similar setting (27%)
9. Status as a thought leader in the field (25%)
10. Experience as a psychologist or therapist (13%)

Wasylyshyn (2003) came to similar conclusions from a survey of 87 executives who used the following criteria for choosing a coach:

1. Graduate-level training in psychology (82%)
2. Experience in business/general management (78%)
3. Coaching experience and positive reputation (25%)
4. Experience in client's industry/knowledge of company culture (15%)
5. Trust in judgment of person who recommended coach (12%)

Happily, they seem to value training in psychology!

The top three personal characteristics mentioned by the executives in Wasylyshyn's study were ability to form a strong connection with the executive, professionalism, and use of a clear coaching methodology.

Consider the sources of your own *authority and expertise*. What is your authority as an executive coach? (Note from the aforementioned surveys that your wonderful, hard-earned experience as a psychotherapist is not highly regarded.) Why should someone take a chance on you? There is much more than money at stake for most coaching clients. They (or their organization) need serious help, and they need it to help quickly and effectively. Clients need help to be able to succeed in a new job, they need it to keep their present job, or they need it to keep an organization afloat. People depend on them to succeed. Ask yourself why they should listen to you. Why should they put themselves and their organizations in your hands?

Only 13% of the experienced coaches in the Harvard survey reported that previous experience as a psychotherapist was an important calling card, whereas more than half pointed to a coach's experience on the job as key. What should a novice coach do to break into the field? This is an important question for someone lacking experience as an executive coach. Here are some possible sources of your attractiveness:

Possibility 1: You have a track record—Maybe you have demonstrated effectiveness under the same or similar circumstances. You may even be able to produce letters of support or recommendation from a small number of former coaching or organizational clients. This is the most effective kind of authority in the marketplace. Some prospective clients will demand it. Consider offering services to local community organizations at no cost and let the director know that you would like a letter of support later if your services are helpful.

Possibility 2: You have experienced the same circumstances as your client—You have worked in the corporate world and served as a vice president of marketing or human resources or finance. You have been there and you understand what it takes to succeed. Or perhaps you ran a small clinic or a university counseling center or a drinking driver program. Maybe you served as an officer in a professional organization. Perhaps you managed a budget and a staff. Consolidate these experiences and describe them in a way that emphasizes the business components of your experience base.

Possibility 3: You have taken (or given) a lot of training in business coaching—It is increasingly easy to find training in coaching. Take some of your mandatory continuing education credits in this area. Read extensively in appropriate areas, and make sure to read the things that potential clients are reading. Do not limit your reading to coaching books. The *Harvard Business Review* is a must-read source for executive coaches. It is an expensive journal, but you can find copies at the library and some articles online.

Possibility 4: You have written about the subject—Maybe you have conducted a study in the field of coaching. Perhaps the newspaper printed an article you wrote. Write a regular column for the business section of a local newspaper or Internet site. You might be surprised to know that most editors are eager to find new writers to fill their pages. Perhaps you have your own newsletter about business coaching and related topics.

Possibility 5: You have a Web site that highlights your accomplishments and presents information and news about coaching—There are already many of these on the Internet from which to learn.

Possibility 6: You have years of experience as an effective psychotherapist— This one is actually quite valuable, especially if you are the kind of therapist who can readily translate previous work into business coaching, but it is a hard one to sell to many corporations. They typically are not interested in sending their execs to therapy, so you have to package your experience in a practical and attractive way. What are the core components of your therapy experience that can be packaged as attractive to industry? For example, if you have been a psychotherapist you probably have exceptional listening skills.

Possibility 7: You are smart, shrewd, and know how to develop quick rapport to influence people—This is a very important set of skills, but it is hard to convince people that it is true ahead of time. When you try to convince them directly, you are liable to come across as bragging or as needy. Smart people do not advertise their smarts, they demonstrate them, and other smart people notice. But those who keep their talents hidden do not fare well, either. Solid interpersonal interaction skills are often enough to keep you in the door once you get there.

Possibility 8: You are able to articulate a clear and powerful, convincing methodology for your coaching in general and for the client in question— This possibility, combined with one of the others on the list, might be enough to carry the day. Anne Scoular wrote about the importance of this task in an essay in the *Harvard Business Review* (2009, p. 31): "If a coach can't tell you what methodology he uses—what he does and what outcomes you can expect—show him the door."

Since this is such an important way to enhance your ability to gain work, it deserves much attention and some serious time. Ask other coaches about their own methodology, search out written descriptions of coaching methods, write and rehearse your own. You may notice that few are able to articulate a clear and plausible methodology, as it is distinctly challenging to do so. When someone actually does it, though, it makes a strong impression.

Assess yourself. Take a good, hard look at yourself, your strengths and weaknesses, your values and interests and figure out how hard it would be to make the transition and break into the field. There is actually a self-assessment instrument designed specifically to help accomplish this task. It was designed by Samuel Modoono (2002) of the Hay Group and can be purchased online.

Transition D: Mixing Relationships

Psychotherapists develop a special relationship with their clients, and they rarely, if ever, mix professional relationships with social ones. They do not party with clients; do not go out on clients' boats; they do not play golf with patients; and rarely even attend weddings, funerals, or graduations with clients. There are good reasons for these restrictions and, in some situations, such contact with clients is actually against the law.

But things are different in the business-coaching world. Consultants are *expected* to socialize with clients. It is an essential and important part of the culture, and serious feelings will be hurt if you routinely decline invitations. You must do some socializing with clients in the business environment. If you do not, they will think you are disinterested or weird.

This difference has two important implications. First, when socializing you have to behave in a way that engenders confidence in your judgment and ability. You are always on in these social situations. These events are work, not necessarily play or fun. Businesspeople know this and they are used to it. Second, this means that you must be especially conscious of the level and kind of confidentiality that you can offer clients. In therapy, the fact that you have a professional relationship with a client is, itself, confidential. This is called contact confidentiality. Such a duty does not exist in the business world, and it is not feasible anyway. People will know that you are a coach and they will know that Bill or Sally is working with you. Discuss this with clients at the beginning of the relationship.

Be clear about how you will handle confidences. Do not present this in a way that pathologizes the information they will discuss or makes that information sound dangerous. It is especially important that you do not make promises you cannot keep. Consider discussing confidentiality in terms of discretion. Assure them that you will be discreet (careful of preserving prudent silence). Let them know that you intend to respect their confidence and their reputation. You are in their corner and your main goal is to enhance their career. It is usually possible to frame the coaching as a positive. Only those with high potential get this service, therefore it is prestigious to be coached, not a sign of weakness. In any case, learn to adapt to this new social aspect of your work.

Transition E: Contracts and Business Arrangements

Negotiate explicit contracts that are fair to all parties. The service you provide is a valuable one, especially when it goes well. Do not underprice or undervalue your work. Skills that may seem relatively simple or second nature to you are quite valuable to many businesspeople who have never spent a day in a psychology class or a human relations seminar. If you underprice your work, you will lose respect and feel abused in the end. If you overprice it, you will feel like an imposter and be discovered and unlikely to get more work in the future.

Create contracts that are clear. Make expectations explicit for you and for your client. Agree on a policy for no-shows, as they are inevitable (and do not take them personally, unless they are chronic; even then, they are worthy of interpretation). When an opportunity pops up for a client to close a lucrative "deal" with a prized client of their own, they will certainly miss their appointment with you. Be prepared to charge them fairly if you charge by the hour. They will understand, especially if you have a contract and an agreement about this in advance.

Your contract ought to include *deliverables*, explicit ways to know if and when you have accomplished your goals. What outcomes will you deliver, and how will you know when you have done so? This will require clear thinking and conversations about those goals. Choose them carefully so that they are measurable and achievable. Make them modest at first, and build on success in stages. This is not often easy, but it is always possible. Think in terms of what will be different as a result of successful coaching. Remember this from Chapter 1: Everything can be measured.

Finally, check with your malpractice or liability carrier. Let them know that you are doing executive coaching as part of your practice. They, too, know about coaching, and may have a policy in place. It is unlikely that the change in your policy will place any demands on you. You will not be the first new coach to call them. Do not give up this insurance policy (assuming that it covers your coaching).

Conclusion: Be Exceptional

Develop a vision for yourself and your new work. Make this vision real by writing it down in a sentence or two. Massage it until it speaks for you, motivates you, and keeps you focused. Refer to it regularly. Keep it real. Turn this vision into a concise mission statement, if you wish, and if you do so, make your mission statement memorable. It must be brief and it must remind you of the most important aspects of what you are all about. You can turn to it later for focus and guidance.

Remember that all consulting is relationship-based. Nurture personal relationships in business. Put long-term relationships ahead of narrow or momentary business matters. Be gracious and generous with your words and your resources.

Go the extra mile to become excellent at what you do. Get feedback from trusted clients and friends and listen to it. Then make changes or get more training or skills. Read extensively in the management consulting area. Certainly this book alone is insufficient preparation for successful coaching, and there are several similar other books now on the market. Many are listed in the Recommended Readings sections at the end of each chapter. Find a mentor. Use him or her, and pay for their time, if necessary.

Study the leadership and management literature. Become familiar with the core readings as well as the popular books that executives read on airplanes. Learn the business of business, along with its vocabulary.

Tell the truth when you coach. A large study of senior managers in Fortune 250 companies found that the most important factor in effective coaching was "honest, straightforward communication" (Peterson, Uranowitz, & Hicks, 1997, p. 1). This may not be altogether easy, but it is extremely valuable, and people will notice it. Do not be too afraid to say the unpopular thing. Your observation skills, listening skills, and your honesty could turn out to be your *inimitable sustainable competitive advantage*. In the long run, clients will hire those they trust, and they will trust those who tell the truth. They do not need another person who buys into the organization's group think. Accomplished coach David Peterson agrees (Peterson & Millier 2005, p. 15):

My coaching is guided by two overarching principles:

1. Be the kind of coach that I would like to work with.

2. Aim to be a Great coach; do not settle for being a good coach.
   After working with hundreds of coaches from virtually every

background of training and experience, I've concluded that it is relatively easy to be a good coach.

Aim high and enjoy the ride.

References

Berra, Y. (1998). *The Yogi book: I really didn't say everything I said.* New York: Workman Publishing.

Kauffman, C., & Coutu, D. (2009). *HBR research report: The realities of executive coaching.* Available at: coachingreport.hbr.org.

Kotler, P. (1997). *Marketing management: Analysis, planning, implementation, and control.* Upper Saddle River, NJ: Prentice Hall.

Modoono, S. (2002). The executive coaching self-assessment inventory. *Consulting Psychology Journal: Practice and Research, 54*(1), 43. Available at: http://psycnet. apa.org/index.cfm?fa=buy.optionToBuy&id=2002-12515-005.

Peterson, D., Uranowitz, S., & Hicks, M. D. (1997). *Management coaching at work: Current practice in multinational and fortune 250 companies.* Minneapolis, MN: Personnel Decisions International Corporation.

Peterson, D. B., & Millier, J. (2005). The alchemy of coaching: You're good, Jennifer, but you could be really good. *Consulting Psychology Journal: Practice and Research, 57*(1), 14–40.

Scoular, P. A. (2009, January). How do you pick a coach? *Harvard Business Review, 87*(1), 96.

Wasylyshyn, K. M. (2003). Executive coaching: An outcome study. *Consulting Psychology Journal: Practice and Research, 55*(2), 94–106.

Weiss, A. (1998). *Million dollar consulting. The professional's guide to growing a practice.* New York: McGraw-Hill.

Recommended Readings

Barney, J. (1997). *Gaining and sustaining competitive advantage.* Menlo Park, CA: Addison-Wesley.

Benton, D. (1999). *Secrets of a CEO coach.* New York: McGraw-Hill.

Block, P. (2000). *Flawless consulting: A guide to getting your expertise used* (2nd ed.). San Francisco: Jossey-Bass/Pfeiffer.

Bluckert, P. (2006). *Psychological dimensions of executive coaching.* Berkshire, UK: Open University Press.

Douglas, C., & Morley, W. (2000). *Executive coaching: An annotated bibliography.* Greensboro, NC: Center for Creative Leadership.

Doyle, J. (1999). *The business coach.* New York: Wiley.

Farson, R. (1996). *Management of the absurd: Paradoxes in leadership.* New York: Simon & Schuster.

Gilley, J., & Boughton, M. (1996). *Stop managing, start coaching!: How performance coaching can enhance commitment and improve productivity.* Chicago: Irwin Professional.

Goldsmith, M., & Lyons, L. S. (Eds.). (2006). *Coaching for leadership: The practice of leadership coaching from the world's greatest coaches* (2nd ed.). San Francisco: Pfeiffer.

Hargrove, R. (1995). *Masterful coaching.* San Francisco: Jossey-Bass/Pfeiffer.

Hart, V., Blattner, J., & Leipsic, S. (2001). Coaching versus therapy: A perspective. *Consulting Psychology Journal: Research and Practice, 53*(4), 229–237.

Harvey, D., & Brown, D. R. (2005). *An experiential approach to organizational development* (7th ed.). Upper Saddle River, NJ: Prentice Hall.

Holtz, H. (1997). *The complete guide to consulting contracts* (2nd ed.). Chicago: Upstart.

Holtz, H., & Zahn, D. (2004). *How to succeed as an independent consultant.* Hoboken, NJ: John Wiley & Sons.

Kerin, R., & Peterson, R. (1998). *Strategic marketing problems: Cases and comments.* Upper Saddle River, NJ: Prentice Hall.

Martin, I. (1996). *From couch to corporation. Becoming a successful corporate therapist.* New York: Wiley.

Miller, J., & Brown, P. (1993). *The corporate coach.* New York: St. Martin's Press.

Palmer, S., & Whybrow, A. (Eds.). (2008). *Handbook of coaching psychology.* London: Routledge.

Peters, T. (1999). *The brand you 50.* New York: Alfred Knopf.

Sperry, L. (1996). *Corporate therapy and consulting.* New York: Brunner/Mazel.

Sperry, L. (2004). *Executive coaching: The essential guide for mental health professionals.* New York: Brunner-Routledge.

Stober, D. R., & Grant, A. M. (Eds.). (2006). *Evidence based coaching handbook.* Hoboken, NJ: John Wiley & Sons.

Tobias, L. (1990). *Psychological consulting to management: A clinician's perspective.* New York: Brunner/Mazel.

Waldroop, J., & Butler, T. (2000, September–October). Managing away bad habits. *Harvard Business Review,* 89–98.

Wallace, W., & Hall, D. (1996). *Psychological consultation: Perspectives and applications.* Pacific Grove, CA: Brooks/Cole.

Index